FLORIDA

FOUR INSPIRING LOVE STORIES
FROM THE SUNSHINE STATE

EILEEN M. BERGER

MUNCY G. CHAPMAN

PEGGY DARTY

STEPHEN A. PAPUCHIS

BARBOUR
PUBLISHING

Published by Barbour Publishing, Inc., P.O. Box 719, Uhrichsville, Ohio 44683, www.barbourbooks.com

ecpa Member of the
Evangelical Christian
Publishers Association

Printed in the United States of America.

Florida

A Place to Call Home

Eileen M. Berger

Chapter 1

Tess usually looked forward to the church dinners, but she was forcing herself to go this evening. She told herself she would enjoy eating the delicious food and being with people she had known all her life. And she certainly needed a break from studying.

Hastily she spread peanut butter frosting on the German chocolate cake, all the while hoping that the evening's program as announced from the pulpit and in this morning's bulletin wouldn't be boring. Peter Macfarland had only recently joined the church and seemed nice, but she had had no opportunity to get to know him.

Her week had been awful, and it didn't look like the next one would be much better. *I shouldn't have taken three major courses this term! I knew it would be a headache getting the Endowment and Special Gifts data to be compatible with the college's new computer system, but I didn't realize it would be this bad.* She liked her work and coworkers but—and what a big "but" it was—her major reason for accepting the computer job three years before was that she would be entitled to free tuition while completing her bachelor's degree.

She placed the cake into its carrier, not allowing herself even a glance at the textbook lying open upon the table. She had been preparing all afternoon for tomorrow's test and deserved to relax for an hour or two.

The small church lot was filled, so she parked her five-year-old red Honda halfway down the block. It was a gloriously beautiful October Sunday, the kind of day she associated with football games, walks, and drives in the country. The town's wide street was lined with huge maples, masses of red and gold, while the oaks had hardly begun to lose their brown, maroon, and dark yellow leaves.

Tess placed her cake with the other desserts on one of the long tables and joined the other people at those tables loaded down with salads, meats, vegetables, and breads. She filled her plate and found an empty seat.

Greeting those around her, she asked the tall, muscular man across from her, "When were you in Florida, Pete?" She understood he was to show pictures and tell of work he and others from his church had done in the Miami area.

"Almost immediately after Hurricane Andrew—from the twenty-ninth of August to Labor Day." His grin was boyish. "I barely had time for a few hours' sleep before the first day of school and a new classroom of twenty-four third-graders."

"What a schedule!"

"The rest of our group started back on Saturday, but I stayed 'til Monday. There was so much to be done!" His eyes wrinkled at the corners. He seemed to be looking into the past, seeing not this brightly lit Family Activity Center with about ninety well-fed and nicely dressed people, but the shambles and needs by which he had been surrounded in Florida.

"I. . .I think I'd have liked doing something like that," she said softly, pushing remnants of meat loaf around with her fork.

He leaned toward her, intense brown eyes holding her blue ones. "It's not too late, you know."

Tess drew back. "I really couldn't though—not now."

"Whenever." A slow, encouraging smile softened his urgency. "There are never enough volunteers, Tess. Nor enough time. And there are so many homeless people waiting almost despairingly for help."

A shiver passed up her spine. He was speaking of faraway things, yet he was looking deeply into her eyes and calling her by name. Before she needed to respond, someone asked him another question.

The tables were cleared, chairs rearranged, and Pastor Jim Hadden introduced the speaker of the evening. As Peter Macfarland had been here less than two months, some might not have had the opportunity of becoming acquainted with him. Pastor Jim explained that Pete had recently moved to Fairhills to teach in this school district and was especially interested in history, science, nature, bowling, and softball. And tonight Pete would be sharing accounts and pictures of his experiences while with people from his home church in Connecticut.

Tess couldn't help smiling when a teen on her right said, "I wish he was my teacher!" The girl next to her agreed. "He's really handsome!"

Yes. He is. Tess had been aware earlier of his easy smile and manner, his slightly wavy hair a shade lighter than his friendly eyes, and those muscular shoulders and arms emphasized, not hidden, by his open-collared, short-sleeved cotton shirt.

As he acknowledged the introduction, she realized how comfortable he was with his tallness and with being in front of people. He had grown up, he said, in a town and church about as large as this, the oldest of three children, and with all the kids on the block spending their time at his home.

"Perhaps," he said, "that's the one reason I've always planned to work with children when I grew up. And why I'm enjoying this opportunity of having your third-graders in my classes."

He smoothly made the transition to telling of the trip to Florida. As soon as they saw TV coverage of Hurricane Andrew, several members of his church decided to go on a work tour. Their enthusiasm spread—so much that they filled two vans, and Pete volunteered to drive a truckload of donated lumber and supplies.

Part of his program was presented on video, for he had ridden and walked around in Florida with a camcorder as well as his still camera. "As you can see," he pointed out as he panned a particularly hard-hit district, "there are entire streets where nothing was left standing and others where the damage was so great that nobody can live there.

"Those having insurance coverage are by now on their way to getting back to 'normal,' if there is such a thing in an area this heavily damaged. However, although the government's doing much to help, for many the wait for housing has seemed interminable."

He told of his reluctance to give so much time and energy in August, when major transitions were taking place in his life. "I might have backed out," he confessed, "had they not needed an experienced driver.

"As it happens, in order to help pay college expenses, I'd worked in a lumberyard and driven trucks during vacations and, when my schedule permitted it, during the school year. The owner, a member of our church, offered one of his vehicles and wholesale prices for lumber and supplies if I drove.

"So," he continued, his eyebrows raised as he shrugged, "I found myself in Florida for what turned out to be one of the most unforgettable, exhausting, and blessed periods of my life." He then challenged them by saying, "I understand some of you are active in prison fellowship ministries, scouting, and working with the aging or handicapped. These are worthwhile and if you truly have already full schedules, I'm not suggesting you add more.

"However, for those not so involved, please consider sharing time, energy, and financial resources to help those desperately needing what you have to give—your love."

His last words made an impact on Tess and stuck in her mind. She had no opportunity to speak with him after the presentation, but as she left she saw him look toward her over the heads of those crowding around. Her hand raised in a small salute and his head cocked slightly, as though in question. And he smiled.

When she arrived home, she put away the few pieces of dessert then changed into pajamas before getting back to her studies. After one more review of her notes, she decided she knew the material and, tired as she was, would benefit from a full night's sleep.

Morning came quickly. She arrived early for work and stayed until ten minutes before her eleven o'clock sociology class. Afterward, as she sat alone, eating the lunch she had brought from home, she checked through her book for underlinings and information written in the margins. Had she missed anything important?

She felt fairly confident when she entered the early afternoon psychology class and was relieved to find that the test was straightforward and direct, without the ambiguities and slanted questions the teacher had used the last time.

Tess returned to the computer department where she stayed late to compensate for class time. On the way back to her apartment, she bought a hoagie at the Kollege Korner. With fruit and milk it made the supper she ate while relaxing in the recliner watching the evening news and reading the paper.

She turned off the TV and was reaching for her textbook and notes on early childhood education when the phone rang. "Hello?"

"Hi, Tess, I have a message for you," said the masculine voice.

"And a good evening to you, Pastor Jim!"

He laughed easily. "I usually do introduce myself when phoning, but it didn't seem necessary with you. So, how are you?"

"Fine, thanks. And you?"

"Okay. And now, as to my message: Pete Macfarland just called. He'd looked in the directory and called the operator to get your number—"

"Which is unlisted," Tess put in, as though it didn't matter that the handsome young teacher had tried to reach her.

"He discovered that, so he asked me to give it to him."

"Did you?"

"Of course not—though you might not have minded this time. You two seemed to be having an interesting conversation over dinner."

Was that a question? "The people at our table got a preview of his later presentation. He and I had never said more than 'Good morning' or 'Hello' before, but I enjoyed getting to know him."

"He's very personable," Pastor Jim agreed. "And a bachelor. And he likes you."

"Because he asked for my number?" she asked. "He probably wants to follow up on my saying I'd like to do something like he did. . .but I also said I wouldn't be able to."

"Could be, Tess." The words might have indicated he agreed, but the tone wasn't convincing. "His number's 555-4421, so you can find out when you call."

Tess hesitated. "I. . .really don't like phoning men."

"But you're the one who's unlisted."

She sighed, knowing she was too curious about Pete's call to not check. Pastor Jim spoke of the dinner the evening before and, as she was on the Board of Christian Education, they also discussed a situation in the junior class before they wished one another a good night.

She sat with the phone in her hand for a time before punching in Pete's number. The receiver was lifted on the first ring and she said, "This is Theresa Kenneman. Pastor Hadden just told me you wished to speak with me."

"Hi, Theresa, or do you go by 'Tess'?"

Of course he would have heard others calling her that. "It's always 'Tess.' I don't know why I introduced myself like that." *Probably because I was uncomfortable about phoning.*

"I appreciate your calling. I want to thank you for keeping the conversation going at our table last night. You helped immeasurably in my getting to know people in a new place."

She smiled in the privacy of her apartment. "I was genuinely interested, so the questions were mostly for my own information."

"Anything else you might want to know?" His voice sounded friendly and warm.

There was a lot she would like to know—about Pete. Pastor Jim had just said he was a bachelor, for example. But it wasn't proper to ask personal questions. "What kinds of things did you personally do after getting your lumber delivered?"

"Mostly cleanup. Backbreaking heavy work of cutting up and dragging trees and gathering trash—and that often meant all the furnishings and treasures that had made these places home. I also helped with digging trenches, putting up scaffolding, and replacing shingles on roofs that weren't too awfully damaged."

"That would be satisfying."

There was only a moment's pause. "How serious are you about wanting to do something like this?"

She had been afraid he would ask. "I am interested, Pete, but there's no way I could free up that much time in the foreseeable future."

He didn't say anything right away, and she rushed in with words to explain about the computer mess throughout the campus and specifically in her department. "It wouldn't have been so bad if things had been done in a logical fashion, instead of the administration's announcing that by a certain day everything will be switched to the new system.

"Until now, each department kept its records in its own way—and for the most part this worked fine. However, the people setting up any of these methods had a great deal of freedom. You can't believe the bizarre and original ways similar problems have been attacked."

"Sounds challenging!"

"To put it mildly! I'm in charge of getting several systems on-line—mainly everything that has to do with gifts of alumni, their families, corporations, and things like that."

"I don't envy you!"

She thanked him for his sympathy, then briefly explained that she had earned her associate's degree in computer science and had been employed by an accounting firm before coming to work here. She was now taking as many courses as possible each semester toward her degree in early childhood education and counseling.

"I'm impressed!"

Considering the schedule she had been keeping, she felt justified in advising, "Don't be. It's probably a form of insanity."

He laughed. "If so, it should be contagious." But then he became more serious. "So what else do you do?"

She laid the textbook on the floor, not wanting to look at it. "Oh, there's church and Bible study, and I enjoy reading, and I sometimes go to dinner or a concert or something with friends."

"Am I 'friend' enough for you to consider dinner with me? Including a concert or anything else you'd like, of course?"

She did not respond with a definite yes or no, but afterward she wasn't sure exactly what she had said. Something about seeing him at church next Sunday.

Why didn't I come right out and say I'd love to go with him? It was next to impossible to involve herself in the assignment for the following day. She unwillingly kept remembering their conversation. Given the opportunity, she felt he would ask her to go to Florida if a group went from their church.

And she couldn't spare the time. She really couldn't.

⚓

It was on Wednesday, while she was making a tuna, lettuce, and tomato salad, that he called again. "Hi, Tess. Pete here. Going to Bible study tonight?"

"Hello, Pete," she responded, wiping her hands on a paper towel and balancing the phone between her ear and shoulder. "I was planning to go. Are you?"

"Um-hmm. Thought I'd try it tonight, and remembered you said you usually go. Can I stop for you?"

There was no reason to refuse. Not that she wanted to. "It may be out of your way—I'm on South Elm."

"How far out?"

"Seven-thirty-three."

"No problem. Look, have you eaten?"

"Not yet. I was late getting home again, so was in the process of making a salad."

"Can it keep 'til tomorrow?"

"I. . .I suppose so."

"In that case, how about my coming right away and we can stop at a restaurant on the way to church?"

Why not? "That sounds like an excellent idea," she agreed. "At the moment I'm wearing pants, a sweater, and joggers. We're not very formal on Wednesday evenings. Should I change?"

"Depends on where you'd like to eat. How about the Midway Steakhouse? I've never had a meal there that I didn't enjoy."

"I like it too. When will you get here?"

"I'm leaving in about thirty seconds. Barring the traffic lights turning red at the wrong time, I should make it in under five minutes."

It was nearly six when he arrived, although if she had not looked at her watch she wouldn't have believed it. She put the salad in a sealed container and quickly straightened the newspaper, books, and pillows.

She had just finished putting a touch of color on her full lips when she heard him at the door. She shrugged into a lightweight jacket. "You made it through on the green lights."

"Just." His eyes sparkled, enjoying her comment. "I saw in my rearview mirror that it was yellow by the time I passed. Now," he said, placing his hand beneath her elbow as they started down the walk, "perhaps we'd better make sure we know where we're going."

She glanced upward. "I thought it was the Midway."

"Only a suggestion. Is there a place you like better?"

She smiled. "The Midway will be fine."

After placing their orders, they helped themselves at the elaborate salad bar. They were soon seated opposite one another in a maroon upholstered booth with the soup, bread, fruit, and dessert they had chosen.

They were halfway through their meals when he asked, "Why are you smiling like that?"

"I didn't realize I was doing anything unusual."

He reached across and covered her left hand with his. "Not unusual, Tess. You have a lovely smile, as though you'd been given a present, or something wonderful had happened."

She looked at their hands, then back up at his face. "I'm going to have to be careful, Mr. Pete Macfarland, if you read me this well."

"Then it is something good?"

She nodded. "I just realized we were conversing comfortably. I think that's good."

He gave her hand a firm squeeze before letting it go, but his eyes didn't release hers. "I agree. That's very good."

They did not speak again of things that could be taken too personally. Rather, they talked about the church and how Tess had grown up in it and had many special memories of the people and things that had happened.

He told of his playing varsity basketball in high school and being involved with track. "I wasn't an awfully good student in those days," he said. "B's seemed plenty good for anyone, and I couldn't understand why my folks weren't satisfied with that, especially when I could get them without studying."

"Being very intelligent can sometimes be a handicap."

"It can be—and was," he confessed. "My first job involved holding a sign telling motorists whether to stop or to go slow around road crews—and I was proud to be making more money than a lot of kids graduating from college."

Pete grimaced with self-deprecation. "It took me longer than it should have to realize I wasn't going to be satisfied doing something like that for the rest of my life."

"That's when you returned to school?"

"Um-hmm. And I held on to my job while taking night courses at the community college for several terms. Up 'til then I hadn't been motivated to save money."

"And you got all A's?"

"And I got all A's," he admitted. "With a lot of studying, I must add. It was worth the effort though, for I was then eligible for grants and financial aid. With that, my working at the lumberyard, and getting loans, I made it."

"I commend you." And she did, knowing from experience how hard it was to work and go to school. She shifted to a more comfortable position as she changed the subject. "How did you happen to come to our town?"

He leaned back in his seat and said thoughtfully, "I'd expected to get a job in my own area, but for two years my only teaching was as a substitute for various school districts—and that is far from being ideal."

She knew this to be true. "The financial crunch has hit school systems here too. As teachers retire or quit, many districts choose to have larger classes and part-time employees, rather than to hire replacements."

"I resolved to try many places, and your school apparently liked my résumé well enough to have me come for interviews. And here I am!" He looked pleased with himself—or the situation—as he added, "So, in answer to how I got here, I'd say this must be where the Lord wants me."

Elbow on the table, chin resting on her loosely clenched fist, she smiled. "I like that—you're giving Him the credit."

He smiled at her approval. "And you, Tess. How does that concept fit with your situation?"

The piece of steak she had lifted an inch or two above her plate was set back down. "Most of the time I've loved my work, and it's given me the opportunity to get additional credits toward my degree. I prayed for guidance before coming to the college three years ago. It seemed the right choice then and it still does, although right now, with this computer system mess, I have to keep reminding myself of that. Thanks, Pete, for making me remember."

🌴

It felt strange to enter the church with this man. She noted raised brows and nudges and knew that some were reading too much into this. She had never "brought a date" to Bible study before, so they were probably jumping to conclusions.

The pastor and others greeted Pete, and some mentioned his presentation at the dinner three days before. By coincidence (Tess corrected her thinking to *providentially*) the Scriptures being emphasized that evening were those of Jesus' commending the giving of even a cup of water in His name.

Her hand started to reach for Pete's in recognition that his work in Florida had been like giving gallons of refreshment to thirsty sufferers. She drew it back in time, hoping nobody saw her gaffe.

At the door, when he brought her back to the apartment, Tess said, "Good night, Pete. I have pages and pages to study yet this evening."

But his smile and voice kept coming between her and the words of her book.

Chapter 2

Pete wasn't at Bible study the next week and she saw him at church only in passing. *Have I offended him? Why hasn't he called?* she thought in confusion. *Well, I don't have time to worry about him or any other man!*

Most of the secretaries were cooperating well with her as she strove to get the computer systems in conformity, but she was still exhausted by the stresses of her job and the long hours. What conceit had made her think she could engineer this technical transition and handle three courses besides?

She considered dropping a course, but which one? She was learning a great deal in each and actually looked forward to attending classes.

She disciplined herself to concentrate on every word her instructors spoke and refused to let anything interfere with study time. Each night she activated her phone's answering device and fastened a notepad on her door for messages.

Weeks flew by. Shortly after getting home from church and changing clothes one Sunday, Tess frowned at the ringing phone, annoyed with herself for neglecting to switch it to automatic. Wiping her hands on one paper towel, she protected the receiver by holding it with another. "Hello?"

"Hi, Tess. It's Pete."

She sank down onto a chair. "Hello. How are you?"

"Good, thanks. And you?"

"Messy, actually." There was humor in her voice. "You caught me in the final stages of stuffing a turkey for tonight's annual Church Family Thanksgiving Dinner. Are you going?"

"Wouldn't miss it. That's why I called. Can I pick you up?"

It sounded delightful. "Sure. And you can carry the roaster, if you wouldn't mind. It will be bulky, with this twenty-four-pound giant in it and being hot from the oven."

"It would be my pleasure."

The words were almost formal, but his expressive voice made her believe he really would like to help. "Great. And if you manage that, I'll bring table service for both of us."

"Fine." There seemed the briefest of pauses before he said, "Well, I'd better not keep you from getting Big Bird into the oven. Shall I come about five-fifteen?"

"Perhaps a bit earlier? There has to be time to carve the turkey once we get there."

Five o'clock or a little earlier was the decision. Tess left the phone off the hook as she hurriedly finished preparing the turkey and getting it into the preheated oven.

She studied until four-thirty before changing into brown wool pants and her new gold sweater embroidered with autumn leaves. She brushed her long hair and fashioned it into a flattering French braid.

"Umm. I like!" Pete admired when he arrived.

She wished he would make complete sentences. Not wanting to assume more than he meant, she indicated the sweater. "I couldn't resist buying it when I saw it at Lawry's recently."

He touched her hair. "The color's a perfect match."

She led him to the kitchen, turned off the oven, and let him lift the roaster to the stove's top. He removed the lid to admire the turkey. "Done to perfection!"

"I hope so. It's larger than I usually roast, but according to the directions, it had plenty of oven time."

Everything was wonderful with the evening—food, fellowship, being with Pete—everything! She especially enjoyed the surprise presentation.

Tess was in the kitchen drying dishes and assumed Pete was helping fold and put away the extra tables and chairs, but he wasn't around when she finished her work. Pastor Jim was missing also.

She was visiting with several elderly women when Molly Eckers, chairwoman of the Social Committee, thanked everyone for coming and hoped each had had enough to eat. The response was a chorus of affirmation, made up partly of mock misery groans of those who had eaten too much.

Molly asked everyone to be seated so the evening's special guests could be introduced. Tess found two chairs together, laying her purse on the second to save it for Pete.

The door near the rear of the big room opened, revealing two clowns. The tall, bold-looking one with moplike orange hair wore a loose-fitting outfit of white with huge multicolored polka dots and wide ruffles at the throat, wrists, and ankles. The second was probably as tall, but he wore oversized work overalls with varicolored patches, held up by one over-the-shoulder strap. He looked around, afraid of the place and the crowd of people.

Tess laughed out loud, recognizing Pastor Jim in the orange hair and Pete under the whiteface decorated with exaggerated worry lines and a huge downturned mouth. Pastor Jim pulled Pete forward, silently miming reassurance that he didn't have to fear coming to the front of the room.

Molly verbally asked questions and said words to which Jim exuberantly responded in mime or by digging into his ugly purple plaid sack for boldly printed signs that he held up for all to see.

Pete hung back, trying to hide behind a supporting pole then fearfully peeking between the spindles of a cane-bottom wooden chair. Molly included him in the "conversation" with firmly direct questions he "answered" by drawing from his ragged burlap bag first a hammer and large nails then, when appropriate, a crowbar, some shingles, a piece of torn tar paper, and a road map of Florida, the lower portion of which was circled in fluorescent red.

Shoulders shaking with sobs, he cried silently into a torn red bandana. He indicated the problem by huffing and puffing Molly's papers until they fell to the floor, and then he blew a paper roof off a Lincoln Log house, which he also partially destroyed.

He cheered up though as he pointed to Pastor Jim, Molly, and himself and, with an all-inclusive sweep of his arm, to the audience; he mimed their going to the Miami area with tools and supplies to repair damage from the big wind.

By Pastor Jim's "driving" with Molly behind him and Pete in the rear, they showed they were going in a big vehicle to southern Florida and indicated they needed time, muscle, and money from the people in the church to make their trip possible.

When near the exit, Molly held up an immense calendar with highlighted dates of December 26 through January 3, and the clowns gave each person a handout.

Tess joined in the enthusiastic applause and was pleased when the clowns came running back in, ostensibly for "curtain calls" but actually so that, wigs in their hands and now speaking, they could answer questions and go into more detail concerning the plans.

Tess had heard that a construction detail was being sent but was amazed by the work already done. Hank Jameson, an older member who owned the local lumberyard, regretted he wasn't well enough to accompany them but volunteered to make available and pay all expenses for any size truck necessary to haul donated lumber, other materials, and sleeping bags.

In addition to giving an account of the plans about which they were being told, Tess saw that the handout had a tear-off portion inviting volunteers to participate. There was a list of ways they could make a commitment to help with the venture: going on the trip; providing funds toward expenses; supplying a van in case these could be used instead of renting a bus; buying materials; continuing in prayer for the hurricane victims and those helping to alleviate suffering; and ended with "Other Offerings."

Many parents with small children and some of the others left immediately after the skit, but most stayed to discuss what had taken place or to crowd around the clowns, asking questions.

Tess went to help a single mother get her two preschool youngsters—one sound asleep—to their car. Fastening the four year old in his car seat, she kissed him and said, "See you Sunday, Mickey, okay?" The drowsy child kissed her back and continued waving as long as he could see her.

She was welcomed back with a smile and half a wink by Pete, still in whiteface. Smiling back, she joined the outer ring of those around him.

Tess and Pete were among the last to leave. It took him some time to remove his makeup and change back into normal garb. Tess looked up at him as he carried the empty roaster to his car. "You did a great job! I had no idea you were into clowning."

"See what an exciting guy I am?" he teased, grinning crookedly. "Full of surprises."

She suspected this was true. "I can hardly wait to see what's next."

"I'm still a novice at clowning," he said modestly. "I never thought of doing it until I went to a Sunday school conference last winter. Just for variety, I sat in on their clown workshop—and loved it."

"I can tell you do. And you're good at it."

"Pastor Jim thought he wasn't ready for it tonight." Pete laughed. "He really got into it, though. I believe he won't need much arm-twisting to do it again."

"I wondered. I've never known him to do anything like that, so I was more surprised at him than you. After all, I don't know you very well."

He helped her into the car. "We'll have to do something about that."

But she decided he didn't mean it when she heard nothing from him for several days. *Why should I let that bother me?* she demanded of herself as she sat alone in church for the Thanksgiving Eve service. Still, she wondered why he was not there.

She spent all day Thursday with her father, who lived several miles away in the house where she had grown up. She didn't feel right in the big old place now that Mother was dead—or, more exactly, now that Dad was married to Jeannette, who was only nine years older than she.

Dinner was delicious and nicely served. Tess made a special effort to admire changes in the house, but she missed the way things had been. It must be difficult for a new wife brought into a house that had been made into a home by a deceased, beloved first wife.

She thought of her own apartment, which was comfortable and adequate. Although it had everything she needed and was a good place to come back to, she didn't think of it as "home."

When Tess invited them to her apartment for Christmas dinner, her father looked from her to Jeannette. "What do you think, Jeannette?"

The dark-haired, slender woman's hands clasped tightly in her lap. "Either there or here, Richard. Whichever you prefer."

He shook his head. "I need your honest opinion. It would be easier for you. . ."

She hesitated. "You know I love cooking, so that's not the question. But I'll go along with what you want."

He rubbed his hand through luxuriant reddish brown hair just beginning to turn gray at the temples. "Well, I've had Christmas here for the past twenty-eight years, two years before you came along, Tess."

Tess could tell he would prefer that tradition. "And it would be nice to keep it that way," she finished for him.

His face wore an almost apologetic look of gratitude. "If you don't mind."

Partly to make him feel better, she said, "I'd have loved having you, but it will be simpler for me to come here this year. I wasn't sure if I'd even decorate a tree this season."

Her father leaned forward, and she knew he was about to insist on being at her place if it made that much difference. She rushed an explanation, "A work group from church is leaving for the Miami area the day after Christmas to do construction or whatever's most needed by that time in cleaning up after Andrew. I'm planning to be with them if I can get clearance at work."

She was committed.

When did I decide to do that? she asked herself on the way home. *I've been thinking of it a lot since the clowns' presentation but hadn't realized I'd come to a conclusion.* The subconscious was a marvelously complicated entity; she was pleased with its decision.

She went to the college the next day "for just long enough to work out that problem that came up Tuesday" and was amazed when she looked at the clock. She had spent over five hours in her vacation-emptied department. The rest of the long weekend, however, was hers, so she shopped for Christmas gifts and met friends for lunch on Saturday—things she had not taken time for since the fall term began.

On Sunday afternoon, she made stops at three different nursing homes to visit elderly people from church and deliver small potted poinsettias. Only during the late afternoon and evening did she get out books and notes to prepare for these last weeks before finals. Frowning, she glanced at the clock as the phone rang. Nine-forty-nine. Who would be calling at this hour? "Hello?"

"Hi, Tess. Have a good Thanksgiving?"

It wasn't too late at all! "Hello, Pete." Perhaps she shouldn't show her pleasure after his not even contacting her since last Sunday, but. . . "Yes, I spent it with my father—traditional turkey and all that."

"Me, too. Pumpkin custard, pecan pie—the works. I've returned at least several pounds heavier than when I left."

"You were in Connecticut for the holiday?"

"Yes. I thought I'd mentioned that. But with my not wanting to speak of the clowning 'til I did it, I probably missed other things too. My brother and sister were home for the day with their families, so we had quite a time!"

"It sounds like fun. How many of you are there?"

"Let's see. . .five of Matt's, four of Lynne's, two grandparents, an uncle and aunt, and my parents. Seventeen of us. We had a great time."

Had he miscounted? Or had he had a guest with him? Maybe she'd rather not know. "How old are the children?"

They talked about the little ones, ranging in ages from nine months to seven years, and then he asked what she had done the rest of the long weekend. "At least I'm glad you got away from computers and studies for a little while," he approved.

Tess said she appreciated that but, since she had been foolish enough to take three subjects this semester, she would have to live with the consequences. Apparently, he took that as a hint to let her get back to her books, for the conversation ended shortly thereafter.

She sighed as she replaced the phone on its cradle and reached for her lesson. She certainly had a lot to learn socially as well as scholastically!

Why hadn't she told him of her decision to go to Miami? Because he hadn't asked, that's why! She wanted him to want her to go with them—or at least be interested enough to ask. She sat there staring at the offending phone, then picked it up and dialed.

"Why, hello, Tess," the voice responded. "Is everything okay?"

She glanced toward the clock. "I'm sorry, Pastor Jim. I was studying and didn't realize it was after ten. Were you getting ready for bed?"

The minister laughed. "I'm ready—yes; going—no. In other words, I put on pajamas and a robe when I got back from a call, but I'm here in the recliner reading a book on spirituality and the church."

"Sounds deep."

"Actually, it's not as interesting or helpful as I'd expected. But I'm only on chapter three, so there's still hope."

"I won't keep you." She still felt apologetic, particularly since her reason for calling didn't bear close scrutiny. Just because she had been miffed at Pete's not asking about her decision was no reason for deliberately giving the news to someone else.

"I could have waited 'til tomorrow or Wednesday night—or next Sunday, for that matter."

"Don't worry about it, Tess. I'm not, that's for sure." His voice was reassuring. "I'm glad you called. Can I help you?"

"Sometimes I forget you're the preacher and are always getting calls for help," she said slowly. "This is something different. I've decided that if I can get vacation time I'll go with you to Florida."

"Great!" She couldn't doubt his enthusiastic approval. "I—we'll love having you!"

"There's still room?"

"Of course. If there weren't, we'd make room, even if it meant arranging for an extra van."

"Oh. . .well, thanks," she stammered. "I wanted to make sure at this end before notifying the school. . . ."

The next day she received that approval. She wondered many times as the weeks sped by if she had been out of her mind to say she would go. She could have used that class-free period to get caught up with things that had been put off much too long. Or she could have gone to bed early at night and treated herself to reading a novel.

One day, she hand-delivered to the head of the social studies department a proposal she had been working on. Occasionally, the college gave credit for an independent studies project, so she asked Dr. Prentiss to consider her getting graded if she did research and presented a major paper on volunteerism.

She would like to present a well-documented account of her group's trip and activities, along with various individuals' reasons for going, whether they had done anything like this before, what they got out of it, and whether they felt they would be willing to do it again.

Dr. Prentiss asked a number of questions that, having already been thoroughly considered, she answered to his satisfaction. He had to clear this with others in the department, so she didn't get the affirmative reply until the twenty-third.

In the meantime, she took finals in all three courses—and earned A's in each.

Pete went home the weekend of December 19 for his family's holiday celebration. When he saw Tess on the following Thursday as they were leaving the seven o'clock Christmas Eve candlelight service he said, "Having off from school only this one day, I've been running around like crazy helping load the truck and finalizing trip plans."

"What about tomorrow?"

"Tomorrow?"

"I was wondering. . .are you celebrating Christmas with someone from the church—or something?" She felt herself blushing—maybe he had plans of a personal nature and would think her prying.

"Nope. Afraid not." Apparently seeing her dismay at his being alone on this most wonderful of holidays, he put his hand on her shoulder. His voice and face showed he was comforting her. "I'll be fine. . .I promise."

If only she were hostessing the noon meal at her apartment! It was too late for that now.

She waited until nine-forty-five before going to the phone. "Jeannette, are you planning for anyone else there tomorrow?" she asked after the usual greetings.

"No, it's just the three of us. Would you like to bring someone?"

She was making it so easy. "Do you know Peter Macfarland, the man who's coordinating our trip to Florida?"

"Who he is—but we don't know him."

"Well, I was talking with him for a minute after the early service tonight. As it turns out, he has no plans for tomorrow and I. . .well. . ."

Jeannette's warm voice covered Tess's hesitancy. "We can't have him eating a solitary dinner in a restaurant or at home on Christmas Day," she stated. "Bring him with you—or have him meet you here, whichever's best for both of you."

Tess didn't tell her father's wife that either choice would be excellent as far as she was concerned. She would call back tonight if Pete would not be joining them.

She half expected difficulty in telling Pete she had made these arrangements, but he accepted as soon as she quoted Jeannette's words of invitation. "What time shall I come for you?" he asked.

"Would eleven-thirty be okay? Dinner's an hour after that, but perhaps I could help with something. If she lets me."

"Problems?"

She hesitated. "This is her first Christmas as my stepmother and. . . sometimes we're not sure what or how to say things to one another."

"That can lead to uncomfortable moments."

She agreed. "We're still overly conscious of 'working' at making things go well. The important thing is our both loving Dad and wanting him to be happy. And we don't choose to be rivals in any way."

His voice had a quality that seemed to come from some deep-seated well of understanding. "You'll make out great, Tess. And I'm looking forward to being with all of you tomorrow."

She had wrapped gifts for the other two last weekend but now tried to figure what to give Pete. It didn't seem right to have nothing for him when they opened presents tomorrow, but it was too late to go to a store. For that matter, she had no idea what to buy for him.

She returned for the second time to the tiny "guest room," where her computer and files took up much of the space not occupied by the spool bed and an antique dresser. Standing in front of the tall bookcase, she noticed the Contemporary English Version of the New Testament, recently put out by the American Bible Society.

Drawing it from between two other versions, she opened it and thoughtfully turned pages. He would probably like this—if he hadn't already bought one for himself.

But that's true of any purchase I'd make for him. I've never been in his home. I really don't know much about him. Seeing him at church or in that restaurant hardly counts.

She remembered the leather Bible cover she had bought for her father the previous year. She had later decided not to give it to him when she realized that on the few occasions he came to church he didn't carry a Bible with him and when—or if—he used it at home, it wouldn't need protection.

Let's see, was it—yes, here it is on the closet's top shelf. In its original wrapper. She had been busy and waited so long before returning it to the store that she figured they probably wouldn't refund the purchase price.

Thank You, God, for making something this good of my neglectfulness, she prayed impulsively as the warmth of her expectations for the next day tinted her cheeks.

Chapter 3

Christmas morning! There was a smile on Tess's lips even before she opened her eyes in the early dawn. She stretched, then relaxed again under the warm covers. A few snowflakes had been falling when she went to bed, but she could wait to find out if the ground was white.

It didn't smell like Christmas, and she felt momentary regret. Perhaps she should have gone to cut a tree this year, though it didn't make sense when she would be leaving for Florida early tomorrow.

She rolled onto her other side. She had had no idea how much she would miss not going out to get a tree. According to pictures and stories, her parents had taken her every year since before she could walk. Even last year, when Dad was dating Jeannette, he and Tess drove to Rossiter's Cut-Your-Own Tree Farm on the Saturday after Thanksgiving and spent hours looking for just the right Douglas fir.

She pushed the covers back, got out of bed, and felt with her toes for her slippers. Going to the kitchen, she prepared her first tea of the day and a bowl of cereal. She put Christmas music on her stereo, to go with breakfast, and made a list of things still to be done before leaving for Florida. She had remembered to stop the paper delivery. Mrs. Kirkpatrick, the elderly woman in the apartment next to hers, had agreed to collect her mail and to care for the three plants that Tess had taken to her yesterday. *Maybe that's why I so miss having a tree; there's nothing green and alive here.* But she didn't convince herself that that was the reason.

Returning to her bedroom, Tess counted out the undergarments, socks, and pajamas she would need. Many work clothes were piled on the guest bed, with only a couple of skirts and dressy blouses.

Would there be opportunities for swimming? She doubted it but got out her one-piece blue suit just in case. She added her sleeping bag, soap and detergent, towels and washcloths, several pairs of athletic shoes, work gloves, and rainwear to the pile. She would have to wait to pack her hair dryer, toothbrush, and other everyday items, but she noted these on her pad so she wouldn't forget them and have to buy replacements.

It was after ten when she called her mother's aunt in Florida. "Merry Christmas, Aunt Freddie," she greeted.

"My goodness, it's Theresa!" the delighted voice said. "I hope you're having a good one too, my dear."

"Yes, I am, thanks. A friend and I are going out to Dad's for dinner, and I'm expecting to enjoy myself. But what about you? What are you doing today?"

She need not have worried about Frederica Bollway, she realized, when the eighty-six-year-old woman explained enthusiastically that six of "the girls" had already gone to a "simply wonderful" church service and were leaving in an hour for a restaurant nine miles away that advertised what looked like a "scrumptious Christmas buffet."

"You know how I love buffets, Theresa. Cooking for just myself, I stick mostly to meat, potatoes, and a vegetable, so when I go to a church dinner or buffet I try a little of all sorts of goodies."

Tess said she understood this feeling, then assured Aunt Freddie that all was well with her physically, emotionally, and job-wise.

When told of the trip beginning the next morning, Freddie insisted Tess must come visit. "It's less than two hours away, which is nothing compared with your two-day drive to Miami."

"I don't know what our schedule will be. I'll bring your number and call Monday or Tuesday."

"Make it before eleven in the morning or between nine and ten at night. That way I'm sure not to miss you."

Tess laughed. "What a social life you lead!"

"It's busy, anyway," she stated briskly. "Now you remember to call me—and plan to come for dinner. Bring a friend along, since that will make your drive more enjoyable."

Pete helped carry gifts to his car and didn't seem self-conscious about going for Christmas dinner at her father's home. He fit in comfortably with Dad and Jeannette, and Tess found this helped everyone.

Jeannette welcomed her assistance. Tess mashed potatoes and made gravy, while Dad carved the turkey. Pete transferred pickles and olives to a cut-glass container and carried the filled serving dishes to the dining room.

The conversation and banter were more natural than Tess could remember in these past ten months. "Thank you, Pete," she whispered in a moment they were alone, but she couldn't amplify that to satisfy the question in his eyes, as the other two came to the table and sat down.

Dad gave the prayer of blessing, and Tess's lips moved with the familiar words she had heard since she was an infant. She had often wished he would pray thoughts of his own, and yet today the continuity—the sameness—

warmed and satisfied her. She silently added her own prayer to his.

The meal and the afternoon were most enjoyable. Only after she was alone in her apartment that evening did she dwell on certain aspects of it.

For the first time, she regarded Jeannette as a friend. Although there had been twinges of pain when she first saw Dad with another woman, she was pleased that he had overcome his intense grief enough to go out socially. He took several women to dinner and for evenings out, but had assured his daughter that, since he knew he could never find another wife like Susan, he was seeking only companionship.

Well, Jeannette certainly was nothing like her mother, but Tess could, as of now, thank God for her father's choice. These two, both widowed after years of loving relationships with fine spouses, had been hurting and lonely. But now they were together, happy, and fulfilled.

Christmas music on her stereo accompanied the last tasks to be done before leaving in the morning. And then, with a kitchen towel over her lap, she cracked and ate walnuts while watching a PBS special in which a fine British actor played Joseph. She had never thought much about what he went through as the husband of Mary, the one chosen by Jehovah God to be the mother of God's Child.

Joseph must have loved her very much.

⚓

Tess's right hand fumbled for the switch to turn off the alarm then came back under the covers. Four-fifteen already. With leaves gone from the trees, a wan square of light coming from the streetlamp shone on the wall to the right of her bed.

She started to roll over until the realization struck her—this was the day she was heading to Florida!

Quickly getting out from under the covers, she straightened them and pulled up the colorful handmade quilt she used as a bedspread. She padded to the kitchen and put her tea in the microwave to heat while she showered.

By the time she got back, the tea was very strong, but she thought she would need the extra caffeine. The toasted English muffin with peanut butter tasted really good. She dried her hair and got dressed, then packed all her clothes in either her garment bag or suitcase.

It was time for one last check. Yes, the electric stove was turned off; everything was as it should be. Loaded down with her sleeping bag and luggage, Tess headed for her car, and nearly panicked! A man was coming up the walk toward her. The streetlight was behind him so all she knew was that he was a big, broad-shouldered man—striding purposefully.

Should she drop things and run? But then Pete's voice was saying, "Good morning, Tess. I forgot to ask yesterday afternoon if I could stop for you. And I was afraid you might have gone to bed early."

It was all she could do to keep from showing Pete how he had frightened her. "I. . .thank you," she said, willingly giving up the luggage he reached for. "It probably is best to not have all of our vehicles parked at the church while we're away."

He nodded and smiled as he placed her things in the back of the big closed truck he had parked by the curb. "Excited?"

"I really am, though I slept right up 'til the alarm rang."

"Me too. And that was real early. This Peterbilt was loaded on Thursday but kept in the fenced lumberyard for safekeeping. I had to go there this morning to pick it up."

Tess climbed into the wide seat and fastened the seat belt on the right. "I wonder how many are at the church."

"On my way to pick up the truck, I saw Pastor Jim and others arriving."

"I would have gotten there on time," she said in a small voice.

"I know that, Tess." His hand paused in the act of pulling his door shut. "It's just. . .I wanted to come."

Both doors slammed at the same time. "Thanks."

Head cocked slightly, he looked at her for a moment before pulling away from the curb. He must have decided not to continue with that topic for he began telling her of calls he had had the night before from volunteers asking questions even that late. "I think a few are wishing they hadn't signed on for this."

"I suspect there are more of us who were unsure at first, then got convinced as today approached." She was rewarded with a beaming smile.

⚓

The last three of the twenty-one were late. While the rest waited, initial assignments to vans were made for those who didn't care where they rode. For the first leg of the journey, Pastor Jim would go with Pete in the truck. Anyone wishing to trade places with him or anyone else could do so at the first stop.

In case they got separated, each vehicle was provided with a list of the truck and rest stops where they would be pulling off. Unless changes were announced later, they would wait for stragglers to catch up.

Takeoff was within ten minutes of their schedule, and for Tess the miles passed quickly. They had nibble foods with them, but the three vans and the truck stopped at one-fifteen so everyone could get out and stretch. At that time, they opened up the lunch that had been packed for them—sandwiches, fruit, cut vegetables, and cold drinks.

They already noticed a marked change in temperature, and by the time they stopped for the night at the church in South Carolina, nobody was wearing a winter jacket. Tess was glad she had worn layers, for her lined windbreaker had been shed shortly after lunch and now even her sweater was too warm.

Pete had called ahead from their last stop to give the approximate time of arrival, so the parishioners of First Baptist, where they were going to spend the night, would have enough time to prepare a very welcome baked ham dinner.

"There was nothing to it," the chairwoman of the food committee declared when the Pennsylvanians thanked them for their thoughtfulness and exclaimed over how well everything was handled.

"The butcher presliced the meat and tied it, so all I did was put it in the oven here, take it out, cut the cords, and arrange it on serving platters. The other women made their big pans of baked beans and macaroni and cheese and salads and cakes at home and brought them in time for your coming."

It sounded so simple, but Tess had helped with too many church activities to believe there was "nothing to it." She was pleased when some from the host church stayed to share their song time and evening devotions.

They had brought some camping cots in the truck but decided to sleep in their sleeping bags on the floor of the large conference room. A moveable wall was positioned to make separate areas for the men and women. When that was done, most were more than ready to call it a night. Only a few senior high and college students were still singing around the piano down the hall when Tess fell asleep.

She was one of the first ones up in the morning and, still wearing the sweat suit in which she had slept, she went to the women's three-stall bathroom to freshen up. She was glad to be finished washing before the rush but wished she had gone earlier to heat water for tea and instant coffee.

Pastor Jim was already in the kitchen and greeted her with, "I beatcha, Tess! The hot water's in the pot on the stove, and I just got back from Dori's Donut Shop down the street."

"Our pastor's got fantastic domestic as well as ministerial talents," she teased.

"This is about the extent of them," he demurred, waving his arm toward the things already mentioned.

She didn't argue with what she knew to be true: As a bachelor he did his own cooking, cleaned the parsonage, and took care of his laundry. She helped set out napkins and cups and fixed herself some tea that she carried back to the conference room. Most of the sleeping bags were empty; some were rolled up. "Come on, Natalie. Time to rise and shine, Krystal," she said briskly. "Hurry and get up, for we leave in," she glanced at her watch, "thirty-eight minutes."

Natalie, a high school senior, sat up, yawned, then grinned. "This is just like home," she said. "I'm always rushing in the morning." Picking up her towel, washcloth, and toiletry case, she hurried from the room.

Long-haired, beautiful Krystal, however, rolled over with a groan and slid down farther into the quilted bag. Tess looked toward Molly who, at sixty-four, was the senior woman on the trip. Molly walked over to Krystal and said, "Might as well learn this at the beginning, Krystal. We go to bed at night in time to get whatever amount of sleep's needed in order to fit into the group's schedule. So get up and pack. We're now down to thirty-six minutes."

Krystal's face and attitude showed very well what she thought of this, but she pushed herself up and flounced off in the direction of the women's bathroom.

One of the other women raised her brows. "I was afraid we'd have trouble with her."

"Oh, I don't know," said another. "She was active in a lot of things in high school, and she's in her second year at college. I don't think she can be too bad."

"The trouble is, Krystal's always managed one way or another to get her own way. . .to not have to fit in with what others want. I told the pastor we'd have trouble."

Tess was about to respond but Molly beat her to it with a calm, "Let's not borrow trouble, okay? Let's assume she's just overly tired this morning and go on from there."

Doughnuts and hot beverages tided them over until midmorning, when most ordered Pete's suggested "hearty, working man's breakfast" of ham or sausage, eggs, biscuits, fried potatoes, and choice of orange or tomato juice. Krystal was an exception, preferring a sweet roll and soda.

Tess was riding in the same van with her during the afternoon and made no verbal response as the young woman complained at the decision of the entourage leaders to keep going. Tess asked if anyone wanted "nibbles" from the bag beside her. Krystal and a few others emptied several boxes begun in the morning and also ate most of the remaining grapes.

By late afternoon, Tess began wondering if Hurricane Andrew had been as bad as reported. It seemed as though some signs should be apparent by now.

Before the end of the next half hour, however, there was no doubt that a bad storm had struck. As they neared Miami's outskirts, Tess was horrified at the devastation on all sides.

Everyone was pointing and exclaiming. "Look there—at that tree trunk with a washer wrapped around it."

"See that trailer smashed right through the other one?"

"Those cars and trucks—they're almost welded together!"

Entire blocks consisted of nothing but rubble. An elderly couple with drooped shoulders stood holding hands, staring at a convoluted mess that had probably been their home. Small children climbed over what appeared to have been a large trailer that teenage boys were now scavenging.

Krystal said nothing. Tess, sitting beside her for the end of the trip, looked toward her and saw anguish on the lovely face. Unnoticed tears were running down her cheeks.

Without thinking, Tess put her arm around Krystal's shoulders, and the younger woman's agonized eyes turned toward her. "I. . .had no idea! No idea at all." The last word was an almost-silent sob.

Tess shared a look with Pastor Jim, who was presently in the front passenger seat as "navigator." His lips tightened before slowly turning upward at the corners. His nod was almost imperceptible, but enough that she was sure it indicated approval.

Of what he approved she wasn't positive—whether of Krystal's response to seeing the destruction surrounding them or of her helping Krystal. Her response was a slow smile.

The sights caused so much trauma that nobody else seemed aware of her and Krystal. Tess spoke quietly to the younger woman of the needs which they had only heard of before and of the work they had come to do.

They were grateful for instructions sent by the church in Dade County, where they would be staying. Even four months after Andrew, state and AAA maps were almost useless at some points because of detours.

They arrived with little difficulty but questioned whether they were at the right address until a small welcoming committee came to greet them.

From the street, the building looked little better than much of the area through which they had just driven. With its roof almost completely gone, the sanctuary reminded Tess of an after-the-bomb movie set.

Mammoth fallen beams had made kindling of the pews and organ. Stonework and masonry had collapsed, leaving irregular portions of walls, devoid of window glass or, for the most part, of frames.

The voices of the new arrivals were hushed with shock and sorrow as they walked around to the reroofed and repaired Christian Education Building where they would be given shelter from now, Sunday, until early the next Saturday morning.

Krystal, subdued, quietly carried in her own things and came back to help the others. Settling in took little time for, again, bed-making consisted of rolling out sleeping bags.

"At least we have a roof over our heads," Molly said. Tess laughed and decided she was going to enjoy being with this woman.

As quickly as they could get their hands washed, they were seated at the long tables in the social room where food prepared by Red Cross and other volunteers was being served. The meal was simple but adequate and, to Tess, was much better than looking for a restaurant after the tiring drive.

People of the host church told them not to worry about changing clothes or if they would be a little late getting to the evening service that was being held in what had originally been the gym. Everyone understood that they had just arrived, and the Floridians were grateful for the time and talent they were giving and were only too happy to have them.

Most of the choruses and hymns were familiar, and the evangelistic message by Dr. Dunne was effectively presented. Tess appreciated his enthusiastic style of delivery. His delightful sense of humor manifested itself in anecdotes, apt descriptions, and twists of phrases.

Almost exhausted by the trip and afraid she would be too sleepy to get anything from the service, she surprised herself by being sufficiently invigorated to volunteer for table tennis before joining a group around the piano.

After that, she went to one of the rooms the women were assigned to sleep in and she went to bed. Everyone there was sleeping in their clothes on spread-out sleeping bags. But, during the night, Tess must have become chilled enough that she pulled up the flannel sheet she had brought in case she needed a light cover.

In the morning, Tess went to the women's rest room to clean up. Getting all the shampoo out of her hair was nearly impossible in one of the small washbasins, but she managed to finish her morning ablutions before the big rush. She hung her damp bath towel on a line strung across the room and helped stack the rolled sleeping bags with hers in a corner.

She put on her oldest, most comfortable jeans and a long-sleeved cotton blouse so she wouldn't sunburn on her first day. However, in case she would be assigned to indoor work, she also carried a sleeveless top. She was grateful she had brought several pairs of work gloves—Molly had forgotten hers and Tess discovered after breakfast that Krystal hadn't thought to bring any either. It sounded as though they were going to need them.

Chapter 4

Most of them walked the three blocks to their assigned work site. Pete brought the truck from where it had been stored overnight, and Tess saw for the first time the many four-by-eight sheets of heavyweight plywood, long sections of spouting and guttering, bundles of shingles, and long rolls of the black, extraheavy, waterproof material that she heard one of the men call roofing felt.

Their first job was a beat-up rectangular building with tattered large plastic sheets covering the area where shingles and even some planks had been blown away. A mother and six children came out, introducing themselves as the Beaufant family.

Mrs. Beaufant welcomed them with big smiles and said how pleased—how honored—she felt that these fine Christians had come to help them. Somebody offered regrets that the house had been so damaged by the hurricane, but she stood there, head high. "We're sorta lucky, though. None of us was hurt or killed. . .and we still have a home. Lots of folks here sure wish they was us."

Under the supervision of Hank Sorrison, a contractor from their home church, the men climbed up the provided ladders, checking to see how many of the remaining shingles were in good enough condition to leave. It had been established previously that, since the damage involved less than one-fourth of the total roof, it would be repaired, not replaced.

The other group of men, with Molly, Krystal, and one other woman, were soon on the roof of the house next door. They removed its torn plastic, which did little good after four months. With flat-tined potato forks and roof shovels, they began ripping off all the shingles needing to be replaced.

The Ehrharts, who lived here, admitted that things got wet in their house when it rained, but they preferred staying here to moving into a tent city.

Mary Sue, as Mrs. Ehrhart insisted they call her, told them, "If we'd gone, bands of looters and worse would have destroyed what little we had left, and I wasn't about to let that happen. My kids need a place to call home."

At first Tess thought nobody could possibly live in the house on the next block where she and the rest of the women and an older man were about to clean up. One end of the roof was barely there, but the exterior walls appeared intact.

Tess sighed as she stood near the curb, gloved hands on her hips, shaking her head. "It's hard to know where to even begin!" Then, squaring her shoulders, she moved into the yard and began to carry or drag fractured pieces of wood, metal, plastic, cardboard, and tree branches to pile along the street.

When they stopped for a midmorning break, Matt Loomis commented, "At least people can see we've been here!"

Tess nodded. The front yard still didn't look too presentable with its weeds and gouges, but it was a debris-free island in these surroundings. It took the rest of the morning to partially clear the backyard. They finished that after lunch, before working on the inside of what had, until August, probably been quite comfortable living quarters.

Anything that could be used had been moved into the two crowded rooms still covered by a fairly good roof. They lugged rubble fallen from the ceiling, interior walls, and roof along with smashed, waterlogged furniture and beds. Tess was dismayed when she began wheezing, undoubtedly from the mildew and molds growing on the pillows and throw rugs she was carrying. Even the broken chairs, tables, and dilapidated chests of drawers were damp and discolored.

She used her inhaler and took her asthma medicine, then put on one of the mouth/nose masks she always carried though hadn't needed for years. She kept on working in spite of the severely restricted breathing that was sapping her strength and energy. She wasn't sure how much longer she could continue.

At first her coworkers weren't aware of what was happening to Tess. When they did realize, they tried unsuccessfully to get her to return to the church. Molly, Pastor Jim, and Pete were especially concerned when they saw her condition at the evening meal.

"I'm sorry. . . ," she began, but was interrupted by another spell of violent coughing. "I took shots for years. . .to desensitize me against. . .mold and mildew and haven't. . .had this bad an attack. . .for a long time. But then, I haven't been. . .handling the stuff like today. Perhaps wearing the mask. . .all day tomorrow. . ." She was embarrassed at her wheezing and the necessity of stopping every few words to gasp for air.

"Come on, Tess!"

Pete sounded angry or provoked, and she flinched. "I know it seems. . . irresponsible, but I didn't. . .consider the possibility of. . .breathing problems after. . .all this time."

"I didn't mean you shouldn't have come," he protested, placing a hand on her arm. "It's just that, if you insist on working, from now on you'll be on a different team."

"I'm not good. . .with ladders and heights." She could have cried, from frustration and disappointment as much as from feeling so bad physically. "I'd at least hoped. . .to spend my time in Florida. . .lugging trash and debris."

Pastor Jim's smile from across the table was meant to be encouraging, but there seemed a sadness there. "We'll see. The important thing now is for you to get over this attack."

It was while trying to finish her dessert that she overheard two of the roofers commenting about the Florida rulings being much more stringent than those in Pennsylvania. For one thing, here the plywood must be thicker—five-eighths of an inch—and that made handling the big sheets more difficult.

The thirty-pound-weight asphalt/felt roofing paper (which could be fifteen-pound back home) was bulkier to handle and must be fastened down with nails, not staples. This in itself would make things more difficult, but even worse was the stipulation that these nails must have special rings or discs between the nailhead and roof. "I could go twice as fast if I could just pick up a nail, pound it in, and keep repeating that."

The other roofer agreed. "I can't believe how time-consuming it is to drive each nail through a disc before using it! I haven't built up any kind of rhythm at all."

"Where are these. . .nails and discs?" Tess asked.

Puzzled, they said they had been put in the room opposite the pastor's study. She asked them to go there with her. When they returned, the men were lugging boxes of nails and discs, while she carried several empty containers.

A group of eight went to play table tennis and the rest visited, while Tess tried pushing or pounding nails through the two-inch-diameter discs. She made little progress. *Dear God, please don't let me be a burden,* she prayed. *Help me feel good enough to keep going. . .to stop wheezing.*

Some time later, when Pete came to where she was sitting at the edge of the group, she looked up at him. "Did you win?"

He smiled wryly. "I never did excel at Ping-Pong and was worse than usual tonight." He took hold of her hand as it reached for another nail. "The important question is, how are you?"

"Fine."

He caught her other hand and silently held both of them until her eyes were raised to his. "That's not an answer, Tess. Let's try again—how are you feeling?"

She wanted to look away, but his brown eyes did not release hers. With dismay, she realized hers were misting. "I feel. . .better than during the afternoon."

Why didn't he say something? She tried unsuccessfully to control her wheezing. "All right, I don't. . .feel good. It takes so much. . .energy to breathe I. . .have little left for anything else."

He lifted the boxes from her lap and the chair beside her and sat down. "You don't have to keep working when you feel rotten, Tess. If you'll notice," his right hand arced to indicate those in front of them, "nobody else is, even though we're well."

"But I feel. . .so useless." She was stopped by violent coughing. "I came all the way down here. . .and wanted to be an addition. . .to the group."

"You are, Tess."

She coughed again and his arm came around her shoulders, pulling her close for a moment. "Do you hurt—physically?"

"Not. . .too much."

"Tell me about it."

She struggled to draw a deep breath and was afraid he would hear or feel its passage. "It's mostly the tightness. . .and wheezing and coughing. . .that bothers me. And my muscles are sore."

"Your chest muscles?"

"Across my back. . .and shoulders. And. . .I'm so tired." She had seldom felt so spent, so exhausted.

He moved one of the low-backed wooden chairs in front of her. "Lean your forearms on that and rest your head on them. I'll massage your back and shoulders and see if that helps."

She tried doing that but straightened almost immediately, shaking her head. "It's too difficult to. . .breathe when I lean over."

His fingertips gently touched her cheek. "That was stupid of me." He stood up and gently turned her so she was sitting sideways on her chair. "Let's try it this way."

His hands were warm and strong, yet gentle, as he massaged her shoulders, up her neck, and then across her upper back. She shivered, and he stopped immediately, his voice solicitous. "Did I hurt you?"

Her left hand covered his where it rested for a moment on her shoulder. She shook her head. "It helps. . .it feels good," she admitted to him as he continued his ministrations.

He did most of the desultory talking—speaking of Thanksgiving and Christmas, of his growing up, and of their trip here.

Her voice was small as she finally said, "I feel guilty. . .keeping you here with me."

"Are you keeping me?"

His voice sounded relaxed and lazy. She whispered, "You're not. . .with the others."

His hand patted the top of her head, as she might do to a child. "You worry too much, Theresa Kenneman. If I didn't want to be here, I wouldn't be."

She hesitated before asking, "Even if you thought. . .it would help me?"

He squeezed both upper arms and tilted her backward until she felt herself resting against him. "Even knowing you as little as I do, I'm aware you wouldn't ask for help. If I find something on my own to make you feel better, I claim that right."

"Oh." She would have loved to stay leaning against him but forced herself to sit upright again. He said nothing and the silence grew long. She didn't know quite how she began to speak of her mother and how close they had been. "She was young in her. . .outlook on life and enjoyed. . .all sorts of activities.

"I was thinking recently of. . .Christmas seasons when she went. . .as advisor on youth trips to. . .New York City for a day of. . .wandering and going to. . .the famous Christmas show."

"Um-hmm. I—" She thought he was about to bring the conversation to himself, but after the briefest of pauses he said, "I'm sure you enjoyed them."

"And going shopping together. Though I usually. . .don't enjoy that. . .but with her it was fun."

The silence lengthened again before he said, "You miss her very much."

"Yes." She nodded, blessedly aware of his strength, his gentleness. "But I think—I know—I'm adjusting better now. It was for the best, you know. Her death from cancer was agonizing."

"I'm sorry, Tess."

She felt a touch on her bowed head and knew it had to be that he had leaned over so his head had rested there for a moment, for his hands didn't leave her back. She had not cried about her mother's death for a long time, but might very well do so any minute.

She slowly turned on her chair and felt his hand slide up to her shoulder again, so that his left wrist was against her neck. "Thank you, Pete," was all she said. She hoped he would realize it was for more than the back massage for which she was grateful.

Yet it was better that he not know everything for which she was thanking him.

Those who had been playing table tennis came over to tease Pete about quitting after losing three times in a row. "What a poor sport you turned out to be," Terry, one of the students, accused.

"It takes great wisdom to know the right time to move on," Pete intoned with mock solemnity.

To which the young man responded, "Or cowardice."

Pete sauntered over to where cans of sodas were being handed out.

Reaching for two Cokes and a handful of pretzels, he challenged, "We'll find out who's the better worker when we start putting roofing paper on our house tomorrow, Terry. You'll have to go some to beat me there."

As he handed Tess her drink and some of the salty snacks, she murmured, "Couldn't resist that, could you?"

His eyes crinkled at the corners. "It was deliberate, of course. Terry's got a lot of leadership qualities and does a good job when he wants to. However, he goofs off a lot, and the younger kids follow his lead."

Pastor Jim, Molly, and Hank Sorrison came over also. Hank, seeing how difficult it was to get nails through discs, disappeared for a short time. He returned with two-by-fours fastened just far enough apart that she could center a disc over the space and pound the nail through.

Molly got hammers for herself and Hank, and the three worked together for the next half hour. Pastor Jim brought empty gallon jugs from the kitchen and cut off the tops, leaving handles attached to bottoms. The prepared nails were dumped into these carriers, ready to be taken to the roofs.

Tess had difficulty getting to sleep. As she hadn't expected to need a pillow, Molly insisted on her own polyester-filled one being used to elevate Tess's head and perhaps make breathing easier. She also gathered the women to pray for her.

In the morning, Tess felt more like herself, although she was bone-tired from the effort to get her breath and from lack of sleep. The horrible wheezing had let up appreciably, but her chest still felt as though confined by leather lacings.

She insisted on being told which place was next on the list for clearing a yard, and plugged away at dragging brush, roofing and siding fragments, and portions of furniture too damaged for use even by those who had lost everything.

She was almost too exhausted to continue when she saw the gloved hand beside hers on the end of a four-by-four beam and heard a worried voice saying, "You don't have to manhandle these heavy things, Tess."

She was sweaty and filthy, but so was he—and Pete had never looked better to her. "I am ready for a break," she said, but that was as far as she would let herself go in admitting her need for rest—and also the need to prove to herself that she could pull her own weight.

He must have realized how nearly spent she was, for Pete's arm remained around her as they walked the long block back to where he had been working. People were resting in the shade of the faded green cement blockhouse with its small gable over the front door. Some were seated, leaning back against it, while others sprawled on stomachs or backs.

The first strip of builder's felt had been applied along the lower edge of the roof so Tess asked, "Who won the workmanship challenge, Terry?"

"Technically, he did." The lanky, young, dark-haired man rolled over, crossed his legs, and put clasped hands behind his head. "But he cheated."

She looked at Pete with feigned horror, then back at Terry. "Pete cheated?"

"I wasn't keeping an eye on him, so at first I didn't realize he was going so fast because he was usin' those nails you fixed for him last night."

She was overjoyed. "It does work then—putting the discs on the nails ahead of time?"

Pete nodded. "Sure does!"

"Fantastic. Then that's what I'll do for awhile before going back to that yard."

She drank cold water, ate salted crackers, and visited. When the others returned to the roof, she continued sitting in the shade with her back against the western side of the house.

As her hands worked, her mind wandered. Had any more crises arisen in the computer department? Were the secretaries continuing to make inroads on the backlog that must be changed, or were they just keeping up with current work?

She felt herself tensing and was conscious of the increased huskiness of her cough. She emphatically reprimanded herself. *Let it go, Tess! You're here, where you got permission to be. And where you want to be. Stop worrying about your absence from work. Somebody will take care of problems if—as they arise.*

It was enjoyable to hear the banter and comments coming from the men and women above her. She wished she could feel secure on ladders or heights for she would love to be with the others, doing physical work directly involved with these restorations.

Oh, well. It wasn't as though she weren't helping.

As they ate lunch, Tess looked around the big tables. "Where's Pastor Jim?"

Molly set down her glass. "It was shortly before you came for break that one of the coordinators stopped by. A volunteer from Tennessee who was doing canvassing got called back home, so they asked if we had someone to fill in."

"To 'canvass'?"

"To find out where groups like ours should be assigned. As I understand it, Pastor Jim will go from house to house and talk with people. He'll find out if they have insurance or are underinsured, how much damage was done, and what people like us can do."

"Oh." Tess hadn't considered how this was accomplished. "There are more aspects to volunteering than meet the eye."

Molly nodded. "And I wouldn't have missed this for anything."

Krystal, who had been silently eating beside her, murmured, "Me too," and Tess smiled at her.

While washing her hands in the women's rest room near the church office, Tess asked the stranger next to her, "Are you putting roofs on also?"

A wry expression crossed the face of the frazzled woman who was probably in her upper sixties. "I wish I were."

Tess reached for a paper towel. "Why? What are you doing?"

"I almost feel like I'm here under false pretenses." The short, plump woman smiled slightly as she too dried her hands. "I am a volunteer, but not in the sense you are. I'm Carrie Jane, a member of this church, and since the hurricane have been trying to help out as temporary secretary. But I'm having such awful problems!"

"Problems with people?" Was the influx of volunteers straining things too badly for the church?

"Not people. Equipment—or use of equipment. And computer software. Everything!"

"I can relate to that!" Tess exclaimed. "I'm something of a troubleshooter for the computer department at a college in Pennsylvania and—"

"You are?" The troubled face lit up with hope. "Could I ask you a favor? Would you please come over to the office and see if you can 'troubleshoot' my mess?"

Tess looked from her to Molly, then back. "That's the least I can do considering all your church is doing for us."

Molly said to take her time—which was good, since Tess wasn't finished even by a quarter 'til six when Pete sauntered into the office, hands in the pockets of his relaxed-cut jeans.

Tess looked at him, then her watch. Pushing several computer keys to close down the system, she started to rise. "We've been so busy here we lost track of time."

She introduced Pete, and Carrie Jane declared, "This woman is the answer to my prayers!"

Pete's brows raised as he nodded. "I'm sure she is." Tucking her hand though his arm, he led her to the doorway as the women confirmed they would meet there again at eight o'clock tomorrow morning.

Tess wasn't sure how to react to his recent statement, but didn't have to when he asked, "What kind of difficulty have you got here?"

She looked sideways at him. "You'll never believe it, but it's the same sort of thing I've been dealing with back home. I suspect the secretary—the real one, not Carrie Jane—didn't have help or training when this first computer of theirs was purchased. Apparently, she taught herself a few basic things and did what she could day by day.

"She may have been able to call up a few files she wanted or needed, but she must have done time-and-nerve-draining searches for almost everything. There was no order nor organization, just hundreds and hundreds of entries."

"How frustrating for her successor!"

"It would have been easier if Carrie Jane were her 'successor,' for then she'd have felt she could call for professional help. As it is, she's filling in for what was expected to be a few weeks, but became months."

She wasn't completely over her asthma yet and had to cough. "The secretary lost everything with the hurricane, so was moved to the tent city. And now she and her husband are on an extended stay with a daughter in Kentucky, since his diabetes and blood pressure went way out of control."

"Those poor folks. And poor Carrie Jane!"

"She's been trying to work within the restrictions of this system—or lack of system. But she'd decided this morning to tell the church board they must get someone to take over immediately—that she couldn't stand it anymore."

He hugged her hand against his body and beamed at her. "And then there was you."

She was warmed by his approval and touch. And yet. . .

"But this isn't what I came to Miami for."

They walked several steps before he said thoughtfully, "It's not what we thought you were coming for, Tess. Apparently, God knew better."

Tess thought he looked very serious about this. "Taking that idea through logical reasoning, I might have to consider the possibility He wanted me to have asthma?"

He held up his right hand, palm toward her, a definite stop. "He often makes something good out of situations that appear all bad while we're going through them. I'll confess I'm never good at seeing what He's up to 'til after it's accomplished, but then I look back and realize, 'So that's what it's all about!' "

Several friends coming down the hallway after having finished their meal engaged in good-natured banter about her spending the afternoon in the church's air-conditioned comfort while they slaved on hot roofs. She tried to laugh, but it was Pete who told what she had been doing—and would be continuing with the next morning.

Pastor Jim's "final" cup of coffee was sitting on the table as they joined him. He was overflowing with stories about people he had talked with, what they had gone through, and their tremendous needs. The others were totally engrossed, not even asking questions or making comments.

Tess was finishing her cake when she saw Pastor Jim thrust out his hand, his voice roughened by emotion. "Thanks, Pete. Had it not been for you, we wouldn't be here."

Pete's hand firmly clasped his. "You're the one who picked up the challenge and ran with it."

"It was both of you—and Molly, here," Tess said, reaching out to stop the woman passing by on her way to the empty tray area, "who got the whole church involved by giving that clown performance."

Molly slid her tray onto the table and sat down. "That reminds me. We brought our clown outfits in case we wanted to do something here."

There was an upward lift to the end of that sentence, making it a question. Her bright eyes looked from one man to the other and Pete nodded. "I was thinking about that this morning when I saw all those kids playing in the street and climbing through the wreckage."

"So what's wrong with right now?"

"Have compassion, Molly," he groaned, reaching toward her pitifully. "Some of us aren't as young as we used to be and may find it difficult to roof all day, then clown at night."

Tess loved his infectious grin as Pete asked, "So which of our vast repertoire of three semiprepared productions do you recommend for this evening, Madam Director?"

Chapter 5

Molly leaned across the table. "How about David and Goliath?"

"With just you three?" Tess asked.

"Nope—four," Pastor Jim corrected, pointing. "He—David; she—King Saul." Drawing himself up as tall as possible and beating his thrust-out chest in the manner of Tarzan, he announced in a deep bass, "Me—Goliath and," with a gleeful look in his eye, "you—Narrator. You give the background and stuff like that, then are David's father and brothers and Goliath's backup army or whomever you choose to be."

"Lucky me!"

"Just so you appreciate the honor bestowed upon you of working with this renowned troupe."

"I've never even tried this."

Molly laughed. "These are persuasive chaps, in case you hadn't noticed. They first talked me into doing that skit at church, and now I'll be in full costume!"

Pete was on his feet, heading for the door. "I'll dash outside and tell the kids who are always around while we're working. They can spread the news that the Pennsylvania Players will do a clown presentation in front of the church in," he glanced at his watch, "fifty-two minutes."

Tess looked at the pastor in disbelief. "You're sitting there with that Cheshire cat grin on your face and letting him go out there to advertise a nonexistent show. Have you no scruples?"

He pushed his chair away from the table and stood up. "Scruples, yes; desire to squelch that crazy character, no."

"But look—I wouldn't have to put on the paint and costume and stuff, would I?"

"Worried?" He laughed out loud and reached for her tray. "I don't think you'll need to. Not this time."

She called after him, "What are you talking about, 'this time'? There may never be another one."

Pastor Jim brought the paints and costumes to the junior high department about the time Pete arrived to announce that he had talked not only to kids but some parents and even those working in the kitchen.

Tess groaned as she entered the women's bathroom to see if she could help Molly. "Well, there goes my hope that few people will show up to witness what we're about to do!"

"Things will go fine," Molly assured.

"Maybe for you three, but I have only the foggiest idea of what I'm even supposed to be doing."

Molly took off her shirt and pants and pulled on the baggy one-piece costume. "You grew up in Sunday school and have known the story of David and Goliath ever since I taught it to you when you were in my class of three year olds."

Her gaze met Tess's in the mirror as she applied paint to her face. "One of the really great things in this life is that the truths of the Bible remain that. If you have doubts as to what to do or say, your best course of action is to read what's in the Bible."

"But. . ."

"You may want to give a brief account of the background of the story—who was fighting, the situation back home at Jesse's, and the youngest brother left behind to care for the sheep. You could mention the father's being so worried that he sent David to the battleground with food and drink for his brothers—and about what he saw and heard there."

"You make it sound so simple!"

"Most of the Bible is. It's what you do with it—what it has to do with you that's hard."

"I'm. . .scared," Tess confessed.

Again, their eyes met in the mirror before Molly turned toward her, interrupting the painting of a matching large, dark blue, upside-down eyebrow. "I can relate to that. But I can assure you that you'll do a great job. I've seen you conduct youth groups, and adult meetings and services."

"I. . .want this to be helpful."

Molly's fingertips were colored, which was probably why, as she reached up, it was the back of her hand that touched her young friend's cheek and jaw. "It will be. And you'll find you do have courage once you've begun.

"You love kids. I've seen it in your eyes and manner when you're with them. And you want tonight to be special for them. Remember this from the fourth chapter of the First Epistle of John, Tess: 'Perfect love drives out fear.' "

Those words kept repeating again and again in Tess's mind as she returned to the room where the women slept.

Love. Yes, she did love these dirty little children in their devastated homes and community. . .and Molly. . .and Pete.

Pete? How could she say even to herself that she loved him? But. . .could she possibly say she didn't?

She was not going to dwell on this. No, she wasn't!

And yet the surprise, the shock of that thought made it come between her and the pages of her Bible. Let's see—First Samuel. . .about halfway. Ah, yes, chapter seventeen.

She went back and read chapter sixteen, also, toying with the possibility of putting into her narration Samuel's being sent by God to anoint David. But that wasn't part of this presentation.

She read chapter seventeen several times and from different translations, grateful she had brought with her the parallel version Bible. She jotted notes of specific things she wanted to stress, in addition to the story's progression.

"How ya comin'?" Molly asked from the doorway, a construction paper gold crown topping her mop-wigged head.

"Okay, I think. And you look fantastic!"

Molly laughed. "King Saul was jealous enough of David to try pinning him to the wall. What would he do to me for making him look like this?"

The men arrived, Pete carrying something long and bulky in a bag. They had time for only a brief rundown of the order in which events would take place, for they wanted Tess outside to greet people as they arrived.

How could I have let them talk me into this idiocy? she asked herself as she went alone to the area that had been the front yard of the church. *Dear Lord, please don't let me start wheezing and coughing again.*

The street and floodlights were still pale in the twilight, but things seemed to stand out with unusual clarity. Massive cut stones still nestled against remnants of walls, and the stumps marked where once-proud giants had shaded congregating worshipers. Something magnificent was gone, perhaps never to be restored to its previous grandeur.

But coming from different directions were individuals, parents and children, and other groups. Had any of these people attended, worshiped, in this house? If so, had they ever before arrived barefoot and in clothing less than clean. . .less than whole?

She crossed the courtyard to meet them, to shake hands, to hug the children. She was glad—elated—they had come. . .were still coming.

Molly had been right. She was not afraid.

Glancing at her watch, Tess realized it was time to begin. She had planned to welcome these people, but she found it more appropriate to do otherwise.

"My friends, we thank you for letting us come to your city for this week and to work beside you. We want you to know we admire your courage, strength, and faith that have brought you not only through the hurricane, but through these four difficult months.

"In speaking with the children," she said, smiling at them, "we mentioned our doing sketches or playlets while dressed as clowns. Being good hosts, they invited us to do one for you. You can thank or blame them for this evening."

The older people laughed, and some of the little ones shifted self-consciously, while others looked proud. She invited them closer before introducing the "Pennsylvania Players:" Saul, the king of Israel (Molly arrived, her crowned head high, walking in stately pomposity); David, the shepherd boy (Pete swung boyishly around the corner of the building, barefoot and clothed in burlap); and then Goliath, the Philistine giant.

When Pastor Jim appeared, she laughed so hard that she was grateful she didn't have to speak immediately. He was walking heavily on three-foot stilts, wearing a hugely padded set of "mail" and other protective armor, and roaring angrily as he glared at Saul and David.

She sobered enough to begin. "This is a story—one that happened long ago in a place called Israel or the Holy Land. The Lord God had given the Israelites this land years before, but the people already living there didn't want this, so war after war took place.

"At the time of our story, King Saul"—Molly bowed regally, holding her crown on with one hand—"was the ruler of the Israelites. The Philistines, who lived between them and the big sea, the Mediterranean, were strong and powerful. And they had a secret weapon by the name of Goliath." Pastor Jim raised one hand and gave a curt little nod.

From then on, they acted out what she was saying.

"Goliath was huge, over nine feet tall—higher than ceilings in most houses," she said to help little ones get an idea of his size. "Goliath had been in major fights before and, big as he was, probably always won. Anyway, he or their army leader got what was considered a fantastic idea.

"One day when the armies were squared off from one another across the Elah Valley, Goliath came stalking out in front of the Philistines. In addition to his size, what he was wearing overwhelmed the Israelites. He had on a bronze helmet and leggings and a two-hundred-pound coat of mail. He had a massive javelin strapped to his back and in his hand was a heavy sword.

"His voice thundered, 'Do you need a whole army to decide this? I represent the Philistines. You pick your champion, and we'll settle this in hand-to-hand combat! If your man kills me, my people will be your slaves. But if I kill him, then you become our slaves! I defy your armies! Send out your man to fight!'

"When King Saul and his army heard this, they were terrified. Nobody was big or strong enough to fight Goliath. Not even King Saul, head and shoulders taller than any of his soldiers, could possibly win.

"No Israelite volunteered, so that night and the next morning and each night and morning from then on the fearsome giant came into the valley, bellowing."

The children's eyes were bright with excitement, their eyes on Goliath, waiting to see what he might do.

"In the meantime, Jesse, the father of three of King Saul's soldiers, was worrying about his sons and how the war was going. They didn't have newspapers in those days, or radios, or TVs, so he sent his youngest son, David, to take food to his brothers and the captain of the army and to find out what was happening.

"After making the twenty-five- or thirty-mile trip, David arrived as Goliath came out to give his challenge again. David was horrified when the Israelite army turned and ran. 'What's going on?' he asked. 'Who is this heathen Philistine who defies the army of the Living God?' "

Tess now had to directly answer David's (Pete's) mimed question to her. "The giant has been hurling defiance and insults at us for forty days. King Saul's so upset that he's offered to the man who kills Goliath not only a stupendous amount of money but also marriage to one of his own daughters, a princess. In addition, this man's family will never again have to pay taxes."

"David" moved away from her, toward some of the audience, and Tess continued, "Word got back to King Saul that David was talking to others about this situation. Now, he already knew David, who had been spending part of his time in the palace playing harp music for the king. Saul sent for the young man who assured him, 'Don't worry, King Saul. I'll kill the giant for you.'

"The king was flabbergasted! 'There's no way a shepherd kid like you can kill that monster, who's been a fighting man all his life!' "

Tess could see the littlest boy in the front row sizing up David. Would he really try to kill Goliath?

"David explained that as a shepherd he'd clubbed to death wild animals that took lambs from his father's flock. 'God saved me from the claws and teeth of the bears and lions,' he insisted. 'He'll surely save me from this heathen Philistine who's making a mockery of Jehovah's troops.'

"The king was impressed by the bravery and words of this youth. So, since there were no other volunteers, he finally consented to David's being their representative and prayed that the Lord would be with him.

"In order to give as much protection as possible, Saul put on David his own specially made bronze helmet and royal armor. But when David strapped on his sword and tried to walk, he said, 'I can hardly move in this heavy armor!' And he removed it."

Tess wasn't sure that anyone was listening to her words now. Their attention was riveted on David struggling to lift and remove his invisible armor.

"Goliath was still out there heckling the Israelite troops, calling them cowards and shouting things he was going to do to them. He was infuriated when he saw David walking toward him, wearing nothing but his regular old shepherd boy's clothing and carrying only his shepherd's staff and sling.

" 'How dare you send a little red-cheeked boy out to fight against me?' he thundered. 'Do you consider me a dog, that you come at me with a stick?' And he started cursing David by all of his pagan gods.

"David had by this time gotten to the stream in the valley, so he stooped to pick up five smooth stones. He didn't appear afraid as he walked toward the ferocious giant, who was swinging his mammoth sword and threatening loudly enough for all to hear. 'You keep coming toward me and I'll cut you into pieces for wild animals and birds to eat.'

"David called back, 'You know how to fight with the sword and spear, but I have Jehovah, the God of the armies of Israel, whom you have defied. Today, the Lord will conquer you. He'll make it possible for me to kill you and cut off your head—and the bodies of your troops will be eaten by the birds and wild animals. All the world will hear of this and know that Jehovah is the God of Israel. And all the Israelites here will know that God doesn't count on weapons to work out His plans, nor is He impressed by human might. He will give you and all your men into our hands.'

"The Philistine lumbered toward him, and as David ran forward he fitted a stone into the center of the leather strip. With a quick twirl of the sling, the stone was released and thudded into that small space between the giant's helmet and eyes. With a crash of armor and weapons, Goliath pitched forward onto his face, unconscious."

Tess paused, worried about the condition of her young pastor, whose hand had gone up to cover where the pretend stone had "hit" him. He didn't seem to have had much way of breaking his fall from off the stilts and now just lay there on the ground, motionless.

But the story must go on. "David had no weapon of his own so, grabbing the huge sword of his enemy, he killed the giant! The Israelites, cheering and yelling their battle cries at the top of their lungs, chased after the retreating Philistines, killing and capturing them.

"And they all knew, as David had predicted, that God is in control of everything."

Tess was pleased that the children in front of her were cheering also. But then she looked again toward Pastor Jim, lying "dead" upon the ground, at

Pete, foot on his "conquered foe," and at Molly, crown askew but proud. Tess wished desperately that they had made arrangements for one of them to take over with a tie-in of their story with the situation in Miami.

But they hadn't!

Well, she would have to do something. "Even today, when things look dark and we wonder why bad things or disasters happen or how we can cope with what comes, the important thing to remember is that God really does care for us.

"He loves us and is with us, even through the bad times. It may not be so obvious as His helping a shepherd boy kill a giant, but when a friend lends a helping hand, when another prays with you, when you have the opportunity to help someone else—God is there.

"Jesus said that a person giving a drink of water to another in His name is giving to Christ. You have given your smiles and welcome to us, you have come to hear and see our clown performance and have patiently and courteously cheered us on.

"We thank you very much for showing us Jesus living in you. And yes, He lives in us, as well. If any of you would like to talk to us about this, or about clowning, or about anything else, please stay and visit."

It was late when they got to bed. At least twenty of the "audience" had remained, talking and visiting. A young man and woman went over to sit on a fallen pillar to talk about some spiritual matter with Pastor Jim, still in whiteface though without stilts and armor.

Tess took some of the teens in Molly's van to bring back pizzas, and they all ate and had an enjoyable time together. It was Molly who finally brought things to a close by stating that if they were to work hard the next day, they needed to get to bed.

Tess didn't sink into sleep immediately, even as physically exhausted as she was. She kept thinking of the work she was doing in the office, of the skit they had done tonight—and that she had not called Aunt Freddie! She had waited too long in the morning, so had planned to do it after the evening meal. She must be sure to call after breakfast.

And she must also get back to making more notes on her laptop computer. She had done some on her way down and her first night here, but she had felt so rotten yesterday and this morning that she had neglected this.

These resolves made, her mind returned to this marvelous evening. What fun it was to be with this group—especially the three who did the clowning. How was it that she had not come to know Molly as the terrific woman she was? Memories of her as an "old" woman teaching a Sunday school class must have still remained in Tess's mind all these years, keeping her from appreciating her as one of the "youngest" sixty-something adults she had ever known.

And Pastor Jim. She had respected and liked him, but it was mostly as "pastor," not as friend, a man only five or six years older than herself. She thought back over this evening, at him thumping his chest and growling, "Me—Goliath." And his taking that crashing fall when "killed" by David's stone. And his counseling with that couple.

She rolled over, willing herself to go to sleep, yet finding this not so easy to accomplish as to dictate. There was Pete also to think about—not that he was the least in her consideration. Had her mind deliberately left him until last so it could dwell on his attractive person?

She smiled in the darkness, glad nobody could know of her thoughts. He was so funny. So kind. So caring. It was he who had come for her at the office—and helped when her asthma was so bad. It was he who had massaged her back and shoulders and neck.

She could almost feel his strong capable hands doing this, and hear his concerned voice telling her not to push herself, but to relax and get better.

And yet, even though his arm had been around her shoulders then, even though he had held her hand snug against his body as they walked back from where she had been working, even though their gaze frequently met laughingly or warmly or with friendship, he had made no effort to be more than just a friend.

Well, that's what she wanted, wasn't it? Her plans had been laid out precisely: She was going to put everything she had into doing her work and taking all the college courses she could manage toward getting her degree. She was not going to get "involved" with anyone as long as she was doing this.

Her twisted smile this time was at her own expense. It looked like Pete was "helping" her in this way also—helping her keep that resolve.

One part of her tried to keep from wishing this were not so.

Tess glanced up at the movement in the doorway and saw him there. Pete's voice and manner were brusque and demanding, though his smile belied this. "Hurry up, Woman. It's lunchtime!"

"I know. But I told Carrie Jane I'd keep going here 'til noon."

"It's after that." He pointed toward the big clock with its hands at twelve and two.

"And then I kept thinking of one more thing to do," she finished, closing down the computer.

Carrie Jane jumped in to justify her. "You have no idea how much she's helped me! Not only has she straightened out the files so I can find things, but she's put in programs for record keeping, and business letters, and the church newsletter, and memos, and all sorts of wonderful things!"

He put his hand on the older woman's shoulder and gave a friendly squeeze. "I was teasing, Carrie Jane. Honest. I know she's talented and generous and always gives her best."

Pete and Tess didn't touch as they walked to the cafeteria area. Her thoughts of the night before ruled out her casually taking his arm; and his approving comments to Carrie Jane, while making her feel great, also made her self-conscious.

In a way she wished he would direct this sort of thing toward her—of course it was best he didn't.

She was reading too much into too little! He thought of her as a friend, nothing more.

They carried their filled trays to where Molly sat at the end of a noisy group, and their conversation moved through discussions of the previous night's activities to the roofing this morning.

Tess remembered to tell them, "This morning I called my elderly aunt who lives over on Florida's gulf side and up a ways. She absolutely insists I visit there tonight. Might I borrow your van, Molly?"

"Of course. You know that."

Tess smiled her appreciation. "Frederica Bollway is my mother's eighty-six-year-old aunt, the last of her generation and one feisty lady! I do want to see her while I'm here."

Pete asked, "How far away is it?"

"She said it would take about two hours, so I'll leave early, about four if that's okay."

He groused to Molly. "Ya just can't get good help nowadays! She sits in that air-conditioned office all morning and leaves at four to go visitin'!"

Molly slapped his arm affectionately (as Tess would have liked to do). "Stop picking on the girl. Her work's every bit as important as ours—probably more so if the truth's known. I just wish I knew something about computers."

Tess was about to offer to teach her but Pete announced, "I'll ride along with you, Tess. You might be glad of even my company when you're making the two-hour drive back."

She felt warm, and suspected she was blushing like a schoolgirl. "That's not necessary."

He frowned at her. "I didn't think it was, Tess. However, you don't know these roads any better than I do, so perhaps a pilot and a navigator are called for. Will your aunt object to an extra person?"

"She'll be glad for it. She suggested I bring a friend with me, but I didn't want to take anyone away."

He picked up his sandwich in both hands, saying, "Since you're 'taking me away' from my work, I'd better eat fast and get back up on the roof. I wouldn't want people thinking I'm not doing what I'm being paid for?"

He bit off a huge mouthful and started chewing rapidly. Knowing she was being teased again because of her overdeveloped sense of responsibility, she rolled her eyes. "You're incorrigible, Pete Macfarland."

He grinned as much as possible with his cheeks bulging with food. He reminded her of a playful chipmunk, but it was better not to say that.

Chapter 6

Tess walked out with Molly and Pete and was delighted to see that their group had finished several roofs as far as possible. The state requirement that their work must be approved by an inspector after decking, flashing, roofing paper, and drip edges were installed meant that another team coming later would have to put on the shingles.

In the meantime, these homes were protected from rain. Those living in them could now begin to use all their space instead of crowding into the driest rooms.

A number of children and some adults came up to Tess, talking about last night's program. She was puzzled that they spoke to her rather than Pete until she realized that she was the only one they recognized. She introduced Pete as "David" and called up to Molly, already on the roof of a small house, to have her wave to her "admirers."

Fearing another bout with asthma, several tried to discourage her from going with them to clear away debris from another yard. She assured them she would be okay if she stayed outside, and was especially glad she had done so when she found she had helpers. Children, still off from school for Christmas vacation and probably bored, were eager to assist.

They wanted to know about Pennsylvania, about snow and sledding, and asked if people really did go out with parents to cut down Christmas trees. A few days earlier, Tess had been sorry she hadn't done that this year, but now reveled in her memories, sharing with her young friends traditions that were taken for granted as a child.

She didn't stop for a break and found when Pete descended from his roof to walk to the church with her that he hadn't, either. They got cleaned up and were on their way northwest shortly after four.

"It's amazing," she said half an hour later, "how quickly we go from devastation to relative normalcy. Few of these homes seem to have been damaged."

"If so, it wasn't bad, anyway." He seemed completely relaxed driving and made comments about things they saw.

"It's nice to have things growing at this time of year."

"But I'd miss the change of seasons. We always did a lot of hiking and skiing and other outdoor activities, so we saw Nature in all her wardrobes.

I loved each of them."

She would have liked knowing who "we" referred to, family or friends. But should it be some special friend—a woman—perhaps it was just as well not to know.

She spoke of Aunt Freddie. "She used to live in Duvall, the town just south of Fairhills. When she retired, she was honored for having taught in that school district for forty-six years!"

"Forty-six?" His amazement was genuine.

"Sounds like forever, doesn't it? She went to normal school the summer after getting her high school diploma and began teaching in a rural one-room, eight-grade building that same fall. From then on, she took college courses each summer and often during the year, as well. Even after getting both her bachelor's and master's degrees, she kept on with continuing education and other courses right up 'til retirement."

"When you described her as 'feisty,' I thought maybe she was quarrelsome or difficult."

"Not Aunt Freddie. Oh, she was ready to fight for any student and for what she believed in, but she was more than willing to listen to the other side and try to work things out."

He shifted position behind the wheel and glanced in her direction. "Family traits?"

She was startled. "I would be. . .honored if people thought me at all like my aunt Freddie!"

🌴

She was waiting for them, perky and spry as always. Tess didn't get to see her often since she had bought this two-bedroom, "low upkeep" house and moved south five years before.

"It's about time you came to visit," Aunt Freddie stated while showing them around.

"You know I've wanted to, but with work and school it was hard to arrange," Tess explained. "And it sounds like you're as busy as I."

Aunt Freddie beamed. "Isn't that wonderful?"

Tess usually didn't think of it that way, but agreed, "It's good to have a lot of friends and interests."

"And it keeps you young."

Pete nodded. "It's certainly done that for you."

She patted his hand. "That's one reason, in addition to my arthritis, for my being here. Many friends back home got into ruts and found it too easy to find reasons for not doing things during the winter. That's no excuse for slowing down here."

On their way to dinner in her big old Lincoln Continental, Freddie stopped at the church to which she had transferred her membership. "If you were staying longer, I'd bring you to Bible study tonight. As it is, you can at least see where I worship and study."

Her guests exclaimed over the beauty of the airy, light sanctuary and how well the Christian Education Building had been planned. She pushed open the door to a smaller, cheerful room with a desk and two chairs by an open window. "This is where I meet with three different children several times a week. The youngest and oldest need help getting their reading skills up to their grade levels, while the other's having difficulty with math."

Pete asked, "What grades are they?"

"Three, five, and eight—and their getting to those levels without anyone caring enough to see they got help is a crime!"

"They have the ability?"

Her fists were planted on her hips. "Definitely! Darrin, the eighth-grader whom I began working with this summer, has already climbed from second to about sixth-grade level. And, most importantly, he has learned to enjoy reading."

"What does he like? Sports? Cars? Space?"

"All of the above. But he loves science fiction. So your old aunt," she said to Tess, "who had read almost none of the genre, is regularly getting these from the library and reading them. Incidentally, there's a lot of trash out there, but I pass on those I feel will help his reading yet not hurt him in other ways."

"He really does read then?"

"I ask questions, and he shows good comprehension and retention. I've begun sneaking in exciting historical fiction and biographies and science too, and bring him my *Smithsonian* and *National Geographic* and even *Biblical Archaeological Review*. He's not reading every word of these, but does some."

"Many subscribers don't read every word, either, for that matter," Pete reminded.

She smiled. "A point well taken. What I'm thrilled about is his not just looking at the pictures. He reads at least enough to answer the questions they raise."

Their stop wasn't long at the Center, a large, low, white structure where Aunt Freddie regularly went to swim and to take lessons in oil painting. As it was less than a mile from her home, she usually walked there each morning. She was disappointed that only a few of her regularly present friends were there to meet her guests.

It was after eight when they got to the Seafood Palace for dinner, and Tess was so hungry that every item on the menu looked delicious. She was glad that her large tossed salad with ranch dressing was brought quickly, for that and her dinner roll were nearly finished before her shrimp threesome was set before her.

Dinner conversation wandered through many topics, from ancient family stories to the political scene to what could not be out of their minds for long—Hurricane Andrew. Aunt Freddie was upset about Tess's asthma attack. "You got those so bad when you were little! You were on the prayer chain many times, especially when you ended up in the hospital."

"I remember all too well, which was a major reason for my resisting your efforts to take me to the emergency room, Pete. I almost always got put in the hospital when I went there." That had been such a terrible period for her that she usually tried to forget it.

"But my shots had helped so much and for so long that I didn't expect even all that mold and mildew to hurt me. Needless to say, I'm not about to take chances like that again." She put an end to that topic after saying how grateful she was for all the prayers on her behalf, which must explain how she had gotten over this attack as quickly as she had.

Pete talked as much as either of them and seemed to enjoy his evening. Tess's suppressed yawn while finishing the lemon meringue pie had nothing to do with being bored, and she tried to convince them she wasn't sleepy.

However, as they started back to Aunt Freddie's home a few minutes later, her aunt insisted they stay overnight. Tess could sleep in the guest room and, "It's no trouble to make the living room couch into a bed for Pete." They could get up and leave as early as they needed to.

A deciding factor was her saying there was always lots of hot water, so they could get their showers either tonight or in the morning. They had both missed being able to do this.

Tess rolled over and checked the time. Four-forty-three. If this were daylight saving time it would be nearly six—none too early to start getting up so they would have time for a full day's work.

At least these clothes I'm getting back into were clean yesterday at four. She used some of her aunt's deodorant and mouthwash, but that would have to do until she returned to Miami. Her aunt didn't own a hair dryer, but Tess could manage without that.

Aunt Freddie was in her kitchen preparing fresh grapefruit juice and visiting with Pete, who was replacing the embroidered pillows onto what was again an Empire sofa. "You're bright and beautiful in the morning, Tess," he complimented.

"And so are you," she assured him. And he was. It was true, as he reminded her, that he needed to shave, but this made him look even more masculine and rugged.

She set the table and visited with her aunt while he showered. Aunt Freddie set scrambled eggs and toast before them, saying they needed good breakfasts to keep up their energy.

She also assured them when leaving that they hadn't been "too much work" and that she had enjoyed every minute of their stay. "You come again if you can get away," she insisted.

"I doubt that we can," Tess explained after thanking her for the invitation. "We have to leave early Saturday."

"Well, maybe you could stay an extra day or so."

Pete suggested, "Perhaps on the next trip we make?"

"You're already thinking of the next time?" Tess asked.

His face lit with that sudden boyish grin. "You betcha!"

Aunt Freddie inquired, "And how soon might that be?"

"Perhaps over Easter—or, to be more politically correct, as public school systems now have to be, 'Spring Holiday.'"

That threatened to bring on a conversation about the government as it pertained to the educational system, but they managed to get away before long. As they drove back, they at first spoke mostly of things concerning their visit. During a companionable period of desultory comments Pete asked, "So what about staying?"

"What?"

"Everybody's planning to leave Saturday morning, spend the night in South Carolina, and arrive home Sunday evening. Do you suppose Pastor Jim might consider staying until very early Sunday, giving the three of us a chance to continue working all day Saturday? With three drivers, we could take the truck straight through."

She had mixed feelings about that. He seemed to take for granted that she would want to stay with them. She decided she was more flattered at being included than annoyed. "Let's ask when we get back."

They had no opportunity for this until the evening meal, since Pastor Jim and the other man and woman conducting the survey were involved in another area and ate their fruit, sandwiches, and beverages there.

A man near them, still suffering from sunburn acquired on his first day of working on roofs, said, "You've sure got it made, Pastor Jim, out doing surveys while we're doing the work!"

Tess almost jumped in to defend the importance of what Pastor Jim was doing, but realized in time that some undoubtedly still figured she had taken the easy way when helping with the church computer. She was relieved at

Pastor Jim's looking innocently toward the speaker. "Would you like to trade places with me tomorrow, Earl?"

"No way!"

"I can go over the information and forms with you tonight, and you can go into those houses and ask questions."

"Hey, Man, there's no way I could do that."

Pastor Jim's eyes didn't release the other's. "Then I'd say we each have an individual niche to fill, wouldn't you, Earl?"

Pete broke the moment's silence by asking Pastor Jim about staying for the extra day. The young minister nodded. "An excellent idea. I'll get the opportunity to work on roofing that way."

Earl looked uncomfortable as he leaned forward over his plate and ate rapidly. Pete went on, "The truck's front seat is plenty wide for elbowroom, and you, Tess, and I can take turns driving and sleeping. It shouldn't be too hard going back to work Monday morning."

"If I recall correctly, that's what you did when you came down before—and that would have been much harder since you were starting with a new class in a new school system that day."

Molly stopped by their table to inquire, "Shall we do the 'Christmas' clowning tonight or tomorrow?"

The men thought it would be better on Friday, and Molly reported she had asked Krystal to narrate this time. They gave Tess hints and suggestions—and the extra clown outfit—for her role as one of the down-and-out strangers seeking the meaning of Nativity. She was grateful to have longer to prepare mentally than the few minutes she had had two evenings before.

Later, while pounding roofing nails through tabs, she decided Pete had deliberately mentioned in front of everybody their staying for an extra night. He had just as openly spoken of their being with her aunt the night before. They had nothing to hide, but she wouldn't have deliberately given more material to possible gossipmongers. On the other hand, it would probably have been worse for people to wonder about where they were and what they had been doing.

The point of a nail jabbed her finger. It wasn't bleeding so she continued her work.

Morning. A new day—the last workday here for most of the crew. After breakfast, she walked out with a group and admired again how much had been accomplished. She was still surprised at the variety of roofs on these one-storied houses, for most shown on TV had seemed to be simple, straight, front and back surfaces. The majority of these had hipped roofs or mini-gables over the front door or other places, thus requiring flashing in gullies and more cutting and fitting.

"Did you notice how slightly slanted these roofs are compared with those at home?" Molly asked Tess.

"With no ice and snow, that's probably more than adequate."

"So there's almost no chance of falling off."

Tess looked at her speculatively, fearing what would be coming—especially when Molly called to a worker already on the roof, "Is the surface dry, Earl?"

"Dry as a bare rock at noonday."

Molly had her hand on Tess's arm, steering her toward the ladder leaning against the house. "You've got so much courage and strength in many ways, Tess. How about climbing up there to hammer in some nails?"

She couldn't help pulling back. "I. . .don't think I can."

"Let's try it, okay? Just hold on to the sides, put one foot on a rung and the other on the one above it. And keep climbing. That's all there is to it."

The idea was mind-boggling. "I couldn't possibly swing around to get off the ladder and onto the roof like. . .like Earl did a minute ago. Even if I managed to climb up there."

"You can. I'll be right behind you and—Pete, you go on up and give her a hand," she commanded.

"Yes, Ma'am," he said, snapping to attention, flattened right hand angled from his forehead, heels of his sneakers coming together silently.

He sprinted to the ladder and climbed up as agilely as a monkey. It looked so easy when others did this, but it was Molly's encouragement from behind her and Pete's smile and outstretched hand from above that made her place a foot on the first, then second, and each additional rung.

She would not look down—she must not. She paid full attention to her handholds on the side rails. Her lips felt dry, hands slippery. Twice, she paused to wipe a palm on her jeans before reaching for another higher grip.

Her head felt funny. Eyes closed with weakness and then in prayer, she leaned her head forward against a rung. *Dear God, please give me courage to go on. I can't do this without assurance that You're with me.*

She felt a strong hand covering her right one and Pete's voice commended, "Good girl!" She looked up into the approving brown eyes and, unbelievably, was able to smile a little bit.

"Keep your hold on the ladder 'til your feet are almost to the line of the roof," he advised. "Good. Continue holding on as you reach out your right foot to rest on the roof. . .over just a bit." The outside edge of his shoe pushed against the inside of hers. "Now there's room for your left one also."

He was not touching her now, but his hands were near enough that she knew he could grab for her if anything went wrong. The roof felt substantial under her athletic shoe—and now under the other one.

She moved her left hand to the right side of the ladder and reached toward Pete with her right one. To her surprise, he shook his head. "You don't need me, Tess," he said softly. "You're doing everything just right."

It didn't feel "just right" to her, but if he said it was, she would take his word for it. She let go of the ladder.

Tess was on a roof! Walking on it! Maybe it was only a step or two, to make room for Molly who, right behind, came to give her a quick hug. Tess looked over her shoulder and saw Pete beaming like a proud father whose baby had taken her first steps. He declared, "You're quite a woman, Theresa Kenneman!"

"Come with me," Molly said briskly, starting up the roof's slant. "As you see, we've got the third strip of the heavy, thirty-pound builder's felt—this waterproof roofing paper—laid down across the roof. The first two were nailed every six inches at the edges and twelve inches otherwise.

"Here's a hammer and one of the nails you've been putting through aluminum tabs. Use them."

Tess stood there for a moment, feeling utterly incapable of taking the several steps to her friend. The tip of her tongue circled dry lips, and she put up her hand to ease the throbbing at her temples.

How would she get back down?

Well, she was going to have to, sooner or later. As it was, she was just standing here while the nine on the roof and goodness knew how many others on the ground saw her acting like a ninny!

She drew a deep breath and held it as she took a faltering step forward. Another. She was near enough to where she was to drive the nail that she could get down on her knees. Reaching for the hammer, she placed the tip of the nail she had been handed in what she hoped was the proper relationship with others. "Okay?" she asked Molly.

"Perfect."

Her first hit was tentative, but the next blow drove it through the builder's paper and firmly into the wood beneath. She reached for several more from the cutoff jug into which the prepared nails had been placed for ease in handling. There was no longer hesitation on her part as she placed and pounded in rapid succession.

Pete gave a long, low whistle. "You've been hiding your talents, Tess!"

"I helped Dad build the garage. And finish off the basement. He's something of a perfectionist, so I learned early how to drive nails."

Molly sat down and motioned for Tess to do the same. "Occasionally, I have to stop what I'm doing and look around. Since there are no hills or mountains, this is as close as we get to a perspective on what happened here and what we're doing."

Tess sat beside her, hugging her knees. From here, she couldn't see down to the base of the ladder or even the yard of this house. The view of the street or beyond didn't give her vertigo, nor did the rooftops.

Pete was on his knees helping pound nails as Molly pointed out to Tess the six houses that had been repaired by their crew. They would be finishing this one soon. The one three houses over, the blue cement block one, should easily get done this afternoon.

The faded pink house across the street, where people were removing the last of the large, heavy, rectangular, cement tiles, had been begun only since they knew Pastor Jim and Pete would be working all day tomorrow.

Perhaps I'll be some help with that also. If they do the work near the edges, she thought timidly.

Tess's arms arced broadly, indicating everything in front of her. "There's so much left to do."

"Yes. There is," Molly agreed. "Every one of those places with plastic covering its roof needs major repairs."

"Are people living in all of them?"

"I think so. At least that's the case with all we've worked on."

"It seemed that way. If we can call that living." Tess shuddered. "In the house where I was carrying all that stuff when I developed that attack, a family of four was crammed into one room. Oh, they could use the commode and the kitchen sink, but the roof's plastic covering had torn, and their belongings in the rest of the house were destroyed."

Her head moved slowly to the right then left. "I never saw people so. . .so overwhelmed by life. He had retired from a reasonably good job, their home and car were paid for and insured, and they thought they were okay.

"And, in one day, they lost almost everything. And then they found that their insurance company was one of those that went bankrupt because of Andrew. They had nowhere to go except to the tent city and figured, whether correctly or incorrectly, that they'd be no better off there."

She sighed. "Their lack of hope made me feel even worse than my wheezing and struggling to breathe. At least my suffering with that is now over."

Molly frowned at her. "You should have left as soon as you realized what was happening, Tess."

"I didn't expect it to get bad." She was silent for a moment before adding, "And yet there was a good side to even that. I keep remembering that, although they'd lived like that for four months, once they saw I was there to help and wasn't leaving with the first twinge of discomfort, the man came out to carry and drag some things too."

"That's another example of the way God makes good come out of bad," Molly said matter-of-factly as she pushed herself up to her feet and reached to help Tess. "And now I'd better get back to work before they fire me."

One of the men unrolling another strip of builder's paper heard her and pretended to scold. "And you wouldn't appreciate our docking your pay, would you, Molly?"

Tess would have liked to go back down the ladder right away—well, she wouldn't like to do that at all, but did wish she were already on the ground.

Pete had completed his hammering of the last nails securing the precious strip and got up to cross to the other side of the roof. His voice was light as he asked, "Ready to help with this one, Tess?"

"I'm not sure I'll ever be ready for that, Pete," she confessed. "But I probably could manage more if that's a requirement for your helping me back onto the ladder."

He was instantly serious. "Look, Tess, I really don't mean to be demanding and nasty. It's just that it's important to deal with fears and hang-ups, even though that's difficult. And I do understand how you feel. I used to be terrified of snakes."

She shuddered. "I don't like them, either."

"Until one day I went to a herpetologist and talked to him about my fears and how this kept me from hiking except in winter. You can probably guess what he did—made me look at pictures of snakes and read about them and finally get so I could touch, then hold them."

She wasn't sure she could ever do that. "You're completely over that fear?"

He laughed ruefully. "Snakes are still not my favorite form of life. And they startle me if I come upon them unexpectedly. But I no longer have a debilitating fear, and I do have a grudging admiration for them."

"So you're saying I don't have to camp out up here to prove I'm not scared to death, but in the meantime I can learn not to let this phobia immobilize me."

"That's about it. If you're positive you want to go down right now, I'll help you. Or," and there was that dancing light in his eyes that often preceded a smile, "if you want to stay up here and practice so you can be our third worker tomorrow, I'll help with that also."

From where she was standing near the center of this shallowly sloping roof, there appeared to be nothing more dangerous than a hillside at home. She drew in a deep breath before saying in a small voice, "I'll stay. For awhile." But she added a qualifier, "If you'll remain between me and the edge of. . .disaster."

He reached toward her, his smile radiant. "Anytime, Tess! Anytime."

Chapter 7

For a moment, she thought he was about to hug her, but instead he leaned over to pick up two hammers and he was all business as he showed her exactly what to do. She was high enough to see that the back of the roof was finished except for the drip edge being attached by men on stepladders.

She enjoyed doing this work that before she had only watched from the ground. She wouldn't let herself dwell on the thought of going down the ladder. But, when the job was completed, she found that with Molly at the bottom to steady it and with Pete talking her through the process, she could do it.

As her foot touched down, she heard spontaneous clapping and looked around at these friends whom she had come to care so much about during this week's time together. They were all smiling, and then she was too. "I couldn't have done this without your patience and caring. Thank you."

A man called from the next roof for more of the "ringed" nails. Tess saw only a few dozen in the large can and asked, "Is this all of them?"

"Afraid so," Earl said. "Everyone was so busy trying to get our jobs finished. . .and I guess we thought these would be enough."

She looked toward Pete, hoping he wouldn't think her offer was an excuse for not going on to the next roof. "We'll need a lot tomorrow too. I'll work on getting nails ready for then. . .and for the rest of today."

Matt Loomis joined her as she lined up aluminum circles along the narrow space between the two-by-fours. "How about my pounding nails in the center of each disc while you continue laying them out?" he offered.

"I'd appreciate that. And after awhile we'll trade off so we get variety in our lives."

This went much faster, and she enjoyed the easy conversation about things here, back home, and, especially, of the early history of their church. She knew he was always reelected as church historian at the annual business meetings, and she had heard him speak at the church's one-hundred-fiftieth anniversary celebration eight years before.

She hadn't been much interested then but was now fascinated by his story of the missionary, Elisha Reichmann, who had come from Connecticut in the 1800s and traveled up and down the valley by foot, horseback, and boat.

Many residents liked and welcomed him, but Elisha had also made fierce enemies, among who were the Doebly brothers. Along with several other drunken men, these two "tarred and feathered the preacher and rode him out of the village and a full five miles away tied him to a fence rail that had one end attached to a horse's saddle."

Tess gasped. "Was he hurt?"

"Sure was. The next morning friends found him in the woods, unconscious, still tied with leather thongs to that pole. They cared for and nursed him back to health and wanted to help him get another horse—his had been stolen or driven off—so he could return to New England.

"But he was a determined as well as dedicated Christian. As soon as he was well enough, he went right back to the same town and walked up to the older of the Doeblys. He stuck out his hand, palm up, and asked that they be friends.

"Jake Doebly was sober that early in the morning, but he still spit tobacco juice on the preacher's hand. That didn't stop Elisha Reichmann, however, for he said, 'That's all right, Mr. Doebly. I'll just keep on praying for you. The Lord God Almighty wants you for His own.' "

"That must have gotten a reaction!"

"Oh, it did. Jake threatened to kill the preacher then and there, but it didn't faze Elisha. He just said, 'In that case, I'll be in the presence of my Lord and God, so even for that I can be thankful.'

"Jake was so mad he drew his gun, but apparently there was something in the bravery—faith?—that got to him. Or, knowing that all the townspeople would be aware of it if he shot an unarmed man, he realized he'd better not do it. Whatever the reason, he turned and walked away.

"And the next summer at an open-air revival meeting, Jake Doebly was one of those who walked down the sawdust aisle and gave his life to Christ."

She had been so involved in what he was saying that she had paused in laying out discs, but she now did more before removing those that had been completed. "That's a great story! And it will be even more wonderful if you tell me he was of the family for whom Doebly's Mills was named."

"It was for him, not his family, that that section of town was named. Once he got straightened out spiritually, the rest of his life changed too. He'd worked in a gristmill as what we'd call a 'gofer,' I guess. He was a hard worker and advanced to more responsibility and finally bought the place and added to it and eventually became one of the most influential deacons in our church and the mayor of our town."

"Fantastic!" she exclaimed. "Do you know what I'm going to do? I'm asking Pastor Jim to have you tell that story in church as a children's sermon."

"Oh, I couldn't do that!"

"Of course you can."

"I'm no good at quoting Scripture and weaving in lessons and doing stuff like that."

She covered his strong, lined hand with her work-gloved one. "That has all the lessons and Bible woven into it, Matt. Any man with the strength of God, the love for His people, and the dedication that Elisha displayed would be an inspiration not only to children but to every single adult present."

He looked dismayed and she smiled. "Don't worry about it, Matt. God will give you courage too. I know He will. It's just that. . .well, I grew up in our church and never even heard that account. Have you written it down?"

"Well, it's in my notes somewhere."

"Don't you see? Perhaps you're the only person in our congregation who knows about this. We can't have it lost when you're gone—which I hope will not be for a very long time," she hastened to add. "Please share these stories of the past that you've searched out and treasure."

Clearly, he was changing the subject when he called her attention to how nearly finished the group across the street was in removing cement tiles from the house. It would take some time for workers on the ground to gather and remove all the heavy, broken pieces of concrete sliding down that improvised ramp.

Several other women also helped drive nails through discs, so Tess was able to carry quite a lot to the house where Pete was securing yet another strip of builder's paper. He waited for her to come partway up the ladder before reaching for the cutoff jug. "Gonna stay and pound?"

She wanted—no, almost wanted—to do this. "I'd better help with cleanup," she said. Forcing herself to look away from those warm, seeing-too-much brown eyes, she focused on the work being done on the pink house. "Do you think that will get finished tomorrow?"

He chuckled. "Depends on the help."

With raised brows she looked back at him. " 'Help'. . .like the people or like what they accomplish?"

"They go together."

"Like. . .perhaps I should get more practice?"

He tilted his head slightly and looked at her through narrowed eyes, as though this was a new thought he had to consider. "Since you mentioned it, yeah, I'd say that's not a bad idea."

Climbing the rest of the way wasn't nearly as bad this time, but she was extremely grateful for his giving a hand to assist her in getting from the top of the ladder to the almost flat roof. He asked, "Wanna look down this time?"

"No!"

She felt her face flushing from embarrassment at having been so emphatic, but she could think of nothing to add that wouldn't make her cowardice even more apparent. She was spared the need by his assurance. "It's okay, Tess. You're doing very well. I'm proud of you."

She looked down at the carefully nailed strips of builder's paper on which her feet were firmly planted. "You shouldn't be, but thank you."

On his way back to where he had been working, he dumped some nails into two other containers for those working on their sections of the roof. She waited for him to drop to his knees before she got down beside him and picked up a hammer.

At first she didn't talk much as she developed the rhythm that would accomplish the most efficient nailing. However, when he said they could review what they would do as clowns in a few hours, she was able to concentrate on that.

This time she had felt more confident, partly because she was better prepared. She had to admit to herself, though, that the main reason she had been able to lose herself behind the paint and inside the costume was that she was no longer Tess then, nor Theresa—she had become the wanderer.

It's strange, she thought while lying in her sleeping bag that night. *It's not that I don't like being me, but it's refreshing to be so entirely in the role of someone else that you even feel and think like that person.* She yawned sleepily. Did professional performers feel like that?

And then it was morning.

Everything was in turmoil. People finished packing their meager belongings, ate breakfast, and started getting into vans. When Molly hugged her and said she hoped the three of them would have a good trip coming back in the truck the next day, Tess found herself almost tearful and wishing she were leaving with this woman who had become such a good friend.

"Maybe I shouldn't be staying."

Molly drew back slightly. "Why not, for goodness' sake?"

"Oh, I don't know. Maybe I won't be that much help."

"And?"

Tess confessed, "I guess. . .I was thinking that maybe it doesn't look good. . .my staying with the two men."

"Worried about your reputation?"

"Not really." She shook her head. "But with Pastor Jim being the pastor and Pete a teacher in the public school system. . .there's not going to be any gossip or trouble for them, is there? If so, I could get my sleeping bag and other things and be back in a few minutes."

"Don't be ridiculous!" Molly said. "If you're up to driving straight through to Pennsylvania tomorrow after putting in a full workday here today, more power to you."

"We'll sleep some on the way. Taking turns driving, it shouldn't be too hard."

"You all have to be at work the next day."

Tess put her hand against the small of Molly's back and gently gave her a push. "Yes, Mommy. We'll be careful."

Pastor Jim, Pete, and Tess stood there waving until the last van turned the corner and was out of sight. Pastor Jim pulled his work gloves from his hip pocket. "Well, there goes our last excuse for not being on the roof."

"Race you to the ladder!" Tess challenged. Her long legs ate up the distance—but both men passed her as they crossed the final yard and took positions on either side of the goal, grinning in triumph.

She was panting from exertion, but laughing. "At least I tried."

Pastor Jim patted her back as though commiserating. "Had the distance been a bit shorter, you'd have won."

Pete sobered. "You did win, Tess. You won in being able to choose the ladder as your endpoint. . .and running like crazy to and not away from it."

"Oh." She could think of nothing more to say as she looked away, not wanting him to read in her eyes how grateful she was for his approval.

He hurried up the ladder and waited at the top to assist her as he had done before. Pastor Jim went to pick up the nails and hammers, and by the time he joined them, they were unrolling the heavy roof covering.

Pastor Jim took her end from her, and she wondered if this was his way of saying she didn't have to be at the very edge of the roof. Only after the unrolling was completed did he put in those nails that would securely hold the beginning of the strip and then worked across to where she had started pounding.

Pete took over the cutting and arranging at the other side of the roof and while he was doing this, she continued pounding nails. There wasn't much talking as they worked steadily at making the strip secure.

The process was repeated and when they stopped for a break, they found Myron, the man of the house, wanting to visit. He had been at work the other days and they hadn't gotten to know him. "I didn't think our roof would get fixed by your group. Dottie, here," he indicated his middle-aged wife who was coming from the cement block house with a pitcher of orange juice, "said everyone was leaving this morning."

They all lounged in the shade of the house, since the trees that had been in the yard had been reduced to splinter-topped stumps. Pete explained, "We're the only ones left, and we'll start home very early tomorrow morning."

"How early?" Dottie asked, pouring juice into unmatched glasses.

"Five, five-thirty. . .somewhere around there."

They talked about Myron and Dottie's family, two sons and a daughter living "up north," and Dottie brought out pictures of their seven grandchildren. "What a handsome family you have!" Tess exclaimed, returning the snapshots.

"We think so." Dottie's round face creased with delight. "We just wish we could be with them more. They were all planning to spend Christmas with us this year—would be here right now if it weren't for Andrew."

Tess reached for her hand, recognizing the sadness that had overtaken her. "Now that your roof's fixed—or will be at least rainproofed by the time we leave—maybe they can come soon."

"I don't know. Much of what was inside—all the beds but one and the living and dining room furniture and most of the rest—is ruined."

"That does present problems," Tess agreed. She had not seen inside and only hoped these people hadn't left the mildew and rot as had been the case where she had developed that horrible difficulty with breathing.

Pete and Pastor Jim were at the ladder, and Myron was carrying a hammer as he came from inside his house and followed Pete upward. Pastor Jim waited for Tess to precede him, and Pete was there to help her should she need it. His presence gave her confidence to step out upon the roof.

They worked steadily for the next couple of hours, during which time two neighbor men joined them. It was noon when Dottie's dark face appeared over the roof's edge. "Y'all hungry?"

Pete answered for all of them. "Starved, actually. I've been trying to get these characters to quit long enough so we could get sandwiches."

Dottie's smile was radiant. "We have a better idea. Instead of you going to get them, we're invitin' you to come eat with us."

Tess laid down her hammer, wiped her perspiring face on her cotton sleeve, and stood up. "That sounds wonderful! I'm so thirsty I can hardly stand it." However, she waited at the ladder until the other woman got all the way down and Pete was beside her.

She desperately wanted his assistance—but he didn't offer it. Holding onto the ladder with both hands, she hesitantly planted one foot upon a rung. She carefully felt with her toes for the next lower one and started her descent.

Looking up as her feet touched the ground, she was rewarded by seeing Pete's right thumb and forefinger forming a circle while the other three fingers were extended. His lips formed silent congratulations: "You made it!"

She felt exhilarated—by having accomplished what she had never thought she could do and by his commendation. For a split second she felt sorry it was only during this last twenty-four hours that she had attempted to overcome her phobia. Her smile answering Pete's before he swung around and scampered down the ladder was one of pure joy.

Adding length to a picnic table and a card table was a long, narrow one created by two-by-four pairs of lumber on sawhorses. The assortment of wooden and metal chairs had been brought from homes on which the Pennsylvanians had worked throughout the week.

Tess blinked to keep from crying as she saw the macaroni salad and baked beans, fried chicken and catfish, steaming corn bread, and even several pecan pies. "What a spread," she exclaimed, looking around at the twenty-five or thirty happy faces. "What a surprise!"

There was a lot of visiting and sharing of happy experiences as well as telling of how life had changed overnight for these new friends. "There have been many times," Effie Mae, a young woman with two small children, said, "when I just wanted to give up. It seemed like no matter how hard I tried, things weren't goin' to get better."

Dottie agreed. "We felt so hopeless. Nobody seemed to care, really care, about our situation. Oh, we were given food and were permitted to go to a tent city or stay on in our homes. But there were so many needin' help that those of us who could 'make do' continued to do just that."

Pastor Jim's face showed compassion. "That was the main feeling of those we surveyed throughout Dade County. Actually, a lot of people and organizations are concerned, but they, like you, are overwhelmed by needs."

Myron slathered butter on the large chunk of corn bread in his hand. "That's an important part of your comin' down here to fix roofs. You didn't have to take from vacation time to help us."

"And you didn't have to give those clown programs, either," Effie Mae stated. "But they helped too."

This led to a discussion of clowning and of how they had gotten into it. The hosts could hardly believe it was here that both Tess and Krystal had had their first experiences with this ministry. They wondered aloud if perhaps they could start something like this in their churches.

Pete promised to send Myron a book about clowning that he had found helpful. He then stood up, saying that since they had already consumed most of the pie, they had better get themselves back up on the roof.

Time and work went speedily, with even more neighbors helping up there and clearing away below. The sun was throwing long shadows by the time the final strip of builder's paper was nailed across the top and the drip edges were securely fastened. Someone on the roof gave a cheer and suddenly everyone was hugging and laughing.

"We made it! We really finished the job," Tess cried, her arms around Dottie, who had been working alongside her husband.

"Isn't it wonderful?" Tears of joy were running down Dottie's cheeks. "You'll never know how much we appreciate what you've done."

There was no sign of morning through the tall windows as Tess, alone in her assigned room in the Christian Education Building, got out of her sleeping bag, fully clothed, and headed for the women's rest room. *It will be good to wake up tomorrow in my own apartment and take a hot shower and get back into my regular routine,* she thought wistfully.

She looked at the tanned, oval face in the bathroom mirror and saw its smile. She would never regret coming here and working and meeting all the people whom she had been able to help even for this limited amount of time. The experience had been so much different from what she had expected or even hoped for.

Bonuses were ticked off on the fingers of her left hand even as she washed with her other one. Getting to know the people of her church better—especially Pastor Jim and Molly and Pete—though not necessarily in that order. Sharing her computer expertise. Getting over her fear of ladders and heights, at least being able to function at a one-story level, anyway. Adventuring into clowning. Having that wonderful time with the people here yesterday.

And the developing relationship with Pete.

She should erase that word "relationship" even from her thoughts. But no! It was a perfectly good word, with an all-encompassing meaning of association or compatibility with another person, and should never have been transmuted, cheapened into implying sexual activity!

Pete was waiting for her inside the door and reached for her luggage. He didn't say good morning as he had done other times when she was looking lovely or wide awake or anything. He just grinned as he said, "You're gonna be surprised."

"What's up?"

With a sideways tilt of his head, he indicated the door and said, "You'll see!"

She preceded him to the cement-and-brick walk and was met by Dottie, who threw her arms around her. "We had to come again and wish y'all a good trip home."

And then the others—nine of them, including two children—were all speaking at once and thrusting candy and homemade cookies into their hands.

Myron was lugging a polystyrene foam container holding sodas, leftover fried chicken, and other things from the day before. Hefting it into the back of Pete's truck, he said in response to Pastor Jim's concern about returning the box, "Don't worry about it. Refrigerated materials come packed in these to the lab where I work. I'm always tryin' to give them away instead of throwin' them out."

Chapter 8

I don't know," Tess said as they were able to get on their way only ten minutes later. "I never expected them to be so responsive. Maybe it was because there were just the three of us."

"Or perhaps because it's the weekend, and the ones who were working all week are home yesterday and today," Pastor Jim suggested from his seat by the passenger window. "During the week, when we were working as a crew, we outnumbered them and they may have been intimidated."

Tess admitted, "You're right. I did talk to people—some. But I'm afraid I didn't try very hard until yesterday. . .except with children occasionally and after the clowning performances."

"None of us was really good at this." Pete sighed. "I didn't make any real effort to draw people out if I didn't get an immediate enthusiastic response." He glanced over at his passengers. "I'm glad God directed us to stay. At least there's a chance that our friends from yesterday realize we really do care about and for them."

Tess nodded. "We had a definite advantage there, because of our clowning. They seemed to appreciate that."

Pastor Jim agreed. "The part I'm especially pleased with is that the sociability was a neighborhood effort. They said that when they were working on the roof with us and helping us clean up, it was the first time some of them had even spoken to one another! Can you believe that?"

"Maybe this will continue now that it's begun," Tess said, hoping this would be the case.

"Even if it doesn't," Pete said, "what a great memory it will be for them. And for us."

Tess agreed. "My grandmother used to tell of wonderful times of spontaneous community kindness as she grew up on her family's farm. Like when the father of some kids showed up at their one-room school with a horse-drawn bobsled to take all of the kids and the teacher for a ride. And another time all the farmers went with their families on a late-fall Saturday and got the corn crop husked and put away for their neighbor who was ill."

"Now that's being good neighbors!"

"It is indeed!"

They spoke of individuals they had met in Florida—of Francis, the man still limping from injuries suffered during the hurricane, who had managed to work on the roof yesterday, and of a child who seemed fine now, although she had been in the hospital due to a skull fracture she had sustained at that time.

They also talked about the church that had hosted them and the Red Cross workers. Tess shifted into a more comfortable position. "I'd expected to get around more while we were there."

"I'm sorry about that," Pastor Jim said. "I saw quite a bit, since I was out talking with people. I should have asked if anyone wanted to take a van and drive around."

Pete put in, "Some of us went out late the second morning we were there. It was awful, even after four months."

He could have come to the church office and asked me to come along, Tess thought. *It would have been nice to be asked—and to have gone. However, as rotten as I felt that day with my asthma and as busy as the secretary and I kept, I'd probably have declined.* Pete obviously didn't seem embarrassed when he mentioned it. He certainly had not meant to hurt her feelings in leaving her behind.

They made a practice of frequently pulling off the highway to stretch and at least walk around the truck a few times. Pastor Jim took the second turn behind the wheel, and it was when Tess finished her stint that they broke out the chicken and salad.

They ate quickly at a wooden picnic table, and Tess still had Coke left when she climbed into the truck to fasten the center seat belt around herself.

It wasn't until late afternoon that talk became more centered on things at home. She suspected Pastor Jim's thoughts must have many times been on their church, just as hers had to be dragged back from worrying about things in the computer department.

She and Pastor Jim included Pete in their discussion of how to improve the senior high Sunday school class and get the students involved with activities. "I assumed this trip indicated they were active," Pete said. "Aren't the three who were with us leaders in the youth group?"

"I wish they were," Pastor Jim admitted. "They have lots of leadership potential, and use it in varying ways at school—sports, drama, music, what have you. All good things, mind you, just not church-related."

"Their parents?"

"Not too active themselves, nor inclined to push our activities. Of course, it is hard to fit everything into busy schedules. . .and they're all good students."

They talked about the three, one of whom had been raised in the church while Terry and the other had come within the last three or four years. Pastor Jim pulled himself into a straighter position. "I'm encouraged that they all worked hard on this project and seemed to really enjoy doing it."

Pete said thoughtfully, "You mentioned awhile back that you wanted us to tell about our trip at the beginning of next Sunday's service. You were planning to include the young people?"

"Of course."

"I was wondering. . .could you perhaps have a separate session for them with their peers, like a pizza or spaghetti supper? I know they got some pictures, as we all did."

"I didn't get as many as I expected." Tess had hoped to take a lot. "And I'm not sure mine will be too great."

"But you did the writing," Pastor Jim said. "How much did you get on your computer?"

She hadn't realized she had been so obvious about it. "Quite a bit." And then she talked about her intention to use the material for independent studies projects.

"I saw you talking to folks from other areas. Did they help?"

"Um-hmm. Especially those working on different details, like those spending weeks cooking for groups like ours."

"That takes dedication!"

"It certainly does."

Pete asked, "Do you have a specific plan as to utilizing the information you've collected?"

"Not firm," she admitted. "Not yet. I've been doing a lot of thinking and will finish my first-stage proposal to submit before the end of this week."

"Will you be using your pictures?"

"I'm. . .not sure. The head of the department wasn't enthusiastic about that. I suspect she saw it as my way of wanting to let pictures do the talking, instead of my words.

"Since she doesn't seem to want that, I checked with the journalism department just before Christmas to see if I can do an independent studies photojournalism project there. With that, I understand that successful publication of the article is a necessity for receiving a good grade."

Pete looked surprised. "They do that sort of thing there?"

"I know of people getting credit for similar things but don't know all their circumstances. Actually, I'd enjoy either project even without college credit, so I've nothing to lose by trying."

"And probably a lot to gain," Pete agreed.

Pastor Jim offered, "If you could use my pictures or if I can help in any way, just ask."

"Thanks, Pastor Jim." It was so typical of him to offer. "I've seen some of your photography. I may very well come knocking on your door."

"I'll be waiting, Tess."

Pete said nothing, but she was certain he would also help if she asked.

Darkness seemed to come awfully early, and she turned the headlights on before she ended her stint of driving. They pulled into a truck stop where the meals were large, flavorful, and nourishing. Pete relaxed against the back of his captain's chair. "I'd planned to have dessert but don't have room. How about you?"

"I'd prefer stopping for something a little later on," she told him, and Pastor Jim agreed.

Tess shivered as they crossed the lot. "Next time I leave the truck I'm wearing my jacket!"

There was a coziness, a feeling of peace, warmth, and rightness, as they rode through the darkness. There were longer lulls between conversations, but these were friendly, comfortable silences.

They stopped and ate dessert around ten, and the men teased Tess about her large butter pecan ice cream cone that turned out to be huge. She still had much of it left when the men had finished their black coffee and pie, so she took it along to enjoy in the truck.

She napped briefly before her next turn to drive, and was asleep when Pastor Jim pulled up in front of her apartment. She looked around, surprised. "We're home already."

Pete laughed. "It's only 'already' for the one who slept away the past hundred miles."

He opened the door and got out, then helped her, which she appreciated, as she was a bit stiff from being in one position for so long. Pastor Jim went to the back of the truck, and they joined him there to retrieve her things. Pete insisted on delivering them, laying them on the Early American tapestry sofa in her apartment before heading for the door.

"Get a good night's sleep, Tess, and be rarin' to go come morning."

"You too, Pete. I suspect you'll need it even more than I, with your post-vacation third-graders waiting to greet you."

He didn't look tired as he smiled. "We'll both make it. I have confidence in us."

She closed and locked the door. Yes, he apparently did have a great amount of confidence in himself. And he inspired it in others. She could still hardly believe she had climbed that ladder, and not just once, but several times. And she had actually worked on that roof!

Her morning shower was every bit as hot and refreshing as she had remembered. Maybe it was good that she had "done without" for a week if it made her more appreciative of everyday blessings. She stepped out onto the shaggy pink rug and dried herself with one of the soft, absorbent pink towels that she wrapped around herself. With a second large towel, she made a turban around her wet hair. Then she went to the kitchen to prepare tea and toast.

She had plenty of time to get ready, especially since she brought her tea and a sandwich of toast with peanut butter into the bedroom to eat. She breakfasted while dressing in slacks, shirt, and blazer.

Even bundled warmly, she shivered from the cold as she hurried to her car, which started with no problems. There was light enough to see without headlights, but the day seemed drab and colorless. The houses on her block were all white, not the pinks and blues and yellows of those that she had been helping repair.

Ah, but these houses had intact roofs, the shrubbery was well tended and manicured, and the bare tree branches still arched over the street. *How blessed I am, Lord. Please help me be more grateful. And help those poor people we met and the thousands of others who are in as bad or worse situations.*

She parked in her reserved space, got out, and hurried toward the Bachman Administration Building, one of the oldest structures on the century-old campus. Its dark red bricks were well-appointed, and the pillars, window frames, and wide trim wore fresh white paint.

She went up the four steps to the wide porticoed area that graced many of the university's publicity shots, through the wood-and-glass door into a large entryway, and from there to the third door on the left, her office. It's true she shared this with her secretary, but she had arrived early as usual, and for the moment this was hers.

She hung her coat and hat on the brass rack and walked over to sit at her desk to shuffle through the stack of mail.

Envelopes that appeared to be Christmas-related were separated then slid into her purse for reading at home. Professional journals and advertising information were stacked on the far corner of her desk and next to them was a separate pile of business letters and memos that had to be taken care of immediately.

Oh, great! The permission to go ahead with the journalism project was in her hand! How much material did she have? She was certain there was enough for both endeavors. She transferred the high-density microdisk from her pocket to her computer. As the file was printing, she continued going through the pile of mail.

There was a special department meeting called for 11:30 today, and her secretary, Alicia, had left a note saying that the treasurer wanted her to call as soon as she got back. Apparently, there were additional questions concerning the endowment fund, about which Tess had notified people prior to her leaving.

She reached for her phone, back on the job and needing to touch base with everyone. She would be expected to give up-to-date information at the meeting concerning how things were progressing, even though she had been out of the office for a week.

The high-speed printout was completed before Alicia and some of those from other offices arrived. They wanted to know all about Tess's trip, and whether there really was as much damage as it appeared from what was shown on TV—or was this just "more media hype"?

She assured them things were worse than she had imagined—even four months after the hurricane. She couldn't go into detail, however, with so much work waiting to be done.

Alicia was unashamedly relieved by her return. "I was scared you'd have car trouble or something, and I'd maybe have to fill in for you at the meeting!"

"Maybe I should have waited to come until this afternoon." Tess laughed shortly and glanced toward her desk. "I'll need all your input from this past week if I'm to get through."

The tone of the meeting was better than at any other time over the past two months. Christmas happiness? Probably not. There was usually more post-Christmas blues than euphoria in the dark month of January.

On her way home, Tess dropped off a roll of film and stopped to pick up the plants and week's mail from her neighbor. She was delighted to find that prints from film she had sent last Tuesday had already arrived. Sitting on Mrs. Kirkpatrick's couch, she shared them, telling of pertinent things that had happened and what she and her group had done.

"It's exciting, Tess, that you got to use your computer skills like that!" The loose-skinned, frail-looking hands were clasped in the lap of the lavender plaid wool skirt, and the older woman's blue eyes sparkled.

"At first I was disappointed that I'd gone all that way, only to be doing what I do at home. But it wasn't long 'til I realized this had to be of the Lord. There's no way I could have predicted getting my worst asthma attack in fifteen years on my very first day of work."

Then she confessed, "I felt sorry for myself—and for my coworkers being stuck with me—and there He was, providing me with a job that nobody else was as well equipped to handle. And, by the time that was done, I was pretty much my old self again."

"Did you go to the hospital?"

"No—though Pastor Jim and everyone else thought I should."

"Why didn't you go?"

"Partly because I didn't want to be a bother." She rushed in more words as the woman began to scold her. "I'd gone down there to work and was afraid that would end it. I've gone to emergency rooms before when this happened—and ended up being admitted."

"But—"

"I always carry my inhaler and other medicine with me, even though it's been a long time since I've needed them. With using them and staying away from molds and mildew for the next thirty-six hours—and having the prayers of my wonderful Christian friends—I got through."

"Thank God!"

"I do." Tess smiled as she got to her feet. Her neighbor invited her to stay for soup and toasted cheese sandwiches, but she declined. She was tired and needed to get at least one load of laundry done. "I'm almost out of under-clothes and every pair of jeans and the things I wore in Florida are filthy!"

Mrs. Kirkpatrick carried the two smaller plants as she walked with her to Tess's apartment, but left when Tess was called to the phone.

Tess slid out of her pumps and curled up on the end of the couch as she visited with Aunt Freddie. Yes, she had arrived safely in Pennsylvania. No, she had not had another attack during the rest of her stay. And they had, indeed, done clowning again.

Tess told of the wonder of their last day in Florida, with people coming to help complete that final roof and share food and spend time with them. "Of my entire experience there, that's got to be the highlight—except for our time with you, of course."

Aunt Freddie's hearty laugh hadn't changed with the years. "That was a good 'save,' my dear. But your visit truly was a highlight of this winter for me. And I want you to know that I like and admire your young man very much."

Tess would have liked saying that she did, also, but needed to keep things accurate. "He's not my young man, Aunt Freddie. Just a man whose friend-ship means a great deal to me." In response to questions, Tess reminded her about his coming to town at the beginning of the school term and about his sharing at the church supper concerning his earlier trip to Florida. "That's what inspired all of us to go and do likewise," she said. "And I do admire him."

Yes, things had apparently gone reasonably well at work while she was away. And her neighbor's care of the plants had been excellent, thank you. Her first pictures arrived today and others were being developed. Her family was well, according to a phone call, but she wouldn't see them until the weekend.

As she replaced the phone, she hoped she would see Pete then too, if not before. He had been such a help in many ways.

He was not at the midweek service. He did not call. She told herself he was busy with school and. . .and what else? She saw him at church on Sunday. He smiled over the heads of people between them but didn't come to her.

Thinking back over their time together, she realized she knew little about his social life. Was he dating? If so, was he seriously—emotionally—involved elsewhere?

He certainly had not romanced her. If she had read too much into his kindnesses when she was suffering, that wasn't his fault.

But she wasn't willing to accept—not yet, at least—that her instincts were wrong. He had gone out of his way to show concern for her, and he had chosen her to work with him in clowning—and to work beside him on that wonderful last day.

He was the one person who had reached out to her in that special way—to make her overcome or cope with her fear of heights. If he didn't care for her, would he have bothered? Would he have gone with her to her aunt's home so she wouldn't have to do all that driving by herself on unfamiliar roads?

She didn't know about these things. Or many other things about him.

But she knew a lot about herself. If he didn't call, if he didn't soon indicate some interest in her, she would not be able to keep from feeling hurt—perhaps devastated.

At work she had no time for fretting about it; there was always so much to do. She was good at her job and knew she could get everything she had into the new system—if given enough time. The last major change, which had taken place before she came and primarily involved updating previous work, had been done over a three-year period. This was a complete change. What they expected timewise was unrealistic, and she was missing some important documents and records. . .how many, she still didn't know.

Today was one of those increasingly frequent times when she admitted to herself she would like to resign.

🏝

She always thought and organized best at the computer, but now found herself taking over much of the dining room table for her projects for credit. She got permission at work to use their facilities to tap into library and other information services so she would not have to waste time tracking down sources.

She wrote letters, but primarily used phone calls to interview people who had done a lot of volunteer work. How she wished she could include in her two papers more of what she was learning!

Another week passed. One day after work, she went to the mall and bought clown makeup, colorful wigs, rubber noses, and other things she thought might come in handy. She wondered if Pete had remembered to send Dottie the book on clowning. In case he had forgotten, she bought a paperback one and sent everything with a note to thank her and the others for their friendship.

Pete still didn't call, but Pastor Jim did—several times. As a result of his first call, she went to church early Wednesday evening and sat with him in the Family Activity Center, going over his pictures. She was awed by their quality. Love for the people was evident in the shots he had chosen to take.

She had considered her own pictures to be good, for they clearly showed the tremendous damage Hurricane Andrew had caused and the reconstruction work accomplished by their team and groups from other places. One of the shots she had considered almost professional in quality was of a house trailer's aluminum shell wrapped around what was left of a large tree.

Pastor Jim had taken a picture from almost the same spot. His showed an elderly man leaning on a wooden cane in his right hand while his left hand reached out to touch with all five fingers the scratched, twisted metal.

She whispered, "His home, the sorrow, the grief—it's all there."

Pastor Jim's voice was solemn. "It was his daughter's home. His small grandson died there."

There were tears in her eyes. It was hard to even say, "How awful!"

His eyes remained focused on the picture in his hand. "The heartbreak. . . is everywhere."

"Oh, Pastor Jim." She wanted to comfort him as much as she wished she could ease the pain of the man in the picture.

The next one was of a little child. Tess had photographed boys searching through debris, scavenging, looking for treasures. The picture before her was a close-up of a barefoot girl surrounded by ragged, splintery lumber and broken glass—and the child was crying.

"How did you get this?" she asked, hurting for the subject of this picture too.

"I used the zoom lens. And I'm ashamed of having taken time to do that before I picked my way into that mess to carry her out. Her name's Betsy Ann and she's only three, but she was able to tell me how to find her mother. Her mother explained that they are living in a tent city but were back at their house trying to salvage some more of their belongings. Betsy Ann had wandered away and ended up stuck where I found her."

The pictures continued. She finally looked up at him, her heart breaking. "How do you bear it?"

"Bear what?"

"Seeing the world like this. The pain. . .heartbreak. . .despair."

He riffled through the photographs and drew out several. "They're balanced by the love in the world, Tess. Things like this."

He held out a picture he had taken of her late in the afternoon when she was first helping the church secretary. "I look awful," she protested.

Pastor Jim would not let her pull it from his hand. "You felt so terrible, yet you wouldn't stop. And here you are," he said, showing her another, "that night when you were wheezing and exhausted, but pounding nails through discs. Because of your love and concern."

"Let me destroy these, please. I had no idea I looked that frightful."

"And you sounded that bad too." His troubled gray eyes looked into hers. "I've seldom felt less helpful—more useless—in my life. I was upset you wouldn't go for help."

Her hand covered his. "You were a help. You and all who were praying for me."

"And you couldn't sleep."

"Not much. But," she said, taking a deep breath and reaching for more pictures, "that's enough about an incident that's over and done with. What's important is the other pictures you have here and the stories they tell. You've got to show these—get them published."

"They're not that good, Tess."

"They are. They really are."

She was sure his response of, "We'll see," was simply his way of terminating that discussion. He got up to greet the people coming for Bible study.

When Pastor Jim called the second time, it was to ask whether she would be going to the association meeting, where people from twenty churches would assemble for their winter session. He had received an invitation for the Fairhills church to have a twenty-minute segment of the program to show pictures and tell briefly about its trip. "I'd appreciate your help, Tess."

"With what aspect of it?"

"To share what it meant to you to be with the group and to tell what you did."

"Comments of the other volunteers would be more typical."

"But that's why I need you. It's easy to get so wrapped up in 'purpose' that we lose flexibility. You did something different—and in a way only you could."

She hesitated. "I'll try, if you want me to, but I wish you'd rethink this. I promise not to be offended if you change your mind."

"I won't and you shouldn't, in that order," he said, voice warm with teasing or relief. "Let's go together with Molly and Pete and some of the others to choose slides and pictures on. . ." The rustling of pages showed he was checking his appointment book. "Thursday night at. . .eight-fifteen, right after the Christian Education Board meeting."

She glanced at the wall calendar, penciled in with things she must do. "Sounds okay. Good thinking to do it while you and I, at least, are already there."

She wondered if it would be awkward if Pete felt he was forced to be with her when he was trying to avoid her.

Might he feel she was "after" him? Or that Pastor Jim was trying to throw them together? Perhaps their closeness during the trip had, upon their return, scared him off. Her mind replayed their conversations in the truck, but she saw nothing to explain why he would be angry with or had decided not to see her.

He never gave me reason to think I meant more to him than any other member of the group, she told herself firmly. *I must have read too much into his gentleness—rubbing my back to loosen tight muscles; stopping for me on the way to meals; including me in clowning. And when he hugged me on the roof that last day, it was what we were all doing when the last nail had been driven. . .like his exuberant embracing of Alice and Myron!*

She would not let it get her down.

Chapter 9

Tess wondered if Pastor Jim's frequent calls meant he was becoming interested in her as more than a friend. She hoped not. She admired and liked him as much as any man she had ever known—yet didn't feel the same about him as she did Pete. She didn't love him, though she almost wished this were possible.

She must be strong and not let herself be so disappointed. . .so hurt. . .by Pete's ignoring her.

She consciously tried to keep the coldness of Pennsylvania's January from affecting her emotions, the grayness of the season from tightening around her.

Things at the college were hectic, with pressures building among the secretarial and computer employees. Each department protested that the blame was not theirs for the missing records, and Tess was the one who bore the brunt of this contention. Some days she developed unaccustomed tension headaches.

She found herself praying in the car on frosty or snowy mornings for the calmness and strength needed to keep things going smoothly and to help the transition to progress without more major problems.

And then came a day when everything seemed to go well—no blowups, no short tempers. It was almost like old times, with people laughing, sharing information about families and activities, and just enjoying each other.

On her way home, she rejoiced in the afterglow, the marvelous red, orange, and salmon of the pellucid western sky following sunset. *Thank You, Lord, for the beauty of this marvelous world You created. Thank You for caring for us and helping this day to be so pleasant. Help me, please, not to let things get me down, like my fretting over computer problems. . .and Pete.*

The Christian Education meeting went smoothly, with input by all members. As they entered the Family Activity Center, Pastor Jim was laughing with her about a humorous suggestion someone made, and she wasn't thinking of Pete until her eyes met his across the room.

Time stopped—as did her feet. The smile left her face. Pastor Jim turned back toward her from a step ahead, undoubtedly wondering what had happened.

She looked downward, flustered. The lace of her left shoe was coming untied, so she used that to explain her stopping. She placed her foot on a nearby wooden chair and bent over to tie the shoelace.

By the time she straightened, Tess had prepared herself to participate in the fun stimulated by seeing the pictures of the trip. She had not known that every camera taken to Florida had snapped a picture of her on Monday night and Tuesday, when she was at her very worst!

She protested the first two, then sank down a little lower in her seat as each additional one was projected. She asked that they not show these at the association meeting and was relieved when they agreed.

Again going through those put aside for possible use, they chose ones showing specific things they wanted emphasized. They could show only a limited number of pictures. It was even more difficult to select brief portions of videotapes.

Molly protested, "It's impossible to compress that whole marvelous week into twenty minutes!"

"Especially when we're supposed to be talking in addition to this," Krystal agreed.

Pastor Jim rubbed his jaw thoughtfully. "Let's see. . .only the five of us agreed to speak. Okay, instead of preparing individual talks, let's go through these one more time. If you feel strongly about a particular shot, volunteer to say something about that scene and what it means to you."

Tess was pleased with the response; it would make an effective presentation. Pastor Jim and Pete, who had done the videotaping, would comment on that.

Pete got to his feet and stretched. "Anyone want a ride to the pizza shop for a bedtime snack?"

Tess kept herself from accepting, even when Molly urged her to go along. "I've got so much to do on my independent studies papers," she explained. "I never learned not to overload myself."

She made a hurried exit before anyone else could ask her. It might have been different had the personal invitation come from Pete.

⚓

She was tired the next day but pleased at the amount of work she had completed the night before toward her journalism project. It was good to not have to leave work to attend classes during the January term. Daylight hours were short, and she went out for her major meal at noon, leaving nice long evenings to accomplish her goal.

⚓

Molly had suggested they carpool for the association meeting, so most of them met at the church. Pastor Jim and Pete each had a load, and Tess rode in Molly's van with a number of members who would not be speaking. Her disloyal mind suggested that if Dad had not phoned just when she was about to leave the apartment, she might have arrived in time to go with Pete. . .if he had asked her.

But he wouldn't have.

Oh, stop thinking about Pete! she scolded herself.

A buffet dinner preceded the meeting, and the Fairhills group ate around tables in one corner. Usually this bothered Tess, for one goal of a get-together like this was to mingle with people from different churches, exchanging friendship and ideas.

Tess took a seat next to Krystal, who would not be returning to college until the following week. Tess commended her on the brief skit she and Pastor Jim had presented for the Mission Moment in last Sunday's church service.

Pete sat down across from her. Cautioning herself to regard this as random positioning, she was able to converse fairly easily with him and others nearby. He inquired of her how things were going at work and asked for an update on the independent studies projects.

"I'm almost sure to get at least a B in the journalism one, since the *Courier* has agreed to publish my article. However, since this is a local paper, it won't count as much as it would if it appeared in a major publication."

"Are you trying?"

"Oh, sure. And I think I have a good chance at it. But one major problem is that my pictures were taken with color film."

Pastor Jim spoke from his position beyond Krystal. "I didn't realize that's what you needed, Tess. I'll call you with the phone number of a man I worked with doing the surveys. He was constantly taking black-and-white shots for his hometown paper. I don't know if he could let you use the ones that have already been printed, but he must have a lot more."

Several others got into the conversation before Pete offered to make contact with a friend who was features editor for a major Connecticut paper.

"That gives me a great idea," she said. "With your folks living there, the article could be about you—your having gone before, getting us interested, being largely responsible for the organization of our trip."

She had never seen him so ill at ease. "Hey, wait a minute!" He raised his hand, palm forward. "This is your article. Not about me!"

"But you're the tie-in. Without you, they might not be interested. So," Tess said, shrugging broadly, enjoying the opportunity of making him squirm, "either you want to help or you don't."

Molly offered, "Hey, let me help fill you in with stuff you can tell about that guy," and Pastor Jim insisted she must report how Pete took advantage of people by making them do things he decided they should.

"Like clowning," Molly suggested.

Pastor Jim added a hearty, "Amen, Sister!"

"Or climbing ladders." Tess pretended a scowl in his direction.

He relaxed, recognizing their banter for what it was. Folding his hands in front of himself, Pete assumed a saintly look. "I was attempting to serve as your group's conscience."

Molly hooted. "Just what we needed—an overgrown Jiminy Cricket!"

The group spent the next ten minutes contributing stories, jokes, and tidbits that "should be included in your article about Pete." People from surrounding tables came ostensibly to visit with Pastor Jim and the others they knew from Fairhills, but Tess was sure they were drawn by the laughter and fun.

Pastor Jim was the first to excuse himself, then Pete. Looking at her watch, Tess said they had better go too. Gathering the dishes of some of the older people at their table, she took them along with her own to the passthrough into the kitchen. She stopped long enough to put on a touch of lipstick and run a comb through her hair before entering the sanctuary with Molly and Krystal.

"I wish they hadn't asked us to sit up front," Molly grumbled.

Tess commented, "Just because you sit near the back in your home church doesn't mean you have to do the same here, Molly."

"I started that when my kids were little, so they wouldn't distract other people, and it just stuck."

They sat in the second pew with Pete and Pastor Jim. There was congregational singing, a small amount of business, a few announcements, an offering, and a devotional. Then it was time for their presentation.

They had agreed that Pastor Jim should take care of the preliminaries. He did this with his usual skill and poise and in a few minutes, pictures, beginning with October's dinner at Fairhills, began appearing on the large screen.

Pete was introduced as a major influence on what took place, and Pastor Jim asked him up front to help explain by photo and word how things were organized and scheduled. Pictures of the truck's being loaded with donated supplies, the group's leaving the morning after Christmas, and the stopover in South Carolina were shown.

Pastor Jim explained, "These next shots were taken by a friend who had the opportunity of seeing things from a helicopter. There are all degrees of damage, from here in Homestead—which was so very badly hit, as you've seen countless times on your TV screens—and this area where the fronts are off some of these condominiums."

"Partial responsibility for a lot of the excessive damage, like here," Pete said, "was the way they were built. Notice how whole sections of the front just peeled away, showing the kitchen cupboards and refrigerators and bathtubs. It's almost like looking into a dollhouse. We were told that if they'd been constructed properly, this wouldn't have been nearly as bad."

Tess, Molly, and Krystal were standing now, also, and joined in commenting briefly about scenes projected on the screen. Tess thought she had seen Pastor Jim's pictures often enough to not be unduly affected, but she had to clear her throat as she explained that the crushed aluminum wrapped around that tree represented not only the loss of the man's home and possessions, but of his grandson.

She also found it hard to speak of the little barefoot girl crying in the wreckage of her house, too frightened to make her way back out through the splintered wood, broken glass, and jagged metal to find her mother.

Molly explained about their work on the roofs. "We were involved only with those that were salvageable. Some, like this one, needed just to have these loosened shingles removed and then to have them and the missing ones replaced. These more severely damaged roofs required major reconstruction—replacing beams, like here, and putting on new sheathing before we could begin replacing shingles."

Krystal told them, "I couldn't imagine why we brought flat-tined potato forks with us, but you can see here what we did with them. I'm the one on the right, ripping off those shingles—and discovering muscles I didn't even know I had work.

"These cement shingles make a lot of sense in southern Florida and would have continued doing a good job had not the wood under them been riddled by termites. There was nothing to hold them on, so even a lesser hurricane than Andrew would probably have loosened them."

Tess gasped with horror to discover they had inserted a picture of her in the secretary's office! As she covered her face with her hands, Molly explained, "Tess is upset that we're showing her when, to put it mildly, she doesn't look too great. I asked that one be included, and this is the best shot of her during a several-day period."

Tess groaned, then punched her lightly on the shoulder. Molly went on telling briefly of the asthma attack, its cause, and of Tess's determination to keep going, which led to her programming the church's computer. "This is only one example of the dedication of each volunteer to the mission and of their willingness to use whatever skills were most needed.

"There was also Pastor Jim, who expected to rip off shingles and pound nails, but spent most of his time doing the surveys necessary to set up work sites for volunteers following us. But you tell them about that, Pastor."

Following the slides and the men's narration of the video, there was an informal period of questions and answers. People crowded around them for another forty-five minutes after the session ended, asking for more information and making comments.

A middle-aged woman shared with Tess her own experiences with mold-triggered asthma, and another came to relate her harrowing computer problems and how she had solved them.

Pete's long strides brought him to her side as she stepped onto the parking lot. "So your papers are coming along well, Tess?"

"Fairly well, thanks. I still have a lot to do, but I should meet my deadlines." She smiled up at him. "I'd like to have that editor's name. Could you give it to me now?"

"I could. . .but. . ." He stood still, and she turned to see him looking troubled. "Don't make the article about me."

"But—"

"Please."

"Why not? You aren't that modest!"

"I'm not trying to be modest, Tess. Or difficult."

"But you're my best selling point for a Connecticut paper, Pete. Won't you reconsider?"

"There are. . .reasons why I'd rather not."

He obviously had decided not to discuss those reasons, but she had to ask, "Could I at least mention your name and your enthusiastic challenge to our church? That's what got us to go to Florida. It's my only tie-in with that paper."

The others had moved on to their vehicles, and nobody interrupted what they must have recognized as a serious discussion. "Perhaps—wouldn't it be better to try an in-state newspaper?"

Her eyes narrowed. Why was she in the position of having to plead for something he had suggested in the first place? She adopted a teasing tone. "Did you get run out of town or something? Are you hiding out in our safe little Fairhills?"

He looked startled but then grinned, and they started walking again, he with his hands deep in his pockets. "Nothing that exciting, I assure you. However, there's plenty to write about the rest of them."

She was disappointed that he didn't ask her to ride back in his car. But why had she even thought he might? *He already has a full car. And Molly's over there patiently waiting for you in her van.*

The next day, she went to the college library at noon and found there was only one major paper in Pete's hometown. She wrote down the feature editor's name and number but didn't get through the first time she called. She was pleased when, in midafternoon, a businesslike voice answered with, "Allyson Kaiser speaking."

Tess introduced herself and her purpose. There was a noticeable warming in the other's manner when told that Peter Macfarland had suggested his hometown paper as a possibility for this article. "I am interested in seeing it but amazed he suggested it. He always claimed he didn't like being in the limelight," the editor commented.

"That's a problem," Tess confessed. "He doesn't want anything in the feature about himself, even though I explained that his part in our project could be the one reason you might consider this."

"What would he say if you told him you were right?"

Tess paused. He would be angry—at least disappointed and annoyed—to know she had made this contact. He had deliberately withheld this woman's name and number. "You won't consider the article if he's not in it?"

"Oh, I'll look at it. But Pete's the connection I'd like, since he's a local man. Another thing, do you have good pictures?"

"I think so. However, they're all color prints, so if you need black-and-white ones, I can borrow them."

"Is there a photo supply store nearby? Often, they have someone on staff who could make glossies from your negatives."

"I don't know. I'll check."

Ms. Kaiser was apparently trying to be helpful. "Do that, but in the meantime send good photocopies of the color prints you think might supplement your writing. Identify the pictures on all the sheets, and be sure to keep copies of the pages in case I should ask for glossies."

Tess needed to make sure she understood. "So I should wait to have black-and-white prints made 'til I hear from you?"

"Right. But I'd personally like you to include a couple of your color shots with Pete in them." She then asked, "When will you mail the manuscript?"

"Tomorrow. And one more thing: Our pastor has some excellent color photos. Might I send copies of his as well?"

The editor didn't seem to mind her additional questions. Her voice was still warm. "Put his on sheets separate from yours and mark them accordingly. That way I'll know if he needs to sign a release, and we can send payment to him. Your pictures, of course, would be considered part of the manuscript package."

Tess was grateful for this deadline; it would force her to discipline herself. She used every moment of the evening to rewrite and polish, and finally completed the task.

She had stopped at the parsonage on her way home that day and picked up the pictures Pastor Jim good-naturedly gave her permission to use. When she returned his pictures the following day, she left photocopies, though she considered these poor reproductions of his brilliant originals. They should, however, serve to give the editor some indication of what was available.

Tess smiled as she entered the apartment and walked through to the kitchen. It was good to be able to see the uncluttered top of the cherry table again. She started to put her jacket over the back of a chair, then carried it to the closet and hung it on a hanger. Just because she had cleared away one mess didn't mean she should start another!

After dinner, she got out the file of materials for her paper on volunteers. She hadn't looked at this collection of notes for the last four days. Now, she saw more clearly the wealth of material she had. A smile established residence on her face; this could be better than she had anticipated.

It was true it needed much work, but the organization of data was sound. More formal and less colorful than the article she had mailed today, it was still very readable and accurate.

The ending, however, needed to be more concise. Taking some notes she had made on the back of an envelope, Tess went to the computer to try various ideas. Two hours later, she shut down the system and stretched. She was satisfied with the last revision—as of now. It might not look as good in the morning, but she was going to bed.

🌴

Sunday school went smoothly. That wasn't always the case since one of the girls and two of the boys often tried to see how far they could go to disrupt their class. Luther, the ringleader, was not there, and Tess had to silently ask forgiveness for the fleeting thought that his absence was a blessing. If anyone in the class needed Christian teaching, it was Luther.

One of the kids chose to stay and talk as Tess was always willing to do. Today, however, it made her almost late getting to church. She took an aisle seat a little more than halfway toward the front. The organist had begun his music when Tess felt a firm hand on her shoulder and heard a whispered comment, "I thought you weren't sending that article to Connecticut."

A welcoming smile started when Tess first heard his voice but left as she turned. She greeted him with a whispered, "Good morning, Pete," before she realized how grim he looked.

His head jerked downward in a nod of acknowledgment of her words, not of approval. "Allyson tells me she received your manuscript."

"You're the one who suggested it, Pete," she defended. "And you didn't say I couldn't send it if I left you out of it."

"But you didn't!" His voice carried a sting, even though whispered.

"I wrote, 'A man who recently joined First Church.' I didn't identify you."

"The pictures did. I'm apparently in a bunch of them."

"I didn't offer any pictures of you for publication."

His brown eyes continued looking into her blue ones for an uncomfortably long time. What could she say if he didn't respond? She was almost relieved when he yanked a hymnbook from the rack in front of him and, leaning back against the pew, pointedly began reading.

Could she move back to the empty space beside him? Was he angry enough—or disappointed enough—to get up and leave if she did? For that matter, what would she do if he chose to ignore her completely?

You've created a horrible situation, Tess, she told herself. *You set your judgment and personal goals against what you sensed he disapproved of—and you lost. Now what?*

Tess kept tugging her mind back to the service, but when it was over she couldn't remember any of the hymns and hardly knew what the sermon was about. This troubled her more than she could have expected; not only had she let herself get bogged down with uncertainties and feeling miserable about Pete, but she had permitted that to keep God's Word and the message of His servant from getting through to her.

She would turn around and apologize as soon as the benediction was pronounced—but Pete was gone. He must have moved into the aisle even before Pastor Jim said, "Amen," for he was already at the door, shaking hands with the pastor, as one of the first to leave.

So be it. She wasn't going to let it bother her. *See if I care about your rudeness, Peter Macfarland!* She was seething on the inside. Could the fake smile on her face cover her confusion and hurt? She left the church quickly and hurried to her car.

Why had he called Allyson? Or why should Allyson have called him about the article? The thought that there might be something between them filled her with anger, but whether more at herself or him was a question.

An irregular pattern of snowflakes floated in the air, appearing not to be falling but moving in an erratic dance about her. *They're like my thoughts, the same ones flying by over and over, not settling down into anything that counts.*

She stopped to pick up Sunday's *Philadelphia Inquirer* and a carton of milk. She thought of getting a hoagie or pizza but had no enthusiasm for either. Leftovers would do.

Vehicles filled the spaces along her street in front of her apartment so Tess parked around the corner. Quick steps brought her almost to her door before she heard Pete's voice.

Her feet stopped of their own volition and she turned as he approached.

"Tess. . ." He was troubled, uncertain. "I need to apologize for acting that way. Can you forgive me?"

She was the one who should be saying she was sorry. Taken by surprise, she asked, "For what, Pete?"

His face was an abject study. "I was angry when Allyson told me last night about your manuscript package arriving. But the house of God is the last place where I should confront you about it—if I have a right to do so at all."

She didn't know what to say, but nodded when he asked if he could come in. The cold didn't feel nearly as severe now, even with its swirling gusts of wind.

Tess unlocked and opened her door and they went inside. "Can I hang up your coat?"

"No, thanks. I'll just lay it here on the couch for a minute—if that's okay."

So he was expecting to leave soon. "Can you stay for ham-and-cheese sandwiches, tomato soup, and fruit?"

He apparently intended to decline, for he stammered, "I. . .think it's better n—" Then he changed his mind. "Uh. . .well. . .yes, if it's not too much trouble."

"That's what I plan to eat." She led the way to the kitchen, grateful she had mopped the white-on-white floor and cleared away the overflow of her projects from the pale wood counters. As she put bread, lettuce, mayonnaise, relishes, and sliced meat and cheese on the counter, Pete used the electric can opener then dumped the can's contents and some water into a pan. He put plates, glasses, silverware, and napkins on the table, then, as the soup began to simmer, added milk.

Tess was afraid to say anything that could make the conversation even more strained than it already was. It was after their tea was in front of them at the end of lunch that he asked, "Please tell me what Allyson said when you called."

She had not expected a question this direct. "She seemed willing to look at what I'd written but gave me no guarantee of buying it. She also implied there would be little chance that she would if you weren't included."

"And that's why you sent the pictures?"

"I sent mostly photocopies of my color prints and some of Pastor Jim's. Those that have you in them are the best ones to illustrate the article, but they were not offered for that purpose. She asked me to send a few prints of you—out of personal interest, I assumed."

Pete's questions made her uneasy. "Now I'll ask you something, Pete. Why does this trouble you so much?"

His gaze dropped to his hands, which were slowly rotating the mug between his palms—forward a little, then back. "Good question." His lips thinned as they pressed together for a moment. "And you deserve an honest answer."

Chapter 10

Pete straightened in his chair. "Allyson and I dated ever since high school. During college it was off and on. Once we agreed it might be a good idea to go out with others. And then she married a real jerk right after graduation."

Tess felt her eyelids twitch. *Something connected with Allyson is why he never said or did anything to lead me on. I was too stupid to realize it. But he was in his upper twenties and.* . . "And you. . .were you married?"

"No. I've never been married. And her marriage lasted a total of just over two months. I tried helping her through the emotional trauma of learning that Hank was unfaithful—even during their honeymoon, as it turned out. She couldn't believe he didn't love her."

"How awful for her!"

"Yes."

She leaned forward on her arms, crossed on the table before her. "Pete?" It seemed a long time before his dark eyes met hers. "Is she still grieving over that?"

"It did terrible things to her self-esteem and to her emotional and social well-being. I tried to get her into Christian counseling, but she'd never admit she needed it. She was by then a feature writer for the paper—and very good at it. Being promoted several times, now to features editor, she's convinced she's handled everything wonderfully."

"She's all right now?"

"Professionally, yes; emotionally, no. For one thing, she's become. . .very possessive."

That explained some things. "You still feel responsible for her?"

His smile was crooked. "It sounds sick, doesn't it? Maybe it is. By the way, she wants us to get married."

By the way, he'd said. As though this were a minor matter. The tightness in her chest made it difficult to breathe. She managed, "You're engaged?"

"That, too, is a good question. Allyson thinks so; I don't. I never asked her to marry me and haven't given her a ring. I avoid discussing houses and. . .and things like that which she keeps bringing up.

"I was unbelievably relieved to get this teaching job, hoping that if I weren't there all the time she'd develop more strength within herself. . .would find someone else to lean on."

"Has it worked?"

"Not enough to mention. I drove back the first few weekends, but not anymore."

"Did you go because you wanted to?"

He had not drunk much of his tea but took a sip before answering. "I felt she still needed me and. . .well, it didn't seem unreasonable. It really isn't too far to travel. But as I got acquainted with people, I wanted to be here on weekends. For one thing, I became aware of you my first Sunday at Fairhills, though I had no opportunity to talk with you until that October dinner."

"I remember."

And then the Thanksgiving dinner. . .and Christmas. . .and the trip to Florida. Each time I was with you I came to like and respect you more. But I felt. . .almost guilty."

"Do you love her?"

He drew a deep breath. "As a dear friend whom I've known for a long time. We've been through many experiences, and our lives have been. . .intertwined on many levels."

His right forefinger traced the pattern in the lace cover she had placed on the table. "But as for being in love? No, Tess, I'm not."

"But you've thought about marrying her?" It was difficult to ask this question that filled her with a pain she hoped he couldn't read in her eyes.

He covered her hand with his. "I've thought about it in the past. . .but can't consider it anymore."

Please, God, make him go on. It isn't right for me to ask questions about anything this personal.

"Allyson wanted to know all about you—how old you are, how pretty, how smart. And what our relationship is, whether we kiss or anything."

It was Tess's turn to break eye contact as she felt the flush staining her cheeks. Pete held her hand more tightly as she started to pull away. "I answered her questions, Tess. But when she again begged me to set our marriage date, I put her off.

"It's impossible for me to consider doing that. I can't marry without the First Corinthians, chapter thirteen, kind of love. . .and knowing that my spouse feels the same way."

Tess's throat was so tight she could hardly manage, "I'm sure you can't, Pete."

"But I'm sure she isn't strong enough yet to handle my coming right out and telling her."

🌴

Nothing was resolved when he left. Tess was in turmoil as she leaned her head against the door after they had said good-bye. It was almost as if he had asked her advice about marrying another woman! And he loved Allyson, even if he qualified that as not being the First Corinthians, chapter thirteen, kind of love.

As for herself? Tess pushed herself upright and headed for the kitchen. While she washed their few dishes, she recognized that the only thing he had said about his feelings toward her were that he "liked" and "respected" her.

And yet, if that were really the only response she engendered, would he have come here like this? Would he have told her even as much as he had?

The next morning, she called Allyson Kaiser to withdraw the manuscript from consideration. The editor had already decided to "go with it." It would appear in Sunday's feature section. With lots of pictures!

"You have nearly a week to get something else," Tess protested, hardly caring if Allyson considered this begging.

Allyson's voice showed firmness Tess hadn't heard before. "You obviously know nothing of what goes into each week's paper. And I had every reason to believe you were offering it for publication when you sent it."

"I was." She had to admit to that. "But I've reconsidered. It would be better for an in-state paper."

"You received a better offer." It was a statement, not a question.

Tess hadn't considered this interpretation. "Nobody else has seen it. This was not a simultaneous submission. It's just that. . ." How could she possibly explain something that didn't make sense to her? "Pete does not want any pictures used that include him."

Allyson's laugh didn't sound quite right to Tess, and her words didn't either, though they could have been meant as reassurance. "Don't worry about Pete. I can handle him. I always do."

Do you? Really? Tess looked at the phone, eyes narrowed. "Perhaps you can, Miss Kaiser," she said softly, then added with all the honesty in her heart, "but I don't want to."

"Sorry. It's too late to make the change."

"It can't be. You don't have my photographs."

"You forget you sent some sample shots along with those copies. We'll make do with these. Unless you send additional ones."

"Wouldn't it be too late to get them to you in time?" She didn't care if the editor heard her sarcasm. She didn't appreciate Allyson's deliberately trying to get her in trouble with Pete.

The response was patronizing. "Don't take this personally, Miss Kenncman. If you continue writing, you'll learn that things aren't always what you want in publishing."

Tess controlled an almost overwhelming urge to retort angrily. She forced her voice to remain calm as she requested one more time, "I would appreciate your returning the unpublished manuscript, Miss Kaiser."

"Impossible. We will, however, return your photographs with your check, following publication. If I were you, I'd be grateful for this exposure, but don't expect me to accept anything else of yours. Ever."

The sound of the phone's being returned to its cradle was loud in Tess's ear. Well, she had tried. She didn't know whether Pete would believe her—or whether she would even have an opportunity to tell him what had transpired.

If only she had settled for the article in the local paper with its B-plus! Or perhaps she could have gotten it into a Harrisburg or Philadelphia paper if she had tried. But no, she had gone against Pete's wishes and sent it to his old girlfriend—the woman who considered herself his fiancée.

When she got home from work, she picked up the file folder in which she kept all her material on the trip to Florida. Riffling through pages, she reread portions of what she had put in her laptop computer there at the church in Florida. She hadn't realized how often Pete's name and activities were mentioned.

Over an hour later, her leg asleep from being curled under her on the couch, she became aware that she was no longer angry or even sad. She was thankful for the opportunity she had had of going with the group to fix those houses—and help with the computer—and do the clowning.

It might even be a good thing that the report of this adventure was going to be read in Connecticut next Sunday. If she were a relative or friend of Pete's, she would enjoy reading about what he had accomplished.

So there, Miss Allyson Kaiser! She was smiling as she limped to the kitchen to microwave the homemade soup that had been defrosting in the refrigerator.

🌴

Sunday again. Sunday school and church. She sat back farther in the congregation so she could see if Pete was there.

He was. Her eyes feasted on the sight of his broad shoulders, his muscled neck, the brown, slightly wavy hair irregularly bleached from his rooftop work in Florida.

What was he thinking, this man whom she had once thought she knew well? He joined in the singing and the responsive reading. He smiled as he passed the offering plate to the woman on his left. . .and sour old Miss Henderson smiled back. Tess's lips curved upward too, remembering how good it felt to have that open approval and genuine liking fastened on herself.

She looked down at the Bible on her lap, eyes closing with the pain which that thought brought because it was in the past. Did those smiles for her belong only to the past?

She wished there were some way she could get a copy of the paper in which her article was appearing. Allyson had said they would send her tear sheets, but would she, now that she was angry? If so, when would she receive them? The Connecticut paper wasn't one of the many carried in the college or town library. She had looked in both places before sending the manuscript, wanting to check their format, to make sure hers conformed.

Tess wondered if Nancy Rohrer, her college roommate, might get it. Although she lived in northern Connecticut, it was possible.

She was doing the same thing as last week—not paying attention to the service! Intrigued with the title of Pastor Jim's sermon, "And Then What?" when she saw it in the bulletin, she had already missed the first half of it but now winced, recognizing herself in what he was saying.

"Everyone keeps trying to box in the Lord, telling Him what He should be doing, and how. If things don't go exactly that way, we try second-guessing Him as to why He's not accommodating our wisdom."

Tess's lips turned upward wryly as he requested people to look back over just this last day, week, and month to review what they had asked for and what had been received. "Perhaps there are things you'd still like to be otherwise. Things like illness, death, loss of a job—major things. Or for a friend to call."

Her errant thoughts made her lose track of the sermon again. When she pulled them back, he was asking if there were happenings during that period which had seemed coincidental or lucky, or perhaps too small to worry about.

These might be seeds that would grow and develop into something better than what was requested. Perhaps they hadn't yet borne fruit, needing more time to nurture. He mentioned the apostle Paul, who had excellent reasons to go one way until God changed his plans. He reminded them that those who traveled with Jesus for three years expected to be rewarded in His earthly kingdom.

He mentioned Lincoln and Ulysses Grant and a famous baseball player— three men who had suffered terrible setbacks that changed their careers and lives.

Pastor Jim challenged them to keep looking for God's hand in things around them—to seek, for they would surely find. And he suggested that when these things were made clear, it would be good to share not only the results but the struggles with others who might be wondering and doubting.

"Your witness is needed more than mine. Many feel that as a pastor I'm paid to give encouragement, and it's to my personal advantage to keep you contented. They can't shrug off as easily your going out on a limb to tell of your relationship with God."

I'm lax in this, Tess admitted. *Even when I talk about our experiences in Florida, I don't always give credit for how God took care of us. . .and got us doing things we didn't know we were going to. . .and provided friendships. . .*

She slowly bowed her head and closed her eyes. *Dear Lord, I do thank You for all of these, especially the friendships. Help me in maintaining them. Even with Pete, Lord, help me be more willing to keep just friendship, if that's all that's offered. It's true I want more than that, but only You know if that's best for both of us.*

At the end of the service, as she turned to leave her pew, she saw Dad and Jeanette across the aisle and three rows back. She went to hug each of them and, while they were talking, heard that beloved voice, "Mr. and Mrs. Kenneman, it's good to see you here this morning."

Pete didn't say the same to her, not in words anyway, but Tess welcomed his warm hand upon her left shoulder and his arm around her back as he reached around to shake their hands.

Dad greeted him. "We were about to ask Tess to join us for dinner at Semper's Turkey Ranch. Are you free to come with us—either there or someplace you like better?"

"Okay with you?" he asked Tess as casually as though they had been seeing one another regularly.

"Sounds good to me." *Very, very good!*

"How about the women riding in the back?" Dad suggested. Pete was enthusiastically admiring his new Chrysler and continued asking questions about it.

Tess would have preferred Pete's sitting with her, but it really didn't matter. There was conversation among all four of them on the fifteen-minute drive to the sprawling one-story restaurant with its two added-on wings.

As would be expected, poultry was the specialty. Jeannette chose steak tips, but the other three ordered the all-you-can-eat dinner of turkey and waffles. While waiting to be served, there was an easy give-and-take in catching up with one another's activities.

Her father was modernizing one of the two bathrooms in his free time. Jeannette, in addition to helping with that, had begun stenciling around the tops of the walls in the hallway, having finished those in the living room.

Pete had volunteered to work with the elementary school's basketball program. Their regular practice included every Wednesday evening, precluding his attendance at Bible study.

Tess told about her two college projects. She was getting an A on the first and expected the same on the second.

Pete's dark eyes seemed locked on hers. "It's in the Connecticut paper?"

She hoped her stomach spasm wasn't reflected on her face. "It should be in today's issue." Tearing her gaze from his, she explained to the others, "I needed to get it into a publication outside of the local area in order to be given a higher grade. Pete suggested I submit it to a paper covering his home district and. . .the editor agreed."

She tried to go on, to explain she had attempted to get it back, but her father immediately jumped in with thanks for Pete's efforts on his daughter's behalf. It had to be deliberate that Pete avoided meeting her gaze and quickly changed the topic of conversation.

Other than that, the meal went smoothly. Once the food was in front of them and Pete prayed, he talked with her as freely as with the others, and she hoped that indicated he was no longer angry.

I should have known better! she told herself later when, getting out of the car with Pete when Dad dropped him by his parked Grand Am, she attempted to explain what had happened.

"Look," he said, interrupting her, "I knew it was in. Allyson called last night to 'congratulate' me on how handsome I looked in the photos."

"I want to tell you—"

His head jerked from side to side. "You have, Tess. You wanted an A."

She flinched as though she had been slapped. "You've got to listen, Pete. I tried. I really tried to get the article back. That and the pictures."

"After it was too late to do anything about it."

"I didn't know it was too late. I called Monday morning—as soon as I could—when I realized how very unhappy this whole thing made you!"

His sigh was heavy, his voice tired. "Okay, Tess. It's over now. Let's just leave it."

What was over, the article's being printed in the paper or—*please, God, no*—their friendship? "I didn't think it was right to call her at home even if I had known her number, which I didn't."

He was getting into his car, not looking at her. She wondered what he would think about Allyson's stating she could always "handle" him. But that was irrelevant. Tess wouldn't tell him; it wasn't her place to do so. And Allyson certainly wouldn't!

At least he hadn't slammed the door shut to emphasize his displeasure. She slipped off her glove and touched the back of her right hand against his left cheek. It was cool to her touch, and she risked getting an even colder response as she ventured, "Ever since last Sunday, Pete, I can honestly say I'd rather have that promised B-plus than an A received at the cost of our friendship. Had I known of any way to retrieve the manuscript, it would have been done."

"You might have called me."

"I couldn't."

"Why not?"

"Because. . ." How could she explain this? "If she considers herself your fiancée, how could I possibly go over her head to complain to you?" she blurted out, unshed tears burning her eyes.

He continued looking through the windshield. She removed her hand from his cheek and unseeingly pushed it into her still-warm leather glove. Turning on her heel, she ran up the street to her car.

Quickly, she got in and rushed through the buckling-up routine. She started the faithful Civic and pulled out without glancing back in his direction.

Home. She should be relaxing and enjoying the novelty of having free time on a Sunday afternoon. No homework. No articles. No research.

But no Pete!

🌴

Her week was hectic. Problems with the transferal of data again. She prayed for guidance through much of Tuesday night, asking what she could do at work—and also how she should resolve or begin to smooth the situation with Pete.

She got up early and sat by the eastern window, praying for wisdom. The brightening of the sky took place so slowly there was no point at which she could say "This is darkness" or "This is light." *Is this what You want me to remember, Lord—that I should let things happen gradually?* But that's what she had been trying to do and everything had fallen apart.

Am I to remember that You are the only true Light? She knew and acknowledged that. *What else, Lord? What else should I be learning? What should I do? What can I say to make things better?*

She had enough questions—answers eluded her.

The upper edge of the sun was nibbling an arc of slate from the house roof across the street. She got to her feet and headed for the shower, saying out loud, "Perhaps You want me to know that the sun—and You and Your Son—are always there, even when I can only see the effects, not the substance."

Chapter 11

The phone was ringing as she came through the door of her office but the line went dead as she put it to her ear. Alicia came in, looking worried. "Good morning, Tess—at least I hope it is. I was just handed a memo from the president's office."

Tess reached for the cream-colored sheet. It was a short message, straight to the point. "A special meeting is being held in his office at eleven," she told her secretary. "I'm to be there."

"Is it about the missing information?"

"Probably." Tess tried for a smile. "Who knows what's going to happen? I'm still praying about that."

She discouraged further speculation on the subject but wondered who had been on the phone as she arrived. Might it have been a personal call, someone she could have asked to pray for her? Probably not, for she discouraged personal calls here.

Would she have asked for prayers had it been someone like Pastor Jim? Or Molly? Or Pete? But it couldn't have been him. If it would have been possible to request prayer had Pastor Jim or Molly called her, could she phone one of them?

Molly would be at work. So would Pastor Jim, but his "work" was largely made up of talking with people. She called the church, and the secretary put her through to the inner office. "Good morning. Pastor Hadden speaking. Can I help you?"

"Yes, Pastor Jim, I think you can. This is Tess and I'm calling to ask if you'd pray for me."

His warm voice was reassuring. "I have been, Tess, and will continue doing that. Is there something special—some specific need right now?"

"I. . .yes, there is. I'm at the college and things are falling apart here."

"In getting the material on the computer? Like what you spoke of on the trip?"

She had been afraid he would have forgotten that conversation. She sketched, in a few sentences, the added problem of missing records, telling as much as she could without breaking trust concerning her job.

He asked, "Have you ever seen this missing information? Is it something that was on the computer and is now lost. . .or was it never there?"

"I've never seen it. I suspect it wasn't put on when the system was updated. And yet—I really shouldn't be talking about this."

"I understand." He then asked if she, personally, was in trouble.

She told of the meeting coming up this morning. She supposed she could even lose her job over discrepancies in the endowment funds, although she was the one who had found and reported the problem.

"May I put this on the prayer chain?"

"I. . .think not." She would have liked having more prayers, but the fewer people who knew of this problem, the better. "However, you can tell anyone you run into that I need their prayers."

She kept busy with routine things. Her hand fumbled for the ringing phone some time later. "Tess Kenneman speaking."

She sat up straight, her world tilting somewhat more toward its normal axis as her friend's voice said, "Good morning, Tess. This is Molly. Pastor Jim tells me you're in a jam. Anything I can do?"

"Where are you?"

"At work. He came to my office, knowing I'd want that."

"I. . .appreciate your concern. And Pastor Jim's. More than you can imagine."

"He was going to tell Pete also. . .to ask for prayer."

"I'm. . .starting to cry," she confessed, fishing in her desk drawer for tissues. .

"Wait for that 'til the tears can be from relief—after your meeting," the firm voice advised.

Tess heard her own sniffle through the phone and apologized, "I'm sorry. . .but I'm so worried!"

"You're not in this alone, Tess. Remember that."

"I will. I really will." She swallowed hard and looked at the large wall clock. "I must leave in about twenty-five minutes, so I'm especially grateful you called when you did."

"And the meeting is when?"

"In about thirty. . .thirty-two minutes."

"I won't hold you. Go wash your eyes with cold water or whatever you need to do, then go over there and wow them!" There was an almost humorous note in her voice as she said that, but the final statement was dead serious. "We'll take care of the praying part for you."

How wonderful that Molly cared and was supportive! Along with all the other stresses, Tess now felt guilty about that too, for she hadn't made enough effort to stay in close touch with this woman she had come to admire and love.

But Molly wouldn't want her worrying about that.

She took her purse to the women's room and put on lipstick before returning to her computer, notes from conversations with the comptroller, treasurer, finance chairman, and the head of the computer department lying on the desk beside it.

Twice she refused to accept on-campus calls as her fingers raced across the keys. She printed out what she had written and took that to the photocopier.

Picking up the folder of memos and records she had gathered previously, she added the sheets from the copier and left the building. She was hardly aware of the cold as she walked across the open quadrangle to Old Main.

Tess pulled open the heavy white steel-and-glass door and walked in. Several individuals hurried toward her, asking questions and assuring her that whatever had happened had not been their fault. She put them off with, "Let's wait 'til we get in his office."

She commiserated with the office manager over her two-month-old daughter's getting days and nights mixed up. Gerald Mosseau, the comptroller, accepted congratulations on his paper that had just come out in a professional journal and that reminded a secretary to tell Tess how much she had enjoyed the article on the Florida trip that had appeared in the local paper.

Dr. Joseph Popler's appearance exemplified what Tess would have envisioned for a university president. Nearly six feet tall, he carried himself erectly and wore perfectly tailored suits. In his late fifties, he retained a full head of salt-and-pepper hair that always looked the same, never a hair out of place. His intelligent hazel eyes appeared to see everything.

The right number of chairs, five, were arranged in a semicircle before his large, carved walnut desk. Tess found herself in the center seat, which she would never have chosen. She suspected it had been maneuvered.

Even Dr. Popler's patience was tried as Mr. Mosseau and another department head loudly disclaimed any responsibility for the missing financial records. The president stepped in several times to insist that only one person speak at a time, and then asked a few questions.

He repeated their complaints in a few short sentences, showing he understood the problem. He then turned toward her. "And you, Miss Kenneman. What do you have to say about this?"

She had been afraid she would be tongue-tied before him, but the words came easily as she explained she had been following orders in working toward getting material on the new system within the specified time.

She recounted her discovery of some missing accounts, some missing names, then waited until interruptions were taken care of. Mr. Mosseau angrily implied that she was incompetent and libelous and suggested she be replaced.

"Replaced? By whom?" Dr. Popler asked brusquely. "She's one of our most respected computer experts and has done nothing unprofessional or unpleasant. She had to notify you and me of discrepancies; that's hardly an accusation of anyone in your or any other department."

Tess was grateful he had said that, but she still couldn't relax. She had no opportunity to speak again for a few minutes, until Dr. Popler directly addressed her. "You've apparently checked all the material you have, Miss Kenneman. How do you suggest handling things at this point?"

"I'm still hoping it proves to be simply a matter of differences in the way information was recorded within departments. We've begun an intensive search of individual and corporate donors in relation to the dates on which gifts were received, and we're exploring other possibilities."

She handed out copies of reports detailing how each department had cooperated thus far and what was in progress. "In one of these areas I've highlighted, there has to be misfiled hard or soft copy records. In our section, we're putting in any time we can spare—plus much of our own—to search for information, mostly for improperly recorded entries prior to the last computer updating. I suggest that all departments do that."

There was near silence for a moment or two before several changes in the wording were made, but none to the content of the reports.

"Take this back to your departments," Dr. Popler said. "Get your colleagues involved with the search, and assure them there's no penalty for an honest mistake. With changes of responsibility through the years, it's a marvel something like this hasn't come to light before."

He flipped open his appointment book and poised his pen above it. "Return here at the same time next week. In the meantime, I'll listen to suggestions. But only if they come in a positive way—if they clarify and are not made," he said with a mirthless smile, "to obfuscate."

Tess tried to keep her face from showing humor at his deliberate choice of the word. It contained a warning to not hide behind things confusing or "academic."

They were dismissed as surely as though he had stated this. There was something about his demeanor as he stood beside his desk that discouraged their lingering to visit or rehash. Tess stepped aside to allow the others to precede her but glanced back as she started to follow them. His right hand lifted from the shiny desktop in the hint of a salute, and his lips parted to form an almost silent, "Thank you."

Her smile was genuine. Giving a slow nod that was almost a little bow, she left the room. *It has to be those prayers that kept me calm before and through that meeting.*

She would call Molly and Pastor Jim as soon as she got back to her office.

Her walk back was more free and joyous than it had been less than an hour before. She ran up the steps of her building, across the porch, through the door—and collided with a tall man standing there reading notices on the overcrowded bulletin board. "Oh, I'm sorry. . . ," she started, then gasped, "Pete! What are you doing here?"

He had reached to steady her, holding her so close his breath was warm against her face. "I can tell you don't need my shoulder to cry on."

She would always want those shoulders. Did he know that? "Don't you have school today?"

He nodded but continued searching her eyes with his beautiful brown ones. "I had to know you're all right. Pastor Jim came to tell me you were worried about the outcome of your meeting. I want you to know you had—you have— my prayers. All the time." His voice was husky. "I wish you had called me."

"I would have liked to." How did she have courage to say that after his not contacting her?

It felt as though he was pulling her closer, but she must have been mistaken, for he then released her. "In less than fifteen minutes I must be in school with my children. When do you finish?"

It was his lunchtime then that he was using to be with her. "How about you?"

"Probably four-thirty. A parent's coming to talk with me after he gets off work."

"I'll be home by then."

His large hands cupped her face, fingers caressing her ears then tangling in her hair. "I'll see you then."

She continued to feel his touch long after he left her to hurry back to his pupils. She walked slowly to her office, no longer in a hurry to share news of the meeting. What seemed to be happening with Pete seemed far more important—and private.

She ate lunch with coworkers at the Student Union Building, and nobody mentioned it if she occasionally drifted into a world of her own. Often at noon she would get a full meal then fix just a sandwich and salad in the evening. Today she ate little. She hoped Pete and she would be together for dinner. He would be hungry since he had missed lunch.

Time toyed with her through the afternoon, going slowly yet not allowing opportunity to get much accomplished. She was usually the last to leave—today she was the first.

She straightened the few things that were out of place in her apartment, including the dishes she had put in the drainer to dry. She had planned to call Pastor Jim to report on the meeting, but there wasn't time before Pete arrived at her door.

In response to his knock on the door, she hurried across the room then stood there, savoring the moment, eager yet shy. She ran her palms down over the front of her slim wool skirt and opened the door for the man she loved. It was so good having him here, tall and handsome and wonderful. "Pete!" She reached out both hands. "Come in."

He held them in his, pressing them to his heart. "I'm glad you said that."

"You couldn't have doubted I would."

"Well, I did give you warning." His smile was fleeting, however light his words. He closed the door and led the way to the couch.

The sun had not set, but Tess suddenly wished she had turned on a lamp or two. His eyes seemed shadowed as he said, "Tell me about your meeting."

Tess had almost forgotten the meeting in her anticipation of what might occur now, but briefly explained what had taken place. He continued holding her right hand tightly as he asked specific questions.

She finally protested, "That's enough about me. Tell me about your day or week or whatever."

He faced her directly. "I'll start with Sunday afternoon—after dinner and what you said there at my car. I realized how miserably I've been treating you."

"It's all right, Pete."

"No." His headshake was emphatic. "It isn't. You've been far more patient than I deserve. First, I try to help you, then am angry because you take my advice. You try to straighten things out and I jump down your throat. Why do you put up with me, Theresa?"

She should give some reason other than the real one. What if he didn't love her? Her words came slowly. "I think you must know why." He waited for her to go on, so she whispered, "I love you, Pete."

He drew her close. "Can you forgive me?"

She nodded as much as was possible. "Of course."

"I went to see Allyson after we parted in the street." He hugged her yet more closely as she started to draw away but then must have thought better of that and released her. She straightened on the couch, confused, and he didn't touch her as he continued. "I hadn't seen her for a couple of weeks and decided it was time. . ."

Her eyelids closed in their effort to hide pain but then reopened.

Pete's voice went on. "That we straighten out exactly where we stand. As I told you, we've been friends for many years, and in all honesty there have been times I considered marrying her."

More pain—sharp, continuing.

"But that was for all the wrong reasons, Tess—getting along well, having fun together, knowing and doing things with the same people—that sort of thing. When I thought of spending the rest of my life with her. . .having her be the mother of my children. . .coming home to her every day. . .knowing she doesn't have a commitment to Christ, which should have been my first consideration—I just couldn't do it."

He drew in a deep breath and let it out very slowly. "I went to see her Sunday and told her this. She accused me of letting you come between us, which is logical from her point of view, but I explained how relieved I'd been to get this teaching position, and that was before I knew you existed."

Was he telling Tess that Allyson didn't really matter to him?

"I said I had needed space and time to sort things out. And she asked if I'd done this. I said I had. I was sure, now, that we could be nothing more than friends.

"She let me know that was unacceptable. . .that it was marriage or nothing."

He got up and walked around the coffee table, hands stuffed into his pockets as he faced her. "So, it's nothing."

Tess looked up at him, this wonderful man whom she loved more than life itself. And yet he still had never said or done anything to give her reason for believing he loved her. Oh, yes, they had hugged on the rooftop, and he had held her here on the couch a minute ago, but. . . "How do you. . .feel about that?" she asked into the silence.

"Good."

"Somewhat. . .empty?" She had to know.

"Not empty. More like. . .free. Free to speak to you of things I've kept bottled up so long. Free to tell you that I love you far beyond what I've ever felt for anyone else. Free to hold you in my arms and kiss you—if you'll let me after the beastly way I've treated you."

"Then," she said, standing up, happiness in her eyes to match that in her heart, "why are you way over there?"

Tess met him halfway, trusting her kisses and hugs to show her otherwise inexpressible joy. The heartache, loneliness, and longing were over. *He loves me. He loves me!*

The tuna and tossed salad they made together and ate at the kitchen table were flavored by the zest of their newly expressed love and were enjoyed more than anything they might have ordered in the finest restaurant.

"I'm so glad I went to Florida with you," she said, leaning over to kiss him again as she placed a dish of ice cream on the table before him.

He tousled her hair. "Me too. I liked you before. . .I loved you then."

"It took you long enough to let me know," she murmured, remembering her insecurity.

"I had to be sure. To be positive this wasn't a. . .rebounding from Allyson. And that it really was what I thought—a forever, 'til-death-do-us-part kind of love."

Later, he told her, "I want you to know it hasn't been easy for me all these weeks, either, Tess. I was miserable much of the time, afraid if I didn't speak up I'd lose you to Pastor Jim."

Even though she herself suspected Pastor Jim might be interested, she hadn't realized that Pete would think such a thing. He added, "Pastor Jim's such a great guy I was afraid God, knowing he needs a helpmate like you in the parsonage, might have that in His plans."

She couldn't help feeling a little glad that he had suffered also. But she asked softly, "And you, Pete, do you also need a helpmate like me?"

His passionate kiss was the immediate answer that left no doubts in her mind or heart.

The answering machine at the parsonage indicated that Pastor Jim expected to be back from his meeting around nine. Tess and Pete drove to her father's to share their news and on the way back stopped at Molly's. She welcomed them into her home with, "So what's new with you young folks?"

"There is something—something wonderful," Tess began.

Molly unerringly read the beaming happiness on their faces and wrapped her arms around them. "You're getting married! I've been praying about this every single day, but then I'd see you sitting alone and coming and going separately. I was beginning to wonder if I was wrong."

"Had you given up on us yet?" Pete inquired.

"I couldn't do that."

Pastor Jim, when they found him, was even less surprised. "I've known how you felt since those days in Florida, Tess. Your climbing that ladder and working on the roof with Pete told me the love you had for him was sufficient to cast out long-lasting fears.

"And, Pete, I would have had to be blind not to recognize your pain and what you were suffering as she coped with her asthma. And how you admired her. Couldn't have been that solicitous and caring without a personal reason."

Pete started to say something, but Pastor Jim went on. "So I've been praying along with Molly for the resolution of whatever was keeping you from acknowledging your love. I'm delighted you're planning for the future together."

They began making arrangements for a simple wedding to be held at the end of a Sunday morning worship service. "Neither of us wants a lot of pomp or extravagant show," she told Pastor Jim. "We'd like our marriage to be a worshipful, blessed experience with those we know and treasure here in the church. And our families and Aunt Freddie and a few others, of course."

Prior to that, they would have their six counseling sessions with Pastor Jim. "We don't know yet which of our apartments we'll live in when we're married," she said. "Logically, it should be Pete's, as he has the longer lease—"

"But she still hasn't seen it," Pete finished.

They received Pastor Jim's blessing and then left for Pete's apartment. He unlocked the door but hesitated before opening. "It's a bachelor pad, Tess."

Her eyebrows raised in question. He responded with, "I'm not a housekeeper, I'm afraid. I just live here."

She smiled up at him, saying nothing.

"It's sort of. . . ," he began as he reluctantly turned the knob.

"It's home, Pete. We've been together in some awful places, remember? But wherever you are, Florida, or here, or anywhere—if I'm with you, I'll be home."

His arm drew her close. They went through the doorway—together.

Never had it been so marvelous to be "home."

EILEEN M. BERGER

Eileen lives in her native state of Pennsylvania, is the wife of a minister, and is the mother of three grown children and grandmother of seven. She and her husband own a choose-and-cut Christmas tree farm. She worked twenty-five years as a medical technologist, but she wrote on the side and had numerous books published. She also became an active member of the St. David's Christian Writers Association, whose annual conference is the second oldest in the country. She has taught workshops and special courses at numerous conferences. She loves helping writers write.

What Love Remembers

Muncy G. Chapman

For Herb,
who taught me to believe in myself.

Chapter 1

To Kristen, the ominous black cloud hovering over the narrow, unfamiliar highway seemed appropriate.

"I've had a black cloud following me for the past week!" she muttered cynically.

More precisely, it had been six days and fifteen hours since Mr. Robert Weston Bradley III had completely shattered her euphoria like a fine crystal goblet dropped from great heights, and left her not just heartbroken, but humiliated as well. And now here she was, making this ridiculous trip in a last-ditch effort to recapture her dignity and salvage what was left of her wounded pride.

That day last February when she first met him, if she had known what she now knew, she would have walked—no, run—toward the nearest exit. Instead, she had sat in the plush reception area of his law firm, wondering how she ever imagined she could qualify for the opening they had advertised.

As a recent graduate of Paula Powell Business College, she had about as much experience as a newly hatched bird pushed out of its warm, familiar shell. A smaller firm would have been a more likely target, instead of the most prestigious law firm in Atlanta. Sitting there, waiting for her name to be called, she had sneezed three times, a nervous habit she had carried over from her childhood.

"*Gesundheit!*" Her eyes had been drawn to the hall doorway, seeking the source of the deep bass voice. She had tried to look away, but his gaze had held her eyes like a magnet and refused to turn loose. His tall, muscular frame had filled the doorway with a stance that appeared at once relaxed and yet in complete control of all his surroundings. Indeed, everything about him had seemed contradictory. Dark, curly hair and heavy brows had created a distinct contrast to the sparkling springwater blue of his eyes, and deeply bronzed skin had revealed that not all of his time was spent inside the office.

He had walked toward the receptionist ("Miss Neal," according to her nameplate) and placed a thick sheaf of papers on her desk. Kristen had been annoyed to feel her heart hammering and her blood pulsing through her veins like a silly schoolgirl's. She had come here to seek employment, she reminded herself; not to swoon over the first handsome man she encountered. First the sneeze and now this silliness. It was time for her to start remembering that she was a mature woman now and to begin acting like one.

With renewed composure, she had watched him speak a few words to Miss Neal, then turn and disappear into the dark hallway from which he had come.

Miss Neal had risen and called her name. "Miss Kelly, would you follow me, please?"

When Kristen stood, her recently revived composure had dissolved, and her knees felt as weak as two used tea bags. She'd hoped she wouldn't need to offer a handshake; her palms had been as cold and as clammy as Jell-O. Was she headed for a meeting with the man she had just seen in the outer office? Oh, no! Another sneeze?

"Excuse me," she had apologized, and groped in her handbag for a tissue.

She had to step lively to keep pace with Miss Neal, whose heels fell silently against the plush carpet. Passing several closed office doors, she had been ushered into a small, austerely furnished room and offered a chair beside a large walnut desk.

Behind the desk sat not the man she had expected to see, but a tall, thin woman who had appeared to be in her fifties, and whose dark brown eyes had seemed to bore right into the center of her very soul.

Kristen's warm smile had not been returned, and the woman's abrupt voice had done nothing to alleviate her nervousness. "You're Kristen Kelly, and I understand that you have no experience at all. Is that correct?"

"Yes, Ma'am, but I—"

"My name is Jane Blakely. I'm the office manager. I do all the hiring and firing of the secretarial pool in this office. If you are selected for this position, you will be expected to be here promptly at eight each morning. We close the office at five o'clock, but whenever the need arises, we work late until all the work is finished. Some weeks we must come back in on Saturday. Would this pose a problem for you?"

"Oh, no, Ma'am."

"Good. Then we can proceed with the interview."

Forty minutes later, Kristen had walked down Peachtree Avenue toward the bus stop, her mind still whirling from the effects of Jane Blakely's rapidly fired questions. Some of them had seemed strange for a secretarial interview, but Kristen had answered everything directly and honestly, and although her hands had been tightly clenched in her lap, she had felt she had presented a reasonably controlled appearance.

Miss Blakely had told her that a selection would be made within a week and that she would be notified by mail if they needed to see her again. Suddenly Kristen realized that she wanted this job more than she had ever wanted anything in her life, and she was sure that the week ahead would seem like forever.

All week long, she had watched her mailbox and prayed that she would be chosen for the position, but the only letters she had received were two from Jack and one from her mother. . .and nothing from the law firm of Bradley, Bradley, and Kline.

Kristen's parents had expected that when she finished high school she would live at home and attend classes at the University of Florida in Gainesville, where her father taught. After all, Jack DeHaven was pursuing his degree there, and she and Jack had been "steadies" for the past three years. Their friends just seemed to assume that after Jack's graduation, when he stepped into his father's furniture business, he and Kristen would marry and build their future there.

Kristen was never able to make her parents fully understand her need to go out on her own, to "become my own person," as she had expressed it. Kristen wasn't even sure she completely understood it herself. But, admitting that Kristen had always exhibited a maturity beyond her years, Dr. and Mrs. Kelly had given her their blessing as she launched into the three-year executive secretarial course at Paula Powell's in Atlanta.

Jack too found it difficult to understand.

"But Atlanta's not that far," Kristen reasoned. "I'll be home for holidays, and you can come to Atlanta too. The temporary separation will probably be good for us."

Though Jack was not convinced, he reluctantly urged Kristen to do what she felt was right. He didn't want to create any roadblocks she might grow to resent in later years.

He'd never loved any girl but Kristen. He wanted her to be his wife and the mother of his children, and as soon as he graduated, he hoped he could get her to set the date.

And Kristen knew she loved Jack, really. He was like a wonderful big brother to her.

That was the whole trouble! She didn't feel she needed another brother; she had two already. Instead, she wanted to hear bells chime when he kissed her, like they did in the romantic novels she read. But she knew that was just foolishness. Good marriages weren't built on ringing bells. Jack was a fine Christian man who shared her deep faith in God and supported her goals, and she really did love him. This time apart would help her appreciate her good fortune in having the love of a man like Jack. Already her love had grown stronger through their separation, and she couldn't imagine a life without Jack.

Just a little more time, she thought. To her, marriage was forever. She needed this breathing room first.

Was she being irresponsible? Selfish? Suppose Jack grew tired of her procrastination and found another girl? He was certainly an attractive, eligible bachelor about town, never lacking for social invitations.

The problem will solve itself, she mused. *I'll never be offered that job with Bradley, Bradley, and Kline. I should never have applied here in Atlanta, anyway. I'll contact the employment agency in Gainesville and see who might be interested in receiving my résumé.*

She had almost put the law firm out of her mind when, on the sixth day, the letter arrived. She was to come in right away for an orientation meeting and complete her final paperwork so that she would be ready to begin work on the first day of February.

Could it really have been only four months ago when she began? So much had happened since then. She had discovered that beneath Jane Blakely's stern exterior rested a heart of gold, and, although she ran a very "tight ship," she had helped Kristen in countless ways.

"Miss Neal" had become "Sara," a good friend with whom Kristen found many things in common, not the least of which was her strong commitment to Christ and His teachings. In fact, Kristen liked all the girls in the office. Though their busy schedules precluded frequent personal exchanges, the staff was friendly and helpful, and Kristen soon felt an integral part of the congenial group.

The attractive man who had captured her attention that first day was the younger Mr. Bradley, whose father was the founder of the law firm. In later years, the elder Mr. Bradley had brought in Mr. Kline, an old friend from law school days. Together, the three of them handled only those cases which interested them most, keeping their business small and select.

Over lunch one day, Kristen confided to Sara that Wes Bradley was the most intriguing man she had ever seen. "He's a walking enigma!"

"How so?"

"Oh, I don't know. He smiles at everyone, and seems friendly enough, but at the same time, he's cool and aloof, detached, like a spectator at a sports event. They love all the players but don't really know any of them."

"Don't fool yourself. He knows all of his players. But 'detached' is probably an accurate description, and that isn't hard to understand, given his background."

"I don't know anything about that, Sara, but I can't help but notice that several of the women in our office turn their charm in his direction at every opportunity."

"They're wasting their efforts. Wes's wife died in an automobile accident two years ago, leaving him with a six-year-old daughter to raise. She's plenty spoiled, believe me. But Wes devotes all his spare time and energy to her and doesn't seem to be interested in women at all. He was totally devoted to his wife. It was so tragic."

"But, Sara, that was two years ago. Surely his faith has helped him put his life back together and find some peace by now. He is a Christian, isn't he?"

"Yes, of course. He and his wife used to attend the same church where I'm still a member. In fact, they were our youth leaders, very active and effective. But we haven't seen much of Wes since Louise died. You'd think the church would be the first place he would turn for comfort."

"I take it for granted that you have all tried."

"Oh, yes. And of course, he is always polite when the pastor calls on him, or when any of the congregation try to offer their help. Unfortunately, he keeps all his problems inside himself and doesn't give anyone a chance to support him."

Kristen thought about that conversation with Sara many times. She wondered if there was any way she could encourage Wes to rekindle his faith and find help from the Source she knew to be unfailing. She would add Wes Bradley to her prayer list and look for a way to help him.

In spite of Sara's comments to the contrary, it seemed obvious to Kristen that Mr. Wes Bradley had begun to show more than a passing interest in her. He now asked her to receive all of his dictation, and more than once she had felt his eyes on her as she hustled about the office performing her secretarial duties.

On a busy Monday morning in April, she was filing letters and documents in the file cabinet when she realized that he was standing behind her, looking over her shoulder. She continued to file until the silence was broken by her loud *"Atchoo!"*

"Miss Kelly, are you catching a cold?" he queried in that familiar warm voice.

"Oh, no, Sir. It's just that. . .well. . .er. . .I sometimes sneeze when I'm nervous."

"And are you nervous now?" She detected a slight smile breaking at the corners of his mouth.

"Yes—no—uh, perhaps just a little." She could feel her face begin to flush as she looked up at him in time to catch one of his rare boyish grins.

"Well, you shouldn't be. You're doing a fine job for us here. Just keep up the good work."

As he turned and walked toward his office, she thought for a moment she heard bells ringing.

How foolish, she thought, as she realized she was only hearing the bell from Sara's word processor.

But the little attentions continued, and even Sara began to notice. "It's definitely out of character for him," she admitted, before biting into her grilled cheese sandwich. The two girls enjoyed lunching together at the downstairs deli several times a week. "But don't read too much into it. I've watched too many girls become frustrated trying to get his attention. I'd hate to see a young, innocent girl like you get hurt."

"You forget that I'm practically engaged," Kristen countered defensively, and used her napkin to dab at the spot of coffee she had just dripped on her white silk blouse.

But as the weeks rolled by, Kristen found herself increasingly attracted to this unusual man and began to realize that the racing of her heart each time he was near was more than a mere coincidence. Could it mean that she was really falling in love for the first time in her life? Initially she resisted the idea, telling herself that it was an impossible situation, and trying to concentrate on Jack and the wonderful life they would have together. But it was useless. Every time Wes Bradley came into the room, her heart just seemed to melt like butter on a warm summer day.

Seated beside his desk one afternoon, rapidly recording his dictation in her shorthand book, she was startled when he interrupted himself and asked abruptly, "Miss Kelly, do you get along well with children?"

"Why, yes, I always have. I love children, and they seem to like me too." She felt her pulse quicken.

But after a brief pause, he resumed his dictation and dismissed her. Just those few words played through her thoughts like a broken record, and she seemed to float through the rest of the day.

The following morning, as she waited for him to begin his first letter, she timidly pointed to the oval silver frame on his desk and asked, "Is that beautiful child your daughter?"

"Yes," he replied softly. "That's Janelle. She is pretty, isn't she? She's looking forward to the end of the school year so that she can go to our vacation home for the summer."

"It sounds like fun," she said. "Where is your vacation home?"

"On Gaspar Island, just off the west coast of Florida. It's one of a long string of barrier islands, some completely developed, but some, like Gaspar, have remained unspoiled and only minimally changed since the days of Ponce de León." His features became relaxed and tranquil as he described the beauty of the island. "It's only accessible by boat, with no commercial enterprises at all. Not even a convenience store. Just miles and miles of sugar white sand."

Suddenly, as though waking from a dream, he sat erect in his chair and snapped back to the business at hand. "The first letter is to. . ."

They worked on the correspondence for nearly an hour, and as she rose from her chair to leave his office, he surprised her with another of his spontaneous questions. "Do you know how to handle a boat?"

"Well, my only experience has been with small boats. But I was a counselor at Lettuce Lake Camp for Girls three summers in a row when I was in high school. We had to learn to handle canoes as well as small motorboats." His question puzzled her. Whatever was he getting at? She mustn't jump to conclusions, and yet—

"And you're a good swimmer?"

"Yes," she smiled confidently. "I'm a certified Red Cross Senior Lifesaver."

"You're certainly a woman of many talents. By the way, I'll need to have those letters finished before you leave so that they can get in tonight's mail. Think you can get them finished?"

Kristen recognized her cue to leave and get to work. "Of course. I'll do them right away."

She shared these conversations with Sara over after-lunch coffee the next day, unable to conceal her excitement.

Sara was still unconvinced and apprehensive. She could see that her friend was becoming much too vulnerable, and she thought Kristen too sweet and naive to experience the letdown she felt was inevitable.

And then Sara gave Kristen something else to worry about. "Business always gets much slower in the summer. It's beginning to do that already. Some years we've had to cut our office staff until fall."

Kristen knew, although Sara was too tactful to remind her, that she was the last person hired, and thus at the bottom of the secretarial pool. If there was any layoff, she would likely be the first to go.

That worry hung like a dark cloud in her mind as she began her afternoon work. Deep in thought, she was not immediately aware of his presence, but looking up from her desk, she realized that Wes Bradley was standing in the doorway observing her.

"Could you come into my office for a few minutes? I have something I wish to discuss with you."

Behind his closed office door, she settled her shorthand pad on the desk and poised her pencil in readiness.

"No, don't bother with that. I just want to talk to you."

Kristen's heart skipped a beat, and she prayed she wouldn't sneeze!

"I have given a lot of thought to this," he began. "I want to discuss a proposal with you, and I think it can best be done in a less formal atmosphere.

Could you join me for dinner Saturday evening?"

Kristen's hopes soared as her brain seemed to disengage and let her heart take over. In her mind's eye, she could already picture them seated at an intimate table for two, sharing thoughts and dreams in the flickering candlelight, whispering soft words that could be a prelude to their future together. In spite of Sara's dire warnings and her own misgivings, here was proof positive that Wes saw more than just a legal secretary when he focused his attention on her.

"Yes, I'd be happy to have dinner with you, Mr. Bradley." She found it difficult to keep her voice calm and impersonal while her mind was racing toward the days and weeks ahead. When she left his office to return to her desk, her head was still reeling, despite her efforts to concentrate on the pile of work before her.

His invitation certainly held a promise of more than a casual dinner date. What kind of "proposal" did he have in mind? Would this be the beginning of a beautiful relationship for the two of them? Of course, it would take time for them to get to know each other on a personal basis. Perhaps this was God's way of answering her prayers, by giving her a chance to help Wes regain and strengthen his faith in Christ. And by summer's end, who could predict what exciting things might happen?

It seemed an eternity until Saturday. She shared her news with no one, not even Sara. If she came to work one day soon, wearing a new diamond ring on her finger, wouldn't they all be surprised? She held up her bare left hand, looked at it, and smiled.

The French restaurant he had chosen was small but elegant. Dressed in her best blue silk dress and her graduation pearls, she sat across from him and tried to participate in casual conversation while her heart seemed to spiral out of control.

At last, stirring his after-dinner coffee, he leaned toward her and spoke with slow deliberation. "Kristen, I think that first of all, we should move to a first-name basis outside the office, because what I have to say is a rather personal matter."

"Oh, yes, Wes, I agree," she answered, scarcely able to control the tremor in her voice.

"Kristen, you know that my life centers around my little girl, Janelle."

Of course she knew that. Wasn't that why he had asked her if she liked children? She could think of no happier future than to become a wife to Weston Bradley, and a mother to his children, including the daughter of his deceased wife. Silently she vowed that she would never show a difference.

"I give Janelle all the time and attention that I can, but she is eight years old now, and really needs a mother."

Kristen didn't trust her voice but nodded and smiled through misty eyes, encouraging him to continue.

"Kristen, I think I have found someone who can fill that void. This summer, as Janelle and I take up our summer residence on the island, I need time to pursue this interest, and that means having less time for Janelle. Of course, I have a couple who live in the house all year. Mrs. Baxter runs the house, and her husband maintains the yard and keeps everything in working order. They both love Janelle, but they're not as young as they used to be, and Janelle gets to be a handful sometimes. She needs to have someone she can relate to."

Kristen's thoughts raced ahead of his words. Naturally, as their relationship developed, Wes would want her to become acquainted with his daughter. If this was to be a test, Kristen was sure to pass with flying colors, because she already felt a love for this innocent, motherless child.

Kristen's eyes never left his, and he continued, "I've watched you these last few months. I know you and Janelle would grow to love each other." He sipped his coffee and paused pensively.

"Things at the law firm are easing up, as they usually do in the summer, so the staff could spare you for three months. You would have a nice vacation, with Janelle being your only responsibility, and you would continue to receive your monthly salary.

"I'd be free to come and go, to get to know Marla Morgan better, and I'd plan to bring her to the island to begin getting acquainted with Janelle. Of course, I'd expect you to help Janelle develop a relationship with Marla that would eventually be a strong mother-daughter bond."

The room was spinning in circles, faster and faster. Kristen felt herself sinking into a bottomless pit. None of this was real. It was a bad dream, and she would soon awaken. Hot tears surfaced and burned her eyes, just ready to erupt, when the waiter opportunely interrupted.

"Excuse me, Mr. Bradley, but there is a telephone call for you."

Wes's hasty departure from the table, along with his casual apology for the interruption, gave Kristen the opportunity she desperately needed. Stumbling blindly through her tears, she wove a path between the dining tables and into the ladies' room.

Once inside the shelter of the lounge, she let the tears flow freely, oblivious of passing curious stares. How could she have been so stupid, allowing herself to fantasize a romantic relationship when there was never any such indication? Why hadn't she listened to Sara and the others? They were certainly right about one thing: Wes Bradley had no personal interest in her whatsoever. Even more humiliating, he didn't even need her as a secretary. All he wanted was a nursemaid. Oh, to think that she actually considered marrying such an inconsiderate man! She should label herself lucky that she realized it in time!

Immune to the ambience of the luxurious red-and-gold powder room, she decided with proud and fierce determination that Wes would never know of her disappointment. Restoring her face to order by putting cold, wet towels over her reddened eyes, she began to plan.

She had already indicated her enthusiasm in going to the island. To refuse now would reveal that she had expected something more. Besides, she couldn't afford to give up her job with the law firm just yet. She'd have to play his game for now, and it wouldn't be easy.

He had finished his telephone call and was back at their table when she returned. She apologized for her delay, and with great difficulty, mustered a smile, listening as he unfolded the details of his plan.

Now, here she was one week later, driving to the marina where she would leave her car in the parking garage and catch the water taxi to Gaspar Island, to meet her young charge for the very first time.

It must be around that next curve, she thought, as she passed the fire station marked on the little map Wes had drawn for her.

Yes, there it was. A big sign proclaimed, GASPAR MARINA, BOAT SALES, RENTALS AND REPAIR, DRYDOCK STORAGE, GUIDES— There was more, but she was beyond the sign as she turned her small red car into the asphalt parking lot.

Since her clothes had been sent ahead, she had only a small bag to carry as she stepped out of the car and filled her lungs with the fresh salt air.

Where was the water taxi? She looked for a sign, or someone who could help her.

A scruffy old man was hunched over the tangled lines of a large fishing net. "Excuse me." She walked over to where he worked. "I was told I could hire a water taxi here, to take me to the Bradley dock on Gaspar Island."

He continued to work without looking up. "Yes, Ma'am, we can get you over there pretty soon. Right now, though, the two boats be out on runs, so why don't you just grab a can of soda pop and set yourself down on the bench there on the dock, and watch the boats come and go."

According to the imprint on his T-shirt, his name was Ben. He looked up then and studied the pretty young thing standing before him. She didn't look like the casual island folks who frequented the waterfront. It prompted him to pull the little cap off his head and gently tip it toward her.

"Thank you," replied Kristen impatiently, "but I am in a bit of a hurry to get to the island. It isn't far, is it?"

"Oh no, Ma'am. That's it right over yonder. Barely half a mile as the crow flies. But—"

"I understand you have rental boats. Can't I just rent a small boat that will get me over there?"

"Yes, Ma'am, but do you know how to run 'em?"

"I've handled boats before." Her voice was edged with impatience, and just a touch of uncharacteristic arrogance. "Where do I go to make the arrangements?"

Old Ben pointed to the office and shook his head as she took off at a fast pace. "City girls!" she heard him mutter.

Fifteen minutes later, she was perched in the little dinghy with the motor idling smoothly. Here came Ben, who obviously wanted to talk, and she had no time for that today. He was pointing and shouting something about keeping in the channel, but the direction in which he pointed was not toward the island. Perhaps he had misunderstood where she wanted to go. It was easy to see that she had but to steer her boat right across the small bay, and she would be there. Quickly, she began to accelerate before she got tied up with Ben again.

This is actually fun, she thought, as she guided the little boat toward the island.

Looking back at the dock, she could see that Ben was still shouting and gesturing wildly, waving his little cap in the air, but she purposely ignored him.

He probably thinks I am some city girl who knows nothing about boats, she thought. Well, she'd show them all. Those years at Lettuce Lake Camp for Girls would really pay off now.

Halfway across the bay, she was suddenly aware of a loud, grinding noise, as the boat slowed and then stopped. The engine had shut off. Now what? She checked the gas gauge and felt reassured. She'd just crank it again.

Turning to pull the rope that would start the motor again, she looked down into the water and was startled to see that long tendrils of sea grass completely surrounded her. Directly behind the boat, the water was muddy where the engine had evidently plowed into the bottom of the bay. Carefully lifting an oar from the bottom of the boat, she lowered it over the edge and found that she was floating in less than a foot of water. Was that what Ben meant about staying in the channel? Oh, what was she to do now?

Then she felt the first drops of rain. Within minutes, the drizzle changed into a downpour, and lightning zigzagged crazily across the suddenly dark sky. Kristen was frightened, frustrated, and soaking wet. She tried to push the boat forward, leaning all her weight against the oar, but it refused to budge. In desperation, she removed her new sneakers and gingerly slid her legs over the side of the boat. Standing in the shallow water, she felt the mud squish between her toes, and the seaweed lap at her legs like the tentacles of a hungry octopus. A small fish brushed against her ankle, startling them both, as Kristen screamed and jumped back inside the boat. Tears mixed with rainwater on her cheeks.

"This is all his fault," she cried. "I wish I had never laid eyes on Wes Bradley!"

In the distance, she heard a faint hum which grew louder and louder, until she could see a small flat-bottomed boat being driven by a figure completely covered in a yellow rain slicker and hood.

"Looked like you could use a little help," Ben said, pulling alongside her. He handed her an extra rain slicker. "I tried to stop you, but you left right hastylike. Wanted to warn you about these here grass beds. They's tricky if you don't know where they be."

Ben pulled up a coil of thick rope which was attached to the stern of his boat and deftly tied it to the bow of the mud-mired little skiff. What a strange sight they must have been as they made their way toward shore, with Ben confidently in the lead, and Kristen sitting forlornly chagrined in the bow of her boat, helplessly consigning her fate to this kind old man.

In a matter of minutes, he was pulling up to the dock on Gaspar Island. Skillfully, he secured her boat to the piling and offered her his leathery hand. Children playing on the catwalk, oblivious to the rain that was now reduced to a light mist, eyed her curiously.

"Is some'un comin' to meet you?" Ben was reluctant to leave her alone.

Only now did she remember that Wes had told her to call Mr. Baxter, his caretaker, before she left the mainland, so that he could meet her at the landing. In all the confusion, she had forgotten to do so.

"I'll be fine," she assured him, "if you'll just tell me how to get to the Bradley house."

Ben pointed toward the west. "That's the Spinnaker over yonder. You can just see the top of it over the trees."

It looked like an easy walk across the dunes. After all, Wes had told her that the whole island was less than a mile wide.

Swallowing her pride, she thanked Ben profusely, and began to make her way across the sand toward the Spinnaker. Her wet shoes made a squishy sound as they sucked at the wet sand and shell, seeming to pull her back with each step as she plowed wearily forward. Like a mirage, her destination seemed to get farther away instead of closer. Her whole body ached.

Thoughts of home crowded into her mind. She could be sitting in her parents' cozy home in Gainesville with Jack beside her, warm and dry. Instead, here she was stranded on a strange island without roads, dripping wet, and freezing cold.

Her hair clung to the back of her neck, as rivulets of water trickled down her arms. She hoped she would not have to meet little Janelle Bradley in this condition.

Well, at least Wes was not due in until next week. She took some comfort in that thought as she began her ascent up the steep wooden stairs that led over the last row of sand dunes and toward the Spinnaker.

At the top, she paused to survey her surroundings. Toward the west she saw giant waves, far out in the Gulf of Mexico, hurling toward the shore. Their white crests looked like heaped mounds of whipping cream churning themselves into light and luscious cake toppings, only to disappear as the waves gently lapped the sandy beach.

The pristine shoreline stretched for miles, disturbed only by hungry gulls scavenging among the seashells and the leisurely strolling sun worshipers who left clean footprints along the sand. The late afternoon sun left only small traces of the summer storm that had ended as suddenly as it began.

She turned her attention to the house. Stretching high above the dunes, its rustic clapboard exterior gave the impression that it had risen from the sea, like some ancient, friendly sea monster from the deep. A wide veranda completely encircled the entire structure. A second story extended skyward, surrounded by a sundeck formed by the roof of the veranda below. From this deck, a wide outdoor staircase led still higher to a multiwindowed room perched like an eagle's nest at the very top. What a view it must offer!

Approaching the back door at last, her first impulse was to turn back and run. But where? She knocked gently, still hoping to attract as little attention as possible.

An elderly man with a kind face opened the door, but his expression quickly changed as he surveyed this strange-looking creature. "Who might you be, and what do you want?" he inquired sternly.

"I might be—I mean I am—*atchoo!*"

Before the startled man could respond, a sound came from within the house. First a laugh, and then a familiar voice boomed, "Never mind, Bax, I think I recognize that sneeze. Bring the young lady in!"

Oh, no, Kristen thought, as she entered the room and looked up into the amazing blue eyes of Robert Weston Bradley III!

Chapter 2

S eeing Kristen standing in his kitchen, Wes felt a strange mixture of amusement and admiration and pity. Her wet hair was plastered to her cheeks and shoulders, and her clothes clung to her body like a wet suit. Mud-covered canvas shoes were planted in the middle of an ever-enlarging puddle of brackish water as remnants of the rain and bay trickled from her goose-pimpled body.

Shaking from cold and from the shock of his unexpected presence, she spoke before considering the incongruity of her words. "What are you doing here?"

Wes chuckled. He just couldn't help it. He didn't mean to be insensitive. It was just that she had always appeared so prim and proper, a picture he could not reconcile with the sad little creature dripping her charm on his kitchen floor. And yet, strangely, she had never looked more endearing.

"I live here, remember? The question should be, what are *you* doing here?"

Then, recognizing her embarrassment, he took two giant strides and pulled her into the center of the big, warm kitchen. "Never mind," he told her. "You're here now, and everything is going to be all right."

A door opened and a plump, gray-haired woman sized up the situation instantly. "There's no need for you to stand there and catch your death of cold, Dear. Slip off your shoes, and I'll get a beach towel to wrap around you."

The grandmotherly lady disappeared briefly and reappeared with a large, fluffy towel. "After a warm bath and a change of clothes, there'll be time enough for the formalities. You must be Kristen. We expected you, but just not quite this soon." The sweet old lady kept chattering, covering the awkward silence of Kristen's uncharacteristic loss for words.

"I'm Martha Baxter," she continued, "and if you'll follow me, I'll show you to your room."

Kristen looked up at Wes, who was still watching her with that maddening laughter in his eyes. He nodded, and she turned and followed Mrs. Baxter up the staircase and into a spacious, charming bedroom.

"I'll have Mr. Baxter bring up your things, Dear. Get into your bath right away before you catch your death of cold. We planned to meet you and give you a much warmer welcome, but you surprised us. The bath is just through that door on your left. Take your time, and when you're ready, come back downstairs and we'll all get properly acquainted."

"Mrs. Baxter, thank you so much. I do apologize for the mess I've dragged in. I didn't intend to arrive this way. It was—well, it was just a series of misunderstandings. But I really didn't expect Mr. Bradley—Wes—to be here yet. I understood he wouldn't be coming for another week."

Mrs. Baxter smiled. "You'll find that he has a way of changing his plans when his little daughter calls. Janelle and her dad are very close. But you'll learn all about that in time. Now, hurry and get out of those wet things before you freeze."

Left alone, Kristen looked around the room as she began to pull off her wet clothes. An intricately carved oak four-poster bed was the focal point of the room. The massive oak dresser was topped by a hutch, in the center of which was a large, clear mirror.

"Oh, no!" she gasped, catching a glimpse of herself in the glass. "I look so dreadful, I can't even recognize myself!" She scurried for the bathroom and began to fill the tub with steaming hot water.

Forty minutes later, she looked and felt like a different person. Stepping out of her tub of warm bubbles, she emerged from the bathroom and found her suitcases in the room waiting for her. She selected a pair of blue poplin slacks and pulled a white cotton sweater over her head. She dried and brushed her flaxen hair, and using a pale blue ribbon, secured it into a ponytail.

Sheepishly, she descended the staircase. How could she ever explain her outlandish predicament? Would Wes be disgusted and send her home, deciding that she lacked the maturity and judgment to provide a role model for his little girl?

Wes and Janelle were waiting for her in the living room. They stood as she approached. "Kristen, I would like for you to meet my daughter, Janelle."

Kristen extended her hand to the child and gave her a warm smile. She was as pretty as the picture in the silver oval frame on his desk, golden ringlets surrounding the elfin features of her delicately luminescent face. Only the eyes were enormous, blue and sparkling—exact replicas of her father's. In her pale, thin arms, she cuddled a well-worn teddy bear wearing a faded once-red T-shirt. The only surprise to Kristen was the child's complexion. Here on a tropical island, she had expected to see a healthy tan, but instead, those huge eyes were surrounded by a pallor that suggested either recent illness or personal trauma.

"Hello, Janelle. I've been looking forward to coming here this summer. I know that we'll become good friends and do lots of interesting things together."

Janelle held out one small hand, but dropped her eyes shyly. "I like to read," she said.

"But now that Kristen is here," her father told her, "the two of you can swim and make castles in the sand, and explore the island while I'm gone." With an amused wink, he added, "I'll even see that Kristen receives some elementary instructions in marine navigation so that the two of you can enjoy boating in the bay. Won't that be fun?"

Kristen flushed. Old Ben must have called and told all of them her embarrassing experiences in the boat. Were they all determined to humiliate her?

Janelle looked doubtful. "Don't go away again, Daddy. I feel better when you're here."

"I like to be here, Janelle, but you know that I can't stay. I'll be going back to the office in Atlanta tomorrow, and I want you to help Kristen feel at home on the island. Can you do that?"

"I'll try," she answered sadly. Kristen's heart went out to the little girl, as she remembered the close companionship she had enjoyed with her own mother, and the fun they shared as she grew up in Gainesville. She desperately wanted to befriend this lonely child.

"What is your bear's name?" Kristen asked, trying to establish eye contact with Janelle.

The frail arms tightened their grip protectively around the shabby little bear. "Timmy," she replied. "My mother gave him to me." Tears welled dangerously close to the surface of her beautiful eyes.

"Tell you what!" exclaimed Wes brightly. "If you two ladies care to get an early start tomorrow, you can ride with me in the yacht to the marina. We'll teach Kristen how to read the channel markers." He smiled and winked at Kristen, and she felt the color rise to her cheeks.

"You can catch the taxi boat back to the island," he continued, "and I'll arrange with Ben for you to keep the rental boat here. That way, you can walk down to the landing and use it whenever you want. You'll be perfectly safe as long as you stay on the bay side of the island, and steer clear of the grass beds."

Kristen watched to see Janelle's reaction, but the child held tightly to her father's hand. Her eyes never seemed to lose the reflection of sadness.

"Daddy, will you play a game of Candyland with me now, like you promised? I mean, just the two of us."

If Wes was embarrassed by his daughter's display of poor manners, he covered it easily. "Yes, I'm sure Kristen needs some time to unpack and rest after her trip. Mrs. Baxter will have dinner ready for us in about an hour, so let's all meet in the dining room at seven. The run of the house is yours, Kristen. Feel free to explore the place."

Kristen felt like a schoolgirl being dismissed from the classroom, but she masked her feelings with a smile. "Thank you," she told him. "I do need time to get settled."

Mounting the stairs, she felt her confusion rising. Sometimes she found it natural to dislike Wes Bradley, so why did she experience this warm pulsation surging through her veins each time he was near? It certainly couldn't be an attraction to him, when every time he spoke to her it irritated her like a sandspur in her shoe. Why couldn't she develop a friendly, uncomplicated feeling for him, which is what he obviously felt for her?

She turned at the top of the stairs and entered the room she was to call her own for the next three months. Sitting on the edge of her bed, she cradled her head in her hands.

"I'm not in love with him," she moaned softly. "I'm not!" she repeated, as though saying it would make it true. But even as she heard her own lips utter the words, in her heart she knew that they were false.

The long summer loomed before her with all its challenges. Who was this Marla person for whom she was supposed to pave the way? From the look in that little girl's eyes, it wasn't going to be easy.

She walked to the desk and opened her Bible to Philippians, the third chapter: "Forgetting what is behind and straining toward what is ahead, I press on toward the goal. . . ."

She would put the past behind her and concentrate on the work ahead. When she turned things over to God, she was often surprised at the end results. She felt an overwhelming sense of peace as she laid down her Bible and left the room.

With permission to explore the house, Kristen walked the length of the upstairs hall. Downstairs, she could hear Janelle's giggles as she enjoyed the game with her father.

All of the doors stood open, so she looked into each of the other three bedrooms. The guest room next to her own was separated by the bath. Both these bedrooms had doors leading onto the north side of the deck.

Directly across the hall from her own room was a bedroom so bedecked with pink ruffles and frills that there was no mistaking who claimed this territory. As she stepped over the threshold, her feet halted at a large, hand-lettered poster propped against a chair.

KEEP OUT.
THIS MEANS YOU.
NO ONE ALOUD IN THIS ROOM.
DANGER.

Kristen could only smile at the crudely printed letters and the misspelled word. It seemed she had her work cut out for her if she was to win the affection of young Miss Bradley!

Next to Janelle's room was the master bedroom. She stuck her head inside, reluctant to invade Wes's privacy, yet feeling an unexplainable compulsion to breathe the air which carried the masculine fragrance of his recent presence. Her eyes scanned the perimeters, taking note of the enormous captain's bed in the center. Wide windows overlooked the gulf and beach, and a set of French doors gave view to the outside deck, invitingly furnished with a table, chairs, and a double-wide chaise. No wonder Wes came here to unwind from the stress of city life. Atlanta seemed to be part of another world.

Through the doors she could see the stairs to the "crow's nest," which was actually the third story of the massive house. Instead of entering his room, she returned to her own room to gain access to the outside deck.

Circling the second level, she mounted the staircase and entered a room that appeared to be floating in the clouds. The whole island was visible from here! A large, steel telescope mounted on a swiveling tripod in the center of the room brought distant ships right up to her doorstep! Awesome!

The room was simply but sturdily furnished. A half-bath occupied one corner, a bookcase another, and each wall was almost completely covered with lightly tinted plate glass. She vowed to come here as often as possible.

Returning to her room, she put her clothes away and washed her face and hands for dinner. Tempting aromas from the kitchen drifted up the stairs, and suddenly she realized that she was ravenous. Only then did she remember that she had not eaten since breakfast!

Dinner was served family style in the dining room, with Mr. and Mrs. Baxter joining them at the table. Kristen dropped her eyes and waited silently for the blessing. A lengthy silence was broken by the sounds of silverware against china, as Wes, at the head of the table, began to ladle steaming chowder from a porcelain tureen into one of five soup bowls. She raised her eyes to look at him at the precise moment he noticed her bowed head, and he dropped the ladle back onto the dish with a clatter. Recovering quickly, he said, "Let us pray."

Now, every head was bowed except for Janelle's, whose eyes scanned the table in an effort to understand this unfamiliar ritual.

"Dear Lord. . ." His deep voice paused thoughtfully before he continued. "We ask Your forgiveness that we have neglected for so long to thank You for our many blessings. We come now with grateful hearts to thank You for our family, our friends, and the abundance of our table. In Jesus' name we pray. Amen."

"Amen," Mr. Baxter echoed lustily, with a satisfying smile on his face. Mrs. Baxter too was beaming her approval, as Wes picked up the ladle and proceeded to fill the bowls.

After a creamy clam chowder, Mrs. Baxter served broiled fresh grouper, green beans from the garden, fluffy baked potatoes, and a crisp, green salad. Conversation was easy and interesting, though Kristen noticed that Janelle said little and ate almost nothing. Several times, Kristen looked up to find Wes watching her. She supposed that he was trying to assure himself that his beloved daughter would be in capable hands.

After coffee was served, Kristen offered to help in the kitchen. Over Mrs. Baxter's mild protests, she helped clear the table. Wes went upstairs with Janelle, promising to read her a story if she could get in and out of the tub in fifteen minutes. Kristen smiled, hearing their playful banter float up the stairs.

Mr. Baxter retired to their quarters, leaving Kristen and Mrs. Baxter alone in the big, rustic kitchen.

Although modernly equipped, the room radiated old-fashioned warmth that made Kristen feel immediately at home. As she and Mrs. Baxter worked and chatted, they began a friendship and mutual respect that was to flourish in the days ahead.

"You've had a long day, Kristen. Now that we have the dishes in the dishwasher, why don't you turn in for the night?"

"I am a bit tired," Kristen admitted. "I think I'll step outside for a breath of fresh air before going up. I'll see you in the morning. And thanks, Mrs. Baxter, for all your help and understanding."

Outside, the evening breeze lifted her long, blond hair and filled her lungs with delightful salty air. The sound of the waves drew her toward the shoreline, where she could see dots of twinkling lights from boats far out in the water. Rhythmic beams from a distant lighthouse played across the choppy gulf.

Walking in the semidarkness, she nearly bumped into a man seated on a big mahogany log that had drifted in from the sea. To her astonishment, she recognized Wes.

"Sit down and join me for a few minutes, Kristen. I just walked out here to gather my thoughts for tomorrow."

"I didn't know you were out here," Kristen said, dropping down beside him. She hoped he wouldn't think she had followed him. "I thought you were upstairs with Janelle."

"She's asleep already. She had an exciting day. She's really worn me out, but I sleep better if I come out here first for a little meditation and relaxation. I hope you'll be able to discover the wonderful peace this island can bring."

"How did you happen to find this beautiful place?"

Pleased with her compliment, he told her, "When I was a boy, my parents used to bring me to Fort Myers every summer, so I developed a real love for the west coast of Florida. Then I began to explore the offshore barrier islands and knew that someday I would own a piece of one."

"What made you choose Gaspar?"

"One of my clients needed to liquidate some assets, and I was more than happy to help him." Wes laughed, remembering. "Some of the islands are accessible by bridges, so from a commercial standpoint, they're a lot more desirable and less affordable than Gaspar. But to me, the charm of this place is its isolation and its lack of commercialization."

"Aren't there any stores here at all?"

"No, none. Just six miles of unspoiled beauty. But it never gets dull here. You'll find that out for yourself this summer."

Kristen knew that no matter how things worked out for her, this summer would be anything but dull!

"When I first bought the land and came out here to build the Spinnaker, a group of developers were trying to get a bridge built across the bay, but all the property owners out here got together and vetoed the idea."

"Are most of the residents just here for the summer?"

"No, actually there are a lot of people who just come down here from the North in winter. They come here and enjoy the sunshine and the fishing, and of course, the beaches. Then, when the weather gets hot, they head back north. In the summer, we get the vacationers with kids out of school for three months."

"But does anyone live here year-round?"

"Oh, yes. We have some commercial fishermen who have houses over here. And there are a few retirees, like Mr. Beardsley, our neighbor." She wondered at his quick little smirk when he mentioned the name. "You'll probably meet him while you're here."

"I know I'm going to love it here this summer. It hardly seems like a job. I'll feel guilty getting paid!"

"Nonsense. You'll well earn your salary if you keep my daughter happy and help her accept the changes that may be taking place in her life."

Janelle was not the only one who would need help coping with the changes taking place. Kristen had already turned to a higher Source for her own needs. Now she prayed that she could be an instrument to help this precious child Wes loved so dearly. "I'll do everything I can to help her," she promised, and meant it with all of her heart.

"I'll be getting up early in the morning, Kristen. My boat will get me to the mainland, and my flight into Atlanta will have me back in the office by midmorning."

"Will you be back next weekend?" Kristen hoped her voice did not betray her anticipation.

"Yes, I'm going to bring Marla here next Saturday. I hope you can smooth the way with Janelle. She is resisting the idea." Wes sounded worried. "I've planned a special dinner for Saturday evening. Mrs. Baxter can handle all the arrangements. In addition to Marla, I've invited Jeff Garrett, who is an old friend, and commander of the Coast Guard station over on the mainland. You'll enjoy meeting him, and he keeps an eye on things over here. If you ever need any help, he's the person to call!"

Kristen hesitated before asking the next question. "Is this when you will announce your engagement?"

"No," Wes answered quickly. "Marla and I have not made that kind of commitment yet. It's too early in our relationship to know how that will work out. But, for Janelle's sake and for mine, I have to hope it will happen."

"Wes," Kristen said softly. She hoped he would not think her too personal, but he seemed relieved to have someone to talk to, and she needed to know. "Do you love her?"

Wes hesitated before answering. "I've known real love once, and I lost it." Deep pain was revealed in his voice. "I'm not sure I would want to risk that again. But I might settle for companionship, mutual respect, and a nice, stable home for Janelle."

After a thoughtful pause, he turned to her and asked, "How about you? Is there a special man in your life?"

He caught her off guard. She was grateful for the darkness that prevented him from seeing the flush that spread over her face. Her first impulse was to deny the existence of a special man, but standing so close to him, with her heart overflowing with love, she could only answer honestly. "Yes. Yes, there is."

She stood quickly, before he had a chance to pursue the subject, and as he stood beside her, his arm brushed hers.

"Why, you're trembling," he said. "You must be chilly. Here, take my windbreaker." He offered the light jacket he had been carrying. As he wrapped it around her shoulders, his hands fell upon her upper arms, and he gripped them and looked down into her eyes.

Kristen thought she read a look in his eyes she had not seen there before.

Then, abruptly, he dropped his hands to his side, and said huskily, "We'd better get back to the house. Tomorrow will be a busy day, and we have to get an early start."

Their shoes made soft, crunchy sounds as they walked through the sand toward the house.

"I'll knock on your door early," he told her. "Janelle is happy to be able to accompany me to the marina tomorrow. She prolongs the parting as long as she can."

"Try not to worry about her," she tried to reassure him. "She's a lovely child, and I'm looking forward to winning her confidence. I'm going to make this summer a happy experience for both of us."

Although it was stretching the truth, she felt it her duty to add, "I'm looking forward to meeting Marla too."

"Good. And I hope you'll be able to pave the way for her meeting with Janelle. You'll have plenty of time together with Janelle tomorrow. The two of you can get back on the taxi boat, like we talked about, and I'll ask Mrs. Baxter to fix you a picnic basket for lunch. There are lots of nice picnic areas on the island, and Janelle can help you select one. Picnics are her favorite pastime."

When he told her, "Good night," at the top of the stairs, Kristen felt something akin to an electric current charging the air between them. Did Wes notice it too?

She turned quickly toward her room, anxious to leave lest he read her emotions. "Good night, Wes," she said.

Later, in her room, Kristen lay between the smooth percale sheets and tried to plan how she could make tomorrow's picnic fun for Janelle. She loved children, and she determined that somehow she would break through that hard little shell and become a friend and confidante for the unhappy child.

She picked up her devotional guide from the bedside table, and as she read, she felt the tensions draining from her body. At the end of her time with the Lord, she turned off her bedside light and allowed her heavy eyelids to close. The gentle sound of the waves beating against the shore and the soft, salty breeze drifting through her open windows seemed to have a hypnotic effect, and she did not open her eyes again until she heard a firm knock on her door.

"Time to get up, sleepyheads," she heard Wes's deep voice declare.

Sleepyheads, indeed. Why, it was still dark! But the tempting aroma of fresh-brewed coffee floated on the air. She closed her windows to the early morning chill, and shivered in delightful anticipation of this new day.

Chapter 3

Dressed in her crisp cotton shorts and sailor blouse, Kristen moved down the staircase toward the inviting smells from the kitchen.

Wes and Janelle were already seated at the big butcher-block table, but their conversation stopped as she entered the room.

A wicker picnic basket rested on the table alongside a tray of warm muffins, fresh orange juice, and a steaming pot of coffee.

"Good morning, Kristen," Wes greeted her. "I hope you slept well."

Kristen's voice betrayed the lingering remnants of sleep. "Yes, thank you."

"Mrs. Baxter got up early and prepared this for us," Wes told her. "She's gone back to her room. She and Bax will come out later and have their breakfast. She likes to cook big, hearty breakfasts whenever I come, but I told her we wouldn't want much this early in the morning."

Kristen could hear the Baxters moving about in their quarters. The sounds of their gentle words and laughter filtered into the kitchen.

"How long have the Baxters worked for you?" she asked, sipping her coffee.

"They worked for my parents when I was a little boy. After my mother died, they stayed on and helped my father keep the household running, up until the time my dad sold his big house and moved into a condominium. That was about the time I built this place, so it was natural for them to come here."

"They're like part of the family, aren't they?"

"They're more like grandparents, I suppose. Mrs. Baxter always met me at the door when I came home from school. She was interested in everything I did and always had a homemade cookie and a glass of milk waiting for me. I don't know how we would have done without them then, and I certainly don't know how I could have managed these last two years without them."

"I don't want to make extra work for them this summer. I'll help out wherever I can."

"They're ecstatic about having you here. Mrs. Baxter will smother you with attention if you're not careful. Your presence here this summer will do as much for her as it will for Janelle." He lifted the empty wicker basket. "When you and Janelle get back here this morning, she'll have your basket packed with all kinds of good things for your lunch. I hope you like picnics. I'm afraid they're an obsession with my daughter."

"Janelle, you'll need to show Kristen some of your favorite picnic spots."

Daylight was just beginning to break as the three of them trudged across the dunes toward the boat landing. Wes carried a briefcase in one hand and held fast to Janelle with the other. With her free arm, Janelle clutched Timmy tightly to her chest. Kristen followed along the path behind, marveling that her feet felt light as a feather today, in stark contrast to the weary journey of yesterday.

The dampness of the morning dew lay heavy on the palmettos that lined their path. A frog chorus filled the air, and birds sang a sweet accompaniment from the trees.

"What was that?" Kristen asked nervously, hearing a rustling of leaves from the underbrush.

"Probably a gopher turtle, or a rabbit, perhaps. Or maybe a curious raccoon. A wide variety of wildlife abounds here on the island. It's a bird sanctuary too. We don't have any hunters over here. Most of the islanders are dedicated to preserving the natural beauty."

"I have some books about birds," volunteered Janelle. It was the first time that she had initiated any conversation, so Kristen picked up on it at once.

"I hope you will help me learn to identify them, Janelle. I can only spot blue jays and cardinals, and all the rest are just birds to me."

"Look!" Wes stopped in his tracks. "There's one of the island residents now." He pointed to the path ahead.

Crossing the path was a large brown turtle. Their approach didn't seem to alarm him, as he twisted his head for a better look.

"That's one of our native gophers," Wes explained. "He's a land turtle, quite harmless, and he lives on the island vegetation. There are lots of them around here."

They were approaching the dock now, and Kristen was surprised to see so many people out this early. Sun-browned fishermen lifted their heavy nets aboard anchored vessels as they discussed the weather forecasts and the prospects for the day's catch. Pleasure boats rested indiscriminantly between commercial crafts, their skippers exchanging fishing tips and friendly banter while making final preparations to launch.

Wes seemed to know everyone.

"You'd better take back that briefcase and bring out your spinning rod instead," a neighbor advised. "It's going to be a perfect day for reeling in the big ones!"

"I know it, you lucky loafer! Just wait. I'll be back soon to get mine."

Kristen gaped in admiration at the twenty-eight-foot Pro Line yacht moored at the landing. Surely it must have been there yesterday when she arrived, but she had been too absorbed in her own despair to notice. Bold, black letters stenciled on its side spelled *Janni Lu*, the namesake, no doubt, of little Janelle Louise Bradley.

Wes picked up his little girl as though she were a helium-filled doll, lifting her high in the air before planting her feet firmly on the clean white deck. Then, jumping aboard, he extended a steadying hand to Kristen. She felt the strength of his grip, yet it was as warm and gentle as the summer breeze.

Once the boat was released from its restraining rods, Kristen observed how skillfully Wes maneuvered it into the channel, carefully avoiding the grass beds that had trapped her the day before.

"Stand here, Kristen, and take the wheel. Now, keep your eyes on those red and green channel markers, and just steer the boat between them. That will keep us in the channel. Just be sure to keep your mind on where you're going."

She stood by him and gripped the wheel, and the force of motion pushed her against the hard muscles of his strong, tanned arm. Despite Wes's directive, her mind was anywhere but on where she was going! With a great deal of determination, she tried to focus on the navigation lesson, hoping that she could perform in a way that would capture his admiration for a change.

Approaching the marina, he cut the speed of the motor to a slow idle. A dockhand helped them secure the boat long enough to unload. Later, the men would clean it and dock it until Wes returned from Atlanta.

Kristen and Janelle followed Wes to the parking garage where he kept his Mercedes, and where Kristen's own little Toyota was parked.

When Wes lifted Janelle into his arms and held her, Kristen discreetly walked a short distance away, giving them a few private moments. The two of them formed a sweet picture, and the strong bond between them was apparent. They had been through a lot together, and now Kristen could see that they were working at healing together. She strengthened her determination to help in any way she could.

Kristen expected a tearful parting, but Janelle stood bravely silent and solemn as she watched her father drive slowly out of the marina, waving and throwing her kisses as he left.

"Let's drive to the shopping center before we go back," Kristen suggested, in an effort to redirect Janelle's thoughts. "I need a few things."

An unsmiling Janelle climbed into the seat beside her, carefully adjusting her seat belt to include her beloved bear, and for the first time, she and Kristen were off on an adventure alone together. Conversation was strained at first, and Kristen tried to start a dialogue of small talk.

"I need stationery and postcards, and I thought I might get a few art supplies. Do you like to draw and paint?"

"I don't draw very well," Janelle replied. "And I've never tried to paint except for finger paints."

"Sometimes it's surprising what you can do when you try," countered Kristen. "Perhaps we could start by doing some of your favorite birds. I'd like to try a seascape too!"

She was pleased to note a small glimmer of interest.

Kristen slowed the car and turned into the parking lot of a small shopping center. There on the corner was a craft shop with a sign in the window that boasted, ART SUPPLIES.

It took a long time for them to decide on the colors they would need.

"And we'll need palettes and brushes," Kristen said. She fingered the brushes and chose several different sizes. Knowing that they would have to carry their purchases across the island, they selected only four small canvases.

"We can come back for more when we need them," Kristen assured her. "Besides, I have a sketch pad in my room. We should have enough to keep us busy for quite awhile."

Kristen was pleased to find that the art store also carried stationery items, and Janelle helped her select the postcards.

"Look, here's one with a picture of Gaspar Island. And here's one with the lighthouse at Buena Vista."

"My family and friends back home will love them," Kristen remarked. She paid the clerk for her purchases and held the door open for Janelle.

Driving back to the marina, conversation was easier. Although Kristen had to initiate most of the conversation, she was pleased to coax a few responses from her small passenger.

The sun was high in the sky when they boarded the taxi boat back to the island.

"G'mornin', lassies," shouted Ben from the end of the dock. He was busy cleaning a nice catch of snapper for a fisherman. "Glad to see you're going across with an expert today." He chuckled at his own humor.

Kristen bristled at first but, remembering how he had come to her rescue, returned his smile and waved.

Kristen watched the boat pilot guide them toward the channel and thread his way to the island wharf. How easy it was when you knew where to go!

Back at the house, Mrs. Baxter did indeed have their lunch packed. They sat at the kitchen table and drank sweet lemonade from tall, frosty glasses while Mrs. Baxter listened to them relate the experiences of the morning.

"And where are you going for lunch, Janelle?" she asked.

"I think we'll walk up the beach to the point. They have nice tables there under the pines."

Mr. Baxter walked through the kitchen. "Don't go swimming at the point, girls. The currents in the pass are vicious. The gulf is nice and smooth today, though, so you should be able to get a nice swim right in front of the house."

Kristen and Janelle went upstairs to change into their bathing suits and pack their beach bags. Along with the usual towels and suntan lotions, Kristen included her sketch pad and colored pencils, and Janelle selected a favorite book and, of course, Timmy.

After eyeing the girl's fair complexion, Kristen gently applied sunscreen, first to the cherub face and then over the thin little limbs that would be exposed to the midday sun. Naturally tanned from weekend outdoor activities, Kristen nevertheless applied the same precaution to herself.

It was nearly a mile to the south end of the island and, swinging the basket between them, they walked along the edge of the surf, kicking up a path of fine, salty spray. The sun beat down on them with pleasing warmth.

The little park under the pines, with its rustic tables and benches, sat high in the dunes on the tip of the island, giving view to the Gulf of Mexico to the west, the blue bay to the east, and directly across the pass, another of the barrier islands.

"It looks as though we could just walk across to the neighboring island," Kristen observed.

"That's the dangerous pass Mr. Baxter warned us about." Janelle was proud to exhibit her knowledge of the island. "Look across there," she continued. "That island is called Buena Vista. There's a bridge connecting it to the mainland. The old lighthouse on the end of it is the one on your picture postcards. You'll be able to see its beam after dark."

"I think I saw that last night from the crow's nest," Kristen told her. "Let's drive over there in my car someday soon."

"Oh, could we? There are little shops and art galleries and all sorts of neat things in Buena Vista. Sometimes we go in the car, and sometimes we go in Daddy's boat. But we always go on the Fourth of July and watch the parade."

A sad, faraway look clouded the little face, and Kristen guessed that she was thinking of happier days when she watched the parade in the loving circle of her family, now broken forever.

"Let's go make a sand castle," Kristen urged, in an effort to divert Janelle's attention.

Kristen showed her how to make a "drip castle," letting fists full of very wet sand slip slowly through their fingers. As the peak reached higher and higher, it began to resemble a castle, complete with turrets and towers.

"Let's dig a moat to protect the beautiful princess who lives inside," Kristen said.

Janelle, an avid fan of fairy tales, was caught up in the fantasy. "But we need to make a drawbridge for the handsome prince."

They cast wary eyes toward the rising tide that threatened to sweep their masterpiece into oblivion.

"We'll leave this one for the tide, and make another one tomorrow," Kristen promised. "Let's stop and have our lunch."

The brisk walk and the salt air had stimulated their healthy young appetites. They spread the red checkered cloth and laid out sandwiches, apples, grapes, boiled eggs, and snack cakes. A jar of lemonade covered with ice had kept everything cool.

After lunch, lying on beach towels in a partially shaded spot, Janelle dozed while Kristen studied the cloud patterns and thought.

She must talk to Jack. He deserved the truth, and the truth, she now knew, was that she would never be his wife. Although there had been no promises spoken between them, there seemed to be an assumption on the part of those who knew them best, and it was time now to set the record straight.

He would always be very dear to her, but the love she had to offer him was not the kind good marriages are made of.

Deep in her own thoughts, she hadn't realized that Janelle was awake and watching her. Kristen picked up her sketch pad and began to draw.

"Can you draw my daddy's boat?"

Janelle's eyes grew wide as the distinct likeness of the *Janni Lu* appeared on the paper. On the deck, Kristen drew two figures, one of a dark-haired man, and one of a curly haired girl. As she began the outline of another figure, Janelle grabbed her pencil.

"No. That's all. Just my dad and me."

Kristen tore the sheet from the pad and handed it to Janelle. "Would you like to color the picture?"

Janelle was quiet as she added colors to the drawing. Pressing it between the pages of her book, she stored it in her beach bag.

Suddenly, without preamble, she stated matter-of-factly, "Stepmothers are mean!"

Kristen tried to conceal her shock. "How did you get an idea like that?"

"Oh, I read about them in my books. Haven't you ever read about Cinderella?"

Kristen paused before answering. "Of course I have. I love fairy tales. But we both know they're just fantasy. How about those big white mice that pulled Cinderella's coach. Do you believe they really exist?"

"No–o–o," Janelle admitted. "But stepmothers really do exist, don't they?"

"Yes," Kristen was forced to admit. "Stepmothers really do exist. Sometimes they can be very loving and wonderful."

"Well, I don't want one. I don't need anybody but my daddy."

"Janelle, what do you remember about your mother?" Kristen hoped that her gentle prodding was the right approach. She had no formal training in child psychology, but common sense told her that sometimes it helped to bring hidden things out in the open.

At first, she thought that Janelle was not going to answer. Had she driven a bigger wedge between them? But then she heard the small voice, scarcely more than a whisper.

"I don't remember everything. I was only six years old when she died. Mostly I remember that she was beautiful, and that she was always nice and never angry."

"I'm sure that she was beautiful, and sweet too, but everyone gets angry sometimes. Love has a way of remembering all of the beautiful things and forgetting the rest. It's one of the wonderful things about love."

"I didn't want her to go away." She was crying now, and Kristen put her arm around her and pulled her close.

"Of course you didn't. And I know that she didn't want to leave you and your father, either. We don't know why those things have to happen. But because of your love for her, you'll always have her close to you, deep in your heart, and you'll go on remembering all the beautiful things about her forever."

"And I won't have to have a stepmother?" She raised her eyes hopefully.

"I can't promise you that. That's something we don't know. But there's one thing I can promise you. Your father loves you very much, and he will always choose what's best for you. He would never allow anyone to hurt you, and he'll do whatever is necessary to make sure you always have a safe and happy home. Don't you know that you can trust him to do that?"

Kristen watched the lines of concern soften on the child's tearstained face as she nodded her head, but the worry lines that creased her forehead remained. What else could she tell her that would help?

"Janelle, do you realize that a part of your mother is still alive in you, her daughter?"

"No, Daddy told me she lives with Jesus now. I know all about that, but I need to have her here with me."

"Wait here just a moment." Kristen went to the picnic basket and pulled out a big red apple and a knife. Janelle watched without comment.

"Did you know, Janelle, that there's a star in every apple?"

"Not really. You're making that up."

"No, really. See?" Kristen had sliced the apple in two, horizontally. With the tip of the knife, she pointed to the star in the center. "Every apple has one."

Janelle was intrigued. She had eaten dozens of apples, and she had never seen a star in one before. "I usually cut mine the other way, and I can't see the star."

"That's right. You can't see it, but it's there every time. And look closer to see what's inside the star."

"I don't see anything but some seeds."

Kristen dug a seed from the core and placed it in Janelle's hand. "Look at that seed, and think very hard, and tell me what you see."

At first Janelle was puzzled, but gradually a half smile curved her lips. "I think I understand. You mean, if I think real hard, I can see an apple tree."

"Exactly!" What a wonderful mind this child possessed! "A tree with lots more apples and lots more stars and seeds. So that even after the apple is gone, it will still leave part of itself with us to enjoy."

"I thought we were talking about my mother, not about apples."

"Of course we were. It was just my way of reminding you that, like the apple, your mother left part of herself here for you to love and enjoy. Janelle, *you* are the star in the apple. All your beautiful memories of her are inside you like the seeds, and you can plant them and make them grow."

"I'll always think of that when I have apples," Janelle told her. Even at eight years of age, she had a good grasp of Kristen's words. She was a star, with seeds to nourish, and that was enough to sustain her for now.

"Look at our castle!" Kristen diverted her attention. "The waves are crossing the moat. Next time we'll build on higher ground. Anyway, we should gather our things and start back. Help me look for some pretty shells along the way."

Walking back down the island through the sand and surf, Kristen tried to break through Janelle's silence. "Let's go for a swim when we get to the beach in front of our house. It's so hot today!"

"No, I don't want to. I don't like to swim."

"We can just splash in the water and cool off. We don't have to really swim." Kristen's training as a Red Cross instructor alerted her to the fear she saw in those big blue eyes.

"No, I don't like to go in the gulf." A hint of panic was beginning to sound in her voice.

"Janelle, are you afraid of the water?" Kristen gently prodded.

The ensuing silence gave her the answer she already knew. Relentlessly, Kristen hit at her most vulnerable spot. "Your daddy would be so surprised and happy if you learned to like the water this summer, even if you don't learn to swim."

She could tell that Janelle was thinking about that, so she continued. "The gulf water is warm and friendly when the weather's nice. It's not as cold or as rough as the ocean."

She moved close to Janelle's side and held her hand. "Let's start by walking out together, just until the water reaches your waist. I won't let go of your hand."

They were directly in front of the Spinnaker now, and the low tide provided a long expanse of flat, white beach leading into the calm water.

"I don't want Timmy to get wet."

"No, we won't let him. Just hold him up, and we'll walk out slowly so that we don't frighten Timmy." Even as she spoke, Kristen was leading the little girl gradually, deeper and deeper into the water. Gentle waves lapped against their legs. The tightening grip of the small hand was the only evidence of Janelle's nervousness, but Kristen was aware of the fear she was bravely trying to conceal.

When the water reached Janelle's waist, Kristen stopped, and together they stood, feeling the warm blue water lap gently against their bodies.

"You know, Janelle, most of the things that frighten us do so because we don't understand them. It's like that with people too. Sometimes when we don't know people, we decide that we don't like them, but when we get to know and understand them, we find that they're really quite nice." She paused to give Janelle time to absorb that thought.

"The Gulf of Mexico is like that. When you get to know it better, you're going to find that it's warm and friendly."

"It tastes salty, and it burns my eyes," Janelle protested.

"Actually, the salt is friendly too. It helps to hold up your weight when you learn to swim."

"I want to go back in the house now."

"All right, Janelle. This was a start, and I'm proud of you for being such a big girl. But let's walk out here like this every day and see if you can make friends with the gulf this summer."

They paused at the foot of the porch steps to rinse the gritty white sand from their bodies. The outdoor shower felt cold on their sun-warmed skin, and their squeals brought Mrs. Baxter to the door with clean, dry towels.

"My goodness, look who's back. Kristen, you had a phone call while you were out. He didn't leave a message, except to tell you that Jack called, and would call you again tonight."

After a warm refreshing shower, Kristen donned a comfortable pair of Hawaiian-print shorts and a bright green T-shirt and opened the door into the hall to enjoy the cross-ventilation of the fresh gulf breeze. She glanced across the hall where Janelle had retreated to the privacy of her own room. Kristen smiled to see through the partially open door that the KEEP OUT sign had been removed. Perhaps she was making headway!

That evening the four of them had a casual meal around the kitchen table. Janelle picked up her fork and then dropped it abruptly as she noticed the three bowed heads around the table. Without comment, she lowered her eyes as Mr. Baxter raised his voice in praise and thanksgiving, just as though he had never missed doing so for all his prior meals. The look of satisfaction on Mrs. Baxter's face affirmed that she heartily approved of the practice, and Kristen took it for granted that this was the normal routine. Only little Janelle looked around with curiosity and wondered at the changes that seemed to be sweeping into her life by leaps and bounds these days. She hadn't decided yet which ones she liked and which ones she didn't. She'd just have to wait and see.

They were finishing dessert when the phone rang.

"That'll probably be your young man, Kristen," predicted Mrs. Baxter. "Why don't you answer it?"

Kristen looked first at the wall phone near the kitchen sink, and then back at the three people sitting around the table. Mrs. Baxter read her thoughts. "Go in Mr. Bradley's study, Dear. There's a phone in there where you can be private."

Kristen gave her a grateful smile.

Entering the small study, Kristen was immediately aware of the air of masculinity surrounding her. She closed the door and reached for the phone.

"Hello," she said, picturing Jack on the other end of the line.

"Hello, yourself! Kristen?"

Suddenly her knees felt as weak as wet cardboard as she recognized not Jack's, but Wes's voice floating across the wire. She inhaled sharply, and struggled to sound unruffled. Oh, where was her voice when she needed it?

"Kristen, are you there? Are we still connected?"

"Yes, Wes," she finally managed to say. "I'm here. Do you want me to put Janelle on the line?"

"Later. Not just yet. Are you trying to get rid of me?" She could almost see the teasing smile on his lips.

"No. No, of course not. *Atchoo!*" She covered the mouthpiece and hoped he had not heard that sneeze.

"What have you ladies been up to today?" If he had heard the sneeze, he chose not to embarrass her by calling attention to her telltale nervous habit.

In a deliberately modulated voice, she related the day's adventures. She told him about the trip to the shopping center, and how she and Janelle were opening up some lines of communication, but she was careful not to mention the revealing conversation they had shared on the beach.

"I feel relieved knowing you're there with her, Kristen. I can't tell you how much this means to me. I just hope you won't find a whole summer on an isolated island too boring."

"I don't see how anyone could ever find Gaspar Island boring."

Reluctantly, she called Janelle to the phone. Her hands were shaking as she transferred the receiver. She returned to the kitchen to afford Janelle the same privacy that had been extended to her.

It took time to regain her composure, so she was glad that Jack did not call until nearly ten o'clock. She was readying for bed when the phone rang again. Mrs. Baxter called up to her, and she answered on the bedside extension.

"Hello."

"Kristen, Darling! It's so good to hear your voice. I miss you very much."

Jack told her all the local news, and Kristen found herself enjoying the call she had been dreading. She told him about the beauty of the island and the activities she planned in the coming weeks. "It doesn't seem like a job at all. More like a vacation. Janelle's a very sweet little girl. Not at all the spoiled brat I expected to find."

They talked for twenty minutes before the conversation took a serious turn.

"Kristen, I've thought a lot about the things you said to me before you left."

Her heart lunged. Here at last was the part of the conversation she had been dreading. How would he react to the things she needed to tell him? She listened while he talked.

"I know you're right about each of us feeling free to see other people, to be sure of our feelings before making a lifetime commitment. I haven't changed my mind, and I don't think I ever will. Still, I want you to know that I'm taking your advice. I'm taking Ann Wilson to the Fourth of July barbecue next month. I wanted to make sure you heard this from me, and not one of our friends."

Kristen supposed that she should feel at least a little jab of jealousy, but instead she experienced a tremendous feeling of relief.

"Jack, Ann's a lovely girl. I know you'll both have a good time. Tell all my friends 'hello' for me, and be sure to write me all about it."

After a few more moments of friendly banter, they hung up, and Kristen leaned back against her pillow. Things have a way of working out sometimes, beyond anything a person could plan. Jack was attractive and popular. She didn't think she would have to worry long about his social adjustments. At least, she hoped not. He would always be very special to her.

Chapter 4

Kristen had lived on the island for almost a week before she encountered Jake Beardsley. What a grouch!

On Thursday, when she and Janelle took a shortcut through his backyard, the old man came bounding out the back door. Like a little bantam rooster, he jumped up and down, waving his arms and shouting, "Get out of here. I'll not have you nosing around my property. Can't you see the boundaries?" He pointed to some crude stakes joined with nylon fishing line, obviously erected to define his property lines. "I'm tired of people tramping around trying to look into my windows!"

Frightened, Janelle ran as fast as her small legs could carry her and headed for the shelter of her own house, but Kristen stubbornly held her ground.

"Well, *excuse me!* Obviously, I have offended you by stepping on your sand." She drew herself up to her full five feet two inches. "But," she continued, "I can assure you that neither Janelle nor I have the slightest interest in looking in your windows, and you can rest assured that we will not walk through your yard again."

Not to be so easily pacified, he ranted on: "Baxter tries to outdo me on everything. He thinks he's the checker champion of the world. Now he even sends his spies around to keep up with what I'm doing. Well, I'll not have it, I tell you."

Kristen tried to control her temper, making allowances for his advanced age. Feeling a small prick of guilt, she forced a smile and bade him good-bye.

When she returned to the house, Mrs. Baxter was comforting a visibly shaken Janelle. Mr. Baxter tried to look sympathetic, but mirth sparkled in his eyes.

"Jake Beardsley's okay, Honey. I guess I should just let him win at checkers once in awhile."

"He reminds me of Rumpelstiltskin in my fairy-tale book," declared Janelle, the beginnings of a smile starting to show.

"Rumpelstiltskin!" repeated Mr. Baxter. "That's a good name for him."

And it was a name that stuck. Since that day, each time they passed his cottage, Janelle would point to it and say, "There's Mr. Rumpelstiltskin's house," and they were ever so careful to give his yard a wide berth.

On Saturday morning, Kristen and Janelle were on the beach early to find the prettiest seashells washed ashore by the morning tide.

"Look at this one, Kristen! A perfect lady's slipper." Janelle added the tiny pink shell to her growing collection. Even as she worked, the girl kept her beloved toy bear tightly cuddled in one arm.

"Time now for our walk in the water," Kristen announced. Since their first experience of going into the gulf together, they had made it a daily adventure. The biggest breakthrough was the first day that Janelle consented to let Timmy sit on a blanket and watch from the shore. Now she placed him on his perch and took Kristen's hand.

Gone was the tense, death-grip hold of those first few adventures. Now the petite hand Kristen held in her own was almost relaxed. Stepping forward, they stood in water that gently lapped at Janelle's chest and Kristen's waist.

"If you can stand here alone for just a minute, I'll show you how I like to float."

"Okay, but don't go off and leave me."

"You know I wouldn't do that." Slowly, without causing a splash or a wave, Kristen placed her face in the water and floated with arms outstretched.

Standing beside Janelle once more, she held her hand and said, "I wish you could see what it looks like under the water!"

"What does it look like?"

"It's beautiful. You can see the bottom, and you can almost pretend that you're a mermaid."

"I can't see the bottom," Janelle complained, as she leaned forward, almost letting the tip of her tiny nose touch the water.

"You could if you put your face into the water and opened your eyes."

"Will it burn my eyes?"

"It didn't burn mine. But you have to remember to hold your breath."

Janelle stood thinking for several minutes, and then slowly, slowly, she lowered her solemn face into the water. It rested there for only a few seconds, but when she stood up, her eyes were shining with delight. "It is beautiful. I really did feel like a mermaid!"

Kristen hugged her. "You're the nicest mermaid I ever met. Shall we go up and dry off now?"

"I want to look just one more time."

This time, the face was submerged deeper and longer, and when she came up for air, Janelle gleefully held her hand high in the air. "Look what I found!"

"A beautiful white sand dollar. What a treasure. Be careful with it, though. They break easily."

The excitement of her newfound treasure made Janelle forget to hold

Kristen's hand as she splashed her way back to shore. "I'm going to save this to show my daddy," she squealed happily.

"I'm very proud of you, Janelle." And Kristen was. They had a long way to go, but they had made a good start. She fervently hoped to help Janelle overcome this and some of the other fears in her young life before the summer ended.

"Did you know that there's a legend about the sand dollar, Janelle?"

"A legend? What's that?"

"It's a story that's been handed down through the years. This is a very old one. Would you like to hear it?"

"Yes, I would." Janelle cradled her treasure in her little hands as Kristen began to recite the age-old tale.

"The sand dollar represents Jesus. Do you see the holes in it?"

"Yes, I see four around the sides, and one bigger one toward the middle. Do they mean something special too?"

"The four little holes represent the nail holes where Jesus was nailed to the cross, and the one in the middle is where the spear pierced His side. Now, look for a star."

"I think I see it," Janelle chirped.

"Of course. Etched right there on the face of the sand dollar. The star stands for the Star of Bethlehem that led the shepherds to the manger where Jesus was born. And there's one other thing."

Janelle studied her treasure for the one remaining secret. "I don't see anything else."

"No, you can't see it because we don't want to break it open. Perhaps we'll find a broken one someday soon, and I can show you what's inside."

"Can you tell me anyway?"

"Inside are five perfect little white doves. They're a symbol of praise."

Janelle had a moment of indecision. She wanted to see the doves, but she didn't want to break her prize.

"If you sit right here, I'll swim out to the sandbar and get another for you to break open," Kristen told her.

Janelle sat in the sand and watched Kristen's smooth, fluid strokes carry her the short distance to the sandbar. She made it look so easy. Then her head disappeared beneath the surface of the water as she dove to search for a sand dollar. In minutes, she was back on the beach, the sand dollar in her hand larger, though not as nearly perfect as Janelle's. Its edges had been chipped and battered by the tides, but it still carried all the outward signs of its legend, and as Kristen broke the fragile shell in the middle, five white porcelain dove-shaped pieces fell free.

Janelle gasped as she retrieved them. "Could I keep these with my sand dollar?"

"Of course. I got them for you."

The sun rose higher in the sky, the morning grew warm, and they began to gather their shells and sea treasures, along with Timmy and the blanket. "Are we ready for a glass of Mrs. Baxter's own special lemonade?" Kristen asked.

"Oh, yes, let's hurry!"

In the house, Mr. and Mrs. Baxter were busy getting everything in tip-top order for the guests. Wes and Marla would be arriving in the afternoon, and Jeff Garrett was invited for dinner at seven.

"Here, let me help you with that," Kristen offered, picking up one end of the leaf Mr. Baxter was adding to extend the dining table.

Mrs. Baxter was busy in the kitchen, rolling dough for her piecrusts. "You girls will have to fix your own lunch today," she said cheerfully. "There's plenty of fixin's for sandwiches in the fridge."

"Don't you give a thought to us, Mrs. B. We'll all pitch in and help. Janelle and I will set your table, and we'll make sure it looks beautiful enough to do justice to your cooking."

"I can't wait to see Daddy. He'll be surprised when he sees our shell collection, especially the sand dollar."

"Will you show him your drawings and paintings too?"

"Some of them," she replied. "But the special one I'm doing of the *Janni Lu* is going to be a surprise for his birthday in August."

Kristen felt a stab of sadness as she thought of August, her last month here on the island.

What did the future hold for her? Could she go back to Atlanta and continue to work at Bradley, Bradley, and Kline, just as though the summer had never happened? Could she see *him* every day, concealing her love for him, knowing he had pledged his heart to another? And how about Janelle? Would she ever see her again after the summer ended? These questions and more weighed heavily on her mind as she moved up the stairs to her room.

Kristen spent the afternoon cleaning her room. Then, remembering that she would be sharing the bath with Marla, she scoured and mopped, polishing the chrome to a lustrous shine. Fresh, fluffy towels were hung on the racks, and the pink ceramic soap dish was filled with dainty, shell-shaped soap. With everything sparkling, she sat down to write some cards and letters to her family and friends back home.

Her door was open, so she heard Janelle when she crossed the hall. "Come on in," she invited. "Will you stick the stamps on my cards for me?" With her willing helper beside her, she put the finishing touches on her correspondence and stacked it on her desk.

Late in the afternoon, they went downstairs to help with the dinner preparations.

Mrs. Baxter found a large glass bowl and asked Kristen to make a salad. While Kristen washed and tore the salad greens, Janelle selected the silverware and began to set the table.

Kristen was as jittery as a jumping bean just thinking about the impending visit, but she tried to project enthusiasm for Janelle's sake.

They were working so hard that they almost missed hearing the crunch of shoes across the yard.

"Why, they're here already," exclaimed Mrs. Baxter as she threw open the back door.

Janelle flew by like a zephyr and flung herself into her father's arms.

Laughing, he twirled her around. "And this, Marla, is my daughter, Janelle."

The three stepped into the kitchen for further introductions, and Kristen extended her hand. Marla's glance went from her head to her toes before she responded to the gesture by offering her own hand in return.

"So you're Janelle's little friend," she said coolly.

Very tall and very slender, Marla looked as if she had just stepped from the pages of *Harper's Bazaar.* Her stylishly cut short hair was the color of orange blossom honey, and her eyes seemed to match. She was chicly dressed in white gabardine slacks, a white silk blouse, and a red linen blazer. Her slender neck was encircled by a massive gold chain that matched the one that dangled from her wrist. Kristen looked at her delicate white sandals and wondered how she had managed to get from the wharf to the house.

Little friend, indeed! Looking directly at Marla, Kristen forced a weak smile.

"I'll carry your bags upstairs, Honey, and show you your room," Wes volunteered.

Kristen winced at his term of endearment, then chastised herself silently for stooping to such petty jealousy. Wanting to extend the "olive branch," she offered, "I'll finish setting the table. Mrs. Baxter has everything else ready, so you can all go get ready for dinner and leave the finishing touches to me."

Wes, Marla, and Janelle made their way upstairs, while the Baxters retired to their quarters. Kristen surveyed the table critically. The sterling silver flatware sparkled brilliantly, attesting to Mrs. Baxter's constant polishing. China and crystal gleamed against the white damask cloth, but there was no centerpiece.

Kristen remembered admiring some brilliant hibiscus blossoms on the south side of the house. *I'll run out and cut a few, and still have time to dress for dinner.*

The big bushes were ablaze with color, their graceful flowers unfolding bright petals to catch the last of the day's fading sun rays. Kristen chose the loveliest blossoms, in shades of pink, red, yellow, and gold.

In the china cabinet, she found a shallow Spode bowl, elegant in its simplicity. Deftly, she twisted and poked each stem into place. She set the arrangement in the center of the table and stepped back to critique her work. It was pretty, but somehow it did not seem complete. What was lacking here?

Back outside, her eyes swept the landscape, and then she saw exactly what she needed! Sea oats, growing in mass profusion over the sand dunes. She had admired it since her first day here, its long, slender stalks generously tipped with graceful oatlike plumes. She snipped the willowy ends from six or eight stalks and laid them in her basket.

In the dining room, she added them to her bouquet, then clapped her hands in delight. She stepped back and admired her work from every angle. Beautiful! Even Wes would have to be impressed with her artistry. It was about time that she did something right in his eyes! She hurried up the steps to her room.

She had showered earlier in order to leave the bathroom free for Marla. Now she only needed to wash her hands and slip into her clean clothes. Since Wes had told them that dinner would be informal and would probably be followed by a beach get-together later, she chose a pair of casual navy blue slacks and topped them with a white jersey pullover.

Marla's words kept ringing in her ears and rankling her spirit: *Janelle's little friend!*

She untied the ribbon and shook out her ponytail and began furiously brushing her thick blond hair. She pulled it into a bun on the back of her neck and scowled critically into the mirror. "Too matronly looking!"

She tried again. Leaning over as she brushed, she piled the great, wavy profusion of hair onto the top of her head, twisting it into large, fat curls. No ribbons tonight. She lifted her pearls from their box and looped them gracefully around her new upswept hairdo. Standing back, she smiled into the mirror with satisfaction.

Then realization took hold. Here she was, Kristen Kelly, trying to compete with glamorous, glitzy Marla Morgan. How foolish. Now, the formal hairdo looked ostentatious, almost ludicrous, with her casual sports outfit.

Again she released her hair and began to brush. This time, she let it hang loose around her shoulders and returned the pearls to their box.

I want to be my own person, she confirmed to herself. *Whatever Wes and his friends see in me will be real, and not an imitation of someone else.*

Promptly at seven, the diners began assembling on the front porch. Mr. Baxter was in the kitchen helping Mrs. Baxter carve the meat. Kristen was downstairs first, followed by Janelle, Marla, and finally Wes.

Suddenly the usually shy Janelle bolted down the steps and ran toward the beach.

"Here comes Uncle Jeff now!" Clutching his big hand in her small one, she pulled the visitor toward the porch.

"This is my Uncle Jeff. He's not really my uncle, but we pretend he is, don't we, Daddy?"

Wes made introductions around the circle. "Marla Morgan, my friend from Atlanta, and Kristen Kelly, who's with our law firm—meet Jeff Garrett, who keeps us safe and secure out here on Gaspar Island. Jeff is commander of the Coast Guard station on the mainland."

Jeff's rugged good looks were softened and enhanced by a big, wide grin that swept easily and often across his freckled face. Curly red hair seemed to rebel against its careful combing and, like an unruly child, went in the direction of its own choosing.

It would have been impossible not to like him at once.

"Why, you sneaky old goat," he joked, grinning at Wes. "You're hiding a virtual harem over here." He included Janelle in the wide sweep of his arm, and Janelle giggled with delight.

"Can I help it if I'm irresistibly attractive?" Wes countered with a laugh.

After a few moments of getting acquainted and exchanging small talk, Wes steered the party in the direction of the tantalizing smells drifting from the dining room.

As they circled the table, Kristen stole a glance at Wes to see his reaction to her floral masterpiece.

He was smiling with pride as his eyes traveled over the perfectly appointed table, until they fell upon the flowers. Suddenly, he froze, the color draining from his face, and all traces of his smile disappeared.

Looking at Mrs. Baxter while pointing toward the center of the table, he spoke with a carefully controlled voice. "Mrs. B, who is responsible for this?"

Mrs. Baxter blushed and stammered, "Oh, Kris—that is, I—oh, Wes, someone should have told her. She couldn't have known."

Kristen's anger and her inherent good manners were at war with each other as she glared defiantly across the table at her host. "Is there a problem with the centerpiece?"

Such ingrates! What could possibly be wrong with adding a touch of beauty to the dining table?

She looked around the circle and noted that the Baxters both wore expressions of concern. Marla looked mildly amused, while Janelle was obviously troubled, as she looked at her father and wondered what had suddenly made him so unhappy.

"Let's all sit down," Wes suggested, trying to regain his composure.

After a few moments of strained silence, he proceeded, in a voice of exaggerated calm, to explain as though he were talking to a small child. "Sea oats, Kristen, are an endangered species of island vegetation, protected by the laws of our land. Very steep fines and penalties are imposed on those who irresponsibly disobey them. You see, the sea oats act as a natural barrier against normal beach erosion. The winds and the tides wear away at our beaches all the time, and we lose a little each year. Sea oats help prevent that loss."

"Thank you, Professor Bradley." Jeff hoped that his attempt at humor would lighten the mood.

Kristen looked crestfallen. She fought back the tears that were stinging her eyes.

Mrs. Baxter spoke up. "We should have warned her. She had no way of knowing."

"I know that, and I'm sorry I reacted so strongly." Wes's tone was apologetic now as he realized the rudeness of his initial reaction. "Don't worry, Kristen. You've learned a valuable lesson, and no real harm was done. The flowers are a lovely addition to the table, and this will just serve to remind all of us to be careful to protect our beaches and not take our natural resources for granted."

Placing his napkin in his lap, he smiled broadly. "Now, let's pause for our blessing!"

Marla raised her eyes in surprise, and then lowered them as she saw everyone else with bowed head. *Knowing Wes Bradley,* she decided, *was a surprise a minute.*

Mr. Baxter echoed the final "Amen," and Wes raised his head and declared, "Now it's time to pass that platter of beef!" Everyone began to breathe easier as bowls and platters of food circled the table, and laughter and cheerful chatter filled the room.

Janelle was ecstatic to have her father beside her. "Will you be here again next weekend, Daddy?"

Wes raised his eyebrows and gave Marla a questioning look before answering.

"Don't forget, Darling." Marla addressed all her conversation directly to Wes. "Vivian and Ted are having a party on Friday, and there's the Belleview Ball on Saturday night."

"Tell you what, Janelle. We'll be back for the Fourth of July. That's only two weeks away. We'll take the boat over to Buena Vista for the big parade and barbecue, but we'll come back here in time to watch the fireworks from the beach."

The child's momentary disappointment was partially dispelled by the excitement of the annual holiday celebration. As they all joined in the planning, earlier dissensions seemed to be forgotten, and an air of merriment prevailed.

"Uncle Jeff, will you go to the parade with us on the Fourth of July, like you usually do?" Janelle obviously adored her adopted uncle.

"Wouldn't miss it for the world, Punkin, unless I have to work that day. But I'll see what I can arrange."

Mrs. Baxter was just bringing out her apple pie when the doorbell rang.

"I'll get it!" Kristen's chair was closest to the front door, and she was eager to be helpful after her earlier mistake. She was soon to regret her decision, however, because as soon as she opened the door, she sensed trouble brewing. There stood Mr. Beardsley, wearing the same angry look she remembered so well from their earlier encounter in his yard.

"Who is it, Kristen?" Wes called from the dining room.

"Oh, it's Mr. Rumpel—uh—Mr. Beardsley," stumbled Kristen. "Won't you come in, Mr. Beardsley?" She stepped back to let him enter.

"Look here, Girl. I saw you out trampling in the sea oats today. Now, don't deny it."

Kristen caught her breath. Before she had time to answer, his bony little finger pointed right in her face, as he warned, "And I'd best not see you cutting any of it!"

Hearing the angry voice, Wes came to the door. "Why, Mr. Beardsley, what a surprise."

The little tyrant ranted on as though he were completely unaware of Wes's presence. "You city people think you can come over here and destroy our little island. Well, I'm warning you. I'll report any unlawful activities I see!"

Wes moved to Kristen's side and put a protective arm around her shoulders.

"Calm down, Mr. Beardsley. I can assure you that I and all of my guests are as anxious as you are to abide by the laws, and to protect our beaches. You won't see any of us doing anything to damage our priceless *good nature*." His accent of those last two words left little doubt that they carried a double meaning.

"Now, come in and join us in the dining room," he continued. "We were just getting ready to have some fresh apple pie and hot coffee."

The old man, wanting to remain angry, began to decline, but the tantalizing aroma drifting from the dining room weakened his resistance. Living alone, his meals usually came from tin cans, and everyone on the island knew the reputation of Mrs. Baxter's pies!

"Well, just to show I'm neighborly," he relented.

Kristen's heart sank. What was Wes thinking? How could he have forgotten the centerpiece? Now she was doomed for certain. Her heart was pounding like a sledgehammer as she turned back to the dining room.

Guiltily, her eyes riveted to the center of the table. There sat the lovely Spode bowl, but it was *empty!* Had a miracle occurred?

"Pull up a chair for your friend here, Bax. He's going to join us for dessert."

"Come in, come in," Mr. Baxter invited jovially as he reached for another chair. Beside him, Mrs. Baxter's chair was empty.

His voice was drowned out by the sudden noise from the kitchen—a big, gushing swoosh of water, accompanied by the loud churning and grinding of the garbage disposal.

Amused glances were exchanged around the table as Mrs. Baxter entered from the kitchen, all smiles, carrying a still-warm, deep-dish apple pie.

"How many for coffee?" she asked sweetly.

Kristen breathed a deep sigh of relief and rolled her eyes heavenward in a silent prayer of thanksgiving.

Chapter 5

The beach was almost deserted as the two young couples strolled along the edge of the surf, shoes abandoned and pant legs rolled up. The cool water lapped at their feet, and the north wind gave a crisp pleasant chill to the evening air.

"A fire would be nice," Jeff suggested. "Let's gather some driftwood and see what we can do, Wes."

Marla and Kristen returned to the blanket where they had left their shoes, while Jeff and Wes began scavenging the beach for firewood.

Although Marla seemed aloof and distant, Kristen tried to make pleasant conversation. "Isn't it lovely here? It's like something out of a picture book." The moon casting its reflection upon the rippling water made a shimmering path to the horizon. Far out, distant boats looked like fireflies winking at the world.

"I can't imagine living out here without cars," Marla mused.

"Cars are easily accessible. It's just a short boat ride to the parking garage. Besides, there are a few emergency jeeps and three-wheelers on the island," explained Kristen.

"It sounds inconvenient, but I suppose it's all right for a short visit now and then. But no stores! Just imagine! Wouldn't you think they'd at least have a convenience store? I think this place would get old in a hurry." Marla shifted her weight on the blanket and turned her head to see when the men would be coming.

"The convenience of stores seems a small price to pay for all this peace and natural beauty. I felt as you did at first, Marla, but this place grows on you."

Marla nodded, but Kristen could tell that she was still skeptical.

It was almost half an hour before Wes and Jeff found enough driftwood to make a good fire. In a spot well away from the trees and tropical shrubs, Jeff struck a match to light the dry kindling and logs. Fanned by the breeze, it ignited easily, and a warm, blazing bonfire sent its smoke and orange flames swirling into the air. The fire snapped and crackled and radiated a circle of instant warmth.

"I used to camp out on the beach when I was a boy," Jeff told them, settling himself comfortably on the blanket beside Kristen. "I'd bring a few supplies and my pup tent, and stay for days at a time."

156

"Have you always lived in this area?" Kristen thought how fortunate he must have been.

"Yes, my dad was a commercial fisherman. Back then, there were only a few houses on this island, mostly owned by fishermen and their families. I used to travel to school on the boat they send for the children who live out here."

"You mean like a school bus?" Kristen's interest mounted. "I know the mailman comes to the island on a boat every day, but I had no idea the schools provided transportation."

"Yes. You weren't here during the school year, but if you had been, you would have seen the children lined up by the dock with their books and tablets, waiting just the way you might have waited for a bus when you were a little girl."

"It must have been terribly lonely growing up out here," offered Marla sympathetically.

"Not on your life! I had the kind of boyhood other guys dream of. After school, I helped my dad with the nets and the boat. Some of the other fishermen had sons too, so I had plenty of friends. No, I was neither lonesome nor bored here on the island. Now I just count myself exceptionally lucky to be stationed here, and I don't even like to think of the possibility of being transferred, but of course, I'm at the mercy of the United States Coast Guard."

"Life on the island can get pretty exciting," Wes agreed. "In fact, sometimes, it can make city life seem dull by comparison."

It was obvious by Marla's look that she was unconvinced, but she tried to be a good sport and even joined in when Jeff suggested they sing some familiar songs.

As they sat by the fire singing, others wandering along the shore stopped to join the fun, and the sounds of laughter and music floated across the cool water and warm sand and blended into the starlit night.

A young man who joined their group recognized Jeff. "Aren't you the Jeff Garrett I went to high school with, way back in the dark ages?"

"Yep, the very same. We used to play on the same football team."

A young woman remembered them both. "We used to come out here to the beach on weekends, play volleyball, and sing, and you guys would try to terrorize us girls with your ghost stories."

"I remember," admitted Jeff.

"Jeff's favorite trick was to try to convince us that the ghost of Josefa still stalked the beach. He made it all so real, honestly, sometimes we thought we actually saw her."

"Who was Josefa?" Marla wanted to know.

"Yeah, Jeff. Tell us about her."

"Well," Jeff began, "Josefa was the lady-love of Jose Gasper. And Gaspar's story is real. That's how this island got its name."

A hush fell over the crowd, and all eyes focused on Jeff, his face ominously illuminated by the flickering fire.

As he began his story, Kristen looked over to see Marla's reaction, and was surprised to see her sitting alone. Wes was nowhere in sight. Had he returned to the house? She hadn't seen him leave. Marla's eyes were focused on the storyteller, and Kristen wondered if she even realized her companion had left.

"Jose Gaspar," Jeff told his spellbound spectators, "was a notorious pirate who razed and terrorized ships and their crews in the Gulf and Caribbean in the early 1800s. His favorite treasures were jewels and beautiful women, and he had no qualms about helping himself to either. He used this little island as a hideaway where he stored his loot and held his lovely ladies chained in captivity. This went on for years. He successfully evaded all his would-be captors. Then one day he found the beautiful Spanish princess, Josefa, and carried her away to his island. For the first time in his life, he fell truly in love."

Jeff paused and looked around the circle. The only noise came from the wind and the pounding surf as his audience waited for him to continue. The smoke from the fire rose in graceful, pearly spirals generously studded with glistening sequins of orange sparks.

"For the first time in his life, the pompous pirate proposed marriage, but much to his surprise, Josefa just turned up her pretty nose and refused his offer. Well, he kept begging and pleading, and finally one day she got so tired of his ardent attentions that she cursed him and spat in his face!"

To heighten the drama, Jeff leaned forward and spat angrily into the fire, and waited while the flames sparked and sizzled. His voice grew suddenly loud. "Gaspar was enraged! He drew his saber and beheaded the beautiful Josefa."

Now he dropped his voice almost to a whisper as his audience crowded closer in anticipation.

"Afterwards, he grieved at his impulsive action, but it was too late. And it's said that her headless ghost still stalks the island, dragging the chains that bound her."

As he finished his tale, there was a moment of silence before they all heard the sinister sounds coming from behind a nearby dune. There was no doubt about it! It was the rattling sound of a heavy chain being dragged through the sand!

Kristen heard the startled gasps and surrounding shrieks and squeals, and she watched in amusement as several of the young boys in the crowd took full advantage of the excuse to protectively embrace their dates. Now she realized why Wes had disappeared so quietly. She couldn't suppress her laughter.

"Come on, Marla; let's catch us a ghost," she said, scrambling through the sand and over the nearest dune. Marla was right behind her.

Sure enough, there was Wes, caught red-handed with his chain, grinning sheepishly. They dragged him down to the fire, where he made a full confession to the amused audience.

When the party finally disbanded, Jeff led Kristen toward the house. Marla and Wes lingered behind, gathering up the blanket and covering the dying embers with sand.

"I've enjoyed this evening more than you can imagine, Kristen." Jeff's voice was deep and sincere. "I'd like to call on you again soon."

"I'll look forward to seeing you, Jeff. Come by anytime. Janelle's so very fond of you, and I can see why."

"Wes has told me a lot about you, all good. He certainly has a lot of admiration for you. And the way you're beginning to bring Janelle out of her shell is truly a miracle."

"She's a lovely child. This is probably going to be the most challenging summer I've ever had, but the most rewarding too, if I can help Janelle."

"There are many unique features of this island. I hope you'll let me share some of them with you in the coming weeks."

On the porch, he took both her hands in his and bent to kiss her cheek. "Thanks for a wonderful evening, Kristen."

"Jeff, I—" She drew back hesitantly.

"Don't worry, Kristen. I only want to be your good friend. I won't deny that I wish it might grow to be more, but Wes has warned me that you already have a special man in your life, so I won't get any romantic illusions."

"Oh, Jeff, I do need another good friend here on the island. I'm so glad we've met." She ignored the reference to her romantic interests. Evidently Wes believed the reply she had given him on the beach that night. Thankfully, he hadn't guessed the identity of the man who had captured her heart.

"Kristen, look at me." She looked into his green eyes and warmed to his unpretentious smile. He winked at her before he asked, "Would you be surprised if I told you I'm well acquainted with that special man in your life?"

For a moment she was startled. How could he know? She had told no one. "Am I that transparent?" she asked.

"No, not to the general public. But I could feel the vibrations all evening. Sometimes I have a sixth sense about things like that. But don't worry; your secret's safe with me."

Kristen blushed. He really did know. Suppose it showed to everyone. She neither denied nor confirmed his suspicions, but his expression told her that he had no doubts.

"All I can say," Jeff continued, "is that sometimes my best friend has very poor judgment. If he lets an opportunity like this escape him, he must be out of his mind."

Wes and Marla were coming up to the porch now, so their conversation ended. Kristen gave his hand a little squeeze as she said, "Thanks for everything, Jeff."

"I'll call you next week." He turned toward the steps then, and while he was bidding good night to Marla and Wes, Kristen slipped quietly inside and went upstairs to bed.

The cool air drifting through her window had a salty fragrance, with a lingering hint of smoke from the extinguished bonfire. She took deep breaths of it, wanting to store it in her memory among the other treasures she was collecting there.

The house was quiet, and Kristen could picture Wes and Marla sitting together on the couch, mapping out their plans for the future.

Much later, she heard Marla in the bathroom they shared, running the shower and humming to herself. Jealousy was wrong, so Kristen would have to guard against it. Perhaps she could help Marla learn to love the island as she did. For Janelle's sake, she hoped so. That little girl deserved a family. She missed her mother so much.

Louise must have been a lovely person. I wish I could have known her, she thought as she drifted off into dreams.

When Kristen opened her eyes on Sunday morning, her first thoughts were of the small neighborhood church she attended in Atlanta. The congregation would be assembling now for their early service, and she could almost hear the organ playing the familiar hymns she loved so much, hymns she had learned as a child no older than Janelle was now.

She had gently probed into Janelle's religious training and learned that Louise had been a good Christian mother, dedicated to nurturing her daughter's faith. Apparently, since her death, Wes had done little to nourish that faith. How sad.

How far did her own authority reach in teaching Janelle about Christianity? She had already initiated a few talks with her, and Janelle was quite receptive. She hoped to lead her into a realization of the great source of comfort available for the asking.

There was no church here on the island, and no plans had been discussed for an excursion to the mainland. She'd have to be content with her own private worship in her room.

After Bible reading, meditation, and prayer, she dressed and went downstairs. Janelle and Wes were already seated in the dining room, having breakfast together and talking. Apparently, Marla was still sleeping.

"Wes, I'm sorry about the sea oats last night. I'm going to be a good environmentalist for the rest of my stay, I promise!"

"Forget it, Kristen. I apologize for my outburst too." She could feel his eyes follow her as she moved toward the buffet.

Breakfast consisted of a chafing dish of hot buttered grits, a warming tray of sausage and scrambled eggs, and a variety of homemade muffins and biscuits. A pitcher of juice and a pot of hot coffee rested beside cups and glasses at the far end of the buffet.

Kristen poured a glass of orange juice and a cup of black coffee and joined them at the table.

"Can we have a picnic today, Daddy?" Janelle seemed happy to have Wes by her side.

"I'm afraid we're going to have to wait for that picnic, Sweetheart, but you can count on it for the Fourth of July."

"But why can't we have one today too?" Her childish whine always softened his heart, and, like most children, she knew just how to turn it to her best advantage.

Wes squirmed in his chair. "Well, today, Marla thinks we should get an early start. She has a couple of stops she needs to make on the way. We'll have to grab lunch at a restaurant along the way. But don't worry, I'll make up for lost time when we come again on the Fourth."

"Did I hear my name?" Marla descended the stairs like a queen, her perfectly coiffed head held high as she smiled down at the people below.

Janelle glared at her without speaking as Wes stood to greet her. She wore a striking navy blue jumpsuit which accented her lean, statuesque figure to perfection. "Am I late for breakfast?"

"Not at all, my dear. You are just in time." Wes poured himself another cup of coffee while Marla filled her plate from the buffet. He poured a cup for Marla and refilled Kristen's cup at the table.

"And my little sweetheart over here is still working on her glass of orange juice."

Instead of returning his smile, Janelle pushed out her lower lip and sulked. "Can't you at least stay until afternoon?" she pleaded.

Still hoping to coax a smile, Wes came up with an alternate plan. "When Marla and I have to leave, why don't you and Kristen take your lunch up to the crow's nest? You can see the bay from there, and you can wave to us as we leave.

We'll wave back, and I'll blow the horn three times. That will be our special signal that says, 'I love you.' "

"No! I won't! I don't want to watch you leave!" She jumped up from her chair and ran up the stairs.

Wes excused himself and followed her.

"She's certainly spoiled, isn't she?" commented Marla. She spread marmalade on a biscuit and bit into it. When Kristen didn't answer, she continued, "What she needs is a firmer hand. I could cure that attitude of hers in a hurry."

"Marla, she's really a very sweet child, but she's experienced a lot of trauma for an eight year old. She's making progress, but it takes a lot of patience."

"Oh, I suppose you're right. And I know I don't have a lot, especially with sulky children. Well, when we come back for the Fourth of July, I have an idea that I hope will help win her over. I have a special present in mind. One I feel sure she'll like. You can tell her I'm bringing her a surprise, so she'll have a reason to look forward to my visit. All children like presents."

"That's a nice idea." Privately, Kristen thought that it would take more than a present, especially for a little girl that had all the material things her heart desired. But at least it showed that Marla intended to make an effort. Maybe it could be a beginning.

After breakfast, Marla returned to her room to pack her bags, and Janelle and Wes sat at the table playing Candyland. Soon the child was giggling again as she beat her daddy at their favorite game.

Kristen took a magazine out onto the porch. Even though the sun was high in the sky, the gulf breeze kept the porch cool and comfortable. She settled onto a lounge chair, leafed through her magazine, and began to grow drowsy. My, but she was getting lazy. Would she be able to get herself back into the workforce in the fall? She'd have to if she planned to eat!

She was drifting off into the nicest dream. Wes was saying to her, "Come along. We must get started." Her eyes popped open, and she realized that he actually had spoken those words, but not to her. They were leaving.

She and Janelle did go up to the crow's nest after all. Mrs. Baxter had fixed them sandwiches and lemonade. But the atmosphere was not festive, as Kristen tried in vain to cheer the dismal little girl. Although Janelle refused to turn her eyes to the bay, they finally heard the *toot, toot, toot* that meant "I love you," and Kristen longed to be included in its message.

She could see the strain written on Janelle's sad face and knew that she would have to work hard for the next two weeks to keep her busy and happy. Paving the way for a smooth holiday when Marla and Wes arrived was going to be a major task!

Chapter 6

True to his word, Jeff called her on Wednesday. "How would my two best girls like a boat ride tomorrow night?"

Janelle's joyful anticipation of the outing made Kristen glad she had accepted the invitation.

"Next to Daddy, Uncle Jeff is my favorite man in the whole world," she told Kristen, walking the path toward the bay. Jeff had asked them to meet him on the dock at seven so that he wouldn't need to tie up his boat. When they arrived five minutes early, he was already waiting for them.

Kristen smiled approval at the sight of his sleek blue pleasure craft. Although it was smaller than the *Janni Lu*, it looked just as comfortable, and spotlessly clean. Jeff lifted Janelle into the boat, and when he was sure she had a firm foothold, he helped Kristen aboard.

"Is this a Coast Guard vessel?"

"No, this one belongs to me. Those others are used strictly for business." He turned the key, and the engine responded with a steady hum.

He guided them along the coastline, and directed their attention to points of interest along the way. Many of the estates that were visible from the water belonged to famous people, and he named them as they passed. Unlike the strictly zoned areas of Atlanta, Kristen noted that here small vacation cottages and rustic fishing shacks were interspersed among the more lavish hideaways of the island's wealthiest residents. Occasionally, people on the land waved or called to them as they cruised by, and they laughed and shouted their greeting in return.

Laced into a small life jacket, Janelle sat in one of the swivel chairs in the stern and waved to every boat they passed, and always the gesture was returned. Kristen loved to see the happy look on her face. *It's beginning to occur more and more often,* she observed.

Jeff maneuvered the boat along the channel, reading and heeding the red and green markers, and Kristen told him about her misfortune on the day of her arrival. She could laugh about it now.

He chuckled too, but not without sympathy. "Those grass beds have trapped a lot of unwary boaters over the years, and even some of the more experienced ones who should know better."

As they rounded a wide bend and turned toward a neighboring island,

Kristen could hear music and see bright lights a short distance ahead.

"That's the Pelican, one of the nicest restaurants in the area," Jeff told her. "We'll give it a try some evening soon." He circled the boat in a wide arc and turned toward home. The ride had a hypnotic effect on Janelle, and her eyes grew heavy. Jeff gently positioned her on some life preserver cushions. Kristen stood beside him at the wheel while he followed the channel markers and guided them back to their wharf.

Kristen roused Janelle enough to stand between them, and each of them held one of her hands and started down the path toward home.

Mrs. Baxter met them at the door and took Janelle upstairs to bed. "There's fresh coffee and pie in the kitchen," she called over her shoulder.

Kristen took plates from the cabinet and cut generous wedges of the warm apple pie. She filled two mugs with the steaming brew, and she and Jeff wandered to the front porch.

In cane-bottomed rockers, they sat in silence, slowly sipping the hot coffee and enjoying Mrs. Baxter's pie. Already their friendship had developed into an easy, undemanding one that did not require constant small talk.

The stars were out, and the moon was growing larger each night, approaching the full moon stage.

"When the moon is full, I'll be back to show you another of our island surprises," he promised.

"No hints?"

"No hints. Just wait and see."

Kristen felt so comfortable with him. He was easy to talk to, and he was fun. How she wished she could transfer her affection for Wes to Jeff. Why couldn't people control such things?

As though Jeff could read her thoughts, he asked, "Have you spoken to Wes since he left?"

"Yes, he calls Janelle almost every night. He usually talks with me to get a report on her behavior and to be sure we have everything we need."

"You're so good for Janelle. She is really beginning to blossom under your care. Already her cheeks are filling out, and she's acquiring a healthy tan. She seems to be gaining more self-confidence too!"

"I hope I've been able to help her. It's going to be hard to give her up."

"Well, just remember, it's not over 'til the fat lady sings."

Maybe not, but it sure seemed to Kristen as though the fat lady was warming up her voice in a hurry.

They said good night on the steps. "Don't forget what I promised. I'll be back when the moon is full, to show you my surprise."

"I'll remember," Kristen promised. She watched him disappear down the brushy path and felt a rush of affection for him. But it was not the kind that made bells ring.

Kristen and Janelle had fallen into a ritual of daily routine. Mornings, after gathering shells from the incoming tide, they cleaned them and added them to their growing collection. As the day warmed, they made their daily venture into the gulf waters. Janelle had already learned to float, and Kristen was confident that it was only a matter of days before she would be swimming. That was to be her big surprise for her father when he came for the Fourth of July weekend.

Janelle loved the birds. They liked to throw crumbs out and watch the terns and gulls squabble over them, but Jeff warned them that it was not in the birds' best interest to be fed by human hands. "Birds need to retain their inherent skills of finding the food of their natural diets, rather than relying on man to feed them," he had explained.

Almost every day, they took the rental boat out into the dark blue-black waters of Gaspar Bay. Sometimes they fished, though their catches were either small or nonexistent, and sometimes they just drifted, Janelle dangling her small feet in the murky water. And not once did they even get near the grass beds!

Afternoons were usually spent up in the crow's nest. Kristen was fast filling her sketchbook with island memories. Janelle was showing remarkable talent with the oil pencils and canvases. Her biggest challenge was the picture of the *Janni Lu* that she was drawing for her father's birthday surprise.

"Don't tell him," she kept reminding Kristen.

"Of course I won't. Your secret is safe with me."

No matter what they did or where they went, Janelle always kept Timmy close by her side. Kristen suggested once that they wash his T-shirt, but Janelle wouldn't hear of it.

"I want him to stay just the way he is. Just like when Mommy gave him to me."

In the evenings, they read, played games, and often walked on the beach before retiring, leaving their footprints for the nocturnal tides to sweep away.

Long gone were the KEEP OUT signs that Janelle had positioned when Kristen first arrived. Instead, the two of them had become close friends, and frequent visits between the rooms were welcomed.

Just two nights after their boating date with Jeff, they walked along the water's edge, and Kristen noticed that the moon had rounded out to a full circle. Jeff must have forgotten his promise, because she had not heard from him since Thursday, and tomorrow the cycle would begin all over with a new moon.

As she readied for bed, she drew on her robe and stepped out on the deck to have one last look at the full moon that bathed everything in its soft, silvery light. She could see the bay sparkling over the treetops and the graceful palm fronds swaying in the gentle night breeze. She inhaled deeply of the salt air and was just turning to go back into her bedroom when she saw a figure approaching the house from across the inland dunes.

When she realized that it was Jeff, she called down to him. "Jeff, it's almost eleven o'clock. What are you doing here at this hour?"

"Come down to the beach, Kristen. Bring Janelle with you. I have something to show you both."

"Jeff, Janelle has been asleep for over an hour. I don't think you realize how late it is." *What could he be thinking?*

"I know, Kristen, but this is something really special. Wake Janelle and both of you hurry down. Trust me. You'll be glad you did."

"Won't this keep until tomorrow?"

"Indeed, it won't."

It was difficult to wake the sleeping child, and Kristen wondered if she were doing the right thing. But, "Trust me," he had said, and trust him she did.

Twenty minutes later, a sleepy-eyed little girl and a very curious lady met a grinning Coastguardsman on the steps of the Spinnaker. "This had better be good, Jeff."

"It's good," he assured her. "But I'll let you be the judge."

With Jeff leading, they headed for the beach. Jeff carried a flashlight, but the bright light of the full moon made it unnecessary.

"Look!" He pointed down the beach.

The largest turtle Kristen had ever seen was lumbering out of the gulf and up the beach toward the dunes. Now she realized that there was not just one, but several. They were awesome! Their shells were flat, quite unlike the boxy shells of the land gophers who inhabited the island, and each was fully a yard wide. They must weigh several hundred pounds apiece!

Janelle was frightened until Jeff assured them that the turtles were harmless and had but one thing in mind—motherhood!

"At this time of year, on the night of the full moon, the female turtles come up out of the sea and lay their eggs along the beaches. Come along, and we'll watch them."

"We don't want to frighten them, Jeff."

"You needn't worry about that. When it's their nesting time, they aren't distracted by anything. It takes them about an hour to make their nests, lay their eggs, and get back to the water. During that time, barking dogs, curious bystanders, or even hunters don't distract them."

"Hunters? You mean they're in danger?"

"Yes, very much so. They're in danger of becoming extinct, so our state and federal laws try to protect them. It's illegal to take the eggs or harm the turtles. But poachers are always trying to find ways to steal them."

"Why would they do that?"

"Turtle steak and turtle soup are considered delicacies. And turtle eggs, they say, make cakes rise higher, taste better, and stay fresh longer."

They were very close now to one of the turtles as she dragged her heavy body up the beach. Her progress was slow and clumsy. She seemed intent on reaching a point high above the first dunes.

"Sea turtles have flippers instead of legs like land turtles," Jeff explained. "They can travel fast in the water, but on land, they're not very mobile. The males never come ashore, and the females only come in to lay their eggs."

The big turtle was working now, using her hind flippers to dig a hole. Farther down, other turtles were feverishly working too.

"These are loggerheads," Jeff told them. "There are about five different kinds of sea turtles, but the loggerheads are the ones we usually see here on the west coast of Florida every year."

By now, the female turtle had finished digging and had positioned the back half of her body into the newly dug nest. As she began depositing her leathery eggs, Jeff shone his flashlight into the big hole.

Janelle, who had been quiet up until now, said, "Look, Uncle Jeff. They don't look like eggs. They look like Ping-Pong balls. And there's lots of them!" She danced with excitement.

On and on the turtle worked, depositing what must have been a hundred eggs in the sandy nest before she stopped to rest. Then, as furiously as she had worked to dig the hole, she began using her front flippers to cover it with sand.

"If each turtle lays that many eggs, I don't understand why they are in danger of becoming extinct," Kristen declared.

"Out of a hundred eggs, she'll be lucky if fifty make it to the sea. When they hatch, the little turtles will have to scurry into the water before a crab or a dog or any of many predators can catch them. Then even in the water, some of them will become prey to fish or birds. They're so small when they're first born that a big fish can swallow one whole. It's a dangerous life!"

"Can't they pull into their shells and hide?"

"No, sea turtles can't do that like land turtles. That's one reason they need all the help we can give them."

"Can we see them hatch, Uncle Jeff?" Janelle was wide awake now, and full of questions.

"It takes almost sixty days, Honey. Let's make a date that on the full moon two months from now, we'll come to watch for them."

Kristen counted the time in her mind. By then she would be preparing to leave the island forever! Janelle's school started the first week in September, and the Atlanta office would be expecting Kristen's return.

"Why such a sad look, Kristen? Don't you want to come back to watch the babies hatch?" Jeff's concern brought her thoughts back to the present.

"Of course, I wouldn't miss it for anything. Look—what's she doing now?"

The mother-to-be turtle had finished filling the hole with sand and was now frantically pushing her flippers back and forth over the ground.

"She's trying to cover up her tracks," Jeff answered. "See how she smooths the top of the nest? She hopes nothing will find her eggs before they hatch. Notice that she chose a spot well above the high tide line, too. She's very concerned for the safety of her children."

Now she began her strange, clumsy retreat to the sea. Farther down the beach, Kristen could see others doing the same, while some were still busy making their nests.

A telltale, tractorlike trail was all the evidence she had left behind. The winds and tide would soon remove that, and hopefully, the little eggs would stay warm and secure, hidden beneath the sand.

Kristen said a silent prayer that they would be safe until they could begin their lives in the water.

"The males are right out there close by, waiting for their mates to return. Scientists have traced their routes, and have found that, no matter how many hundreds of miles they travel, the little females, when they reach maturity, will return to this very beach to nest."

"Can we come back and see them when they do?" Janelle asked.

"I don't see why not, Janelle. That won't happen until next summer, but you'll be coming back by then for your next school vacation."

Jeff took Janelle's small hand in his big one and smiled down at her. "But now I think it's time I walked my two best girls home and let them get back to bed."

They looked back for a last glimpse of the big, old turtles, lumbering down to the sea.

"How can I ever thank you for such an exciting night, Jeff?" Kristen felt certain that she had never had a better friend.

They said good night on the steps. "I'll be in touch soon," he told them. "And don't forget that we have a date fifty-six nights from tonight! That's two lunar months."

"We'll mark the calendar," Kristen promised. She took Janelle by the hand and led her up the stairs.

For the second time that night, she put on her gown and robe, and stepped out on the deck. In the distance, she could hear the whir of the motor as Jeff departed the island. Life here on Gaspar Island was filled with surprises. Remembering Marla's comments, she wondered how anyone could ever be bored in this place.

Returning to her room, she crawled into bed and turned out the light. She wasn't at all sure she could fall asleep after so much excitement, but before she had time to wonder about it, she already had.

Chapter 7

The house was a beehive of activity! The floors and the furniture were polished to a high luster. In the kitchen, the oven had been going almost constantly for two days, as preparations were under way for the much-anticipated Fourth of July weekend.

"What time do you think Daddy will be here?" Janelle kept running to the door to look.

"They could arrive any time now, Honey." Mrs. Baxter gave the curly head a pat as it danced by. "Kristen says that Marla is bringing some kind of surprise for you. Any idea what that might be?"

"No. She just said it was a present. Don't tell Daddy about the picture I'm painting. I'm saving that for his birthday."

Kristen came into the kitchen through the back door, her arms filled with summer flowers. "I'll make the centerpiece for the table, and this time I know better than to cut the sea oats." Sensing Janelle's nervous impatience, Kristen tried to distract her. "Let's take a walk on the beach. Your father is going to be proud when we tell him about our new project."

"And what would that be?" Mr. Baxter came in the back door, carrying his toolbox. "What are you two up to this time?"

"We've resolved to be good environmentalists. We found some books in the crow's nest that tell us things we can do to preserve and beautify our beaches."

"You mean like not disturbing the native vegetation?" Mr. Baxter gave her a good-natured wink.

"That too. We're keeping watch over the turtles' nests to scare away raccoons or other animals that might like turtle eggs. And we've been picking up trash from the beach. It's unbelievable that people will drop candy wrappers or drink cans on the beach, when garbage bins are provided."

"Yes," Janelle added. "We even picked up an old shoe that washed in on the tide."

"Well, that's great. If you find two of them, see if they're big enough for me." Mr. Baxter's eyes twinkled like Santa Claus's.

"We'll be on the lookout for something in your size," they promised him. Since most island residents were conscientious about keeping their beaches clean, there was surprisingly little wayward trash to be collected, except what floated in on the tide, but Kristen liked to encourage Janelle's awareness, so they perused the area daily.

Barefoot and dressed in their oldest shorts, they combed the beach, their eyes sweeping the area for debris.

"Look, Janelle. There's an old plastic jug floating in the water. Someone was very irresponsible to dispose of it like that. It's not biodegradable, either." She waded out to retrieve it. "It's an old bleach bottle." She grabbed it by the handle and turned back toward shore.

"Give it to me, Kristen. I'll put it in the trash bin." Janelle was eager to help.

"I can't bring it in. There's a string attached, and it seems to be caught on a rock or something."

Janelle splashed out to where Kristen stood knee-deep in the water. "I'll help." She put out her little hand and tugged, squealing as an incoming wave caught the bottom of her cotton shorts.

"Never mind, Janelle. I've found a sharp shell. I'll just cut it loose. I hate to leave the string, but at least it won't be visible. We don't want an unsightly plastic bottle spoiling our pretty beach today, with company coming."

Kristen waded as far as she could without soaking her shorts and severed the nylon fishing cord. Janelle took the bleach bottle and ran up the beach to deposit it in a trash bin.

"It looks like that's about it for today, Janelle. We'd better start back. Maybe we can get our clothes changed before our guests arrive."

"Daddy's not a guest, Kristen. Only Marla."

"Of course you're right. My mistake."

Far up the beach, Kristen spotted him. Her heart lurched, and she watched Janelle fly to meet him. Hand in hand, Wes and Janelle waited for Kristen. She willed her knees to stop shaking as she walked toward them.

His arm reached out and encircled Kristen with a friendly hug. "I thought I'd find you out here somewhere."

Janelle was ecstatic. "We've been cleaning the beach. We're eek—eek—"

"Ecologists," Kristen prompted.

"That's wonderful. I want to hear all about it."

As they approached the house, they could see Marla sitting on the porch, holding a large, festively wrapped package.

"This is for you, Janelle." She held the box out toward the little girl. "It's the present I've been promising you."

"Thank you, Marla." Even in her excitement, Janelle remembered to use her best company manners the way Kristen had urged her to.

171

"Go ahead. Open it."

"Yes," Wes encouraged. "I'm anxious myself to see what it is. Marla wouldn't even give me a hint."

Carefully, Janelle removed the enormous red bow and unfolded the bright foil wrapping paper. As she lifted the lid of the big box, everyone crowded around to see. Smothered in white tissue, the object inside remained a mystery as Janelle took her time in revealing the contents. Finally, she reached in and pulled out a big brown bear. He was dressed all in red, from his little knit cap and coat, to his shiny leather boots. It was a beautiful toy.

The air was filled with silence as all eyes watched the expressionless little face. Janelle turned the furry body this way and that, examining his face, his body, his clothes. Then, carefully, she replaced the bear inside his box, folded the tissue over the top, and replaced the lid. "Thank you, Marla. It's very nice," she said.

If only Marla had let it drop right there. But she persisted, "I thought it was time for a new bear, Janelle. When I saw how disreputable your old one looked, I thought it was time for a change."

Janelle's usually angelic face was suddenly contorted with rage. *"No!* I won't. . ."

Quickly, Kristen interrupted the tantrum by bending to hug the distraught child. "I have a better idea, Janelle. Now Timmy can have a friend. He's been looking a little lonely lately. Why don't you take the new bear up to meet him. Two bears will be twice as much fun."

Janelle's little body was quivering from shock, but she didn't protest as Kristen picked up the box with one hand and gently led her up the steps with the other. Halfway up the stairs, she could still hear Marla's voice.

"She's a strange child, Wes. I think you should seriously consider my suggestion."

All through dinner, Janelle was quiet and withdrawn. She had appeared at the table with Timmy clutched to her body, and no more mention was made of the new bear. If Wes noticed the tension in the air, he didn't acknowledge it, as he steered the conversation toward the Baxters.

"Well, have you been letting Jake Beardsley win a few checker games, Bax?"

"Oh, he wins in his own right sometimes. But this afternoon he canceled our usual weekly game. He was too upset to play."

"What was his problem? Is he sick?"

"Oh, you know how he loves boiled crab. Well, it seems he went out to pull in his trap, and someone had removed his marker."

"Probably came loose and floated away," Wes said. "I can't believe anyone would deliberately take away his marker."

"Well, you know how he always thinks the worst of people. He thinks someone did it for spite."

"He does seem to have a way of making enemies," Kristen said. "But surely no one around here would be that mean."

"That's what I told him. But he said he had tied it on real tight, and now he's lost not just the crabs, but his biggest trap." He turned to his wife. "Martha, he wants you to save him another bleach bottle so he can mark his new trap when it's finished."

"Bleach bottle?" Kristen and Janelle spoke in unison as their eyes met across the table in horrified realization.

Pale and contrite, Kristen related the story of how, in their cleanup efforts, they had retrieved the bleach bottle and put it in the trash bin. The mystery of the crab trap was solved.

"I'll go over right now and make my apologies to that crotchety old man." She was trembling with dread, but she knew what she had to do.

"Not alone, you won't!" Wes rose to his feet. "First I'll go look for his crab trap. Then, whether or not I find it, I'll go with you to explain how an honest mistake was made. There are plenty of crabs left in the gulf. It's not the end of the world."

Kristen started to protest his generous offer, but as relief washed over her, she managed a grateful smile and rose to join him.

"First I'll change into my swimming trunks," he said. "The tide is out now, so maybe I can spot the trap easily. Do you remember about where you first saw the marker?"

"Yes, it was just this side of the point where we made the bonfire last time you were here. It's not far from the house."

"It was right out from that first trash bin," Janelle offered. It was one of the few times she had spoken during the entire evening.

"Don't let this interrupt your dessert. You all just go right ahead with your pie and coffee, and we'll get this job over as soon as possible and come back for ours."

As Kristen and Wes left the table, Marla's eyes followed them. Her look was anything but genial, but she offered no comment.

Together they walked along the surf's edge. The recently set sun still cast an incandescent glow on the western horizon, edging the low white clouds with a neon border.

"It was right about here," Kristen said, pointing toward the water.

Wes waded out in a big arc, sweeping his powerful hands through the water. Kristen's worried eyes followed his every movement. Back and forth he went, swimming when the water deepened and walking when his long legs could touch the bottom. He kept his eyes fastened to the blue water lapping around him in small waves.

Just when Kristen was about to admit defeat, he called, "Hey, I think I've found it!"

He dragged the old wooden trap toward the shore, and as he came into the shallower water, Kristen reached out to help him pull it in. It looked like an old weather-beaten crate.

"Oh, Wes. I'm so glad. Not just because you've saved my hide, but because I really did feel sorry for poor Mr. Beardsley. He seems like such a sad, lonely person."

Wes looked down on her with wonder and frank admiration. "Kristen, you're a special person, so kind and forgiving. You don't have a selfish bone in your body."

Kristen flushed, amazed to receive such an unexpected compliment, especially since she seemed to cause him so much trouble every time he came.

Together they dragged the crab trap right up to Mr. Beardsley's door. It was the first time that Kristen had crossed his little homemade string barrier since the day he scolded her and frightened Janelle.

A knock on the door brought the sound of slow footsteps, and then a small crack appeared at the opening. "Who is it, and what do you want?"

"We've come to bring you your crab trap, Mr. Beardsley." Wes's warm, friendly voice allowed the door to open all the way as he continued the explanation of what had happened.

"I might have known she had something to do with it," the little man retorted angrily. "I ought to have you put in jail, Girl!"

"I know I've been a lot of trouble for you, Mr. Beardsley, and I'm truly sorry. I hope you'll forgive me."

"How much longer are you going to be around here, aggravating me?" he asked.

"I'll only be here a few more weeks," she responded sadly. "I had hoped we could get to be friends." Perhaps that was an exaggeration, but it seemed the right thing to say.

He wanted to remain angry, but he was unaccustomed to such kindness, and seemed to be groping for a suitable response. He turned his eyes to the crab trap on the porch. The satisfying noise of scratching claws assured him that he would have boiled crab for supper, and his expression mellowed slightly. "Well, just stay on your side of the yard, Girl, and don't mess with my crab trap again."

"Good night, Mr. Beardsley. God bless you."

"Humph!" He lapsed into an artificial bout of coughing as he closed the front door.

Wes smiled broadly as he looked down at Kristen. "You charmed him. You have a way of doing that to people. I don't know what kind of mystical power you possess, Lady, but you seem to cast your magical spell on everyone around you."

It was dark when they reached the Spinnaker. Marla sat on the front porch alone. Wes and Kristen were almost giddy with the success of their mission, and as they retold the events, their happy laughter sounded through the house.

Janelle came out to join them. "Did you really go up on his porch and talk to him, Kristen?" Her big eyes were wide with wonder.

"She certainly did," her father interjected. "She completely subdued him!"

"How nice," Marla commented dryly.

"Why is he always so grouchy, Daddy? Is it because he's so old?"

Wes gave his daughter a thoughtful stare. "Is Mr. Baxter grouchy? Is Mrs. Baxter?"

"No–o–o, but—"

"They're all about the same age, Janelle. Age has nothing to do with it."

"You mean he was born grouchy?"

They all laughed at that, even Marla.

"Probably not, Punkin. I guess he's just reacting to some of his life's experiences."

"What does that mean, Daddy?"

"It means that he probably had some very bad times in his life." He studied the little girl's expression as he continued soberly. "Most people do, you know. When that happens, some people just give up and quit trying, and then they begin to forget how to laugh and love, and they grow grouchy and unhappy. Other people work to overcome the bad times, and they're the survivors, Janelle. They learn to find happiness for themselves and to share it with others."

"I think I understand about that, Daddy. It's like the way love remembers the beautiful things, isn't it?"

The look on Wes's face was pure astonishment. "Where did you learn that?"

"From Kristen. She explains things like that to me. She told me I'm like an apple seed that's left to grow into something beautiful, even after the apple is gone."

Sudden silence enveloped the room like a winter morning fog, so that even the rhythmic, persistent ticking of the grandfather clock in the living room sounded noisy and obtrusive. Finally, Wes was the first to speak.

"Well. Is everyone ready for a big day tomorrow?" He tried to sound casual, but traces of emotion still graveled his voice. "We'll need to get an early start."

Wes began to outline the plans for the day ahead. "I talked to Jeff, and he's going to meet us at the pier over there. He's already reserved bicycles, because the demand is so great for them on holidays."

"Bicycles?" Marla's eyebrows raised like the waves in the gulf.

"Yes, Buena Vista has some of the most interesting bicycle trails in the country. They lead all the way to the lighthouse on the tip of the island. And that historic old lighthouse is well worth all the effort to get there!"

Looking out over the water toward the end of the neighboring island, they could see the sweeping beams of the lighthouse from the porch where they sat.

"Light from that point over there has been guiding wayward sailors for over a hundred years. Jeff will take us inside the lighthouse, and you can see how it works."

"Will we take a picnic?" Janelle asked hopefully. Her obsession with picnics was almost comical.

"No, not this time. I've made reservations at the Pink Shell. After that bike ride, we'll all be glad to sit down in air-conditioned comfort and enjoy a nice lunch."

"Oh, Daddy, aren't we ever going to have a picnic?"

But Janelle's disappointment was short-lived when her father assured her, "We'll have a real picnic on Sunday; I promise."

Sitting on the porch, planning the day ahead, a peaceful contentment settled over them like a blanket. The stars were out in profusion, and Kristen looked wistfully at the waxing moon. It was a romantic evening. Perhaps she should take Janelle upstairs and give Wes some time alone with Marla. "If we are going to get up early, Janelle, perhaps we should go upstairs and get ready for bed."

"Don't go just yet," Wes pleaded. "Let's all go down to the beach and see if the water's firing."

"Firing?" Marla asked. "What do you mean by that?"

"Let's go down there, and if we're lucky, I can show you."

Kristen didn't need a second invitation. He actually wanted her to stay! But of course it was Janelle's company he wanted to savor, and she was just lucky enough to be included.

The evening tide had begun to rise. Standing close to the water, Wes pointed toward the waves. "See the sparks?"

"Oh, yes." Kristen wondered why she had not noticed it before. Lights sparkled just beneath the surface and danced on the ripples like miniature

Christmas lights. "What causes that, Wes?"

"Phosphorus in the water. It's a chemical reaction called 'bioluminescence.' Sometimes it's more prevalent than at other times. It's great tonight. I thought it might be, and I wanted all of you to see it."

"Interesting," Marla commented, kicking the gritty shells from her shoe.

"Watch this," he said as he reached down and raked his fingers through the water. Green, neonlike streaks followed the path of his hand. Janelle ran through the lapping waves, kicking the water up into sparkling showers.

"It isn't always present," Wes explained. "And we can't predict just when it will occur, but it happens mostly in the summer."

"Perhaps it's some of Gaspar's jewels washing ashore," Kristen quipped.

Wes looked at her. "This island is not such an unlikely spot to discover a great treasure." Was there a hidden meaning in those words?

As the three of them walked ahead, Kristen lingered behind, lost in her own thoughts, and lulled by the shimmering waves.

His voice broke into her reverie. "Hey, come on. Some big fish might mistake you for a mermaid and sweep you off your feet."

Together the four of them walked back to the house.

Kristen and Janelle were the first to retire, but Kristen was surprised to hear Marla returning to the guest room a short time later. Although her own door to the bathroom was closed, Kristen could hear Marla preparing for bed. She seemed to be making an unnecessary amount of noise, slamming things around as though she were angry.

Kristen could tell that Marla didn't share her love of the island, but it wouldn't matter in the end. After all, this was only a vacation house to Wes. He probably fit well into the glitzy city life that Marla seemed to crave.

If Marla was irritated about something when she retired, she must have forgotten it by morning, because she was up and dressed when Kristen entered the dining room.

"Be sure to eat a good breakfast," Wes urged them. "You'll get mighty hungry by the time we ride to the lighthouse and back."

Mrs. Baxter brought in a basket of warm blueberry muffins for the buffet. "Will you and Mr. Baxter be coming to the parade?" Kristen asked her.

"No, Dear, we've seen a-many of them, so we're just going to share the day with some friends down the island and watch the festivities on TV. But we'll be able to see the fireworks from the beach."

By boat, it was only a short hop to the next island. Kristen recognized the Pelican as they rode by. People were already seated on the deck having their breakfasts, and they waved to the passing boaters.

Wes moved his boat smoothly into a slip at the Buena Vista Municipal

Pier, and Jeff walked up to help him secure it.

At the local bicycle shop, they were each fitted with a bike of appropriate size, Kristen declining Jeff's suggestion that they use a tandem bicycle. "I want to maintain my independence," she declared.

Marla handled her bicycle awkwardly at first. It was plain that she had not ridden one lately, but after a few unsuccessful attempts, she pushed off and caught up with the rest of them.

As they approached the main intersection of the small town, they saw that all through traffic was blocked in deference to the annual Independence Day parade. Excited children stood on the curb and waved little flags, and street vendors hawked their wares—everything from balloons to T-shirts. Wes bought Janelle a shirt with a picture of the lighthouse on the front and "Buena Vista" spelled out in large letters across the back.

They found a shady spot near the end of the parade route where they could stand and watch the parade pass. The parade marshal marched to the beat of the local high school band as cute majorettes twirled their batons. Clowns threw candy to the crowd, and Jeff and Wes were able to catch several pieces for the ladies. When the local Coast Guard unit filed past, Kristen was sure they all recognized Jeff, even though their expressions remained solemn and their eyes fixed straight ahead.

Colorful floats glided by, each more elaborate and ornate than the last. Girls in billowing antebellum gowns graced the decorative floats and demurely smiled and waved white gloved hands to the cheering onlookers.

Next came the impressive float bearing an impostor of Jose Gaspar himself. Surrounded by swashbuckling buccaneers and beautiful maidens restrained by strong, thick chains, he stood tall and arrogant beside his open chest of jewels. He flung strings of beads and pearls to the ladies lining the curbside, and Kristen caught a shimmering strand of emerald-colored glass beads for Janelle. To the men, he brandished his shining saber in a menacing manner. The crowd roared and clapped in appreciation.

"It was a lovely parade," Kristen enthused, when the last float rolled by. Red, white, and blue were the colors of the day.

"Okay, let's hit the road." Jeff had assumed the role of tour guide, and Kristen followed his lead. Janelle, Marla, and Wes moved in behind them.

The bicycle path led beside the main road, and passersby shouted greetings from their cars, some decorated with crepe paper and banners. The music from the bands still filled the air. Royal palm trees lined their path, and hibiscus bushes bloomed in profusion at every turn.

"What beautiful homes." Marla gazed at them in admiration. "This island seems so much more progressive than Gaspar. I suppose that's because of the bridge."

"It makes a big difference," Wes admitted.

At a city park, they stopped by a water fountain to refresh. Janelle ran to the swing set, but the adults were happy to sit on the benches and rest their legs. Marla slipped off her shoes and massaged her bare feet. After a brief rest, they remounted their bikes and continued toward the lighthouse.

Nearly an hour later, they reached their destination. The lighthouse keeper was expecting them. "Come in, friends. Anna here has just made a fresh pot of coffee. And there's milk for the wee one." He patted Janelle's curly head. They trooped into the welcome cool of the quaint little cottage behind the lighthouse and gratefully accepted the couple's hospitality.

Sipping their coffee, they listened to the story of the historic lighthouse built on this point in 1890.

"Why, it's over a hundred years old," Kristen marveled.

"Let's climb to the top and see what the island looks like from there." Wes looked at Marla and held out his hand.

"After that bicycle ride? No, thanks. I'm sure it's beautiful, but you'll have to count me out on that one. I'm saving my legs for the ride back." Marla leaned back in her comfortable chair and savored her coffee.

"How about you, Kristen? Care for a look?"

She was hoping for the chance. It would be even higher than the crow's nest. The seemingly endless steps were steep and winding, but even though the muscles in her legs protested, Kristen was determined to get to the top.

When she did, she knew it had been worth all the effort. What a view! Up until this moment, she had been certain that the crow's nest at the Spinnaker displayed the world's most spectacular panorama, but now she knew that here was the epitome. Wes stood looking over her shoulder. "It takes the breath away, doesn't it?"

"I'd love to capture this on canvas, but I'm not talented enough to do it justice."

"You have so many talents, Kristen. You are a most unusual lady."

"We'd better go down and join the others," she said. She avoided his eyes lest her feelings should show, as they had to Jeff.

Going down was easier, but it still took a lot of effort. They were both ready to sit down for a few minutes before starting back.

The friendly lighthouse keeper and his wife were glad for the company, and were more than happy to entertain them with tales of the historic landmark.

"She's over one hundred feet tall," he proclaimed proudly. "She's been faithfully guiding lost ships and warning them of the dangerous reefs for over a hundred years, and even though she's had her glass shattered by hurricane winds a few times, she's never failed yet."

"What happens when the electricity goes off?" Janelle's intelligent curiosity amused Kristen. She knew that Janelle was remembering the many times recently that sudden summer electrical storms had plunged their island home into temporary darkness.

"We have an emergency diesel generator that comes on when that happens. The first lights were powered by mineral oil, but we've had electricity for as long as I've been here."

Jeff stood and looked at his watch. "I hate to interrupt this interesting visit, but we have a long ride ahead of us."

His audience moaned in mock protest as he got them onto their feet. After thanking their host and hostess, they said their good-byes and mounted their bicycles.

The path seemed much longer on the return journey, but they pedaled steadily in stoic silence.

"Are you okay, Janelle?" Wes finally asked.

She only nodded in reply. Her face was red from the sun and from exertion, but she pedaled on without complaint.

At last they reached the main part of town.

"Let's return our bikes," Jeff suggested, "so that we don't have to worry about parking them while we have lunch."

Seated in the cool restaurant sipping tall glasses of iced tea, their energy returned. After a salad lunch and huge pieces of Key lime pie, they walked across the street to the pier.

Holiday crowds hopefully dangled their fishing lines into the cobalt blue water, or simply enjoyed the beautiful day.

"Ride back with me, Kristen," Jeff suggested as the two men untied their boats. "Wes always gets the girls, and alas, I sail alone!"

Kristen laughed as she jumped aboard his boat. "Fair damsel here, to your rescue."

Janelle stayed to ride with her father and Marla. Janelle frowned when Kristen left with Jeff. She would much rather she had stayed to ride with them.

Around the dinner table that night, they related every detail of the day's adventures to the Baxters.

"We always used to see the parade," Martha Baxter reminisced. "Now, we just settle for the fireworks. I think they're better seen from here than over there, where the noise is so loud."

Kristen agreed. She thought it would be much nicer viewed from their own beach.

After the sun had gone down, they sat on blankets in the moonlight. Kristen and Jeff shared a blanket with the Baxters, and on another blanket, Janelle snuggled close in her father's lap next to Marla. "How much longer before they start, Daddy?"

As if on signal, her words seemed to call up the first brilliant lights across the water. While the lighthouse turned its steady beam toward the sea, the spectacular Roman candles filled the air with shooting streams of color. Sprays of sparks spiraled into the sky, arched and rained their fire into the gulf water below, and each colorful eruption was greeted with "oohs and aahs" from spectators gathered along the beach.

When the grand finale finally exploded, red, white, and blue filled the sky, and everyone clapped and cheered. Groups along the beach slowly began to disperse, and Kristen suddenly realized how tired she had become.

Mrs. Baxter led Janelle back to the house, while Jeff and Kristen said their good-byes on the steps. Wes and Marla seemed to be in serious conversation and hardly looked up when Kristen passed on her way inside and up the stairs to bed.

Chapter 8

The first sounds that Kristen heard on Sunday morning were the gulls as they swept the beach in their never-ending search for the small fish and coquinas they found along the water's edge.

She stretched lazily between her sheets and smiled, thinking of yesterday. Although the house was quiet, she could smell the coffee brewing. Kristen wished she could just grab a cup and head out for church, but no one at the Spinnaker went to church. Did the Baxters worship together? She reached for her Bible and began her private worship, softly singing one of her favorite hymns. Just as she ended her meditation and whispered her final "Amen," she heard a strange low moaning from the connecting bath.

"Marla, are you sick? Do you need help?" She knocked on the closed bathroom door. When she received no answer, she cautiously opened the door into the bath and discovered that the door into Marla's room was open too.

Marla was seated on her bed, with her head in her hands. "What is it, Marla? Are you ill?" Kristen was alarmed at her appearance. Her disheveled hair hung down in her face, and her whole body was beet red. "Why, you're badly sunburned. Didn't you use the sunscreen yesterday?"

"No, I didn't. I didn't want to ruin my makeup with all that greasy stuff. Anyway, it's not just the sunburn. My legs are hurting so that I can hardly stand on them. My head hurts too. I think I must be coming down with the flu or something!"

Kristen saw that she was miserable and felt sincerely sorry for her. "Lie down, Marla. I'll go down and bring up a breakfast tray. I'll bring up some aspirin for your headache and sore muscles, and something to soothe your sunburn. My legs are a little sore too this morning. It's from the bike riding."

Marla didn't protest as she sank back against her pillows.

Kristen went into the bathroom and came out with a cool, damp washcloth. "Put this over your eyes and relax, and I'll be back in a jiffy."

She hurried down the stairs, where the only person she encountered was Mrs. Baxter. She explained Marla's problems to a sympathetic ear.

"Oh, my. She never should have passed up the sunscreen. But I have just the thing for that."

She went into her own room, and Kristen waited in the kitchen, expecting to see her return with a bottle of lotion or cream. Instead, she carried a small potted plant.

"Now, you take this upstairs and break off one of these spikes, and have her rub the juice all over her body."

"What in the world for, Mrs. Baxter? What is that?"

"It's my aloe plant. Best sunburn medicine in the world. Just take my word for it. It'll feel sticky, but it takes the fire out, and she'll feel better right away."

Kristen knew that aloe was an active ingredient in many of the body lotions on the market. Mrs. Baxter usually knew what she was talking about, so it seemed worth a try.

Together, they fixed a tray of orange juice, hot coffee, and warm muffins, and Mrs. Baxter took a bottle of aspirin from the cupboard shelf. "You're a regular Florence Nightingale," she told Kristen.

Back in Marla's room, Kristen approached the bed. "Marla, Mrs. Baxter says that you're to break off one of these leaves and rub the plant juice all over your sunburn."

"What is this? Some kind of joke? No way am I going to do that!" She eyed the tray that Kristen was positioning on the bed and raised her head to take the two aspirin tablets, swallowing them down with the cold orange juice. "Ooh," she moaned. The movement hurt.

"I know it seems strange, Marla, but Mrs. Baxter assured me that the aloe plant would relieve your suffering. Why don't you give it a try?"

Reluctantly, Marla broke off one of the spikelike leaves and turned up her nose in disgust.

"Let me help you," Kristen offered, as she took the plant and gently began to rub the sticky substance over Marla's face.

Almost at once, the cool juice of the aloe plant relieved the pain of the sunburn, but Marla was still unhappy. "Kristen, don't you dare tell *anyone* about this. Absolutely no one can see me like this." She could feel the skin on her face puckering in response to the gelatinous substance from the plant. "Just tell them that I have a terrible headache and that I'm going to stay in my room today."

"Whatever you say, Marla. Here. Let me rub some of this aloe on your arms and legs."

Marla didn't protest anymore. She just lay back on her pillows, closed her eyes, and silently let Kristen minister to her needs.

Kristen moved the tray to the bedside table and quietly slipped from the room, closing the door behind her. She would let Marla rest awhile before checking on her again.

Back in her own room, she dressed in a pair of bright red shorts and topped them with a blue-and-white-striped T-shirt. She decided that she must have been inspired by all the Fourth of July patriotism. She slipped into her leather sandals and went downstairs for the second time that morning to claim the cup of the coffee that had been tempting her ever since she first opened her eyes.

By now, Wes and Janelle were already having their breakfasts in the dining room. "We must have worn you ladies out yesterday," Wes teased her. "Marla still isn't up."

"Wes, I'm afraid Marla isn't feeling well today. I've taken her a breakfast tray, and she wants to rest and get over a headache." Kristen tried to follow Marla's wishes and tell him only enough to explain her absence from the breakfast table.

"You're sure it's nothing serious?"

"Absolutely certain. A few hours of rest and she'll be good as new."

"I hate to go off and leave her here alone. Janelle and I have just been talking, and I'm afraid I've promised her a picnic." Wes looked at Janelle with concern. "Honey, do you think we could put this off until another day?"

"Daddy, you promised." Tears were already beginning to run down her little cheeks.

"Wes," Kristen intervened. "I've talked with Marla, and I honestly think she would prefer to be left alone today. I've given her some aspirin, and she'll probably sleep most of the day. Besides, I'll be here, and so will the Baxters. You and Janelle go ahead and have your picnic as planned."

"But Kristen," Janelle protested, "what about our surprise? I can't do it without you."

Then Kristen remembered that this was the day she planned to show her father how she could swim. They had worked so hard to reach this goal, and all along the incentive had been the final moment of triumph when she would surprise her father with her brave new accomplishment.

"What's this about a surprise?" Wes wanted to know. "There's no reason in the world why Kristen should stay here all day if Marla wants to rest. The Baxters will be around if Marla needs anything. I'll just run up and check on her before we leave."

He stood up, but just as quickly Kristen stood beside him.

"Oh no, Wes. Really. I don't think Marla wants to see you right now. Er. . .uh. . .she's not dressed, you see. I'll run up and check on her myself." She hurried up the steps before Wes could object. Marla would die rather than have Wes see her with the sticky aloe all over her face, and without her makeup. Kristen was sure of that.

"Marla." She tapped gently on the door.

"Go away."

"Marla, listen. It's either me or Wes. He's determined to check on you, and I volunteered instead." With that, she opened the door a crack and peeked in.

Marla hadn't moved. She was still stretched out on the bed, the sheet covering her body, her arms outstretched over her head. The aloe juice had dried now and made her skin look like parchment, but the redness had subsided, and Marla looked much more comfortable than she had been earlier.

"Do you feel any better?" Kristen walked over to the bed.

"How do you think I feel? Just look at me!" Gratitude wasn't exactly rolling off Marla's lips.

"Wes wants to know if you feel up to a picnic today."

"No, I don't feel up to a picnic today, or tomorrow, or any other day, for that matter. And if you let him see me like this, I'll find some way to get even with you, I promise."

"Just asking," Kristen said softly. She left the room, closing the door behind her.

Mrs. Baxter promised to check on Marla later in the day. She'd take her a nice lunch at noon, she said. Kristen told her to be sure to get permission before entering the room.

Mrs. Baxter was humming as she packed their picnic basket. She seemed unusually cheerful, as though harboring some happy little secret all her own.

"You're feeling mighty chipper today, Mrs. B," Kristen called over her shoulder as she and Janelle went upstairs to get into their bathing suits.

⚓

Wes, waiting on the porch, was not able to conceal his admiration as Kristen approached. Her conservative black bathing suit gave perfect contrast to her long blond hair, lightened even more from its recent exposure to the sun.

Janelle joined them wearing a cute little ruffled two-piece.

"The summer is agreeing with you, Janelle. You've put on a few very becoming pounds, and you've grown roses in your cheeks."

"Let's go, Daddy. I can't wait to show you my surprise."

Janelle had selected a spot toward the north end of the island, in a little cape that was usually smooth and calm. It was nearly noon by the time they got there.

"When do I get my big surprise?"

"Let's show him now, Kristen."

Janelle put Timmy on the table beside the picnic basket. Kristen exchanged a look with Wes, whose expression told her that he had already received his first big surprise of the day. Janelle was actually going to leave the toy bear on the table while she ran barefoot toward the water!

Kristen waded beside her through the shallow surf and thought how far

185

they had come that Janelle no longer needed the security of her hand as she worked her way into deeper water.

When the water reached her chest, Janelle gave herself a little push directly into the gentle waves and kicked and paddled as though she had been swimming for years.

She laughed when she turned and saw the look of utter amazement on her father's face. "Who is this little mermaid?" he asked her. "Not my daughter, certainly. Not the one who won't get her face wet."

Giggling, she swam back and forth again and again, stopping each time to look for his smiling approval and hear his enthusiastic applause.

Kristen looked on like a proud mother hen, especially when Wes turned to her and said, "Kristen, I don't know how you've done it. I've tried every way I know to overcome her fear of the water. In just a few short weeks, you've turned my shy little darling into a self-assured young lady."

"Not yet, Wes. But we're working on it."

You, too, have made leaps and bounds in the self-esteem department, Wes thought.

When her energy was spent, Janelle remembered the picnic basket. "Swimming makes me hungry."

"Now I see how Kristen has managed to get a little meat on your bones. She makes you work up an appetite."

Sandwiches never tasted better than they did that day under the shade of the ancient Australian pines. If a little sand blew into the food, it was hardly noticed. Janelle shared the crusts from her sandwich with a squawking gull who swooped down to eye their lunch.

Far out, a school of porpoises playfully rolled in the waves. "Those are truly the gentle giants of the deep," Wes observed. "They're so big they could scare you out of your wits when you encounter them, if you didn't know how sweet and friendly they really are."

Why, you've just given a perfect description of yourself, Kristen thought as she watched him gaze out over the water. *A gentle giant if ever there was one.*

He surely did scare me before I knew how sweet and friendly he really is! Kristen reminded herself.

Aloud, she said, "Yes, and they're highly intelligent too. Jeff told me that the navy is doing research to learn how they communicate with each other."

Wes had a sudden inspiration. "See that sandbar out there?" He pointed into the water, where the waves were breaking over the rise of sand that extended along the beach, about fifty yards offshore. "Could you swim that far, Janelle?"

"No, I don't think so, Daddy. I wish I could. I'd like to find some more sand dollars."

Wes looked at Kristen. "Are you thinking what I'm thinking?"

"Let's go!"

They grabbed Janelle's hands between them and splashed into the water. When the water reached Janelle's chin, Wes lifted her to his shoulders. Kristen plunged forward, cutting through the water like a knife, hardly causing it to ripple. Her smooth strokes took her to the sandbar in less than two minutes. Wes walked out until he could no longer hold his chin above the water. "Now, Janelle, swim to Kristen," he told her, giving her a big push that landed her almost in Kristen's arms. A few of his big, powerful strokes put him at their side.

Janelle was thrilled. She had never been on the sandbar before. Here the water was only six inches deep, clear as crystal, and she could easily spot the coveted sand dollars, which were in plentiful supply. She reached down and scooped up a large one and held it above her head.

"Look, Daddy. Did you know there's a legend about these?"

"A legend?"

"Yes. Do you want to hear it?" Without waiting for his reply, his usually quiet little girl launched into a lengthy explanation of the ancient story of the sand dollar, just as Kristen had related it to her.

"Interesting! You're certainly learning a lot of new things this summer!"

The three of them frolicked in the water, nearly losing track of time.

At last Kristen reminded them, "We'd better get back to shore. The tide is coming in, and soon it will be too deep for Janelle to swim across."

They left just as they had come, except that Wes swam toward shore first, and stood to catch Janelle as Kristen gave her a mighty heave toward the waiting arms of her father.

They were nearly exhausted as they approached the beach, splashing up the bank through the shallow ripples.

"Ouch!" Kristen sank to the ground and clutched her foot. Blood spurted forth, coloring a bright red circle in the white sand beneath her foot.

"Kristen! What happened? Let me see that!" Wes held her foot in his hands and applied firm pressure with his thumbs until the bleeding slowed and then stopped.

"I must have stepped on a sharp shell. It's all right, though. I don't think it's very bad. It hardly hurts at all."

"I don't think you'd better walk on it. It might start bleeding again. Janelle, do you think you can handle the empty basket so that I can carry Kristen?"

"Sure, Daddy. Is it very bad? Will you have to have stitches, Kristen?"

"No, I'm sure I won't. And I feel perfectly able to walk."

Without further words, Wes swept her up in his strong arms and started for home. Kristen started to protest again, but when she leaned her head against his hairy chest and heard the strong, steady beat of his heart, she relaxed and did not argue at all.

She felt his heart beating faster and his breath coming harder as he hurried toward home. Her heart was beating faster too, but she knew that his accelerated pulse was due to exertion rather than emotion, and her conscience pricked her into admitting once more, "Wes, you can put me down now. I'm okay, really."

"Kristen, you're as light as a feather. We're almost there." He seemed reluctant to release her. "It's obvious that you haven't been 'pigging out' like my chubby-cheeked mermaid here."

They were laughing when they reached the top of the dune leading up to the porch steps. There, sitting in a rocker watching them, was Marla, evidently at least partially recuperated from her morning malady. Although her skin was still a glowing pink, she had showered and dressed in a white, bare-shouldered sundress and her white strap sandals. A white gardenia was pinned to her hair.

"My, that must have been quite a picnic! Let me in on your little joke."

"Put me down, Wes."

He gently lowered Kristen into the nearest chair. "Marla, I'm glad to see that you're feeling better. Kristen, I'm going to get a pan of soapy water for your foot, and after we make sure it's clean, I want to have a better look at it."

Janelle followed Wes into the house to get the first aid supplies, and Marla turned to Kristen. "Did you feel you had to get into the act?"

A sharp answer on the tip of her tongue was quickly swallowed as Kristen realized the foolishness of the situation. Here they were, two grown women sparring like a couple of schoolgirls. She refused to be a part of it.

"It's nothing really, Marla. Just a small cut. I'll clean it up and put on a Band-Aid, and it'll be as good as new. After supper, I'm going to bed early, so you'll have the whole stage to yourself!"

Wes returned to the porch with a basin of water in his hands and Janelle at his heels, carrying a tray of gauze, adhesive, scissors, and various medicines. He stooped and put the basin at her feet. "Just soak in that for a few minutes. It may burn a little; I've added a disinfectant to the water. Sometimes shell cuts can be very painful."

A few minutes later he knelt before her, tenderly cradling her foot in his hand, toweling it dry with soft, gentle pats. "I'll make a butterfly bandage to make sure it heals properly. I don't think it will give you any trouble."

He applied an antiseptic cream to the cut and snipped the corners of a wide piece of adhesive to draw it together. His hands on her flesh felt warm and comforting.

Then she was aware of Marla's eyes upon her. "Thank you, Wes." She pulled her ankle from his grasp and stood. "I'm going up to rest awhile before supper. I'll see all of you a little later."

She stood and hobbled toward the stairs.

"Let me help you," Wes offered, but she hurried off alone. As she climbed the stairs, she heard Marla comment, "I think you've helped quite enough for one day," but she didn't linger to hear his reply.

In the sanctity of her room, Kristen relived those happy hours on the beach. Thankfully, Wes and Marla would be leaving tomorrow, and she could try to put him out of her mind.

She would try to see as little of him as possible until he left. That should be less painful for her, and certainly it would please Marla, who did not seem to be in the best of moods, anyway.

Marla! She might be the right choice for Wes, but how about Janelle? Kristen thought of the promise she had made to the little girl, who trusted her father to provide a happy home for her. Was he making a wise decision? She had no right to speculate on that, but her love for Janelle had grown so deep that she couldn't bear to think of having her hurt. She had felt too much pain and sorrow already.

At supper that evening, Kristen sat between Mrs. Baxter and Janelle. Across the table, Marla sat between Mr. Baxter and Wes. Janelle was still excited over the picnic she had finally been able to share with her father. Uncharacteristically, she chattered nonstop.

Wes was pleased and amused at her performance, and his encouragement just seemed to add to her efforts. Kristen wondered if all this excitement would be too stimulating this close to bedtime, but it was nice to see the two of them so happy together.

Marla looked regally beautiful, her pink glow rather becoming. Although not talkative, she was sociable and pleasant, and there was no sign of the strain Kristen had felt earlier on the porch. Evidently, Wes had smoothed everything over.

After dinner, true to her promise to Marla earlier, she announced that she was going up to her room for the night.

"So early?" Wes sounded disappointed.

"Yes, I have some letters to write."

"Well, you tell him that I think he's a lucky guy." He grinned impishly at her.

She was glad to let him believe that she was writing to a sweetheart that didn't exist. That was a balm to her pride.

Upstairs, she picked up her nightclothes and headed for the shower. What a mess. Marla had enough cosmetics strewn around to open a beauty parlor. Without disturbing anything, Kristen showered and slipped into her muslin gown. She brushed her hair and let it fall upon her shoulders. Then she retired to her room, closing the bathroom door behind her.

Kristen slept fitfully, tossing and turning as unrealistic and disturbing dreams kept entering her mind uninvited. Finally, she got up and took her terry cloth robe from its hanger.

The half-moon was high in the clear, starry sky, and the little clock by her bed told her that it was two A.M. She never took sedatives—she didn't even own any—but she needed her sleep. Perhaps some warm milk would help.

Opening her door a crack, she listened. The house was bathed in silence as she crept down the stairs. In the kitchen, she had just warmed a cup of milk when she heard voices on the porch. Who could that be? She thought everyone else had been asleep for hours.

She heard the front door, and then their voices in the living room. *Wes and Marla!* Suddenly aware of her inappropriate attire, she stepped into the pantry. After they went upstairs, she could retreat to her room without being noticed.

Her worst fears were realized when she heard them enter the kitchen.

"Well, Darling, it's been fun." It was Marla who spoke. "I guess we both should have known from the start."

"We've had some good times, Marla, but it's over between us. It never would have worked."

Panic seized Kristen as she listened to a conversation she had no business hearing. Her heart was pounding like a hammer. If only she hadn't come downstairs. She looked for an escape route, but it was already too late for that. A familiar and dreaded feeling began to spread over her as she pressed her forefinger to her nose, hoping to stop the twitching she knew to be a prelude to disaster. *"Atchoo!"*

"Kristen!" His voice sounded sharp and angry.

There was no choice for her now. Sheepishly, she stepped into the lighted kitchen, pulling her robe closer around her. Her loosened hair hung around her shoulders in blond, bouncy profusion. Her eyes were wide with embarrassment.

"I'm sorry! I didn't mean to—"

"Why, you little eavesdropper," Marla snarled viciously.

Wes's expression showed more disappointment than anger. "Kristen, you of all people!"

"Just let me explain."

"There's been too much said already for one night. Let's all get to bed before it's time to get up." With that, he turned on his heel and stomped out of the kitchen.

Marla followed, but not before giving Kristen a cold, contemptuous look. "I know what you've wanted, but I didn't think you'd stoop this low."

Now it was Kristen's turn to be angry. Judging her like that, without giving her a chance to explain. *Well, let them think what they want.* She would soon be leaving this place, and the sooner the better!

⚓

Breakfast was strained that morning, as events of the earlier hours were studiously ignored. Suitcases sat by the back door, awaiting departure time. Soon they would be gone, and Kristen could try to regain her rationality.

"Kristen, may I talk with you in my study before I leave?" Wes was cool and formal.

She followed him into the study. At least now she could explain what a terrible mistake they had all made. "About last night, Wes—"

"Kristen, I don't have time for that now. We'll address that later. I wanted to tell you that I won't be able to come here again for several weeks."

"I can't think of any reason we'd need you." Her cold reply was intended to mask her anger and humiliation as she tried to avoid his eyes.

"I have a very important case coming up," he continued, ignoring her uncharacteristic rudeness, "and it's going to demand all of my time for awhile. It's the malpractice case against the doctor."

"Oh, yes. I remember that case. I typed some of your depositions for it."

"Yes, that's the one. That case is grossly unwarranted. I've told him the evidence is all in his favor. He's a good man who's been unfairly accused."

"If anyone can help him, you can."

"I certainly intend to try. But it's going to take a lot of work. I want to be ready when the time comes."

Kristen knew his reputation as a defense lawyer. He had a strong commitment to justice, and he limited his clients to those he felt were on the right side of the law. Consequently, his percentage of successes was very high. Despite whatever personal differences the two of them might have, she always admired his professional ethics and his legal expertise.

"In a few weeks it will all be over. Then I'm coming back here. Alone." His voice displayed no emotion at all. Was he angry, hurt, or indifferent?

"There'll be plenty of time then for any explanations you care to make," he continued. "But for now, I have to give my full attention to the malpractice suit, and I'm depending on you to take good care of Janelle."

"That was our agreement from the start, and I certainly mean to fulfill my part of the bargain." There it was again. Another reminder that her presence here was simply a business arrangement. Nothing more!

"If there is anything you need—anything at all—you know how to get in touch with me. Meanwhile, Jeff enjoys keeping an eye on you. He's certainly making that abundantly clear."

Why did he sound so undone about that? It was his idea in the first place.

She thought he should be happy that Jeff took such good care of them in his absence.

"And you know that he's just five minutes away if you need him."

He hesitated momentarily, looking as though he had more to say. Then abruptly, he hurried out the door and left her standing alone in the empty room.

Not wanting to be downstairs when they left, she went upstairs to the sanctity of her room.

Just keep busy, she told herself.

Both doors into the bathroom which connected her room with Marla's stood open. Marla had already packed her many cosmetics, but her towels were strewn about the bath. Kristen was gathering up all the dirty linen to drop down the laundry chute when Marla came in to say good-bye.

"I don't expect our paths will ever cross again, but I didn't want to go away mad."

"I appreciate that, Marla. I'd really like to explain about last night. It was truly an accident, you know."

"No, I don't know, but I really don't care, either. I'm not cut out for island life, and I'm certainly not ready for motherhood, either. I just want to blot out this chapter of my life and get on with something else."

She turned to go, paused thoughtfully, then turned back toward Kristen. "I don't know why I should do you any favors, but then again, why not?"

Kristen didn't understand. "Favors?"

"Yes. I just thought you ought to know that Wes is crazy in love with you."

"That's impossible. He's never shown any indication." Kristen remembered how she had once thought he wanted her to be his wife. It had taken her a long time to get over the pain of that mistake.

"Oh, that's because he doesn't know it himself yet." Marla's laugh was low and throaty. "But he will, in time."

This time when Marla left the room, she didn't pause or look back. Any connection the two women had was clearly severed.

Wes, in love with her? No, that was certainly not true. Was this some cruel joke of Marla's? Was she trying to get even? Even if Wes did ask her to marry him now, she'd have to refuse. Wes only wanted to establish another home for his daughter, and as much as she loved Janelle, she knew now that she would need more out of marriage than that. Good marriages were made of everlasting love and deep respect. She did love Wes, and she always would. But she would never marry a man who did not love her in return.

She stayed in her room, and didn't hear them when they left, but later she heard the *toot, toot, toot* of the boat horn that told Janelle he loved her. How she wished those notes included her!

Chapter 9

Robert Weston Bradley III sat behind his massive oak desk and groaned. Even within his sealed, air-conditioned office, the noise of late afternoon Peachtree Avenue traffic distracted him. *Everything* distracted him. The tapping of computer keys in the adjoining rooms, the stir of air from the ceiling vents, and even his own thoughts. *Especially* his own thoughts.

He looked at the pile of evidence on his desk. This was an important case, and time was of the essence. Why couldn't he focus on it?

Was it because of his recent breakup with Marla? He tried to think of her, and found he could hardly call a clear picture of her to his mind. Was he really so fickle?

He had no such trouble remembering Louise, every endearing little freckle. What was it Janelle had said about love remembering all the beautiful things? Yes, and that part about the apple seed. Janelle was the seed all right; the part of Louise she had left with him, to love and cherish forever. Janelle was a beautiful reminder of their love. But now Louise was dead, and where did he go from here?

He had almost made a serious mistake. It scared him to think of the possible consequences of a marriage with someone like Marla.

He stood and moved into the front office. "Sara, please put a record of my calls on my desk. I'll return them later."

"Yes, Mr. Bradley. Will you be out of the office the rest of the day?"

"I don't know, Sara. I'm not sure."

When he walked through the Peachtree Avenue exit, the July heat bounced off the sidewalk and hit him like a solid wall. "Taxi, Mister?"

"No, thank you. I'm walking."

Anyone watching him start down the avenue would have believed that he was hurrying toward an important meeting, but in truth, he had no idea of his destination. He just wanted to keep moving, to concentrate on this action of his feet so that he would have no room in his mind for other thoughts.

Perversely, the traffic noises that had invaded his thoughts when muffled by his office walls were scarcely noticeable to him now as he walked and walked and walked.

The pavement burned through the leather soles of his shoes, and his shirt was wet with perspiration. How long had he been walking? How far had he come? This corner was an unfamiliar one. He loosened his tie. No one in his right mind would dress in a long-sleeved shirt and tie for a walk in this weather. His breath was coming fast and hard, and he needed to sit down somewhere and rest.

He looked around for a bench, but saw none. A large gray structure blocked out the sun and shaded the corner, and he turned toward it gratefully. A sign read, CHAPEL OPEN FOR PRAYER. Why, this was a church. Slowly he climbed the old stone steps.

Inside, it was cool and beautiful. Candles burned on the altar, while sunlight seeped through the tall stained-glass windows. The chapel was empty. Wes took a seat just inside the door.

The only prayers he had offered in years were the few times he had said grace at the table for Kristen's benefit. Would God still hear his prayers?

He removed a Bible from the pew rack and turned the leaves randomly. He knew that he needed help, but he wasn't sure how to find it.

"Lord, help me," he prayed, letting the pages sift through his fingers. A passage caught his eye. From Philippians, he read: "Forgetting what is behind and straining toward what is ahead, I press on toward the goal. . . ."

As he continued to read, a strange, warm peace enveloped him, and a heavy door in his mind seemed to open, while at the same time another gently closed. Suddenly he knew exactly where he was going, and with God's help, what he must do.

Descending the church steps, he saw a small tree that he had failed to notice earlier. Its tender young branches shaded a tiny patch of ground, and he walked toward it. It was an apple tree! He cradled a shiny red apple in his hands. There were seeds inside that, if given care and nourishment, would flourish and produce good fruit.

On a busy Atlanta street corner in a sparse patch of shade, he said goodbye to Louise, and left her there beneath the apple tree.

⚓

It was mid-August before Wes came to the island again. They were long weeks for Kristen, as she tried to keep busy writing letters, working and playing with Janelle, and seeing Jeff whenever he could get away.

Wes had promised they would talk when he returned. Now that the time was near, she had mixed emotions.

She wanted to talk to him, to explain how she happened to be in the pantry the night he and Marla terminated their relationship. Yet she dreaded the confrontation too.

It would likely be their last personal conversation. He probably intended to discuss her transition back into the office now that summer was ending, but she had already made up her mind about that.

As much as she loved her job and her fellow workers, she planned to resign and seek employment elsewhere. She could not continue to see him day after day without letting her feelings show. With a good recommendation from Bradley, Bradley, and Kline, she was sure to get a good job almost anywhere she chose.

Often after supper she walked on the beach, sometimes sitting on the log she had shared with Wes that first night on Gaspar Island. Alone, with only the soothing sounds of the eternal tides, she felt his presence there beside the sea.

Even with all the heartaches, it had been a good summer. Janelle had emerged like a butterfly from her sheltering cocoon and was spreading her wings in preparation to fly.

And Kristen recognized her own growth. She was not the same insecure girl who had trapped herself in the grass beds in June. Like Janelle, she had shed the restricting tentacles and now felt ready to face her life ahead.

Though neither of them ever voiced it, Marla's departure had lifted a weight from Janelle, and Kristen too. It had nothing to do with any personal delusions of Wes's feelings. She had finally been able to admit that his interest in her was entirely related to Janelle. Even if, by some remote chance, he ever asked her to marry him, she now knew that she would refuse.

As much as she loved him, she could never be happy in a marriage arranged for convenience, even for someone as lovely as Janelle. Wes Bradley had never given Kristen any indication that he loved her. If he simply wanted to find a mother for his child, he would have to look somewhere else. To her, marriage meant sharing a lifetime of mutual love, and she could never settle for anything less.

Finally, the weeks of waiting were over. She and Janelle, and of course, Timmy, were on the wharf to meet Wes when the *Janni Lu* pulled up.

"Ahoy, there, mates!" he called to them.

Janelle was beside herself with joy. Kristen wisely left the two of them together when they reached the house. She and Wes would have their time to talk later.

After dinner, it was still daylight when the three of them walked together on the beach. It was good to see him relaxed and having fun.

He had won his case, he told her. He must have been even more concerned about that case than she had realized, because the difference in him tonight was profound. He was like a new person. In all the months she had known him, she had never seen him appear quite so content and peaceful.

They walked all the way to the point, Janelle between them. *Just like a family*, Kristen thought wistfully.

On the way back, Janelle pulled Wes by the hand, up above the tide line. "Look, Daddy. Right here is where we watched the turtles." He listened intently while she told him in great detail how the giant sea turtles came ashore to bury their eggs. Kristen was sure he had witnessed that spectacle many times in the past, but he listened patiently to every word.

Not until Janelle was snugly tucked into bed by her father did Wes suggest that he and Kristen should talk. "I'll ask Mrs. Baxter to listen for Janelle while we're gone."

"Where are we going?"

"A moonlight boat ride would give us a chance for uninterrupted conversation. What do you think?"

"I think it would be lovely." Her heart was pounding so hard against her rib cage that she was almost afraid he could hear it. For weeks she had thought of being with him, just the two of them alone together, and she had rehearsed all the words she wanted to say. Now she hoped she could trust her head to rule over her heart.

Wes maneuvered the boat with ease as they surged through the channel, his eyes focused on the strategically marked waterway. All tension seemed to have oozed from his body. Then, turning into a wide lagoon, he idled the motor and dropped anchor. Turning to her, he said, "Of course, you know that Marla and I are through."

"I heard that. And I *wasn't* eavesdropping."

"I know that. You were caught off guard. I should have realized that at once."

"I was pretty mad when you wouldn't let me explain."

"There was no need to explain. I knew we had a lot of things that needed to be said, but that was neither the place nor the time to say them."

He touched her chin and lifted her lips to his. His kiss was gentle at first, and then more demanding, causing her head and her heart to reel. As she encircled his neck with her slender arms, all her earlier resolutions melted into oblivion as she surrendered herself to his embrace. Loud and clear, she heard those bells ringing at last!

Then abruptly, almost as suddenly as he had kissed her, he released her. So suddenly, in fact, that she stumbled backwards and almost lost her balance.

"What—"

"Forgive me, Kristen. I had no right to do that. Believe me when I say that I surprised myself even more than I surprised you. I intended coming out here to discuss your plans for returning to the office. I guess I just got carried away."

"But, Wes—"

"Never mind, Kristen. I know what you are going to say. You gave me fair warning that you are in love with someone else. I want you to find the happiness you deserve."

Kristen wanted to shout her denial, to tell him that *he* was that special man who held all the keys to her heart. Yet in the deepest recesses of her mind, she finally heard the alarm that reminded her of her earlier resolve, warning her that even when he kissed her, he had never once said that he loved her. Once again she was reading too many of her own dreams into Wes's actions and words. She loved Janelle almost as much as she loved Wes, but both she and Janelle deserved better than a half family. Although it took every ounce of her will-power, she pulled her eyes away from him and stood beside him in silence.

Oblivious to her distress, Wes continued. "What I especially wanted to tell you was how much I appreciate the way you have helped Janelle. You will never know what a big impact you have had on both of our lives, because as you have helped her, that help has filtered down to guide me into making some important changes in my own life as well."

He pulled a small box from his pocket and placed it in her hands. "Kristen, I wanted you to have a token reminder of our appreciation, Janelle's and mine. I wanted it to be something that would help you remember us in the years to come."

Remember them? Did he think for one moment that she could ever forget? With trembling fingers, she opened the little velvet box and caught her breath when she saw the beautiful white porcelain dove dangling from a gold serpentine chain. "Oh, Wes. It's the most beautiful present I have ever received. I will cherish it always. Here, can you help me fasten it?"

His fingers felt warm against the back of her neck, and she felt the goose pimples rise on her arms.

She longed to turn to him and unburden her heart, but, "Thank you," was all she said.

He turned the key, the engine roared, and they moved forward, into the murky bay.

Wes ran the boat at high speed all the way back, his thoughts racing too, as the motor droned and he stared straight ahead. What was the matter with him? He had always disapproved of men who made romantic advances toward their employees. It was unfair to put that kind of pressure on a woman, especially one who belonged to someone else. She couldn't know how much he'd grown to admire and respect her these recent weeks, but that didn't excuse his thoughtless behavior.

Back at the dock, Kristen didn't even wait for him to secure the yacht. She couldn't face him now, with so much of her heart written on her face. She'd never let him know how much she loved him—would always love him. He must never know.

When he kissed her, she'd listened for those three important little words, "I love you," but they had not come. And without them, their relationship was friendship; nothing more, ever.

Kristen ran all the way home. Even the rustlings in the bushes didn't slow her return to the Spinnaker. She hurried through the kitchen door and was almost to the staircase when Mrs. Baxter stopped her.

"You had a telephone message, Honey. I tried to write down everything he said." She handed Kristen a piece of paper. "Is something wrong, Dear? You don't look well!"

"Oh no, Mrs. Baxter. I–I just have a little headache, that's all. I'll be fine as soon as I lie down."

"Oh, my! Let me get you some aspirin." Motherly concern wrinkled her brow.

Kristen wanted to get away before Wes came in. "Thank you, but I have some in my bathroom. I'll be fine. I'll see you in the morning."

She bolted up the stairs without giving the old lady time to protest.

In the privacy of her room, she sat on the bed and opened the folded paper. Mrs. Baxter had painstakingly written:

From Jack: Had business in Fort Myers. Staying at Wayside Inn tonight. I'll arrive at Gaspar Marina in A.M. I'll phone you for instructions about getting over to see you. If okay, will plan to spend the day.

Jack! What a sense of timing. He was about the last person she was prepared to see right now. On the other hand, having Jack around would keep her from being alone with Wes and might cement the impression Wes held about another man in her life.

No need to worry about it, anyway. He was almost here, and she couldn't send him back home without seeing him. She'd just have to take things one step at a time and see what happened.

What happened was actually much more pleasant than she had imagined.

At the breakfast table, she shared her note, telling everyone that a good friend wanted to spend the day on the island.

"That's fine," Wes told her. "When he calls, we'll run over in the *Janni Lu* and pick him up. Janelle, you can come along with Kristen and me."

Her delight was obvious. "Can we have another picnic today? Remember how much fun we had on our last one?"

Wes smiled indulgently. "I certainly do remember that day." He looked across the table at Kristen and smiled. "Unless Kristen wants to be alone with her guest today, I don't see why we can't all plan one together."

How could she refuse? He was offering to provide transportation for Jack and the hospitality of his summer home as well. "That would be lovely," she said, hoping her apprehension did not show.

Janelle giggled with glee. "I'll go upstairs and get ready." The phone call came just as they finished breakfast, and the three of them left to meet Jack at the marina.

Mrs. Baxter stopped them at the kitchen door. "I may be gone to the grocery when you get back. But I'll leave you a nice picnic lunch, all wrapped up to keep it fresh. I'm frying some chicken now, and I'll put in some of those deviled eggs you like so much. Just get the lemonade out of the freezer before you leave, and put it in the bottom of the basket, and lay the lunch on top of it. That should keep it fresh."

"Thanks, Mrs. B. If you're ready now, you two can ride over to the parking garage with us."

Kristen hoped that the Baxters would. The more the merrier. But they politely declined. "It'll be a few minutes before we're ready, and Kristen's gentleman is already waiting. You go on ahead."

Mrs. Baxter dismissed them with a wave of her hand and began directing her husband to help her finish her chores. "Bax, Dear, don't forget this is garbage pickup day. Better get it out in the can early."

Kristen gave her a quick kiss as she headed out the door. "You just do too much for us, Mrs. Baxter."

Janelle's constant chatter directed at her adored and adoring father relieved any strain Kristen might have felt alone with him, and it was a smiling threesome who greeted Jack on the wharf of the marina a few minutes later.

Wes took Janelle by the hand and led her into the store, discreetly giving Kristen a few moments alone with Jack.

"It's great to see you," Jack told her. "Island life apparently agrees with you." Admiration shone in his eyes. "You look like the magazine ads for tanning lotions."

"And you look like a real Florida tourist in your white shorts and island-print shirt!" It really was good to see him. "Come over here. I want you to meet the Bradleys." They held hands and smiled as she introduced him to Wes and Janelle.

The men shook hands. "This is an impressive boat," Jack told Wes, letting his eyes move from bow to stern.

"Come up front with me, and see how smoothly she runs."

Kristen and Janelle sat in the stern in the swivel chairs. Looking at the two men at the helm, Kristen wondered once more how her emotions could be so unmanageable. Here was Jack, loving and kind, the perfect choice for a life mate. Then there was Wes, whose only interest was his child. Wouldn't Jack be the logical choice for her heart? Life was strange where love was concerned!

Janelle sat beside her, chattering, her words and her golden curls blowing in the wind.

At the island wharf, Jack helped Wes tie up the boat, and the four made their way to the Spinnaker.

Mrs. Baxter had left the electric coffeepot on, and a tray of still-warm coffee cake lay on the table.

"Mrs. Baxter thinks of everything. I'm afraid she has us all quite spoiled," Kristen told Jack as she passed the cake.

"We're going on a picnic," Janelle declared happily.

Jack looked puzzled until Wes explained. "I'm afraid I have a daughter who's a picnic-aholic. She never lets up. I hope you won't mind if the two of us join you and Kristen today."

Dependably polite, Jack assured him that he and Kristen would be happy to have the pleasure of their company. "Where do you suggest we have this picnic?"

"There's a beautiful state park only accessible by boat. Why don't we pack our lunch and go over there?" Wes took the big basket down from the shelf. Remembering Mrs. Baxter's instructions, he put the frozen lemonade in first. It would be thawed to a cold slush by lunchtime. Spying the brown paper-wrapped bundle by the sink, he placed it over the lemonade to keep it cool. Then he covered everything with the red checkered tablecloth Mrs. Baxter had laid out.

"Okay," he directed, "let's get started."

Kristen wondered if Jack was getting tired of walking back and forth to the boat. Little beads of perspiration stood out on his forehead. She remembered how her feet and legs had ached until they became accustomed to the sandy pathway to the wharf.

There was not a storm cloud in the sky. Gliding through the bay on the *Janni Lu,* Kristen watched the two pilots through half-closed eyes as she leaned back in her swivel chair. Two wonderful men, and she loved them both, but in such totally different ways.

The state park was as beautiful as Wes had promised. Janelle spotted the playground at once. "Come push me in the swing, Daddy. Please."

Wes dutifully answered her summons, and Jack and Kristen were left alone at last.

"I had to see you, Kristen. I know by our telephone conversations and letters that we've both changed a lot this summer. So what are your plans for the future?"

"Jack, I wish I knew. But I'm not coming back to Gainesville. That much I know." She looked at him with tenderness. "You are so special to me, Jack, and I'll always love you. But I'm not *in* love with you, and there's a big difference."

"I've known that for a long time. Accepting that was the hardest thing I've ever had to do. But I've come to grips with it now, and I just want you to know that, no matter what happens, you can always count on me to be there for you, Kristen."

She kissed his cheek, just as she would have kissed her brother's, and they looked at each other with a new understanding.

"Now, tell me all the news from home."

He told her of all the social activities of her friends back in Gainesville, and she was surprised to realize that she scarcely remembered some of them. It was fun to reminisce, but Gainesville was no longer "home" for her. Where was home? Atlanta? Gaspar Island? She didn't know.

Squeals from the playground drew her attention. "Kristen, look at me!" Janelle was swinging high and loving it, while Wes was pushing her, perspiration running down his face.

"Let's break for lunch, Punkin." Wes let his arms drop to his sides as the swing idled and stopped. "I need some of that lemonade."

Janelle ran to keep up with his long strides as Wes moved toward the picnic table where Kristen and Jack were seated.

Kristen lifted the lid of the basket and removed the cloth and the neatly wrapped bundle, while Wes eagerly gripped the jug of the partially thawed lemonade and began to pour into four paper cups. Cold and slightly tart, it was wonderfully refreshing.

"Help me spread the cloth, Janelle, so we can see what Mrs. Baxter fixed for our lunch." Kristen pulled at one end of the red checkered cloth while Janelle held the other. The wind whipped it into billows so that they had to anchor each corner with their silverware.

Wes lifted the paper-wrapped bundle and untied the string. Unfolding the tidy wrappings, he smiled in hungry anticipation as he looked down upon the carefully packaged—*lunch?*

What met his eyes and assailed his nostrils was not freshly fried chicken and plump southern biscuits, but a heap of old, wet coffee grounds, broken eggshells, bones, and assorted smelly refuse.

Kristen watched his horrified expression as her mind formed a vision of the delicious food so painstakingly prepared by Mrs. Baxter earlier that morning, resting at that very moment in the Bradley garbage can. The two packages, each so neatly wrapped, had been placed side by side on the kitchen counter, and it was not hard to figure the rest.

Her suppressed laughter caught in her throat, then surfaced like bubbles in a glass of ginger ale, bursting uncontrollably from her lips.

Wes glared at her. "You have a very strange sense of humor." But then, she saw the corners of his mouth begin to twitch, and in moments, he too was laughing heartily.

Jack and Janelle looked on without comprehension, and Janelle's little face began to pucker as she struggled to keep back the tears.

"Never mind, Sweetheart," her father consoled her. "It seems like fate is working against our picnic today. But we won't go home hungry. Let's drive over to Buena Vista and have a nice lunch on the deck of the Pelican."

Kristen tried to look properly remorseful for Janelle's sake but just could not contain the laughter that continued to bubble up from within her.

Explaining to Jack that Mr. Baxter had evidently put their lunch in the garbage can by mistake, leaving his garbage bundle on the table for Wes to pick up, Kristen wiped the moisture from her eyes. Now, even Jack began to laugh, so that in the end, Janelle forgot her disappointment and shared in the hilarity with the grown-ups.

Lunch at the Pelican was delicious and fun, and the lively music lifted the spirits of even little Janelle, as she feasted on lobster and smiled across the table at her father.

"Let's walk across to the center of town and see what Buena Vista looks like on a normal day." Kristen had loved the quaint little town when they were there for the parade, but she still had not explored the shops.

They visited the shell shop, where Kristen called Janelle's attention to a mirror with shells glued all around the edges. "I think you could make one of these for your room."

"Look at this. I could make this too." Janelle picked up a tiny jewelry box covered with small shells.

Wes bought her a craft book that promised directions to make thirty-five beautiful and useful gift items. Janelle was happy, and assured them all that they could look forward to beautiful and useful Christmas presents this year.

Tropical boutiques and small specialty shops lined the streets, but except for Janelle's craft book, they contented themselves with browsing and window-shopping.

They passed the bicycle shop, and Kristen told Jack about their trip to the lighthouse.

At a sidewalk art show, several local artists were at work before their easels. "You should have brought some of yours, Kristen. They're even better," Janelle told her.

"You have an admiring fan, I see," Jack observed.

"I'd say she has quite a few," Wes agreed.

Next stop was the local ice cream shop, where thirty flavors were made on the premises, with an assortment of fruit and gooey toppings to choose from.

Four banana splits later, they headed for home. "Buena Vista is a fun place to visit," Kristen told Jack, "but Gaspar is the best place to come home to."

"I'd have to agree with you, Kristen. It's easy to see how you've formed such a quick attachment to it."

Late in the day, as the sun was setting, the four of them set out for the marina to take Jack back to his car. Kristen walked with him to the parking lot, leaving Janelle and Wes sipping sodas on the marina patio.

"This really is good-bye, Kristen. I don't know when I'll see you again."

"It will never really be good-bye for us, Jack. I'll let you know when I come to visit my parents, and if I'm lucky, you'll come by to see me and tell me all the local news."

" 'Til then," he said huskily as he squeezed her hands in his and turned to go.

She watched him drive away and waved until she could no longer see his car.

Wes and Janelle were waiting for her on the boat. Wes stretched his steady hand to help her aboard.

"He's nice, Kristen. Just the kind of man I would have expected you to choose."

"I—" She almost corrected his mistaken impression before she remembered. "Thank you, Wes. I hoped you would like him."

Back on the island, she did not wait while he secured the yacht. "Want to walk home with me, Janelle?"

"I think I'll wait for Daddy."

Kristen was glad for the time alone, to sort her thoughts and make some sense of her confusion. She had counted on this weekend to resolve a lot of her problems, and in a way, it had. Now she and Jack had verbalized the change in their relationship, but there was no resolution to the deep and painful spear that pierced her heart. If there was ever to be any peace for her, she had to get away from here, from all the daily reminders of Wes Bradley and her hopeless love for him.

As tiring as the day had been, sleep did not come easily to her that night. Mixed emotions seemed to be waging a war within her. When daylight finally dawned, she stayed upstairs with her door closed, trying to blot out the muffled rattle of dishes below, mixed with an occasional burst of little-girl giggles.

It was almost an hour before she finally heard the familiar *toot, toot, toot,* and only then did she go down for breakfast.

Chapter 10

Kristen sat alone on the old wooden pier overlooking the bay and relived the past weekend.

It frightened her to think of how close she had come to revealing her feelings to Wes on his boat Saturday night.

It must have been moon madness, she thought, as she looked up at the almost-full moon.

She had to get away. Make a new beginning and try to put together the shattered pieces of her heart.

She would write a letter to Paula Powell Business College, to begin again to explore the employment market. She'd search for something in another area and try to erase from her mind every little memory of Robert Weston Bradley III. Impossible? Of course. But she had to try, and she had to begin at once.

Engrossed in her own thoughts, she did not see Jeff until he was standing beside her.

"It's almost full again." His eyes lifted to the sky, matching her gaze. "Only two more nights until the full moon. Don't forget our plans."

"I've kept track of the days. I was wondering if you'd remember. Do you think our baby turtles are going to survive?"

"We certainly hope so. I'll keep a lookout on the beach, and as soon as I see any action, I'll come calling at your window like I did before."

Remembering that night, Kristen confessed, "I thought you were out of your mind."

Jeff was such a good friend. He spent as much time at the Spinnaker as his busy schedule allowed, and although she had been shocked to realize that he could read her heart and mind, there was a certain comfort in having at least one person in whom she could confide.

"Why the long face?" he asked. "I see storm clouds on that usually sunny face. And speaking of storms, that's one reason I stopped by. I only have a few minutes, but I wanted to let you know that there's a tropical disturbance just below Cuba. We're watching it pretty carefully in case it continues in this direction."

Afternoon thunderstorms had been a regular occurrence on the beach all summer. They cleared as suddenly as they burst from the clouds. Fierce rolls of thunder and daggerlike flashes of lightning would play across the water like fireworks, accompanied by torrents of pelting rain. Then, in seconds, it seemed, the sun would overpower the cloudburst, and in its wake, the air swept in crisply clean and fresh. Kristen found these storms refreshing and had actually come to enjoy them.

"Why would we be so concerned about a storm in Cuba?"

"Because we're just getting into the hurricane season," he explained. "Sometimes these tropical disturbances escalate in speed and intensity, and there's no way to predict which way they'll turn. But worry at this point is probably premature. I'll keep you posted."

Kristen rose and walked with him to the end of the pier where his boat was anchored. "Thanks for stopping by."

"I wish I could have left you with a smile on your lovely face. Just keep remembering what I told you. It's not over—"

"I know. Until the fat lady sings." This time she did smile, but the ache in her heart remained.

Two nights later, she sat on her upstairs deck at midnight, dressed in her jeans and T-shirt, and watched and waited. The full moon was high in the sky, and it cast a rippling reflection on the gulf waters below. The night air was strangely still.

True to his word, by the brightness of the full moon, Jeff came hurrying up to the house, waving to her as she sat on her second-floor perch. "Hurry up. Get Janelle. It's time to go."

He didn't need to say any more this time. She knew what they were going to do, and excitement sent her running across the hall to Janelle's room.

Shaking the sleeping child gently, she whispered, "Wake up, Darling. It's time to check on our babies."

She only needed to call her once. Janelle had gone to sleep in her clothes in anticipation of Jeff's visit, and in just five minutes from his first call, Jeff's "girls" were joining him on the shore.

Holding hands, they ran down the beach. The night was almost as bright as daylight. As they approached the spot where they had watched the big turtle deposit her eggs, Janelle looked disappointed. "I don't see anything happening!"

"Just watch and listen." Jeff shined his flashlight on the flat sand. The first sign of life was a slight shifting of the sand, barely visible, but unmistakable movement!

A scratching noise and the appearance of little brown claws fighting their way to the surface confirmed that the small baby turtles were indeed cracking

205

out of their round, leathery shells and frantically clawing their way through the fine sand toward a new life.

Kristen felt as though she were witnessing a miracle, as hundreds of little turtles, scarcely two inches long, began to populate the beach and travel toward the sea.

"How do they know which way to go?" Janelle asked.

"It's a natural instinct," Jeff told her. "They never hesitate about which direction to take."

But the little band of fascinated human spectators were not the only ones watching for the turtles' birth. Crabs seemed to appear from everywhere, more than Kristen had ever seen on the beach at one time. They had but one mission, it seemed: baby turtles for dinner!

Janelle screamed at them. "Go away! Go away!" In vain, the three of them kicked at the crabs, clapping and shouting in an attempt to scare away the predators, but their best efforts went unheeded, as many little turtles fell victim to the hungry scavengers.

"I used to like crabs," Janelle wailed, "but not anymore!"

"It's just all part of nature, Janelle." Jeff put his hand on her head. "Just look at all the ones who are making it safely to the water."

As soon as the turtles hit the water, their chances of survival improved, for they were swift little swimmers. They lost no time in heading out to sea.

Janelle walked several feet ahead of them going home, lost in her own thoughts.

"I'm so glad we were able to see the completion of the turtle cycle," Kristen told Jeff. "It's something I'll always remember."

"If you're here next year, you may get to see the same little turtles return as adults, to begin the cycle all over again."

"I'm afraid not," she said sadly. "Janelle's school starts next week. She's flying back to Atlanta on Sunday, and my work here will be over."

"So you'll be putting on your career clothes and stepping back into the famous offices of Bradley, Bradley, and Kline."

"I've been giving that a lot of thought lately. I think not. I need to make a new start, but I don't have it all figured out yet."

Jeff didn't speak for a few moments. Finally, his tone became more serious. "Kristen, don't let stubborn pride make you miss out on a chance for happiness."

"What do you mean?"

"I guess I'm overstepping my boundaries. Good friends do that sometimes. But just don't be afraid to follow your heart," he counseled.

She thought about that as they walked along in silence. Good friends didn't always have to talk, either. Sometimes they could just share the pleasure of understanding and companionship. That's the way it was with them.

At the door, he said, "I didn't want to bring it up before, to spoil our party tonight, but I don't like the looks of that tropical storm. It's moving this way and gathering strength as it passes over the water."

"Well, if it comes, we'll just close everything up tight and wait it out."

"It may not be that simple. But let's not worry about it yet. I just wanted to put you on your guard in case anything develops."

Kristen invited him in. "Let me fix you a cup of coffee before you drive back to the base."

"No, I'll have to take a rain check. Things are pretty busy, and I have to get up early in the morning."

The next day was dark and rainy, and Jeff called her again. "Kristen, that tropical storm has just turned into a full-fledged hurricane—the first of the season. They're calling her 'Amy,' and she seems to be a pretty mean lady."

"Is there anything we should do to be ready?"

"Yes, that's why I called. These things turn most of the time, so you may not need to worry, but it's better to be ready just in case. Bax knows what to do. Just tell him to be sure he has what he needs to board up the windows and secure everything. And fill all your available jugs with clean water."

"I'm not sure he could handle everything by himself." She knew Mr. Baxter was a good carpenter, but he was getting up in years. She didn't want him to get hurt.

"Don't worry about that, Kristen. He knows some teenage boys who live nearby, who are always happy to make a few extra bucks. Just make sure he doesn't wait until the last minute to make arrangements."

The next time the phone rang it was Wes. News of Amy was on all the television broadcasts, and he was watching her movement. "If it even looks like it's headed your way, take Janelle and the Baxters, and get a couple of motel rooms on the mainland. Don't take any chances, Kristen."

She was touched by his concern for his child. "I'll take care of Janelle. And Mr. Baxter will take care of the Spinnaker." Her knees had turned to jelly at the sound of his voice, but she retained her composure and continued in her strictly business tone. "All the fishing boats have come in off the water, so there is a good supply of manpower on the island, and everyone seems eager to help." She gave the receiver to Janelle, who had danced impatiently, waiting for her turn to talk.

All day, people were preparing for the possibility of an emergency. Men with long hooks were pulling coconuts out of the palms. "Why are they doing that?" Kristen asked Mr. Baxter. "I should think there'd be a lot of things more important just now than coconuts."

"They aren't trying to save the coconuts," he explained. "Anything that heavy becomes a lethal projectile when it is picked up by a two-hundred-mile-an-hour wind. Right now they are clocking Amy at 148 miles per hour, and she is still growing."

"Sounds like a bad one." Kristen listened to the wind, which had picked up in the last few minutes.

"Yep. Better pray she turns out toward the sea."

"When will we know if she's going to hit Gaspar?"

"Oh, Honey, there's no way to predict that. Sometimes they twist and turn around and tease you for days. Then other times, they just rush in like a wild boar."

Kristen pulled on her rain gear and helped gather coconuts, piling them into baskets. She worked all morning, collecting loose boards and bottles, bringing in beach chairs and porch furniture, and anything that looked like it could blow in the wind.

The neighborhood boys, under Mr. Baxter's watchful eye, were nailing the shutters over the windows of the Spinnaker.

"How about the crow's nest?" Listening to the nearly howling wind, Kristen thought of those wide plate-glass windows.

Mr. Baxter reassured her again. "Those are double windows of tempered glass. We have storm shutters made to fit them too. The boys will use an extension ladder from the second-floor deck."

"How about Mr. Beardsley? He doesn't seem to have many friends. Will someone help him?"

Mr. Baxter chuckled. "You're right about friends. But, yes, in times of trouble, island people put aside little petty grievances and help each other. I saw some men over there earlier this morning, nailing on his storm shutters. His cottage is small. It won't take long."

"Why don't you call him, just to make sure? I'd be glad to help him if I could, but he doesn't want me near his place."

"You're a fine girl, Kristen. I'll call him right now."

But there would be no more phone calls in or out. Mr. Baxter reported that the phone was dead and that service was probably out on the whole island. "Must be a downed line," he guessed.

By noon, most of the workers were finished. The house was dark as a cave with all the windows boarded up. Mrs. Baxter had been gathering emergency supplies and had them set on the dining room table.

"Let's see. There's candles, matches, jugs of water, our battery radio, canned goods, a manual can opener. . ." She continued to inventory her supplies.

Kristen shed her wet outer garments by the door and sank in a chair to catch her breath. A sudden knock at the front door brought her to her feet.

As she opened the door, the wind caught it and whipped it back all the way. Even covered with his rain slicker, boots, and hat, Kristen could recognize that a uniformed Coastguardsman stood at the threshold.

"Come in out of the weather, and pull that door behind you," she said. He obeyed her instructions, then spoke quickly.

"I just came by, Ma'am, to tell you folks that we're going door-to-door, evacuating the entire island. It looks like Amy's going to hit here by midnight, unless she changes course."

"But our boats have been taken in to the marina. Can the taxi boats handle everyone?" Kristen asked him.

"Don't worry, Ma'am. We have Coast Guard cutters down at the wharf. We'll see that everyone is taken to a shelter." He paused before leaving and asked, "Is your name Kristen Kelly?"

When she nodded, he held out his hand. "Commander Garrett asked me to give you this note."

She reached for the piece of paper and thanked him. She held it under the flashlight and read aloud.

Kristen, don't try any heroics. Just get Janelle and the Baxters down to the wharf and get on the first boat. The bay is getting rougher by the minute. Wes called on the shortwave radio, and he's frantic. I promised him I'd see you all to safety, but right now I just can't get away. I'll try to get by the shelter later to make sure you are all okay. Just leave now!

Your friend, Jeff

"We'd better do as he says," Mr. Baxter told them. "We can't carry much with us. Just put a change of clothes in a beach bag, and get on your raincoats and we'll go. The longer we wait, the worse it will get."

"I'll get my things and some things for Janelle," Kristen volunteered. In the near darkness, she could see that the little girl had fallen asleep on the living room couch. "No need to wake her up until it's time to leave. She's already troubled enough about all this upheaval."

She hurried upstairs and threw a few clothes in her canvas bag. She ran into Janelle's room and grabbed the first things her hands touched, hardly bothering to see what she had. It wasn't important. Jeff told her to leave now, and she didn't want to take any chances where Janelle or the Baxters were concerned. She had given Wes her word that she would take good care of his daughter, and she intended to keep her promise.

Downstairs, the Baxters were ready. Mrs. Baxter carried a small bag, and Mr. Baxter carried Janelle. "I didn't see any reason to wake her up. She's not very heavy."

"I could carry her, part of the way, at least," Kristen volunteered.

"No, indeed. I'm the man of the family today, and I'll get all my ladies safely ashore. Now let's get moving."

It was hard walking against the wind, with the rain pelting down upon them. The wet sand seemed to pull at their feet, and movement was slow. Other people too were making their way toward the pier. In the background, Kristen could hear the loud voice of a Coastguardsman as he shouted through his megaphone. "Complete evacuation of Gaspar Island has been ordered by the United States Coast Guard. Repeat. Mandatory evacuation of Gaspar Island immediately. Transportation is provided from the main pier."

Over and over again, the message was repeated up and down the island. Kristen looked up as she heard the loud roar of helicopter blades chopping the air above. On through the sand they plodded. It had never seemed so far to the bay. Mr. Baxter's face was red, and his breath was coming faster.

"Please, Mr. Baxter, put Janelle down and let her walk. I don't know how she's sleeping through all of this, but we can wake her. She's too heavy for you."

"No, it's quicker this way. It's not much farther."

And it wasn't. As they approached the pier, Kristen saw two large Coast Guard vessels. The first was almost full of people, but they managed to board and find a place on a bench where they could rest.

Kristen didn't like the way Mr. Baxter was breathing, fast and hard, his face flushed from the exertion. Mrs. Baxter was watching him closely, concern written on her face.

"This boat is loaded to capacity," came the announcement. "We will depart momentarily. The second boat will leave in twenty minutes and will have room for all additional evacuees."

As Kristen lifted the sleeping child from Mr. Baxter's arms, Janelle opened her eyes and looked around. "Where are we?" she asked.

"Don't be worried, Janelle," Kristen soothed her. "We're going over to the mainland. Your daddy wants us to leave the Spinnaker before the storm hits." She cuddled the little girl close to her.

Suddenly a wail such as Kristen had never heard poured from the abruptly awakened child. Her eyes wide with terror, she screamed, *"Timmy! We left Timmy!"* and jumped up. It took the three of them to restrain her as she tried to climb out of the boat.

"I'll go back for him," Mr. Baxter offered. "I can get back in time for the second boat."

"No way," Kristen commanded. "I'm a fast runner. You just stay here and take care of Janelle. I'll get Timmy and be back in plenty of time. But Janelle, first you must stop crying and promise to be a good girl for the Baxters. I'll get Timmy and meet you at the shelter."

"I promise," Janelle sobbed penitently. "But hurry, Kristen. He'll be afraid there by himself."

Kristen's legs ached as she ran through the wet sand toward the house. Everyone else was going in the opposite direction, and the second boat was already half loaded. She'd have to hurry. A catch in her side caused her to slow her pace, but persistently she plodded on. Once she reached the wooden walkway, it would be easy to run. She could see it just ahead. In the path, she stumbled, then caught herself. She thought she had moved all the debris from the path. What was this? She was just about to step over the impediment when she heard a low groan. Bending over the dark heap, she realized it was a person!

Alive or dead? She had heard the sound. That was encouraging. She knelt on the soft, soggy ground and lifted the head that was partially submerged in water.

"Mr. Beardsley!"

Chapter 11

He was breathing, but just barely. She would have to run for help. But she couldn't leave him here, his head in the rapidly rising water. He would drown before she could get back to him.

"*Help! Help!*" She screamed with all her might, but her voice was like a gentle hum against the raging wind.

His eyes were open now, and he looked at her intently. "You! Well, don't stop here. Just get on your way while you still can."

"I can't leave you here alone, Mr. Beardsley. We're nearly at the Spinnaker. Let me help you, and we'll try to get you inside."

She tried to lift him in her arms. He was a slight man, and she thought she could manage to carry him, if he would only help a little. As she tried to raise him to his feet, he cried out in pain. "I can't do it, Girl. My leg is broken."

Kristen looked now at the rain-soaked pant leg, and even through the denim cloth, it was obvious from the strange angle of his leg that he was right.

Frantically, she looked around. A small, jagged board lay nearby. The blood on the board and the gaping cut on the old man's forehead told her that this was the wind-borne weapon that had injured him.

Her mind groped for a possible solution. Without a second thought, she whipped off her raincoat and began tearing strips from the bottom of her cotton blouse. It was hard to tear, but she bit and tugged at it until it finally gave way to her determination.

Using the cotton strips and the wayward board, she constructed a makeshift splint. He had lost a lot of blood from his head wound, and he seemed to bounce back and forth between extreme pain and complete disorientation.

"Grace, I knew you'd come for me. I've been waiting for you." He spoke in a trembling voice, then lapsed into unconsciousness again.

"Mr. Beardsley, you've got to help me. We have to get you inside. Then I can go for help."

He seemed to understand as, groaning in pain, he raised himself and let her lift him up on his one good leg. Slowly, painfully, he hobbled along, and using Kristen's thin shoulder as his crutch, he finally, somehow, made it to the door.

Kristen retrieved the key from her pocket and fumbled with the lock. She pulled him over the threshold, where they both collapsed onto the kitchen floor.

"Thank You, God," she murmured.

Automatically, she reached for the light switch, but the room remained in darkness. Of course! No electricity!

Remembering the supplies Mrs. Baxter had laid out on the dining room table, she found matches and candles and soon had a soft glow to work by. She tried the faucet at the sink. No water, either. Then she remembered that they depended on an electric pump for their water.

She pulled a glass bowl from the cabinet and filled it with cool, clean water from one of the jugs on the table. Using a clean dish towel, she began to wipe the grime from the old man's face. She examined his head wound, and although it had bled profusely, it seemed to be superficial. A large knot had risen beneath the cut. She placed a cool compress over his eyes and forehead. "Can you hear me, Mr. Beardsley?"

"Course I can hear you, Girl. I'm not deaf!" His voice was beginning to sound much stronger and more stable. "Look here, I don't know what your game is, but if you've got any sense at all, which I doubt, you'll get yourself down to that dock and get on one of those boats they brought over."

"I'm afraid it's too late for that, Sir. I just heard the final blast of the whistle."

"Then you're just as big a fool as I thought you were. Don't you know there's a hurricane coming?"

"So they say." She gave him a small tolerating smile. "The Spinnaker has come through several hurricanes already, and I feel sure it will weather this one, and us along with it. Now, let's see if we can get you onto the couch."

She knew he had no choice but to do as she directed. For once, she held the upper hand, at least for the moment.

Supporting his body again, she managed to make him as comfortable as possible on the living room sofa, gently placing a pillow beneath his head. "You need medical attention for that leg, Mr. Beardsley. I'm afraid I can't do anything but try to make you comfortable."

Although he had not complained, she saw in his eyes that he was enduring intense pain. "I'll get you some aspirin. I'm afraid it's the strongest thing that I have."

She supported his head with one arm while she gave him the aspirin and a cool drink of water. She covered him with the afghan on the back of the sofa and began to make her plans.

Fortunately, there were enough provisions laid out for them to survive a day or two of isolation. The head wound did not look life threatening, and he seemed to have come out of his delirium, but she didn't like the looks of that leg. Well, she was neither equipped nor trained to do anything about that. They would just have to wait it out until help arrived.

No one would realize she was missing until the second boat arrived and people were taken to the shelter. By the time the Baxters reported her missing, would it be too late to send help?

Mr. Beardsley was dozing, snoring softly. She was thankful for that. She walked to the living room window and peeked through the crack between the storm shutters. The wind had become much stronger, and the tide was rapidly rising. Water was almost up to the front door! The usually calm gulf churned up dark, angry waves as it roared its way to the doorstep. If it rose much higher, it would flood the lower floor of the house. It wouldn't be easy to get Mr. Beardsley to the next level, but they could do it if they had to.

"Girl!"

He didn't sleep long, she thought. She went to him.

"You've got yourself into a real mess, Girl. And all on account of me. I guess I should say 'I'm sorry,' but those kind of words don't come easy for me."

"Never mind, Mr. Beardsley. You don't need to apologize. I've done this of my own free will. We'll get through this. But there is one favor I'd like to ask of you."

"Can't do anything at all. You see my leg. Can't do any favors for you now. But I figured you'd be wanting something. Well, what is it? Money?"

"No, Mr. Beardsley, I don't want money. And I don't want you to do anything that will hurt you. It's just this." She knelt beside him and looked directly into his eyes as she spoke. "I have a name, Mr. Beardsley. My name is Kristen. I'd truly appreciate it if you'd use it when you speak to me."

"Hmmph. Never heard of such a name."

"Well, it's mine. My parents gave it to me when I was born, and I intend to use it for life. So, if you don't mind, please call me Kristen from now on." With that, she rose from the floor and took some of her supplies into the kitchen.

She emptied the contents of a can of chicken soup into a small pan and lit the spirit lamp with her matches. When the soup was hot, she divided it into two bowls. On a plastic tray, she placed a stack of crackers and a banana beside the bowl of hot soup.

When she took it to him, he mumbled, "Thank you," but he didn't call her anything. She brought her own tray into the living room, and they ate in silence.

Then she remembered the battery radio. "Let's just hope this thing works," she said, tuning it to the local station. It crackled and popped, and for a moment she thought it would not respond.

She was about to turn it off when, through the static, she could discern the words of the announcer. "We bring you this word from the National Hurricane Service. Amy, the first hurricane of the season, and one of the worst in recent history, appears headed for the west coast of Florida. With winds up to 158 miles per hour, and gaining intensity as it passes over water, all barrier islands and coastal residents have been evacuated. It is expected that, continuing on its present course, the storm will strike the mainland in the Englewood area about midnight. Storm warnings are posted as far north as Tampa."

"Where is Englewood, Mr. Beardsley?"

"Just up the road a few miles. If that man's right, we'll be smack-dab in the path of the hurricane."

"Have you ever stayed out here during a hurricane before?"

"Sure, several of them. But never one this fierce. Nobody in his right mind would stay out here during this. I'm afraid we've got trouble, Gir—Kris—what's that name again?"

She smiled. He was really trying to be pleasant for a change. "Kristen."

She took the dirty dishes to the kitchen and washed them in only about a cup of her preciously hoarded water. With so much water everywhere around them, it was ironic that she should be so concerned about their limited supply.

Her concern changed to alarm when she saw that water was now seeping in the front door and soaking the living room carpet. The pounding of the waves against the house sounded as though giant sandbags were being thrown against it. It was going to get worse before it got better. She would have to take action.

"Mr. Beardsley, we are going to have to get you up the stairs to the next level. I know it's going to be painful, but we've no choice."

"I can see that. Well, it's a slow process, so we'd better get moving, Christine."

"Kristen."

"Whatever."

In spite of the seriousness of their predicament, she couldn't help but smile. She was impressed by his brave efforts as she helped him up the stairs. She knew that the pain must be excruciating, and yet he said nothing, except for barely audible groans each time he moved the broken leg.

As gently as she could, she eased him onto Wes's big bed. Then she proceeded to bring her emergency supplies up to the second floor.

It took several trips, and by the time she finished, she paused to catch her breath.

"It's a good thing we did that," she told him. "The water is already a foot deep all through the house."

She gave him two more aspirins and sat in a chair at the foot of his bed. "Your family will be worried about you, won't they?" she asked him.

"Don't have any family."

"None at all? Weren't you ever married?"

"Yep. I was married to Grace for forty-five years. When she died, so did I."

"I'm sorry, Mr. Beardsley. You must have loved her a great deal. But you never had any children?"

He didn't answer for several minutes, and she thought he hadn't heard her. Had he dropped off to sleep again?

"No. No children. At least, not any that I count."

"What do you mean? Did you have a child that died?"

"No, but she's dead to me. I don't ever want to see her again."

"I can't believe that, Mr. Beardsley. Would you tell me about it?"

Again, he was silent for a long time. Then he began to speak softly. "Dorothy was her name. When she was born, I thought she was the most beautiful little girl I had ever seen. Her mother and I loved her, and I thought she loved us too. I sure was wrong about that!"

"What makes you think that Dorothy doesn't love you?" She was asking questions that she knew he didn't have to answer, but at least she was getting his mind off the pain of his broken leg.

"When her mother died, we were living in Englewood. We came out here for weekends and vacations and just about every chance we had. That's why I wanted to move out here when Grace died. Seemed to be closer to her, somehow."

"Well, I don't see—"

"Dorothy—she was eighteen then—wanted the house in Englewood, with all her mother's things. I didn't want any strangers in there, so I just gave it to her."

"That was very generous. Did she appreciate it?"

"I thought she did. At first she lived in it while she was going to college. She could commute. And she kept inviting me for dinner, and then one day just about the time she finished college, she up and told me she was getting married."

"And did you like her fiancé?" Kristen kept looking for the missing piece of the puzzle that would explain his anger at his daughter.

"Oh, sure. He was okay. I thought they would set up housekeeping right there in our little house. It had everything they needed."

"So they married and lived in the house you had given her?"

"For about a year. Then one day she up and tells me her husband has taken a job in Louisiana, and she's selling the house."

"And you didn't want her to go?"

"She could go wherever she wanted, but she had no business selling that house that had been our home all those years. She tried to give me the money, but I wouldn't take it. I wasn't about to take money for that house."

"Did she become angry with you?"

"No. Said she wasn't. But I told her the day she let strangers have that house was the day she would be dead to me. I told her I didn't ever want to see her again, and I don't."

Kristen was shocked by what she had just heard. She thought of her own parents, and how tolerant and understanding they were. They hadn't approved of her decision to leave home, either, but they had supported and loved her just the same.

She told him then about her own life and about how much she appreciated the understanding she had received. "I think you should seriously reconsider your attitude, Mr. Beardsley. You are missing out on so much of life. Why, you could be enjoying your grandchildren instead of growing old and bitter alone." Perhaps she shouldn't have said that. She spoke without thinking. Now he'd probably quit talking to her at all.

Her thoughts were interrupted by a crash of glass from below. "What was that? The windows are all boarded up."

"From the sound of that wind, I'd say a shutter probably blew off. Look, Gir—Kristen. Go in yonder and open up the window a crack in the east bedroom."

"*Open a window! Are you mad?*" She wondered if the delirium was coming back.

"The wind is coming from the west. You need to equalize the pressure in the house. Just do like I tell you, and maybe no more windows will blow out."

Apprehensively, she did as she was told. He had a lot of experience with hurricanes, and she had none.

She turned on the little radio again.

"The National Hurricane Service reports that Amy is approaching the barrier islands off the west coast of Florida. Tides are ten feet above normal and rising rapidly. Wind velocity is 165 miles per hour. Hurricane warnings extend northward to Jacksonville. Small craft warnings are in effect up the entire eastern seaboard as far north as Savannah, Georgia. Stay tuned for the latest news on Hurricane Amy."

She switched off the radio and went back to check on her patient. She didn't want to alarm him with the news.

The wind now sounded like a giant freight train bearing down upon them. The constant roar was accompanied by spasmodic pounding upon the house, as flying debris seemed to be striking the house every few minutes. It was terrifying.

She took her candle and held it at the top of the steps. The water had risen now, almost to the second floor. Whatever could they do? Nothing. They had done all that they could. There was nothing to do now but pray and wait.

Sitting beside his bed in the rocking chair, she listened to his even breathing. Thank goodness he was able to get a little sleep from time to time. Sitting in the semidarkness with only the candle glow, she drifted into a light sleep herself. When she awoke a short time later, she listened in wonder. The wind had died down to a moderate gale. She heard the old man stir.

"Oh, Mr. Beardsley, we made it. God has answered our prayers in a wonderful way! The hurricane is over. Just listen to the stillness outside." She was elated. "And just in time too. Look, the water has already risen to the second floor. Our carpet is soaked. But we made it! We survived!"

"Not so fast, Girl—er—Kristen. It's far from over. We're in the eye right now."

"The eye? What's that?"

"Why, that's the very middle of the storm. It whirls around and around, and directly, we'll get it from the other side. Go now, and close that window, and put a crack in the one on the west side before she hits again."

"Oh, no!" She wailed in disappointment, but she went to do as he instructed. "I thought it was over."

The ominous silence surrounded them for at least thirty minutes before they heard it begin again. Now the giant waves were pounding against their second-story windows, and Kristen knew it was only a matter of time before the room would be flooded. They would drown unless they could do something.

Mr. Beardsley knew it too. "Go on up to the crow's nest quick, Kristen. It's your only hope. I can't make it, but I've been doing a lot of thinking, and I need you to do something for me."

"What can I do to help you, Mr. Beardsley?"

"Well, if you get out of this alive, I want you to call Dorothy." He paused, and she could tell that it was a very difficult thing for him to say. "I don't want to die without letting her know. I reckon I owe her that much."

"Well, you're not going to die if I can help it. You're going up into the crow's nest too. If there's a way to get out of this thing alive, we'll find it together."

She put as many supplies as she could in a backpack. She knew that if they made it to the crow's nest alive, she wouldn't tempt fate by trying to make two trips.

The French doors leading onto the outer deck were securely boarded. She opened the doors and began hammering against the shutters with a big boot she found in Wes's closet. It seemed hopeless at first, but gradually one of the shutters began to creak. Fortunately, the wind was coming from the east now, so she was able to push open the shutter.

They were wading through several inches of water as she helped Jake Beardsley through the door. They would have to walk several yards to the staircase and get up those stairs without being blown away.

As soon as they stepped into the open, the old man was nearly swept from her arms. She lost her balance and they both fell.

"Crawl!" she commanded. And he did, dragging his broken leg across the deck. The wind and the waves lashed against their bodies as they slowly made their way to the staircase.

"You go first," Kristen ordered. "Use the handrails for crutches."

Grimacing in pain, he slowly pulled himself up the stairs, with Kristen right behind him. She had to hold on to the rails with all her strength to keep from being swept away. Debris sailed through the air, and Kristen prayed that they would not be hit.

Fortunately, the door to the crow's nest did not have any glass panes, so it had not been boarded. It was not even locked. She reached over his shoulder and opened the door. The force of the wind propelled them into the room and nearly blew the door off the hinges as it hit the inside wall. Rain poured in, and they had to press the full weight of both their bodies against the door to close it.

They sank to the floor and rested. They had no radio now—Kristen could only carry a limited amount, and water had seemed the most important thing.

She remembered seeing some candles in the drawer when she and Janelle were up here painting. Rummaging around in the dark, she found three candles and a book of matches.

After she lit a candle, she helped Mr. Beardsley onto the couch and took inventory of her supplies. A jug of water, aspirin tablets, a box of crackers, a couple of apples and bananas. That was all. Well, neither of them felt like food, anyway. She found a glass in the bathroom and filled it with water for the strange little man. "We made it this far. How much longer do you think it will last?"

"There's no way to tell. Sometimes they turn around and come right back over where they've been. We'll just have to wait and see."

The dark crow's nest was shaking from the fierce winds, and Kristen wondered if it would be blown away. If this was to be her last day on earth, she wished that just once she had let Wes know how much she loved him. Even if he didn't love her in return, she wanted him to know.

The walls were trembling and heaving, and it seemed as though the whole structure would topple at any minute. Suddenly a crash louder than any they had heard before, and a cracking sound like splintering wood, rocked the crow's nest and sent Kristen teetering over to the north window beside the door.

Through the crack in the shutters she soon saw what had happened. The twisted framework of the stairway that led to the crow's nest had been ripped from the wall and caught in the wind like a giant glider, spinning into the raging sea. Now they were really stranded! Even if they survived the hurricane, there was no way to get down to the deck below. Through the night, they waited and prayed, and as they prayed, Kristen felt a warm peace settle in her heart. They had done everything they could humanly do, and now it was all in God's hands.

When had the wind died down? Had she been asleep? It was blowing, but not with the howling force of a few hours ago. The candle had burned itself out, but a flicker of light peeked through the cracks of the shutters. Kristen went to the door. Dare she open it a crack? She remembered how hard it had been to close it once the wind grabbed hold.

Slowly, she opened it just an inch. Daylight was breaking, although the sun was veiled by clouds. Waves lapped hungrily over the deck below, and the wind had not given up. But this was no hurricane! Had they survived, or was this another eye?

"Mr. Beardsley, look!"

He opened his eyes, and for the first time ever, Kristen saw him smile. Why, he had a rather pleasant face!

"Looks like we made it," he said. "But it'll be awhile before the water goes down enough for us to get out of here. Looks like you'll have to put up with me for awhile longer!"

Oh, they could joke about it now. Wasn't life wonderful? "Do you think they'll send a rescue party for us?" she asked.

"How can they? They don't know where we are. If we're missed at all, they'll probably think we fell off the boat. No one will think to look up here."

When she thought about it, she knew that he was right. Still, there had to be some way. An idea began to take shape. She went to the window and tugged at the sheer curtain until it tore loose from the rod and fell at her feet.

"What are you up to now, Girl?" He didn't even apologize for that last word.

She tied the limp fabric to the inside knob of the front door, letting most of its filmy length hang outside but catching it securely in the closed door. The rain soaked it at once, but it blew out like a giant white flag. "Maybe someone will notice that!" she said.

"Who's to see?" he asked logically. "There won't be any boats out today." She hadn't thought of that.

Their breakfast of crackers, bananas, and water seemed like a feast. With their fears diminished, they were suddenly ravenous.

"Mr. Beardsley, I haven't forgotten what you told me about Dorothy, and I hope you won't forget, either. We both should realize that life is too short to let love pass us by. It's given me some insights too."

Before he could answer, they were surrounded by a great roaring noise. "Oh no, the storm again," she cried. "It's coming back!" Her eyes widened with fright.

"No, no. It won't come back. Go look out the door."

Kristen ran to the door and opened it wide, unmindful of the rain that washed in. There in the sky above her was the most beautiful gray helicopter she had ever seen. She couldn't see who was in it, but she could plainly see the big white letters that said, UNITED STATES COAST GUARD. That was all she needed to know.

Chapter 12

She watched the big gray bird hover over them and slowly lower its basket level with the door. Its sole occupant, a uniformed Coastguardsman, grinned at her from his swinging perch.

"I'll need you to give me a hand, Lady," he said, as his basket lurched this way and that.

Kristen reached out and grabbed the edge of the basket as it swung by, its weight nearly pulling her out of the door. The young man jumped through the doorway, knocking Kristen backward onto the floor. "Sorry, Ma'am."

Kristen could have hugged him. "You're a welcome visitor!"

"Well, the two of you get into the basket, one at a time. I'll hold it steady. Then my friend up there will pull us up." He looked over at Mr. Beardsley. "Come on, Friend, it's time to go."

"Oh, Mr. Beardsley can't do that. I'm afraid he's rather badly injured," Kristen explained. "I'm pretty sure his leg is broken, and he has a head injury too. What can we do?"

"We'll need to bring the medical rescue helicopter in here for him and get him out on a stretcher. But you can come with us now. We'll take you to safety and send help for him right away."

"No, I can't leave him here by himself. You go on ahead and send help, and when the rescue team arrives, we'll both go together. Alone, he's completely helpless."

"Well, Ma'am, I don't even think they will let you go in the rescue unit with him. The stretcher takes up most of the space, and what's left is for the medical technicians. You'd better come on now while you have the chance."

But Kristen was determined. They had made it this far together, and she would not desert him now. "Then you can send someone for me after the rescue team picks him up. I'm *not* leaving here until I see him taken care of."

Mr. Beardsley had been listening in silence, but now he spoke up. "You're being foolish again, Gir—Kristen. I told you before to go while you could, and you didn't listen to me, and see what a mess you got yourself into? Now, *go!*"

But of course, she didn't. She couldn't. This poor old man had been languishing in pain for nearly twenty-four hours with scarcely a complaint. She couldn't go away and leave him here alone.

"All right, Lady. You're the boss. But I don't know how long this will take." He was reluctant to leave her there. "The medical units have been answering calls all night long, but we'll do the best we can to get back to you as soon as possible." He reached into his jacket pocket and pulled out two candy bars and gave them to her. It was all he had with him. "Please, reconsider and come with me."

"No, but thanks for everything. We'll be fine here until help comes, now that we know you've found us."

He grabbed the basket and vaulted in without assistance, and in minutes, the basket was raised and the chopper went sailing through the sky.

"You did a foolish thing," Mr. Beardsley told her.

She didn't answer him, but set about washing his face and giving him his aspirin, with a glass of the cool, precious water. "That bump on your head needs attention," she said. "Your leg too. I hope they hurry back."

Weak from shock and hunger, she sat on the floor beside him. "About Dorothy, you asked me to call her. Where does she live?"

"That was just if I died."

"But we didn't die, did we? And now that we have a new chance at life, let's make the most of it. Agreed?"

"She still lives in Louisiana. Writes to me about once a month, but I never read them. Send them back unopened."

Kristen tried to find words that would show the stubborn, inflexible old man how unreasonable he was being, and how he was actually the victim of his own vicious attitudes. She thought of the hurting young woman who was his daughter, and realized how much she must long for his love.

Without preamble, she spoke the words that came into her mind. " 'Forgetting what is behind and straining toward what is ahead, I press on toward the goal. . .' That's from the Bible, you know. It's in Philippians." She watched him for reaction, and saw none.

Then suddenly he surprised her. "You're right, for once. I came to see that while I was watching you do all those things for me."

"What things?"

"Why, you saved my life. You know that. And I know I've been cantankerous with you. So if you can lay all that aside and help me the way you did, I guess I ought to be able to lay aside a few things myself."

Even in her weakened state, a spontaneous smile spread across her face. "I'm so glad, Mr. Beardsley. Imagine how happy Dorothy is going to be when you call her. I wish I could meet her someday."

"I'm not so sure she's going to be all that happy. After all the things I've said to her, she probably won't even want to hear from me now."

Kristen took his bony, wrinkled hand in hers. "Recently, I told a friend that love remembers the beautiful things about a person and lays aside the rest. Dorothy must love you very much, and I'm sure you've hurt her. But it's not too late to tell her you're sorry and that you love her."

Kristen thought about the strange friendship that had developed between the two of them. What an unlikely pair! They had started out as adversaries, but tragedy had brought them together and made them friends. He said she had saved his life, and she supposed that she had, but hadn't he helped her too? His knowledge of hurricanes had kept her from going out to a certain death during the eye of the storm, and he knew how to equalize the pressure in the house so that the windows didn't implode. Quite possibly, he had saved her life as well.

Patiently they waited now, sure that help was on the way. Weak and tired, they spoke few words, saving their remaining strength for the rescue operation ahead. Kristen breathed a silent prayer of thanksgiving for the miracle of their survival and for the equally miraculous change of heart in her new friend, Jake Beardsley.

It was midafternoon before the medical rescue team arrived. The water had receded enough to let the helicopter drop the workers and their equipment directly onto the second-floor deck. The efficient team of workers erected a ladder, giving them entry into the crow's nest, and from there on, everything went smoothly.

The two technicians went to work on Jake Beardsley at once, giving him emergency treatment and stabilizing him for the trip ahead.

In his semiconscious state, he seemed scarcely aware of his surroundings but rallied enough to express his concern for her.

"Take care of Kristen," he instructed the medics, and she beamed.

Gently he was put on a stretcher and raised into the hovering machine.

The female technician handed Kristen a canvas bag. "There are some provisions in here. Your rescue chopper will be along very shortly. I'm sorry we can't accommodate you on the medical unit, but you won't have long to wait."

"It's all right." Kristen smiled as she gratefully took the bag. "Just take good care of my friend, and tell him I'll visit him soon."

"We're transporting him to the hospital in Punta Gorda. My guess is that they'll keep him a few days, so you'll have plenty of time to visit him. Goodbye and good luck!"

Kristen watched them soar into the sky and felt a great burden lifted from her shoulders. She knew that Mr. Beardsley was in competent hands now and would live to make his peace with Dorothy.

Kristen opened the bag and found the best sandwiches she had ever tasted in her entire life. And the juice was wet and sweet. As her eyes grew heavy, she stretched out on the couch, pulling the soft afghan over her damp, chilled body. For the first time since the ordeal had begun, she felt safe and secure as she drifted into a peaceful, dreamless sleep.

Wes Bradley slammed his fist down on his massive oak desk in dire frustration. All the phone lines in southwestern Florida were out, and all commercial air flights into the area had been grounded.

"Can't you find anything into Tampa? I could rent a car and drive from there."

"We've tried every airline, Mr. Bradley," his secretary assured him. "Nothing is flying into Florida at this time."

"Try the private charter lines, then. Surely there's someone who can get me in there."

His eyes were bloodshot from lack of sleep, and his hands shook from the seemingly gallons of coffee he had drunk during the night.

Thank goodness for the shortwave radio operators. He had been able to learn of Janelle's safety. The Baxters would care for her well until he could get there. But Kristen. Where was Kristen? A check of all the shelters failed to turn up her name. Her car had not been removed from the parking garage. The last time she was seen was on Gaspar Island, running back toward the house. According to reports, she had plenty of time to get back to the dock before the last boat left, so what had happened to her?

He knew well the fury of hurricanes, even in their earliest stages, and how dangerous it could be to go out in one. His mind pictured flying debris and rising water, as his thoughts tortured him through the night.

If anything happened to Kristen, he didn't know what he would do. It had taken him a long time to realize how much he loved her, but he knew now beyond a doubt that without her, the rest of his life would be meaningless.

Of course, she would never be completely his. She had told him that she loved someone else. Probably Jack—lucky guy! But he would at least see that she was well treated. Pity the person who ever tried to harm her, if he knew anything about it! She was the loveliest woman on earth, and he had failed to see it until it was too late.

"Mr. Bradley." His secretary interrupted his thoughts. "No one, absolutely no one, is willing to fly into that weather. What's more, they say that most of the roads into that area are closed because of downed trees and high water."

He slumped over the desk. "Thank you, Sara." He looked at her.

Sara was as tired as he was. She had come to love Kristen like a sister when the two of them had worked together. She had stayed at his office all night, frantically trying to help him get through to the disaster area.

Now he told her, "You go on home, Sara, and get some sleep. It's not even daylight yet. I'm going to get my car and head out in that direction. I'll go as far as I can, and maybe somehow I can get through."

"But you can't drive now. You haven't had any sleep," she protested.

"I'll be okay." He couldn't sleep now if he tried.

Streaking down the wet, deserted interstate in his black Mercedes, he drove as fast as he dared and hoped he wouldn't get stopped by the highway patrol. He didn't have time for that now.

Like a madman, he drove without stopping, passing little Georgia towns sprinkled along the highway. Not until he reached the Gainesville, Florida, exit did he stop.

Sitting at a lunch counter, he ordered grits and eggs. It was the first food he had taken time to eat in nearly twenty-four hours, yet it all tasted like cardboard. He ate quickly, as though it were a job to get done, paid the cashier, and was about to get in his car when he remembered that this was Kristen's hometown.

The telephone directory listed numerous Kellys. He tried six before he reached her home.

"No," said her mother, her voice heavy with worry. "We've been hoping to get some word, but we've heard nothing. The news said that Gaspar Island was completely covered with ten feet of water, but that they had evacuated all the residents, so we feel sure that Kristen is safe in one of the shelters. The phone lines are all down, so she can't get word to us, but I know she will call when she can."

So they didn't know even as much as he did. And lucky they didn't. He wouldn't tell them that she was missing. No need alarming them until it was necessary. But he knew that chances of finding her alive were slim. No one could have survived on the island in that hurricane! His only hope was that she had been able to come ashore and find shelter somewhere.

Tampa was as far as he could drive. Beyond that point, all roads were closed. He had seen plenty of signs of destruction already. He couldn't even imagine how bad it must be farther south.

The day was cloudy and gusty, but the hurricane had crossed the state and blown itself out into the Atlantic. It had diminished in intensity as it traveled over the land and was no longer a threat as it continued to break up over the waters of the ocean.

Wes turned his car into the Tampa International Heliport. He knew several of the fellows there.

"Hi, Kevin. I need your help."

"Man, what happened to you? You look like something the cat dragged in!"

"Thanks!" Wes slapped him on the back. "I need transportation in a hurry."

"I'm your man. Where are we going?"

"Over to Gaspar Island. We'll need to cover the whole island as low as possible to see if there's any sign of life."

"Let's go, then. I'll get suited up. But from what I hear, I don't think you're going to like what you find."

"First, let me use your shortwave set. I need to see if there's been any word yet."

It was difficult to get through to the Coast Guard station because everything was jammed with emergency calls, but finally Wes heard Jeff's weary voice over the static-filled wire.

"I wish I had some encouraging news for you, Wes. We have our choppers out there now covering all the barrier islands, searching for any possible survivors. As soon as they report back, I'll be able to give you a more up-to-the-minute picture, but on the surface, things look very bad."

"Any chance Kristen is somewhere on the mainland?"

The set crackled as Jeff's voice came back over the air. "We've checked every shelter and have turned up nothing. Some of the people who came over on the last boat know her, and no one remembers seeing her get on the boat."

Wes's heart sank as he broke the connection and followed Kevin out onto the heliport pad. The helicopter rocked back and forth in the wind as the blades roared and lifted the two of them into the air.

At the first sight of the island, his despair hit a new low. Utter devastation was everywhere. Big old trees were turned with their roots pointed toward the sky. Houses had been ripped from their pilings like toy game pieces. In the tallest surviving pine trees, Wes saw articles of clothing caught in the highest branches, tattered rags waving like sinister flags signaling disaster. Piers that had held fast to their pilings through many previous storms over the years were twisted and torn and flung about the island like Tinkertoys.

As the pilot skillfully guided them up the coastline, Wes strained to see what was left of the Spinnaker. He was almost afraid to look. But yes, there it stood like a proud sentinel. He could just make out the outline of the crow's nest. It was one of the few remaining structures on the island that stood upright, but it brought little joy to his heavy heart.

"That's my place over there," he shouted over the loud chopping of the copter blades. "Drop down as low as you can and hover over it so I can see what the damage looks like." He didn't even voice his silent hope, because he knew how foolish it would seem in the face of this destruction.

Suddenly he jerked his body forward, striking his head against the roof. "What's that?" Something was flying from the door of the crow's nest. Something white, like a flag.

"Looks like one of the curtains came loose and flew partway out the window. Beats me how it could have done that after the storm. It's a cinch it wasn't there during the storm."

Excited now, Wes was trembling. "Can you lower me down there?"

"Are you crazy, Man? Sure, I could, but—"

"Well, do it! Just do it!"

Kristen was awake, but she didn't want to open her eyes. Not when she was having such a deliciously lovely dream. Wes was there, holding her in his arms and saying her name over and over again.

Slowly and reluctantly she opened her eyes, but the dream didn't disappear. Wes was there, bending over her, cradling her in his arms, tears rolling down his unshaven cheeks.

"Wes. Is this real? Am I awake? How did you get here?"

"Don't you ever run out of questions?" he asked. "My darling Kristen. You're alive and safe, and that's all I asked for."

She still couldn't believe this was happening, not even when his mouth sought hers in an anything but brotherly fashion. Real or not, it was wonderful. She wrapped her arms about his neck and responded with a fervor equal to his own.

When he finally let her breathe again, she said, "Oh, Wes. You came for me."

"Kristen, I never want to let you go. I know you don't love me in the way that I love you, but that's okay. At least I want you to know how I feel. I've loved you for a very long time, even before I knew it myself. I know that you're in love with Jack, and I'll have to accept that. But as long as I know you're safe and happy, I can learn to live with that."

She drew back from him and eyed him quizzically. "How did you come to decide that I'm not in love with you?"

"Because you told me yourself. You said that there was someone else you loved very much. Don't you remember telling me that?"

She broke into a broad grin. This was the happiest, most magical day of her life. The miracles just kept pouring out upon her. If this was a dream, so be it. She hoped she would never wake up.

"You didn't listen very well," she said. "I told you that there was a special man in my life whom I love very much. But I never told you there was someone *else!*"

Slowly, as realization began to dawn upon him, a look of pure incredulity spread across his face. "Are you saying that you do love *me?*"

"More than anything else in the world."

"And you'll marry me and share a lifetime together?" He had trouble taking it all in.

"Oh, Wes, whatever years God grants us both, I want to share with you, and stay with you forever."

This time, when he held her tenderly in his arms and kissed her long and with passion, she was sure that she heard the beautiful ringing of a hundred bells. And not only that. She knew for certain that the fat lady had finally sung!

Epilogue

"Janelle, would you hand me that hammer, please?" Kristen called from the small stepladder. "I want to get this picture hung in the dining room before our guests arrive."

Janelle ran to get the hammer from the table and stretched to give it to Kristen. "I love that picture! It's my favorite one of our wedding."

Kristen smiled. Our wedding! She and Wes had included Janelle in every facet of the wedding preparations, and now almost a year later, all three of them still spoke of it as "our wedding." The picture showed the newlyweds side by side, with a smiling Janelle nestled happily between them.

"Kristen!" Wes's voice boomed from the doorway. "Honey, what are you doing up on that ladder? Here, let me do that!"

"It's done," Janelle told him. "Kristen and I are going outside now to cut some flowers for our party tonight."

"Just don't cut any sea oats," Wes teased, and was rewarded with a playful jab of his wife's elbow.

"Bax, come and help me put another leaf in this table," Martha Baxter called. "I declare, I don't know where we're going to put all these people!" But her smiling countenance dispelled any doubt that she was delighted with the festive preparations.

"We keeping adding guests, don't we?" Kristen admitted, counting them on her fingers. "We started out with just Jeff Garrett and his new girlfriend, but of course, when we found out that Jake Beardsley was in Englewood with his daughter and her family, we couldn't miss inviting them to come too."

"I'll sure be glad to see Jake again," Bax admitted. "Maybe we'll have time for a game of checkers after dinner."

"You'll be seeing more of him soon," Wes told him. "I talked with Dorothy yesterday. She and her husband have already started ordering the materials to rebuild Jake's cottage on the island for him."

"I can't wait to see little Jacob," Janelle said. "Miss Dorothy said when I get just a little older, I can baby-sit whenever she comes to the island to visit her dad."

"That makes thirteen," Kristen counted, running out of fingers, "and the Michaels and their daughter, Kori, make sixteen. That's a nice even number."

"I haven't met the Michaels yet," Martha Baxter said, "but from everything I hear, they're wonderful people."

"They're special people," Kristen confirmed. "As soon as they heard about the chapel Wes is building near the point, Reverend Michael offered to come over every Sunday afternoon and conduct a worship service for the island residents."

"And Kristen and I are going to have a Sunday school for the kids," Janelle added, "and Kori said she'd help. I can't wait. How much longer before the chapel's finished, Daddy?"

"As soon as possible, Honey. We've lined up lots of volunteer labor, but the first priority is getting all the homes restored after the damage last summer by Hurricane Amy. The barges stay busy all day bringing lumber and supplies to the island, and all the available carpenters are working from daylight to dusk. In fact, we're going to need a little more work done here at the Spinnaker."

Mrs. Baxter was on her way to the kitchen when she caught Wes's remark. She whipped around and raised her eyebrows. "More work done here? I thought we had everything back to normal. You aren't going to make this place any bigger, are you?"

Wes laughed. "No, not exactly."

Kristen grinned, and Janelle jumped up and down like a jumping jack. "Can I tell now? Can I tell?"

"Sure," Wes and Kristen agreed in unison. "Go ahead and tell them, Janelle."

"We're going to make a nursery! I'm going to have a little brother, and his room is going to be right across from mine, where Kristen used to stay, and I'm going to get to hold him when he's brand-new, and I get to help pick out a name for him, and—"

"Whoa," her father interrupted, laughing. "Slow down, Janelle! You're going to jump a hole in the floor! And there's one thing you need to remember."

"What, Daddy?" Janelle continued to jump up and down, bubbling over with her excitement.

"Your new brother might turn out to be a little sister. What if that happens? Will we keep her anyway?"

"Oh, Daddy," Janelle said. Standing between Kristen and Wes, she smiled up into their faces and clasped their hands. "Of course we'll keep her. She's part of our family!"

MUNCY G. CHAPMAN

Muncy has four children who magically became eight (i.e., their spouses), and then was blessed with eleven grandchildren. All live in Florida. She says she is married to the most wonderful man in the world with whom she recently celebrated their golden wedding anniversary. Muncy likes to sew, cook, play the piano, and of course, write. She works with the children in her church, and also with the shut-ins as a "Caring Caller." She enjoys writing with her husband. He likes the research, and she likes choosing the words.

Summer Place

Peggy Darty

Chapter 1

W e have a story just breaking at the courthouse!"
Brad Wilson's announcement captured the attention of the
staff in the WJAK television newsroom.

"Is it the Blake Taylor story?" someone yelled.

Suddenly everyone was speculating again over the controversial trial. Was Blake Taylor, one of the most prominent developers in Florida, really a diamond thief? And when he had the money to buy the evidence that had been found in his home, why would he steal it? Or had he been framed by one of the competitors who had been irate over losing a million-dollar development to him, as the defense claimed?

The trial had stretched on for weeks, while the city of Seabreeze buzzed with gossip. From the third desk back, Mary Kate Moore jumped to her feet, unable to endure the suspense.

"Well, tell us!" she cried.

All eyes shot to the petite woman who was flicking a strand of dark hair over her shoulder. The navy sailor dress swirled about her slim ankles, further minimizing her slender, five-three frame.

Ignoring the stares of the more contained reporters, Mary Kate's gold-flecked brown eyes widened on the news director's face, imploring him to answer.

"Not guilty!" he finally reported, after holding his audience captive for a few tense seconds.

His reply was met by a moment of stunned silence. Then suddenly everyone was talking at once. How had Blake Taylor gotten off when the evidence had been found in his home? Was it the slick attorney, or had he really been framed?

Brad Wilson bounded across the room to Mary Kate's desk.

"Take crew three and get over there." He raked a nervous hand through his thinning brown hair. "There's another crew inside the courthouse getting interviews. Just try to get the reaction of the man on the street. And hurry."

"Right!" Mary Kate scrambled around her desk, grabbing a pen and pad. "Thanks, Brad," she added quickly, ignoring the envious gazes of other reporters as she stuffed the pen and pad into her large navy shoulder bag and made a dash for the back door.

"She doesn't know how to walk," someone commented. "She always goes in a run."

"Maybe that's why she gets the stories," Brad replied with a caustic grin.

The words echoed in Mary Kate's ears as she reached the corridor, tossing a doubtful glance toward the closed doors of the elevator, then opting for the stairway instead.

"I get the stories because I work harder," she mumbled, flying down three flights of stairs and pushing the back door open. She blinked into the sudden glare of Florida's noonday sun as she headed across the parking lot. Seabreeze was located only ten miles from the ocean, and the balmy breezes drifted to the town, allowing a measure of relief on this hot day in August.

In the distance, the motor was already warming on the WJAK van, while Coty Brakefield stood loading the camera and Tom Allen worried over the sound equipment.

An amused grin tilted the corners of Mary Kate's pert mouth as she regarded the two men, so different in size and temperament, yet perfectly paired to orchestrate camera and sound into successful news coverage.

"Ready?" Coty's deep voice rumbled over the parked cars, his hazel eyes widening in his bearded face.

"Not guilty, can you believe it?" Mary Kate called in answer as she hurried across to the van, her gaze flicking over the big man dressed in khaki slacks and a loose T-shirt.

"Seabreeze is really buzzing," Tom informed them, folding trailing wires into the backseat. The smaller man, dressed more conservatively in dark pants and a plaid sports shirt, was checking out his equipment one last time.

"Come on, guys. Hurry." Mary Kate climbed into the van. "But of course I don't have to tell *you* to hurry." She grinned at Coty. The gold flecks danced in her brown eyes as she glanced back at Tom jumping into the backseat.

"And no one has to tell *you* how to talk," Coty shot back, starting up the van and whipping the wheel around to make a U-turn. In seconds, they were roaring out of the parking lot.

"As long as she looks good on the tube, no one cares." Tom hung over the seat. "But you'd better brush your hair," he prompted under his breath.

"Give me time, Tom." She glanced over her shoulder, smiling. "I've had less than five minutes to grab my bag and make a mad dash to the parking lot."

As the men chuckled, Mary Kate flipped the visor mirror down, examining her reflection critically. Her gaze lingered indifferently on wide-set brown eyes, sharply arched brows, rosy lips, and a complexion that remained smooth and flawless despite little care. Dark brown hair dipped in long waves about her oval face, and, as usual, it was in total disarray, thanks to her hectic schedule.

"Now where's my hairbrush?" she mumbled, diving into her shoulder bag. The jumble of contents within brought an impatient sigh, and she quickly tossed the bag on its side, dragging out each item in search of the elusive brush. A strange mixture composed of pens, pads, yellow stick-ons, a makeup bag, and a granola bar fell out. Another *thump* sent her New Testament, nestling in the bottom of the bag, to the floorboard.

"Uh-oh." Coty glanced back at Tom. "She's gonna try to convert us!"

Mary Kate looked up, puzzled; then catching Coty's eyes on her Bible, she grinned back. "Not right now, but I'd better get busy. The way *you* drive, I may not get many more chances."

Laughter rumbled from Coty's broad chest, and he accelerated even more, delighted by her squeal of fear.

She glanced at the buildings zipping past as they reached the heart of Seabreeze, a town of about sixty thousand. Glancing back into the visor, she gave up on the hairbrush and yanked a comb from her makeup kit. She dragged it through her thick dark hair in a few hasty attempts then shook her hair back from her face. It tumbled into deep waves that framed her delicate features and enhanced her classic bone structure. She managed to look both delicate and vulnerable, although she could be one of the toughest television reporters in the business. Her striking natural beauty captivated her television audience, but Mary Kate thought little about her beauty. She was far more interested in developing her inner self and devoted hours to reading self-help books in both her profession and her personal life. The small community church was an important part of her life as well, and she attended regularly to strengthen her faith for the hectic days of her life.

While Coty often teased her about her religious beliefs, Mary Kate wondered how he and Tom, like so many others, could face life without the power available to them. She stared down at the cover of her New Testament before gently replacing it in her bag. Even a capsule prayer, at times like this, could provide her with a flash of wisdom and strength for the task ahead.

"Let's see what's going out over the wires." Coty's voice brought her back to the moment as he tuned in a popular radio station.

"It's ten o'clock in Seabreeze," a voice informed them. "The temperature is a sunny eighty-five degrees, with a slight breeze."

A wistful sigh escaped Mary Kate as she thought about spending a day at the beach, picnicking or sunning, or just loafing, doing some shopping.

"Listen." Coty nudged her, turning up the volume.

"This late bulletin just in," the casual voice tensed. "A verdict of 'not guilty' has been handed down in the trial of Blake Taylor. Details later. . ."

"That's the first case the district attorney has lost in a long time." Coty wheeled around the corner, screeching to a halt near the crowd-jammed courthouse. "Ready?" he glanced at Mary Kate.

"Ready," she acknowledged, shoving the heavy door open, then scrambling down, wondering why her instincts hadn't alerted her to wear slacks today.

"Where do you want to start?" Coty asked, the television camera hoisted to his shoulder. Tom, trailing behind, hugged cords and mikes.

Coty scanned the crowd, searching for those who looked willing to express an opinion.

"Look!" Tom's voice halted them. "There's Blake Taylor coming out a side door."

Mary Kate's startled gaze flew to the distant figure. A well-tailored navy suit neatly encased broad shoulders and long legs, now stretched forward in a hurried stride. The man was making his way down the back steps in an effort to escape the waiting crowd in front of the building. His blond head was lowered in brooding contemplation.

⚓

Mary Kate recalled Taylor's other television appearances where he had entranced audiences with his rugged good looks, while the ice blue gaze silenced noisy questions. He could be a real charmer, or he could slice a reporter to shreds.

Blake Taylor always looked cool and poised, despite the charges leveled against him. Shock waves had reverberated throughout the state when the prominent developer had been charged with the theft of a three-carat diamond ring, then a pair of ruby earrings and a matching ruby necklace. Soon, other items were found in his home, and nobody really expected him to beat the rap. He claimed to have an alibi during the robberies, and his alibi was substantiated by at least a dozen men who worked on a shopping center he was overseeing. But how did the jewels get into his house?

It was common knowledge that his wife, now deceased, had been dying of cancer. Public sympathy had almost been in his favor when one reporter suggested these were gifts for his dying wife, that her staggering hospital bills had all but bankrupted him.

The charges against him must have been a real blow to his ego. To approach him now, after the grueling trial, would be like stepping into the cage with a grizzly bear. And yet. . .

"Let's get a statement," she called over her shoulder, taking off across the courthouse lawn.

"Mr. Taylor," she called to him, not caring if Coty and Tom were keeping up as she ran as fast as she could.

He walked faster, ignoring her call, making no acknowledgment of her presence.

"Mr. Taylor!" Mary Kate yelled again, running to catch up, gulping for breath.

He whirled then, a threatening frown clouding his handsome face when he spotted the television camera on Coty's shoulder.

"Mr. Taylor, I'm Mary Kate Moore from Channel 6 News." She smiled brightly, although she was slightly out of breath.

He gave a brisk nod. "I made a statement earlier. I have nothing more to say."

The rich voice was loaded with scarcely suppressed anger, matching the sharp arch of brows and the steel glint in his deep blue eyes. Mary Kate swallowed, scrutinizing the broad-set jaw and jutting chin, marveling that a full mouth could be drawn in such a tight line. Only the look of soft blond hair offset the harsh planes of his face.

She felt a slight nudge between her shoulders and glanced back at Coty, closing in with the camera.

"Mr. Taylor. . ." She blinked at him, inching closer. "Can't you just give us a few words? Aren't you pleased over the verdict?"

"Yes, and now excuse me!" he snapped, turning away.

"Wait!"

The desperation in her voice spun him around again, the eyes blue stones now, chipping away at her self-confidence as he glared down at her as though she were a yapping puppy, blocking his path.

"The public deserves to hear *your* side of the story," she pressed further. "You've maintained from the beginning that you were innocent. Can't you elaborate why?"

He stopped walking and looked her squarely in the eye. "Because I *am* innocent. That's just been proven in a court of law. You can read the remainder of the story in the evening newspaper."

Mary Kate's mouth dropped open, his rudeness striking a raw nerve. If he could make a comment to the newspaper, why not to the television audience? This time her temper and her stubborn nature took over.

She threw an irritated glance at Coty, who motioned her back toward Taylor, focusing the camera squarely on the tall man as the film continued to roll.

Mary Kate stalked after him, mentally berating him for his lack of cooperation, his arrogance, his conceit. There was only one way to gain his attention now.

"Mr. Taylor, how do you think the charges against you will affect your future?"

The question directed upward to the rock-hard jaw had scarcely left her lips when he wheeled around with a cold fury that rocked her back on her heels.

"I've lost a wife, my business is in jeopardy, and my self-esteem has been torn to shreds. I'm not sure I have a future." The blue eyes darkened in wounded pride, the rich voice faltering. "Now you've got your statement," he said wearily, as though the very life had been drained from him, "are you satisfied?"

Mary Kate stood speechless, stepping back from the cutting blue gaze as he turned and walked away, the broad shoulders drooping.

"Hey, you were great." Coty lowered the camera, looking from her to the departing figure of Blake Taylor. "You captured his vulnerable side, and nobody's put that on film."

"Maybe," Mary Kate said, lifting a hand to massage the tense muscles in the back of her neck, "but I don't feel very proud of myself, Coty. In fact, what I feel is pure shame. I've never behaved so badly."

"Ah, come on! It takes guts to be a good reporter." Coty gave her a reassuring tap on the shoulder.

"Then maybe I just lost some of my ambition." Mary Kate hugged her arms against her chest, suddenly feeling a chill despite the warm day.

"Coty, we still have film left, haven't we?" Tom interrupted tactfully.

"Yeah, enough for another interview."

Mary Kate shook her head. "No, I'm finished. Let's go."

"What?" Coty stared at her.

"I said I'm finished," she replied miserably. "If you want to stalk the crowd for an opinion, go right ahead."

With that statement, she turned and trudged back to the van, guiltily recalling the manner in which she had pursued Blake Taylor, circling him mentally, analyzing his weakness, then swooping in like a vulture. She had sensed a vulnerable spot and gone for it, thoughtlessly and shamelessly. It was unlike her to be so callous and insensitive, but then he was the first person who had ever prodded her into losing her temper during an interview.

What was there about the man that set her so on edge? That made her violate the basic Christian principle of compassion? Talking tough was not Mary Kate's style, was not even consistent with her personal convictions. She operated from a code of ethics based on the Golden Rule.

She shook her head, forcing the corners of her mouth into a tense smile as she passed the crowd, but then the smile faded.

She owed Blake Taylor an apology.

Chapter 2

I think you're horrible!" the voice of an angry little girl shouted into Mary Kate's office phone.

Mary Kate gripped the telephone, wide-eyed, trying to ignore the noise of the newsroom in order to concentrate on her caller.

"I beg your pardon?" she managed finally. "Who's speaking?"

"My name's Hanna, and you're a mean ol' reporter!" she repeated, more loudly this time. "You made Dad look awful on television last night and now he's left."

"Your dad?" Mary Kate frowned.

"Blake Taylor is my dad, and you made him feel awful. He's gone to our summer place at Seaside, and I'm going to run away too. *I hate you!*" The little voice cracked a second before the phone clicked in Mary Kate's ear.

She shook her dark head, her thoughts spinning, as she replaced the phone and sat in a daze, trying to piece together the indignant message shouted above the roar of a familiar noise she couldn't pinpoint.

Hanna Taylor. Blake Taylor.

She propped an elbow on her desk, cupping her chin in her palm as she lifted her thoughtful gaze and watched a dark cloud float past.

Searching her mind for information on the Taylor family, she recalled how the death of Charlotte Taylor—Mrs. Blake Taylor—had taken precedence over the local news shortly after Mary Kate had moved to Seabreeze to begin her new job.

Drumming her fingers on the desk, she scanned her brain for the newspaper article on Mrs. Taylor. Slowly, the story came back to her. She had been a fashion model who had made a name for herself before marrying Blake Taylor. Then she had stayed home with their child, and apparently everyone had been happy until she was diagnosed with breast cancer. Surgery and radiation had not prevented the cancer from spreading to her bones, and she had died a painful death after a lengthy illness.

Mary Kate sighed, recalling the little girl's tormented voice. She hadn't realized when she prodded Blake Taylor to make his vulnerable reply that she would be hurting his daughter as well.

"Brad—" She raised her eyes to her lanky boss, hurrying past her desk.

He whirled, brows arched questioningly.

"Brad, tell me more about Blake Taylor. I just got a complaint from his daughter about my interview."

Brad shrugged, raking a hand through his hair. "Taylor is a talented developer who put his unique brand of work on the new shopping center just west of town. He managed to retain a historical look to the center, while updating it with modern conveniences. Aside from his intelligence, I know nothing more. Oh, he and his wife lived in Tallahassee before coming here."

He fidgeted, eager to be gone.

"I see," Mary Kate murmured, her eyes narrowing as his words penetrated. "Thanks."

Was it possible that a jealous competitor had planted the jewels in his house, as he had claimed? His wife had certainly been too ill to shop, and the woman who worked for them was a plain type of woman, not given to fancy jewelry. And he had produced witnesses for his whereabouts on the days the jewelry had disappeared.

The phone pulled at her like a magnet, her clear-polished nails tapping a rhythm again on her cluttered desk. She ignored the papers, the work waiting to be done. She could not dismiss from her mind the voice of the little girl. The misery in that voice seemed to match the misery in her father's eyes.

"All because of me," she said, staring dejectedly at her nails.

"Get tough, Mary Kate," Brad had advised her on more than one occasion. "You'll never make it in this business if you take every interview seriously. Leave your work on the doorstep when you go home."

But home for her was a small duplex with only her cocker spaniel, Bo, waiting when she dragged in hungry and tired. Her parents and older brother still lived up in Dothan, and she visited them as often as possible. She was a family person, not wanting to escape her roots, for she found real pleasure and companionship in being with her family. And yet, she had jumped at the chance to move to Florida and work at WJAK after graduating from college.

She rolled Brad's words over in her mind. *You'll never make it in this business if you take every interview seriously.*

Well, she had overstepped her boundaries, and her conscience was hounding her. She had to try and make amends; otherwise, she was not going to sleep very well tonight.

The dimension of caring that she brought to her work was the very ingredient that had set her apart from other reporters. She believed it was why the public responded so easily to her. She owed Blake Taylor an apology, and she was not above delivering it.

Taking a deep breath, she reached for the telephone directory, her fingernail making a sweep down the column of T's. Locating Blake Taylor's home and office number, she dialed the office, phrasing a conversation in her mind.

An efficient secretary informed her that Mr. Taylor was out of town for the remainder of the week.

Thanking the secretary, she hung up, recalling Hanna's last words. *"I'm going to run away too."*

What did she mean by that? she wondered, brows knitted. In the child's state of mind, that surely meant running away from home! She glanced at the wall clock. It was almost three-thirty. Hanna should be home from school by now.

Quickly, she dialed the home telephone number, tension building within her as she waited for an answer. Finally, a woman's voice came on the wire, announcing the Taylor residence.

"May I speak with Hanna, please?" Mary Kate asked politely.

There was a slight hesitation. "She isn't here. Who's calling?"

Mary Kate took only a second to ponder using a fictitious name, then in her typical straightforward manner, she replied honestly to the question.

"This is Mary Kate Moore."

"Mary Kate Moore? From WJAK?" The woman's voice was cold and flat.

"That's right."

"What do you want *now?*"

"I had a call from Hanna earlier," she explained, overlooking the woman's sharp tone. "I merely wanted to apologize."

Silence filled the wire before the woman continued in a more civil tone. "She hasn't come home from school yet."

"Not yet?" Mary Kate glanced at the clock again. "Isn't she running a bit late?"

"Well, this *is* the first week of school, and—wait a minute, what concern is it of yours?" she asked pointedly, as though remembering the interview again.

Mary Kate scooted to the edge of the chair, ignoring the small voice in her brain that warned her not to get involved. "May I come over, please? I think I should relate the phone conversation I just had with Hanna. I'm afraid there may be a problem and—"

"If you're looking for another story," the woman cut her short, "don't bother."

"I assure you that I'm *not* looking for another story," Mary Kate replied emphatically. "You have my word that none of this will reach the media."

"All right," the woman conceded. "I *am* worried, quite frankly. And Mr. Taylor has gone to his beach house for a few days' rest."

"Please give me your address." Mary Kate grabbed a notepad and reached for a pen. "I'll come right over."

After jotting down the address, Mary Kate ripped off the note and stuck it in the pocket of her white cotton slacks. Saying a hurried good-bye, she hung up the phone and grabbed her shoulder bag, making a dash for the back door. She paused as Carey, the secretary, shot her a questioning look.

"Carey, I'll be out for awhile," she called over her shoulder.

"Oh? Want to leave a number?"

"No." Mary Kate forced a smile. "I just have to take care of some business."

Carey nodded thoughtfully, misinterpreting her words. "Have fun, then." Carey gave her an impish little grin.

Mary Kate merely smiled. Carey probably thought she was meeting someone. She decided to let it go that way. If Carey believed she were up to something, maybe she would quit trying to fix her up with her younger brother. Carey was a happily married woman with three children, and wanted Mary Kate to find a good man.

She flew out the door and down the steps to the parking lot, the big door banging behind her as she stepped out into the warm afternoon.

She glanced up at the sky and saw a scattering of dark clouds. She remembered the weatherman had predicted rain this afternoon. By the time Mary Kate reached her red economy car, she was again feeling that nagging little concern for Hanna Taylor. Did she take an umbrella or rain jacket when she left for school? *If* she left for school. Or had she merely pretended she was going to school, then taken off someplace else? Surely she was all right, or she wouldn't be calling.

Mary Kate slid into the car seat and fished a silver ring of keys from her bag. As she inserted the key in the ignition and started the engine, she found herself pondering the wisdom of a trip to the Taylor home.

Why am I doing this? she wondered suddenly, as a blank expression filled her brown eyes.

Chapter 3

Mary Kate drove through town and turned into the exclusive area where Blake Taylor's home was located. She had continued to ask herself why she felt compelled to deliver Hanna's message in person. But she knew the reason. She was partly responsible if the child had run away.

"I've never been so insensitive in my entire career as a reporter," she said into the silence of her car as she stopped for a traffic light. She reached into her pocket, retrieving the note to verify the street and house number as the light changed and her mental argument continued.

Other reporters pursued, tantalized, aggravated. Such tactics seemed to go with the territory. But she was Mary Kate Moore, a Christian who lived by the Golden Rule and who attributed her small degree of success to her determination to live by her Christian standards.

She glanced around her, aware that she had reached the Taylors' exclusive neighborhood. Neat green lawns stretched past flower gardens to impressive homes of all sizes and shapes. Some ranch style, some Spanish, some Tudor. Rows of protective shrubs bordered the properties to ensure privacy. When she reached the mailbox marked 1507, she turned her car up the sweeping driveway to the quiet, Spanish-style home. Despite the pleasant white exterior and red tiled roof, the desperate stillness of the place brought a shiver racing down her spine as she parked the car and sat staring for a moment at the isolated house and grounds.

There were no shouts of playful children in the neighborhood, no vibrations from stereos or televisions, not even the sound of bike tires on the smooth pavement behind her. The neighborhood was depressingly silent, and she found it hard to imagine a normal active child flourishing here, particularly one who had lost her mother.

Sighing, she reached for her bag and hooked it over her shoulder as she hopped out of the car. She followed the stone walk that curved past a manicured lawn that bore no evidence of children at play, up the circular steps leading to the front door.

Squaring her shoulders, she lifted her hand to the brass knocker and let it fall. The heavy thud magnified in her ears, while a low grumble of thunder echoed from the skies.

Slowly, the door opened, and she stood facing a gray-haired woman, fiftyish and plump, her round face lined with concern.

"Hello." Mary Kate smiled. "I'm—"

"I know who you are." The woman gave a brisk nod and slowly opened the door. It was obvious she was reluctant to admit Mary Kate.

"And you're. . . ?" Mary Kate extended her hand, determined to be friendly.

"Sue Sampson, the housekeeper. I've been with the Taylors for five years." Her work-roughened hand gripped Mary Kate's momentarily before retreating to her apron pocket.

"What did Hanna say to you over the phone?" she asked, closing the door behind Mary Kate. "And why did she call you?"

Mary Kate paused, studying the woman whose eyes held an expression of worry. She was scarcely taller than Mary Kate, yet she was many pounds heavier, presenting the image of a motherly confidante.

"Well, I may be jumping to conclusions," Mary Kate began, wondering if she had overreacted to Hanna's phone call. She shoved her hands into her pants pockets, suddenly feeling ill at ease here.

"Come in," Sue said, her tone softening, as she led the way down a corridor and entered the second door on the right.

Mary Kate followed her into a large room painted a soft cream color, decorated in wines and deep greens in draperies and furnishings. The room was filled with overstuffed chairs and sofas and nice oak tables topped with brass lamps.

"We can talk here in the den." Sue motioned Mary Kate to a chair.

Mary Kate's heels sank into plush, deep green carpet as she took a seat in a chair. Glancing toward the cloudy sky, Sue turned on one of the lamps, bringing a soft mellow glow to the room. Mary Kate's eyes returned to the clouds outside the window, and she decided to get right to the point.

"Hanna called to scold me about the interview with her father. And then she said, 'My father has gone off and now I'm running away too.' Or something like that." Mary Kate shrugged, wondering if she had recited the conversation exactly as she had first heard it.

"Running away?" Sue gasped, scooting to the edge of her chair. "She didn't tell she was going anywhere. Henry—that's my husband, he takes care of the yard work—has checked the neighborhood and didn't find her." She made no attempt now to hide her concern.

"Maybe it's only a threat," Mary Kate said gently, hating to bear the news. Still, something was obviously wrong; that was apparent after talking with Sue. "By the way, how old is Hanna?"

"She's eight," Sue answered absently, staring into space as though lost in thought.

"After all we've been through. . . ," she mumbled, then bit her lip and broke off her flow of words.

Mary Kate suspected she was referring to more than today's problem. She cleared her throat. "Did she go to school today?"

Sue looked back at her and began to nod her head. "She got on the school bus this morning, but when she didn't get off this afternoon, I assumed she had stopped at Molly's house. That's her friend down the street. I just got off the phone with Molly's mother, but Hanna isn't there. Then you drove up. I thought maybe you knew something."

Mary Kate shook her head. "I've told you all I know."

Sue jumped up and rushed to the desk phone. "I'll call her teacher to see if she was at school today." She grabbed a small leather book and flipped it open. Then she began to punch the numbers into the telephone's keypad.

Mary Kate crossed the room and lifted a picture from a table, studying the face of a very pretty little girl. Perfectly chiseled features were framed by long blond hair. A pert nose hinted at mischief, but the smile was that of an angel. The eyes, a deep rich blue, reminded Mary Kate of those of Blake Taylor.

She returned the gold-framed picture to the table, her eyes lingering thoughtfully on the little girl's face. While she had beautiful eyes, they did not reflect the confidence of her father. Perhaps that air of assurance would come in later years, after she had solved the mysteries of her own little world.

"She didn't go to school today!" Sue cried, dropping the phone awkwardly before scrambling for it, then replacing it on the hook. "She may have run away, like you said." She sank into the desk chair, obviously stunned.

Mary Kate moistened her lips, searching for something comforting to say, and yet she knew that Sue had every right to be distraught. "Children often run away just to prove something. Then they're back home by dinner. Maybe that's what Hanna will do."

She heard the sound of fear in her own voice and realized even as she attempted to calm Sue, that other fears, worse fears, were forming in her own mind.

A vulnerable little girl running away from home was bad enough. When that little girl was the daughter of a prominent developer who could pay a hefty ransom. . .

"I've had a sick feeling in the pit of my stomach all week," Sue's voice trembled. "Mr. Taylor's been so involved with the trial that he's hardly had time to speak to the rest of us. Hanna has seemed so lonely lately." She jumped to her feet, reaching for the phone again. "Why am I sitting here rambling? I've got to call Mr. Taylor."

"He's at his beach house, you said?"

Sue nodded. "On the upper end of the beach where it's quiet. Hanna begged for him to wait until the weekend so she could go with him, but he was so worn out after the trial, he said he needed a few days to himself. Hanna didn't understand." She sighed, clutching the phone, waiting for an answer.

Mary Kate thought it over. Since Seabreeze was only a short drive from the beach, Blake Taylor could be back home in twenty minutes or so.

"I have an appointment soon," Mary Kate commented, glancing at her watch. "I must go. If you or Mr. Taylor need to reach me, I'll be at the station until seven. After that, I'll be at my apartment." She removed a business card from her purse. "Here are both numbers, office and home phone."

Sue Sampson nodded bleakly. "You will respect our privacy?" she asked desperately.

"Of course I will," Mary Kate reached across the desk to touch her hand reassuringly.

"Mr. Taylor?" Sue spoke the name then glanced cautiously at Mary Kate.

Tactfully, Mary Kate turned and hurried out of the den. She could hear Sue's voice speaking in a low tone as she crossed the foyer and let herself out the front door.

If Blake Taylor had been notified, then there was nothing more she could do. Except pray. Once she stepped out into the gray afternoon, she looked up at the clouds. It was going to start raining any minute now. Where was Hanna? Her eyes scanned the neighborhood as she hooked her shoulder bag over her arm and crossed the porch.

There was something terribly depressing about the surroundings here, or perhaps it was only the gloomy day. Still, her steps quickened as she hurried back to the car. She was suddenly anxious to get away.

🌴

Mary Kate sat on the edge of a chair in the darkened editing room, going over last week's interview with a local politician. The interview had been one of her typical, on-the-street clips, but this one had been unique in that she had captured the man and his son on their way into a fast-food establishment.

They had spent a few seconds discussing the merits of hamburgers and French fries for growing boys before the politician adeptly maneuvered the conversation back to his upcoming election.

"He's a cool one," the film editor commented as he checked the frames, "but he lacks something."

"Charisma, Bill," Mary Kate nodded. "I noticed that too."

"Too bad Blake Taylor doesn't run for office," Bill offered idly, unaware that the name had brought Mary Kate upright. "Now there's a man with plenty of charisma. Talked his way right out of that theft charge."

Mary Kate frowned. "Do you believe he was guilty?"

Bill shrugged. "That slick attorney's argument of a jealous competitor planting the jewels didn't convince me."

Mary Kate chewed her lip. "But he had airtight alibis during the time the jewelry was stolen."

Bill gave her a sardonic grin. "Mary Kate, that man can buy plenty of alibis!"

She stared at him, weighing his words. Was it possible? Her thoughts darted back to Hanna. She wondered if the little girl had been located. In front of her, the footage of the politician ran on, and she forced her eyes back to the screen. As she stared at the blond politician, she saw in his place the dark commanding presence of Blake Taylor.

Bill's right about his charisma, Mary Kate thought, recalling how she had stood mesmerized on the courthouse steps before she could propel herself into action.

She stood up, her nerves on edge. "I think that looks okay, don't you, Bill? If Brad agrees, we'll use it one night this week."

"Yeah, it's okay." Bill flicked the lights on, grinning across at her. "You're the one who should run for office, you know. You have a way with people."

Mary Kate waved a hand of dismissal at his teasing grin. Bill liked to goad her for fun, telling her that her successful interviews were aided by her good looks and charm. It usually prompted a healthy argument between them, but she ignored him now. She hadn't the time for more jostling. She prided herself on her ability to create rapport with the person on the street. It would have been a compromise of her convictions to use feminine wiles rather than intelligence and skill.

She hurried back down the corridor to the newsroom. Brad's deep voice halted her as she rounded a corner.

"Mary Kate! I took a look at the footage on that Jenkins guy. Good job!" He caught up with her, giving her a nod of approval as they walked back to the newsroom.

"Mr. Jenkins was a delightful interview," she said, smiling up at Brad. "Can you imagine yourself walking five miles a day when you're eighty-three? He never misses a morning, he told me."

Brad groaned. "I can't force myself to do two miles a day at forty-two!" His lanky stride slackened at the thought. "No discipline, that's my problem."

Mary Kate laughed. "Well, you easily cover a dozen miles a day just pacing around this building." They turned into the wide door of the newsroom.

"Mary Kate! You're wanted on the phone," Carey called. "Some kid."

Mary Kate's mind bolted to the memory of Hanna as she raced across to the desk, scrambling for the phone.

"Didn't know you were so fond of kids," Carey called with a grin.

She gave Carey a quick smile as she sat down at her desk and forced a calm tone to her voice as she lifted the receiver.

For a moment there was no reply to her hello, just light breathing.

"Hello," Mary Kate repeated. "Who's there?" She gripped the phone tighter.

"You didn't tell them I'd run away."

Mary Kate blinked for a moment, too confused by the words to grasp their meaning at first. "Is this Hanna?" she asked. Then she thought she knew what the little girl meant. "Who was I supposed to tell?"

The little girl huffed an impatient sigh. In that quiet second, a public address system announced a twenty-five percent discount on a special brand of electric trains.

Mary Kate gripped the phone tighter, listening, aware that her caller was in a large store. But which one? Her eyes flew to the glass window, and she saw that it was pouring rain, and day was giving way to early evening.

"You didn't announce it on television!" Hanna stated slowly, emphatically, as though being sure she made her point.

Mary Kate concentrated on her words, her mind probing for the proper replies. "Did you want me to?" she asked softly.

There was a slight hesitation again, a vibrating hum filling up the silence as Mary Kate closed her eyes, struggling to remember where she had heard those sounds before.

"Well, I *have* run away!" Her voice rose in an indignant protest. "Not that anybody cares!"

"Hanna, listen to me." She took a deep breath, praying for the right words. "Everyone cares about you. Everyone is worried. You need to call home right now."

Another impatient sigh.

"Listen," Mary Kate continued, wondering if she had time to put a tracer on the call, "I'm really sorry about that interview. I upset your father, and that's why he went away. It wasn't because of you, and now he'll be sick with worry. You don't want to do that to him, do you?"

"He doesn't care. All he cares about is his business."

Mary Kate gulped, searching for another argument. "Sue is terribly upset. You need to call her right this minute. She's—"

"Sue doesn't care either. She's always talking to her daughter on the phone. She never has time for me."

Mary Kate gasped, feeling her heart go out to this poor lonely child. Somehow she had to think of the right words to reach her.

"If you'll just come back home, you'll see that you're wrong and—"

"No! I'm never going home," she threatened, her voice trembling.

Mary Kate's eyes flew back to the window, watching the rain pour down. She was making a desperate mental plea to God for a way to help Hanna. Then during that moment of silence, she could hear the public address system and this time the message was distinct.

"Stop in at the Wun-der-ful World of Toys for all your children's needs."

She bolted upright in her chair. "Hanna, if I can get a special news bulletin about you on the air in the next half hour, could you watch it? Is there a television set nearby?"

"Yeah. I can see a television set where I am," she replied slowly.

"Great!" Mary Kate was already getting to her feet, reaching for her shoulder bag. "You stay right where you are and watch that television. I'll try to get that bulletin on within the next half hour. Okay?"

"Okay! But make it good," she added, a note of triumph in her little voice.

"I will. Don't go away from that television set!"

As soon as the line clicked, she hung up to break the connection. Then she quickly lifted the phone again, her fingers zipping over the numbers as she punched in the Taylor residence. A rich male voice answered on the first ring, and she realized with a start that Blake Taylor had returned.

"Mr. Taylor?" she asked tentatively.

"Yes? Who is this?" he barked impatiently.

"This is Mary Kate Moore. I think I've located Hanna." The words burst from her throat.

"What? How? The police are looking everywhere."

"She just telephoned me, wanting to know why I hadn't broadcast her runaway over the news. I distinctly heard a public address system announcing sales at the Wun-der-ful World of Toys. I'm sure that's where she is."

This was a huge toy store in the mall, featuring items of interest for kids of all ages, with a special set of colorful televisions, guaranteed to match any color scheme.

"I thought the police checked the mall. There's a Wun-der-ful Toy store there."

She rushed on. "When I asked Hanna if she could watch a television if I put on a special news bulletin, she was quick to assure me that she could. I think you'll find her in that special little television department. I'm going there now," she added, unwilling to waste more time. "Good-bye."

"I'll meet you," he yelled in her ear before she replaced the phone and hurried toward the door.

"Take an umbrella." Carey shoved a small black one toward her.

"Thanks, Carey. What would I do without you?" she called over her shoulder as she darted out of the newsroom.

🛝

Mary Kate drove through the slashing rain, trying to be careful as darkness began to descend over Seabreeze. In exactly fifteen minutes, she had reached the parking lot near the huge toy store at the mall. The rain had slackened a bit, but it was still a miserable afternoon.

Grabbing the dripping umbrella, she opened the door and hopped out. Sidestepping the mud puddles, she huddled under the umbrella, nodding her thanks to a car that waited for her to pass.

She rushed to the front door, lowered the umbrella, and entered the brightly lit department store, a stark contrast to the dark afternoon. She was familiar with the layout of the store, and she took a shortcut through Little Guys Tools and cut around the floor-to-ceiling shelves of dolls where she slowed down, peering around a life-size doll to the entertainment center. What she saw melted her heart.

Blake Taylor, in khaki shorts and sports shirt, was kneeling beside a stool where a blond head was nestled into his shoulder. His arms were wrapped around the little girl, and he too looked as though he were about to cry.

She hesitated. There was no point in intruding on a family matter. He had found his daughter; that was all that mattered. She was about to turn when Blake's moist blue eyes lifted over Hanna's head, widening suddenly at the sight of Mary Kate. She gave him a little smile then lifted her hand in a reassuring wave. Quickly, she turned and headed back toward the door. She knew Hanna would think she had betrayed her, and she was sorry for that. But she was glad Hanna had been reunited with her father, and maybe everyone had learned a lesson.

"Can I help you?" asked a voice from behind her.

She jumped, whirling to face an equally surprised salesman.

"Hey, you're the girl who does the on-the-street interviews, aren't you?" The older man's eyes widened with interest. "Are you looking for a special toy? Or someone to interview?"

She smiled. "No, I was just leaving," she replied politely and hurried through the door into the light drizzle. The night sky was slowly beginning to clear, and she decided that was a good omen.

Chapter 4

Remembering her hasty exit, Mary Kate decided to check in at the office before going home for the night. Brad, who seemed to eat and sleep in his glass-enclosed office, was working late. As she passed his door, he gave her a silent salute, still cradling the telephone against his shoulder.

Waving back, Mary Kate hurried on, hoping she had misinterpreted the look of quiet panic on his face. Clearing her desk, then locking the drawers, she was preparing to leave when she caught a glimpse of Brad's long legs swiftly closing the distance between them.

"Aren't you overdoing your dedication to WJAK?" he asked teasingly. Before she could answer, he plunged on. "Hal's sick and the drugstore on South Main is on fire." He waved a scribbled note. "Crew three is covering. Could you go, Mary Kate? We'll hold a slot on tonight's wrap-up."

"But—" Her brown eyes widened in protest as she stared up into his pleading face. Then her protest died in her throat as she glanced around the deserted newsroom.

"Okay, but you're a tough boss, Brad!" She yanked the piece of paper from his hand, whirling for her shoulder bag. "You know I don't like fires."

Her lips thinned in frustration as she checked her purse for her pen and pad then took off. A nagging voice within reminded her that it had taken two years to earn the distinction of being one of the station's best reporters. If she wanted to protest overwork, she must do it later in a more businesslike manner. *A point of discussion tomorrow,* she vowed, glancing over her shoulder at Brad. He was back at his desk, slumped in the chair, the phone cradled against his ear.

She trudged out the door, her small chin thrust forward in defiance. *Tomorrow,* she vowed. *But for now there's a building on fire!*

🪔

Exhaustion crept into every bone in Mary Kate's body as she dragged herself up the steps to her duplex. The hour was late, and she longed for a leisurely soak in the tub followed by twelve hours of uninterrupted sleep. The phone was ringing as she unlocked the door. Hurriedly flipping on the light in the foyer, she dashed toward the nearest phone and tripped over a discarded house shoe from the morning's hurried departure. *I have got to slow down!*

"Hello," she shouted irritably, cradling the phone against her shoulder as she leaned over to drag her sandals from her aching feet. Frowning at the blister on her big toe, she was caught momentarily off guard by the rich masculine voice on the other end of the wire.

"Ms. Moore? This is Blake Taylor." He spoke slowly. "I hope I'm not bothering you."

She snapped upright, surprised by his call. "No, that's okay. How's Hanna?"

"She's fine," he answered politely. "I didn't get a chance to thank you earlier."

She blinked and sank into the sofa, reaching for the lamp on the end table. "I'm just glad I could help," she replied, turning the switch and focusing on the circle of light on her carpet. Her thoughts moved on to Hanna and again she felt guilty. "Would it be possible for me to speak to Hanna? I think I owe her an apology, I sort of. . .betrayed her, I suppose."

"She's already in bed." Blake hesitated. "And it might be better to wait. She is a bit upset with you, but then she's been upset with everyone. I hope you understand. She's just a child, after all."

"I do understand." Mary Kate closed her eyes, thinking of the vulnerable little voice that had begged for attention. "Where was she all day? Did you find out?"

"I think she just wandered around the mall, somehow managing to elude everyone who was looking for her. The minute Sue called, I rushed back home. We were frantic," he added, the tension returning to his voice.

"Well," Mary Kate said with a sigh, "I'm glad she's home safely, Mr. Taylor."

"Blake," he added gently. "Since you've been involved in our family trauma, we should at least be on a first-name basis."

"About the interview," she continued, wanting to make amends so that she could ease her conscience. "I really don't know what came over me. I've never been such a pest during my career as a reporter. I'm sorry."

"You were merely doing your job," he answered after a momentary pause. "I respect that, even if you were doing that job on *me.*" He was chuckling softly into the phone.

Mary Kate's brow lifted. So he had a sense of humor, after all. "Well, I think I overdid my 'job,' as you put it. I had no right to provoke you that way."

"Let's just forget the entire incident. I was overwrought from the trial. We've been through a strain. I'm sure you can appreciate that. I'd like to put the matter behind me."

"I'll be happy to join you in that," she replied.

"Now back to my reason for calling. I wanted to invite you to dinner at our house tomorrow evening. Would you join us—Hanna and me? The poor kid is pretty embarrassed about everything. I suppose that's normal."

"I suppose." Mary Kate bit her lip, wondering if anything Hanna had done could be considered normal.

Dinner? With Blake Taylor? And his troubled daughter? She frowned.

His deep voice filled her ear again, this time more persuasive. "I feel we owe you something. Please allow us to make amends. Even Sue insists on preparing a nice dinner for you."

Mary Kate took a deep breath, thinking there was no way she could refuse. "All right, but my work schedule won't allow me to be definite about the hour, I'm afraid. The best I can do is get there between six-thirty and seven. Is that okay?"

"That's fine. Just come when you're free. I'm taking the day off. I intend to spend more time with Hanna. I've learned something from all this, I hope."

His relief at having his daughter back was evident.

"Perhaps we all have," she replied. "Enjoy your day with Hanna, and I'll see you tomorrow evening. Good night. . .Blake." She replaced the phone and stretched out on the sofa.

Mary Kate lay still, savoring the peaceful moment and thinking about the Scripture verse which promises that all things work together for good to those who love God and are called according to His purpose. Perhaps the temporary anguish suffered during Hanna's disappearance had been worth the cost.

Her brown eyes drifted toward the ceiling, a smile lighting her weary features.

"Thank You," she whispered.

Chapter 5

A wrap!" Coty nodded, lowering the camera.

"Thanks, kids." Mary Kate smiled at the students of Winston Elementary, who had agreed to be interviewed about an upcoming bake sale and car wash. They were working hard to help one of their teachers who needed a kidney transplant. It had been a touching story.

She unhooked the microphone and waved to the group. "You can see yourselves on the news at five o'clock tonight."

Her little audience whooped their response, then dashed off to join the line at the side entrance of the school.

"Whew, what a day!" She glanced at Coty as they climbed back into the van.

"Like every other one," he answered, wedging his considerable weight in under the wheel.

She leaned back in the seat, closing her eyes in an effort to relax as Coty started the van and they sped away from the curb. She had spent a hectic morning rushing from one location to another; Brad thrusting an assignment in her face each time she slowed down to catch her breath. While she had performed her tasks with the usual diligence, one part of her consciousness centered on Blake and Hanna, each presenting a different problem.

She prayed that Hanna had forgiven her and that this dinner together would somehow make things right between them. Reaching for her shoulder bag, Mary Kate remembered the two Sea World tickets she had been given as a member of the press. Maybe Hanna would want to go. Regaining her trust would not be easy, but perhaps she could make a beginning.

She thought of Blake Taylor again, wondering why the man lingered in her mind. She had lain awake last night, despite utter exhaustion, debating whether this nervousness was connected to her concern for Hanna or the strange effect he had on her. Blake Taylor set her nerves on edge, like a flash of lightning streaking through a summer sky.

Coty swung into the parking lot and was turning off the engine of the van as she roused up in her seat, a weary yawn escaping her.

"I've had a craving for Mexican food all day." Coty glanced at her. "Want to try that new place over on Union Street?" He reached into the backseat for his camera.

"Nope. I don't have that kind of craving."

"Well, what's next?" he asked, nodding toward the clipboard in the front seat.

"This is it, I hope." She pressed a hand to her forehead, fighting off the dull ache there. "Can you rush that film over to Editing so they can see how it looks? In the meantime, I'll check my desk for messages. Thanks, Coty, and I'll take a rain check on the Mexican food."

She gathered up her clipboard and purse and climbed down from the van. Hurrying across the parking lot to the back door of the station, she prayed this would be her last assignment for the day.

Deep in thought, she stepped through the slow-moving doors of the elevator and absently punched the button, watching the lights flick on the floor numbers as the elevator swung upward. She looked over her still-fresh white silk blouse and navy slacks, deciding that it would not be necessary to change before going to the Taylor home for dinner.

Stepping off the elevator, she headed for Brad's office, ready now for that confrontation about her overloaded schedule. *Nothing is going to prevent me from keeping my date this evening,* she decided.

Later, when Mary Kate arrived at the Taylor house, her neat appearance belied her hectic day. Her efforts to convince Brad that she was overworked had been waved aside with a rash of compliments and a cunning grin. Still, her workload *had* lightened, and now she was arriving before dark, like any other respectable dinner guest.

Hurrying up the walk to the front door, a cooling breeze wafted over the green lawn, bringing with it the pleasant aroma of meals being prepared in the neighborhood. She took a deep breath, settling her hand onto the top of her shoulder bag as she waited.

The front door swung open and Sue stood smiling, her hazel eyes reflecting a pleasant expression this evening.

"Come in, Ms. Moore!"

"Thank you. And please call me Mary Kate." She smiled, stepping into the foyer. She had changed out of her working sandals into dressy navy pumps, freshened her makeup, and brushed her hair. But suddenly she wished she were more. . .sophisticated. . .or glamorous.

You're Mary Kate Moore and that's good enough, she scolded herself.

"Mr. Taylor and Hanna are in the den," Sue indicated with a nod. Then her eyes swept over Mary Kate's white silk blouse and navy slacks and returned to her face. There was an inscrutable expression in her eyes, which left Mary Kate to wonder what she was thinking before Sue turned and led the way to the den.

"Thank you." Mary Kate absently brushed a speck of lint from the sleeve of her blouse. Sue paused in the doorway, announcing that their guest had arrived, and Mary Kate had a brief glimpse of father and daughter seated at a checkerboard in intense concentration before both heads spun in her direction.

"Come in." He stood, motioning her to join them.

Hanna's little cheeks colored slightly, and she jumped up, ready to make a dash from the room. Blake's hand reached out, gently drawing her against him.

"Wait, Hanna," he said quietly. He was casually dressed in tan slacks and a pale blue polo shirt, emphasizing his blond hair and blue eyes. Hanna wore a pink shorts outfit.

"Hello Hanna." Mary Kate smiled, hoping to make friends despite Hanna's obvious unwillingness. She reached into her purse and withdrew the tickets. "I have two passes for Sea World—"

"I don't want to go." Hanna glared at her.

"You don't? Have you ever watched a baby dolphin play?"

Mary Kate's gaze slipped to Blake, who stood observing the parley between them in quiet amusement.

"No. . ." Hanna's tone softened, curiosity and excitement overcoming her anger.

"Then you should definitely visit Sea World. It's lots of fun." Mary Kate smiled warmly, ignoring the child's impolite manner. "I'll bet you a giant bag of popcorn that you'd have a good time, Hanna."

"Sounds great to me!" Blake beamed at Mary Kate, his approval obvious. "What about you, Hanna?"

Hanna merely shrugged and dropped her eyes to the floor in sullen silence. Just then, Sue appeared in the door to announce dinner, and Mary Kate smothered a sigh of frustration.

"Yes, I think we're all ready for one of your delicious dinners, Sue." Blake's broad shoulders drooped slightly as he glanced from Hanna back to Mary Kate. "How about you?"

"Definitely," she answered, trying to recall what she had eaten for lunch and deciding she must have forgotten to eat.

"Then what are we waiting for?" Blake smiled at her.

Mary Kate stared for a moment. It was the first time she had seen him smile, and she was more than a little dazed by the effect of white teeth against suntanned skin, offset by the clearest, deepest blue eyes she had ever seen. Except for his daughter's eyes. She glanced back at Hanna.

The little girl had tilted her face to peer sideways at Mary Kate. Once their eyes met, her glance darted away.

With his arm around Hanna's shoulder, Blake led the way into the dining room. Mary Kate followed, wondering how to bridge the awkward silence with the little girl. *This is not going to be easy.*

The formality of the dining room seemed to add to the starched atmosphere. Blake seated Mary Kate at the opposite end of the table, with Hanna to her right.

Mary Kate tried to force an appreciative smile at the sight of the snowy linen tablecloth, the gleaming silver, and the elegant china. The corners of her mouth refused to budge, however. It occurred to her that a cozy kitchen supper would have been easier for her first meal with Blake and Hanna. They would all be more relaxed. *Or do these two ever relax?* she wondered.

Leaning back against the ornate mahogany chair, she stole a glance at Hanna, slumped over her plate. She seemed smaller and more vulnerable than ever with her thick blond hair hanging about a too-thin face. Mary Kate realized the picture she had seen in the den was a recent one. Hanna had not changed, except for losing more weight.

She turned her attention to the platter of roast beef that Sue was placing on the table. "My, that looks good," she said, watching a parade of accompanying dishes—carrots, creamed potatoes, and green beans.

"I hope you enjoy everything," Sue replied, glancing at Mary Kate with that same peculiar expression before she turned and hurried back to the kitchen.

Blake took a sip of water, his eyes meeting hers over the rim of the crystal goblet. Shaken by a jolting awareness of his masculinity, Mary Kate busied herself with the white linen napkin. It felt clean and crisp against her fingertips. She wondered if he were going to offer grace, then realized he was not when he began to speak.

"Well, tell us about yourself. How did you happen to get into television reporting?"

"Almost by accident," she replied, warming to one of her favorite subjects. "I started out as a part-time reporter for an Alabama television station. I worked during the summers while I attended college. Then after college, I went back full time. I was an anchor on the evening news when Brad—my boss here—was passing through town and caught the telecast. He came by the station the next day and offered me a job." She shrugged lightly, hoping she didn't sound too boastful. "It was merely luck."

"You're doing a good job," Blake said as Sue served the food. "We watched you on television covering that fire at the drugstore. Aren't you nervous about covering an assignment like that? I mean, it could get dangerous, couldn't it?"

She studied the silver meat fork as she lifted a slice of roast beef onto her plate, then added vegetables. "Fires definitely are not my favorite news story," she acknowledged with a grin. "But one of our top reporters is on vacation, leaving the rest of us to pick up the slack." She took a sip of water.

"I think you're being modest." Blake watched as Sue filled his coffee cup from a silver pot. "I've noticed you're covering some pretty important people and events."

"Actually, my specialty is on-the-street interviews. I like talking with the average person, trying to find something fresh and exciting in everyday life. I don't have any strong desire to get into hard news."

"That's very commendable," he complimented, sipping his coffee. "My experience with reporters has often been unpleasant, due to their efforts to make a flashy report rather than an accurate one."

While his remark had been innocently stated, the tense silence that followed hung thickly over the table, as the three of them recalled her brief interview with Blake only days ago.

She lowered her eyes, wondering if she had blundered terribly by even discussing her work.

"Why were you so mean to my dad?" Hanna blurted, glaring at her.

"Hanna—" her father started to scold.

"No, that's okay." Mary Kate put up her hand. "That's a fair question, and I think we need to talk about that." She took a deep breath. "Hanna, I have apologized to your father, and now I would like to apologize to you. I was tired and rushed and—" She broke off, realizing she was not being honest. "That's just an excuse. I guess I wanted a story, and your dad was outsmarting me. I lost my temper. Please forgive me."

"And you tricked me!" she lashed out, tears filling her blue eyes. "You told me I was going to be on television, but instead you called my dad." She jumped out of her seat, sloshing the water from the crystal goblet.

"Hanna," her father called sternly.

She paused at the door, her little shoulders set in a rigid line.

Mary Kate looked at Blake and shook her head. It had turned into a terrible scene, and she was more embarrassed for the Taylors than for herself.

Blake's eyes rested on Mary Kate. "Don't fuss at her," she mouthed quietly.

His eyes swept back to his daughter. "You're excused, Hanna," he said in a low voice.

She darted from the room.

"Actually," Mary Kate said quietly, "she has every right to be upset with me."

"But no right to be rude, when I specifically asked her to behave tonight." Blake dropped his eyes.

As Mary Kate looked down the table to him, she was startled to see this touch of vulnerability in a man who had achieved so much success. Apparently, life at home was a different story.

Mary Kate picked up her fork and began to push her food around her plate, but her appetite was gone. Soon even Blake made no pretense. The room was silent when Sue entered later to check on them.

"Is something wrong?" she asked, looking from one to the other.

"The meal is wonderful, Sue." Blake sighed. "Hanna's behavior altered our appetite, that's all. Would you mind leaving the food in the oven? Maybe we'll have a snack later."

He looked down the table to Mary Kate. "How about coffee in the den?" She nodded. "I'd like that."

She laid her napkin across the table and stood, smiling sadly at Sue. "Your food was wonderful," she said, glancing back at her scarcely touched portion. "I'm sorry," she added.

Sue began to nod her head. "I understand."

Mary Kate decided if Sue had worked here for awhile she must be accustomed to the family's problems. She followed Blake back to the den and tried to clear her mind by looking over the book-lined room. The variety of books on the shelves reflected the personality of an intelligent, well-read man. She moved to the floral sofa and took a seat as Blake settled in the recliner opposite her. Sue entered with a tray holding a pot of coffee and two china cups.

"I'll pour. Thank you, Sue."

Blake walked over and poured the rich dark brew into the cups then glanced at Mary Kate. In the soft glow of the lamps, his eyes were an even deeper blue. "Sugar or cream?" he asked.

"Just black, thank you." She looked away, mentally telling herself that she must not become involved with this man and his daughter. And there was still the matter of the stolen jewelry. *What was the real story?* she wondered, as her heart beat faster.

She took the cup from his hand, feeling the warm brush of his fingers. Something told her to run for her life before she lost her heart. Then as she looked up to thank him, she felt her heart give a leap, and she wondered if it was already too late.

"You're really good with children," he said, settling back in the chair and studying her thoughtfully. "Do you come from a large family?"

She smiled, warmed by the thought of her rowdy brothers and sister. And yet they had always had such a good time together. "As a matter of fact, I do. I have three brothers and one sister. I'm next to the youngest."

"Where did you go to college?"

"The University of Alabama in Tuscaloosa. And you?"

"The University of Tennessee in Knoxville. I was a business major.

Guess I always knew I wanted to be in real estate. That was my minor."

"What about your family?" she asked, eager to know more about him.

"I have one sister who lives in Kentucky. She's married with two girls, thirteen and sixteen. My parents live in Chattanooga and try to visit us as often as they can. They both work for the state and hope to retire in the next five years. Then they promise to spend lots of time with us. When they visit, they always come down together. They're very close and have a wonderful marriage," he said, looking more thoughtful than ever.

In the silence that followed, so many questions flooded Mary Kate's mind, one of the main ones being, *How happy was your marriage?* She had heard conflicting rumors but doubted if she would ever know the truth, unless he chose to tell her. That was far from likely. She would probably never talk with him again after this token dinner to show his appreciation.

He was looking at her again, and she found herself shifting nervously beneath his forthright gaze. Despite her efforts to appear nonchalant about Blake Taylor, she could not remain indifferent each time his penetrating blue gaze held hers.

She turned her attention to the coffee, enjoying its taste. No doubt, this was one of those specialty coffees made from fresh beans and ground daily by Sue, the devoted housekeeper.

"Well," she said, looking back at him, "tell me about your work."

This was always a good, safe subject, she had learned in her years of interviewing. Most people talked easily about their work, even when they detested their job—which Mary Kate secretly found amusing.

He took a deep breath and his tense features visibly relaxed. "My latest project is a special little shopping center near Destin. The design reflects the ocean motif, lots of driftwood, seashells, that sort of thing. It's kind of fun to plan."

"Oh, that does sound like fun. Have you begun work on it?"

"As a matter of fact, we're still in the planning stages, which is one of the reasons I had gone to my beach house near there. Of course, I needed to relax, but I also wanted to go over some of the plans and think about the best way to design the shopping center."

"I see." She nodded. So his trip hadn't been entirely selfish, escaping the press and his little daughter. He was attempting to mix business with pleasure.

"Maybe you'd like to come down with me sometime. There's a wonderful restaurant nearby. I could show you what we're doing."

The invitation took Mary Kate totally by surprise. Her first thought was, *Why is he asking me? He's fulfilled his obligation.* Then her next thought was, *Whatever the reason, I'd like to go.*

Belatedly, she thought she saw the wisdom of his plan. "Would you want me to do some sort of interview for promotion?"

He groaned. "No, please. I've had more than my share of press lately. It's the last thing I want." He drained his coffee cup and placed it on the coffee table. "No, my reason for asking you was purely selfish," he said, glancing across at her. "I thought it would be fun to get away from here and get to know you better. You're a very interesting young lady."

She swallowed, trying to take the compliment in stride. "Thank you," she said at length.

"I'm sorry about Hanna's behavior tonight," he said, turning to her, his full lips drawn in a tight, worried line.

She shifted, propping her elbow against a soft pillow. "Please don't apologize. I can understand how difficult it must be trying to raise a little girl alone—" She broke off, noting the guarded look on his face. Had she said too much?

"We've managed," he said, his tone more formal now. "There haven't been any serious problems—until this trial." His words were heavily underscored, reminding Mary Kate of her own dismal role in publicizing the trial.

She didn't know how to respond. She took a deep breath and tried again. "I just meant I appreciate the problems both of you must have had adjusting to the loss of your wife."

After speaking those words, she could have bitten her tongue off. She watched the handsome face harden to a mask of bitterness. *How could I have become so personal with him in these past minutes when all I wanted was to express concern?* She had assumed enough time had elapsed since Charlotte Taylor's death to allow a gentle reference to her, but Blake's tormented face shouted the truth into the sudden, tense silence.

Somewhere behind them she could hear the tick of a clock as the silence stretched between them. She glanced around the room then met his eyes once again. "Well, I have to be at work early in the morning, and I expect you do, as well. I hope you and Hanna get everything straightened out." It was an innocent remark on her part, but again he seemed to be on the defensive.

"We'll get everything straightened out," he assured her. "But I'm afraid that you're leaving with the impression that our situation is worse than it really is."

"Oh no, I didn't mean it that way. And I certainly don't want to pry. But I was just wondering. . ."

"What were you wondering?" he asked, studying her curiously.

She cleared her throat. "It might help if Hanna had some counseling, and I know a wonderful Christian counselor."

His brown brows arched questioningly. "Are you saying you think Hanna needs to see a psychiatrist?" The blue eyes darkened, and again there was a tightness about his mouth.

"Lots of children see counselors nowadays," Mary Kate answered gently. "Sometimes an outsider who is trained to deal with family problems can accomplish more than a parent who may have become overprotective or—"

"Overworked! I know that's on the tip of your tongue, so I'll say it for you. Yes, I'm overworked. And yes, I should have taken her to the beach with me the day she begged to go. But I needed the time to myself."

"I wasn't about to say anything like that," Mary Kate said, suddenly angered by his quick assumptions.

The sudden silence that filled the room was charged with the electrical tension of strong emotions held in check.

"I must go," she said, reaching for her bag. "Thanks for inviting me."

He hesitated for a moment, almost as though he wanted her to stay, but then he shoved his hands in his pockets and shrugged his broad shoulders lightly. "Thanks for coming," he said, his tone changed.

She sensed that he was sorry for bristling at her remark, and she regretted almost snapping at him, but at least the evening was almost over and she wouldn't have to see him again.

"I imagine everything will straighten out in time," she assured him, feeling awkward now.

He walked her to the door, saying nothing more until they had crossed the foyer. Then as he opened the door for her, he looked across with a question in his eyes. "You never did respond to my invitation for dinner at the beach. What do you think?"

In view of the tense exchange that had just passed between them, she knew he was only being polite, and she had no desire to go now, anyway.

"I'm sorry. I don't think I'll be able to go."

He nodded, as though he had read her thoughts clearly. "Then again, thanks for trying to help with Hanna."

"No problem." She stepped out onto the porch, momentarily taking in the elegance of the neighborhood—and the loneliness. She turned back. "Thanks for dinner."

"My pleasure. Shall I walk you to the car?" He was looking at her as though he wanted to make up for their argument, but she decided this was a good way to end it.

"I'll be fine," she said, then turned quickly and hurried down the steps and across the sidewalk, her heels clicking loudly in the silence of the summer night. He was still watching her as she backed her car out of the drive and pulled away.

Chapter 6

The desk phone shattered Mary Kate's quiet concentration as she studied the script for her next interview.

"Not again," she moaned, wondering as she lifted the phone how many times she had been interrupted in the past hour.

"I decided I want to go to Sea World after all," came a small voice.

Mary Kate had almost forgotten the rumpled tickets in her purse. She blinked, prodding her work-numbed brain a couple of times before she could translate the words and the unspoken plea behind them.

"Hanna, is that you?" She frowned, staring at the mountain of work overflowing her desk.

"Yes. Can we go? Please?"

Mary Kate bit the inside of her lip, recalling her decision to stay out of the Taylors' life after leaving their house two nights ago. And yet, how could she say no to the lonely little voice on the other end of the line?

"Well. . ." She swallowed, closing her eyes to her workload. "If you want to go to Sea World. . .sure, we'll go. When would you like to do that?"

"I could go this weekend," Hanna quickly replied. "I don't have anything to do."

This weekend, Mary Kate thought, recalling how she had planned to collapse on her sofa on Saturday and enjoy the luxury of doing absolutely nothing. Her first day off in weeks.

"Sue already said I could go," Hanna said, as though pleading her case. "Besides, Dad has to go check on one of his projects."

"Okay," Mary Kate heard herself relenting. "I think there's an afternoon show of Shamu around two. How does that sound?"

"Great!" There was no mistaking the excitement in her voice. She sounded like a completely different child than the sullen one Mary Kate had encountered only a few nights ago.

"Okay," Mary Kate replied, picking up the child's excitement. "How about if I pick you up at noon? Maybe we could have a pizza first."

"I'll be ready," Hanna answered excitedly. "And thank you," she added quietly.

"You're welcome. Thank you for calling me."

After she hung up, she sat staring at the phone. She couldn't resist the surge of happiness that flowed through her. It made her feel so good to do something kind for Hanna. There was such a sadness about her and her father, and she was sure it stemmed from the tragedy of losing their beautiful mother and wife.

She leaned back in the chair, her thoughts wandering toward Blake Taylor again. What would his reaction be to his daughter going to Sea World with Mary Kate? Of course he wouldn't mind. He would probably be relieved that someone was entertaining his daughter. That thought brought a wave of disappointment to her. Blake Taylor had a lot to learn about being a father. He should have been spending Saturday with his daughter after what had happened this week. Instead, he was off to one of his projects. When was the man going to learn?

"The dolphins were so cute, weren't they?" Hanna asked, beaming up at Mary Kate.

Steering the car into the slower lane of traffic, Mary Kate stole a glance at her little friend. Her blond hair was combed neatly in place, and she was wearing a blue, two-piece outfit that looked as though it had come from a very expensive children's shop. She smiled at Hanna.

It had been a delightful Saturday for both Mary Kate and Hanna. Mary Kate had joined in the fun with Hanna, telling her stories about her own childhood over pizza as Hanna listened intently, a strange look on her face. It occurred to Mary Kate that Hanna had missed out on so much in her life, specifically a normal childhood. Later, as they sat together, munching popcorn and taking in the antics of the animals at Sea World, Hanna had squealed with delight.

Glancing down at the little girl whose blue eyes glowed with excitement, Mary Kate felt happier than she had in a long time. It warmed her heart to see Hanna having such a good time. *What,* she wondered, *does the child normally do on Saturday?* From their conversation, she didn't seem to have many friends, and Mary Kate wondered about that, although she had refrained from asking personal questions.

"We'll spend another Saturday together sometime if you'd like to."

"I would." Hanna was studying her strangely. "Can I come to see you sometime?"

"You want to come to my junked-up place?" Mary Kate laughed. "Well, sure. But I'll have to warn you, I'm not a good housekeeper."

"Mother wasn't either," Hanna said, turning her eyes back to the road. "Sue did all the work." Then her eyes lit up again as she turned to Mary

Kate. "Maybe Sue could come over and help you out."

"Oh, I don't think I could afford Sue," Mary Kate said, turning into Hanna's neighborhood. "And besides, she's needed at your house."

"Yeah, but she gets bored. She runs out of things to do."

"She does?" Mary Kate glanced at her, thinking it should be a busy life, taking care of Hanna and her father, doing the housework and the cooking.

"She has a cleaning woman who comes in twice a week to help out. And she orders meals from a take-out shop lots of evenings. And sometimes Dad and I eat out."

"Oh, you do?" Mary Kate asked with interest, thinking maybe she had been a bit hard on Hanna's father, after all.

"Yes, he lets me choose a restaurant, and we go out once a week. I like tacos." She smiled across at Mary Kate, who nodded in agreement.

"What else do you do?" she asked, wanting to know more.

"I sometimes go to visit my mother's parents in Memphis."

"Do you have fun?" Mary Kate asked hopefully, although she already suspected she knew the answer judging from the child's sad face.

"Not anymore. All Grandmother wants to do is talk about Mother. And she cries a lot."

Mary Kate nodded. That was exactly the sort of thing Hanna didn't need.

"Mother was an only child, so I don't even have cousins to play with."

"What about your dad's parents?"

Her eyes lit up. "I do have fun when I go to see Grandma and Grandpa. They live in Chattanooga."

"Do you have cousins on your dad's side?"

Hanna giggled. "Rachel and Tina. They're teenagers and they're always talking about dating." She giggled. "When I visit them, they let me play dress-up with their things, and they take me to movies and shopping."

"That sounds like fun. Where do they live?"

"In Kentucky," she replied with a sigh. "So I don't get to go there very often."

Mary Kate nodded sagely as she turned into the drive. It occurred to her that Hanna was probably the loneliest little girl she had ever met. She wondered why she didn't have more friends, and she decided it was time to come right out and ask.

"Do you have many friends in your neighborhood?"

Hanna sighed again. "Not anymore. I used to have friends, but then when Mother was sick, I couldn't have company, and then. . ." Her voice trailed away.

"You could have company now, couldn't you?" Mary Kate frowned at her, thinking something was terribly amiss here. It was bad enough that she had lost her mother; now she seemed to have lost her friends as well.

"I don't want to play with them," she answered defiantly.

Mary Kate stared at her. "Why not?"

Something in her face closed down, and Mary Kate realized she was not going to get an answer to her question.

"I just don't," she said, reaching for the door handle. "Thanks for taking me." Her voice was more formal now, and Mary Kate realized with a pang of sadness that the questions she had asked had put a gap in their friendship. She so wanted to return to the warm funny state they had shared earlier, but she had no idea how.

"Hey," she said, reaching across to touch Hanna's arm, "if you like tacos, do you like spaghetti?"

Hanna looked surprised by the question. Then, thinking it over, she began to nod. "I like spaghetti."

"Then you're in luck. It's the only thing I cook decently. Want to come over sometime and help me make spaghetti? We might even make cookies afterwards."

Hanna's blue eyes lit up again. "When?"

Mary Kate mentally ran her hectic week through her mind and hit a wall. "Why don't I call you? I'd say tomorrow, but I've already promised my Sunday school class I'd go to lunch with them." Then another idea came to her. "Do you go to Sunday school, Hanna?"

She shook her head. "I go to church when I visit my grandma in Chattanooga."

Mary Kate nodded, making a mental note to do something about that.

"Why don't I call you about that spaghetti?" Mary Kate winked at her.

"Okay." Hanna pushed open the door and hopped out, smiling back at Mary Kate. "Thanks." She slammed the door and skipped, swinging her bag of souvenirs, up to the front door where Sue was waiting. Hanna waved to Mary Kate who waved back before leaving.

All the way home, she kept thinking about what an enchanting little girl Hanna was. She would be so easy to love, but she couldn't get involved. *Why not?* a voice in her head questioned.

Because getting involved with Hanna might mean getting involved with her dad, and Mary Kate knew she had to avoid that. *Perhaps one more outing with Hanna wouldn't hurt anything,* she reasoned, humming to herself as she drove home.

⚓

The first part of Mary Kate's week was as hectic as usual, and by Tuesday night she was exhausted. She had already taken her bath, jumped into her comfortable pajamas, and settled down on the sofa with a bag of popcorn when the telephone rang, intruding on her favorite television program.

With a sigh of resignation, she placed the popcorn on the table and reached for the phone. "Hello." She tried to sound more pleasant than she felt.

"Mary Kate?"

She bolted to attention, knowing instinctively that the voice on the other end belonged to Blake Taylor.

"Yes?" She tried to control a ridiculous leap of her heart as she waited for him to continue.

"This is Blake Taylor. I wanted to thank you for taking Hanna to Sea World on Saturday. She had a wonderful time. She's still talking about the dolphins."

Mary Kate smiled, remembering. "Strange that you should call. I was thinking about phoning to see if she could come over for spaghetti on Thursday evening. We sort of discussed doing that."

"Sounds like a good idea, if she isn't overloaded with homework."

"I promise to have her home by seven-thirty," Mary Kate said, wondering why she sounded apologetic.

There was a moment's hesitation, and it occurred to Mary Kate that he might enjoy joining them, but she just wasn't up for another jolting encounter with Blake Taylor, so she kept silent. "I'll mention this to Hanna if you like."

"Yes, would you please?"

"Sure. Hold on a minute."

She could hear the phone being placed on something solid, then steps retreating over a tiled floor. *He must be on the kitchen phone,* she deduced, since it was the only area of the house that was not plushly carpeted. In a matter of seconds, he was back.

"She's thrilled. Shall I drop her off?"

"Er. . .no," she answered quickly, then bit her tongue. "I'm not sure just what time I'll be getting away from the station. What would work best for me is to pick her up after I leave work. I'd say that will be around six, but I'll call first."

"Fine. I'll tell her. Well. . ." He hesitated for a moment. "Thanks again for what you're doing for her."

"Believe me, I'm having as much fun as she is. Maybe more," she added, realizing that this was really true.

"Have a good week," he said before hanging up.

After she replaced the phone, she sat staring into space, trying to analyze her reasons for avoiding Blake. His reputation? There was still some buzz about the jewelry incident, and she had a feeling Brad wouldn't want her seeing him. He would make noises about her "image." But that wasn't really it, she knew in her heart of hearts. The man had a strange effect on her. The truth was, she didn't quite know how to react to him. He was older, more sophisticated; and he had been married to a woman who had died a painful death. He must be suffering terribly. She didn't know what to say to him or how to act in that situation. In fact, the whole thing was so complicated that she couldn't begin to sort through her feelings. What confused her most of all was her own response to him. He made her heart beat faster and brought an odd tingling to her skin, and all the while she felt hot and cold at the same time.

Nerves, she decided, *pure and simple.* And the best cure was to avoid him completely.

It makes perfect sense, she told herself, picking up her popcorn again and trying to catch up on what she had missed of her favorite show. To her disappointment, she had lost interest in television, and now her mind kept straying to Blake.

Disgusted, she got up and went to the kitchen to make herself a cup of hot chocolate. *I'm just overtired from the past two strenuous days. A cup of hot chocolate, early to bed, my nightly devotion, and maybe I'll flip through my Bible—that's what I need.* She needed some peace of mind and in the last hour, it seemed to have fled. Blake's call had left her rattled.

As she waited for the hot chocolate to warm in the microwave, she thought again of what Hanna had said about church. She only went with her grandmother. No wonder the poor little girl was at a loss. She couldn't believe Blake had neglected taking her to church. Surely her mother had, before she became ill.

The bell on the microwave rang, and she opened the door, pondering the thought of inviting Hanna to go to church with her. It seemed like the least she could do. In fact, that was far more important than taking her to Sea World or cooking spaghetti for her.

She suddenly felt better as she headed toward her bedroom, sipping her hot chocolate. She had made a decision, and she knew she was doing the right thing.

🌴

On Thursday evening, when Mary Kate pulled into the Taylor driveway to pick up Hanna, she saw the black European import parked in the driveway. Blake Taylor was already home. She had hoped to avoid him, but now there seemed to be no chance of that. Maybe Hanna would be ready and waiting at the door. Resisting the impulse to merely blow the horn, she got out of the car and hurried up to knock on the front door.

Immediately, it swung back and she was staring into Blake's deep blue eyes. "Good evening," he said with a little smile. His business suit was rumpled, his tie loosened. The blue eyes were weary, haggard, and underlined with dark circles. Mary Kate thought he must work very hard, or perhaps he pushed himself deeper in his work to escape his problems.

She glanced over his shoulder, searching for the little girl.

"Hi. Is Hanna ready? I'm running a bit late."

"No time for a quick cup of coffee?"

She shook her head. "Afraid not."

Quick little steps sounded behind him, and the little girl was pushing around her father, a wide smile on her face.

"Hi," she said, smiling at Mary Kate. She was wearing jeans and the T-shirt she had bought at Sea World on Saturday. Her blond hair was neatly combed, and her face looked as though it had just been scrubbed.

"Hi, Hanna. Ready to go?"

She bolted forward as her dad's hand shot to her shoulder. "Not even a good-bye?" he asked, looking at her with sad eyes.

"Bye, Dad." As he knelt down, she gave him a quick kiss on the cheek, and Mary Kate felt a warm tenderness tugging at her heart.

"I'll have her back by seven-thirty, as I promised," Mary Kate said as Hanna tugged at her hand and they turned to go.

"Have fun," he called after them.

"Thanks," Mary Kate said, giving a quick wave.

Several thoughts concerning Blake were bouncing around in her head, but Mary Kate vowed to sort them out later. Hanna yanked open her car door and leapt into the front seat, as though this was already a familiar routine.

The next hour flew by at Mary Kate's place. While Mary Kate prepared the spaghetti, Hanna played with Bo on the living room floor.

The living room and dining area flowed into the kitchen, and it was easy to peer around a corner to keep an eye on Hanna. Bo, the black cocker spaniel, had become hyper with his new playmate. He had Hanna down on the floor, licking her right in the face. Mary Kate could imagine Blake Taylor's reaction to this scene.

"Bo, stop that!" Mary Kate scolded, although Hanna was squealing with laughter.

Mary Kate hurried to the hall closet to get out a small plastic bucket of his toys. "He likes to play fetch. Maybe if you gently toss the rubber ball, he'll play fetch with you." She turned to Bo and pointed a finger as he wagged his tail happily. "Now, you settle down; otherwise, you'll have to spend some time in the bathroom with the door closed."

He merely licked her hand good-naturedly, too thrilled with his new playmate to be bothered by a little scolding from his mistress.

Mary Kate hurried back to the kitchen just in time to grab the pan of pasta before the water boiled over onto the stove. Lowering the heat, she replaced the pan and turned to pick up a wooden spoon. She was eager to sample the sauce. Her lunch had consisted of an apple, a box of raisins, and a container of juice—all devoured on the run. In fact, she rarely sat down for a relaxed meal. She had to slow down and start leading a sensible life, like she assumed other people did.

When the sauce and pasta were almost ready, she turned to the cabinet and reached for two bright red plates and placed them on the counter. She lived very casually and didn't plan to alter her lifestyle one bit. She opened the silverware drawer, pulled out two stainless steel place settings, then reached into the refrigerator for the salad she had put together the night before. She uncovered the plastic container and placed it on the counter. Now she added salad bowls and dressing to the counter and peered back at Hanna.

"You want milk to drink, Hanna?"

She was squealing with delight as Bo loped back to her side, the ball in his mouth.

"Milk?" she repeated louder.

"I don't like milk." She glanced at Mary Kate.

"Oh? What do you usually drink at dinner?"

"Cola. Or root beer."

Mary Kate frowned. "Sorry, I don't have either one. How about chocolate milk?"

Hanna shrugged. "Maybe."

Mary Kate took that as a yes and prepared it for her, adding an extra scoop of chocolate powder to entice the little girl. *Doesn't her father mind her not drinking milk?* she wondered. Again, she assumed Blake Taylor was too busy with his career to keep a proper eye on his daughter. *And what was Sue thinking?* She wondered about that for a moment, then realized it was probably easier to give in to Hanna than to discipline her.

"Okay, come get it," she called, reminding herself this was not her child to raise, and she should keep her nose out of the Taylors' business.

Hanna ate heartily, turning to offer Bo a bite of spaghetti.

"Please don't do that, Hanna," Mary Kate spoke firmly. "I feed him from his bowl in the kitchen after meals."

For a moment, Hanna looked as though she would rebel.

"I'll let you put his food together later. Okay?"

Hanna smiled, satisfied with the compromise.

The evening went well, and Mary Kate couldn't believe it was already seven o'clock by the time they finished the meal and played with Bo.

"Hanna, look at the time," she said, pointing to the clock. "I promised your dad I'd have you home by seven-thirty."

All the joy drained from her little girl's face. "I don't want to go home," she pouted.

"Then that will give us an excuse to do this again."

"But you promised we would bake cookies."

Mary Kate took a deep breath, wishing she hadn't been so enthusiastic with her invitation. "Well, we'll do that next time."

"You're breaking your promise again!" Hanna's blue eyes darkened as her mouth turned downward.

Mary Kate studied her face and wondered how often she used this ploy to get her way, even though she had a valid point.

"I have to break my promise either to you or to your dad. Since your dad is the boss for both of us on this, if I break my promise to him you might not get to come back. And Bo and I want you to come back again. So, now can we agree on that?"

Hanna chewed the inside of her lip, and Mary Kate could see the mental wheels turning. "I guess so," she agreed with a shrug, turning to give Bo a last hug.

Finally, they were out the door and into the car, heading back home. Hanna was in good spirits again, chatting happily about Bo.

A thought kept nagging at Mary Kate. Another Sunday was coming up, and she wouldn't mind picking Hanna up for Sunday school. It seemed such a waste for her not to attend church.

Don't get involved, a voice warned. But as a Christian, she couldn't help thinking God had put this child in her life for a reason. She felt strongly that one reason was to see that she got in church. If Mary Kate didn't invite her, who would?

She took a deep breath and plunged in. "Hanna, how would you like to come to Sunday school with me Sunday? Last week they were talking about the puppet show they were having this Sunday. I think you'd enjoy that."

"A puppet show?" She swung around on the car seat, her eyes wide. "Why would they have a puppet show in a *church?*"

The lights of a passing car flashed over them, and above the muted lights of her dashboard, Mary Kate saw the doubt in Hanna's eyes.

"Well, you see, the teachers use puppets to tell Bible stories. It's a lot of fun. I think you'd enjoy it, really. Want me to come pick you up Sunday morning?"

"Maybe," she said, squirming. "I like puppets."

"Great." Then she hesitated, realizing she hadn't even mentioned this to Hanna's father.

"I'll ask your dad about it when we get home." She tried to suppress the heavy sigh that was building in her chest. She dreaded another encounter with him, and yet she knew that getting Hanna in Sunday school where she would be surrounded by caring adults and friendly children would be worth the effort.

She turned into the driveway, and as her car lights swept over the sprawling Spanish home, the front door was already swinging open.

He was dressed in jeans and a T-shirt, and seeing him in a more relaxed manner made Mary Kate more cautious than ever. It was easier to think of him as the super businessman with whom she had little in common when he was in business clothes. Seeing him in comfortable clothes and smiling, as he was now, made her want to be friends with him. And she couldn't be.

"Hello," he called to them.

"Dad, you should see Bo."

"Bo?" His blue eyes held a question as he looked from Hanna to Mary Kate.

"My cocker spaniel," Mary Kate explained.

"Oh."

Why does he look relieved? Mary Kate wondered. *Does he think Bo is my boyfriend and that I had made my meal with Hanna a threesome?*

"Won't you come in?" he asked Mary Kate.

He looked more friendly than before as he glanced from Hanna, who was smiling happily at him, back to Mary Kate. Even though she knew the man had no interest in her beyond his daughter's friendship, Mary Kate felt unsettled by his blond good looks and the intense blue gaze in his eyes.

"I have to go. Thanks anyway." She hesitated, glancing down at Hanna. "Bye."

"Bye. See you Sunday," Hanna called over her shoulder as she disappeared into the house.

"Sunday?" Blake looked back at Mary Kate.

She caught her breath. In the confusion, she had forgotten to ask his permission. She cleared her throat. "Would you mind if I took Hanna to Sunday school?"

He stared at her for a moment, then his eyes moved on to something in the darkness. "I've already made plans for the two of us," he said, his tone more formal now.

Mary Kate realized she had struck a nerve with him but failed to see why. "Well, maybe some other time," she suggested.

When he did not acknowledge the offer with further comment, Mary Kate was scarcely able to hide her irritation. She had a strong urge to tell him just what she thought of his method of child rearing. She couldn't do that. After all, it was none of her business. There seemed to be nothing more to say, so she turned to go.

His hand reached out, gripping her arm. The warm strength of his fingers brought a catch to her throat, and she whirled back to him, her brows lifted questioningly.

"Thank you for entertaining Hanna this evening," he said, suddenly releasing her. He seemed to regret having touched her. It was as though he reacted before he thought. They were both silent for a moment, causing her to linger just when she would have pulled away.

Mary Kate didn't like the way she felt pulled toward him, wanting to stay and talk. But she had to keep her distance. "You're welcome," she replied. This time she was the one whose tone was formal. "Good night," she said, hurrying down the steps.

As she walked quickly to her car, she tried to figure the man out. What went on inside that complicated brain of his? His voice told her one thing, while his eyes, his touch, revealed something else entirely.

As she drove back to her apartment, Mary Kate couldn't stop thinking about him. She even rubbed her arm gently where his fingers had rested. Her experience with romance had been limited to a high school boyfriend who was really just a friend, and several dates in college. There had been a brief fascination or two, but she had never been in love. Her mother had told her she was too picky, but the truth was she kept waiting for that special magic she saw between her parents. She had always thought she might prefer someone older, but she dared not consider Blake Taylor a possibility.

He had been married with a child. And there was still a cloud over his head concerning the jewelry theft. No, she couldn't feel anything for the man, even though the song on the radio stirred a deep longing in her soul.

She pondered over the tension between Blake and her. Strong vibrations crackled in the air when they were in the same room, so that, inevitably, they ended up snapping at each other or glaring silently, unable to speak at all.

It was just too bewildering to figure out.

☥

As Mary Kate unlocked her door and flipped on the lights, Bo came running to meet her. It was good to have someone waiting for her when she came home at night, even if it was only her beloved little dog.

"You've had quite a night, haven't you?" she teased him.

Glancing around, she heaved a sigh at the disorder of her duplex. She had moved in, months before, with the idea of completely renovating the plain rooms. But there had been no time.

"Oh, well." She turned to Bo and shook her head. "You don't really mind, do you?"

She reached down to stroke his soft fur, and they both wandered back to her bedroom. She wanted a relaxing soak in the tub and then she was going to jump into bed and read for awhile.

As she passed the dresser mirror, she hesitated, studying her reflection. She had changed into jeans and an oversized white blouse after she and Hanna came back, and she noted that the white accented the darkness of her hair and eyes. She found herself wondering what Blake thought of her, as she appraised her petite reflection. She had narrow shoulders, a tiny waist, flaring hips, and legs that were too long for her small frame—attractive, but definitely not the figure of a model.

She turned and moved on into the bathroom, thinking of that relaxing soak in the tub that she had promised herself. Nothing soothed her nerves like lounging in the tub surrounded with bubbles and scented oil.

Suddenly, the phone jangled on the nightstand in the bedroom. She glanced at her watch. Eight o'clock. This had better not be some ridiculous night assignment Brad was asking her to do at this hour. She hurried back into the bedroom and grabbed the ringing phone.

To her surprise, it was Blake Taylor's voice on the other end of the wire.

"Mary Kate, am I disturbing you?" he asked politely.

"No. . ." *Why is* he *calling?* she wondered, fighting a burst of excitement at the sound of his voice.

He cleared his throat. "Hanna's really disappointed about missing that puppet show on Sunday," he said. "So I've canceled our plans. If you still would like her to go, I don't object."

Object? Thank you very much, she was tempted to respond. He should be pleased she was making the effort to take his daughter to church, when he didn't take her himself.

"Fine," she said, matter-of-factly. "I'll pick her up at nine-thirty. My church is only fifteen minutes from your house, and Sunday school starts at a quarter of ten."

"She'll be ready," he said quietly.

Mary Kate sensed that he wanted to say more, but she didn't give him time.

"Tell her I'll see her then. Thanks for letting her go."

"Thanks for taking her—"

"Good night," she said quickly, scarcely hearing his reply before she hung up.

She was on the brink of being rude to him, but she couldn't help it. The man unnerved her, and she knew she had to keep a tight rein on this situation. *In fact, it might be a good idea if I don't continue to see Hanna,* she decided, going into the bathroom to run water in the tub. Maybe getting her started in Sunday school would influence her father to take her, and Mary Kate could drop her role as companion.

The situation was a difficult one, at best. First, she had put Blake on guard in that awful interview. Then he had interpreted her concern for Hanna as criticism of his parenting, and now she was stealing valuable time he had planned to spend with his daughter.

She sighed, opening the cabinet for a towel and washcloth. She would miss being with Hanna. *The little girl is winning my heart,* she thought, reaching for the bath oil.

God, how am I going to handle this? she silently prayed.

Chapter 7

Those puppets were really neat!" Hanna exclaimed, her blue eyes dancing as Mary Kate steered the car out of the church parking lot. "I never had so much fun in Sunday school."

Mary Kate glanced across at her and smiled. She looked so cute today, wearing a pink dress with a Peter Pan collar and delicate pearl buttons down the front. She wore black patent leather shoes and had a tiny matching purse on her arm.

"Glad you had a good time, Hanna. Did you pick out that pretty dress?"

Her eyes darkened as she looked away. "No, Mommy bought it before she got so sick."

The words ripped through Mary Kate's heart. It wasn't the first time Hanna had referred to her mother, and now she could see the pain on the little girl's face. She bit her lip, trying to think what to say. Should she change the subject or encourage Hanna to talk about her mother? She had no idea what to do, but then Hanna solved the problem.

"Mommy's in heaven," she said, turning on the seat to look at Mary Kate. "Grandma told me that at the hospital."

Mary Kate swallowed hard, nodding her head. "That's right. And you'll see her again someday."

"Grandma says I need to give my heart to Jesus. How do I do that?"

Mary Kate was grateful for the red light, giving her a chance to slow down and gather her thoughts. "Would you like to talk to my pastor sometime, Hanna? Or even your Sunday school teacher might be better at explaining it than I am. But I can tell you what I did."

"What did you do?" Hanna turned her head, studying Mary Kate thoughtfully.

Mary Kate thought back to her childhood and the small country church she had loved so much. "Come to think of it, I was exactly your age. Eight years old. It was the Sunday after Bible school, the first week in June—June 7, as a matter of fact. I had been learning about becoming a Christian during Bible school. My teacher told me that all I had to do was confess my sins and believe that Jesus came down to earth to die for those sins. I believed that then, and I believe it now. So I walked down the aisle on

Sunday morning when the altar call was given and told the pastor what I had decided." She glanced at Hanna. "I remember feeling so happy that day, and it still makes me happy to think about becoming a Christian."

Hanna was quiet for a moment, staring at Mary Kate. Then she sank back against the seat and stared out the window. Mary Kate imagined she was thinking this over; maybe even now she was feeling a tug on her heart to do the very same thing.

"Can I come back with you next Sunday?" Hanna looked at her.

Mary Kate remembered her vow not to get further involved after today, but now she knew she had no choice. If she could help Hanna to become a Christian, it would be one of the most wonderful things that could happen.

"Of course," she said tenderly.

The light had changed and as they drove into Hanna's neighborhood, Mary Kate thought perhaps Hanna could influence her father to come to church. The thought of Hanna's father drew Mary Kate's eyes to the car mirror, assessing her image. She had worn a blue linen suit with short sleeves and a blue floral scarf tucked into the open collar. Her dark hair was shining from the morning's shampoo and her eyes sparkled with happiness. She always felt better after going to church.

Her eyes darted back to the street, then to the Taylor house they were now approaching. She turned into the driveway and stopped the car.

"Well. . ."

"Aren't you coming in?" Hanna whirled, her eyes wide.

"I can't, Honey. Sorry."

Then, looking over Hanna's head to the front yard, she spotted Blake walking toward them. He was dressed in casual clothes, and for once he looked relaxed and rested. He opened the car door for Hanna.

"Dad, the puppet show was great!" she said, hopping out of the car. "But Mary Kate won't come in."

Mary Kate noted the little pout forming on Hanna's mouth and knew instantly that she had her own methods for getting her way with her dad.

"Do you have to go?" Blake too looked disappointed, but Mary Kate tried not to think about that.

"Yes, I do."

"Are you sure? We hoped you would stay for lunch."

She sighed. "I really can't. I'm sorry, but thanks anyway."

Blake turned to Hanna. "Run and get your playclothes on. I thought we'd ride over to the beach if you want to."

"Yippee!" Hanna yelled, darting across the yard, her pink skirt flying.

Blake opened the door wider. "May I talk with you for a moment?"

Mary Kate swallowed. "Sure." She stretched one arm across the steering wheel and moved her purse over with the other as Blake sat down.

"I hope you know how much I appreciate your kindness to Hanna. I was hoping you'd have lunch with us and then go to our beach house for the afternoon. I should have asked sooner. Sorry."

"That's okay," she answered quickly, trying not to look into his blue eyes. He was so handsome and so appealing when he spoke in that soft rich tone. It was becoming more difficult for her not to feel a strong attraction to him.

There was a genuine humility in his voice that drew her attention to his face. The blond hair and brown brows were offset by the rich blue of his eyes, and the hard line of jaw and chin were somehow softened by the quiet pleading in his level gaze.

She dragged her eyes away and tapped her fingers on the steering wheel. "Well. . .," she began, trying to assemble her thoughts before she made an excuse. She was suddenly thinking of Hanna's expression of concern about becoming a Christian. How could she hold a grudge against Blake Taylor? As a Christian she wasn't supposed to do that, and she knew it.

"You probably noticed I was a bit sensitive about church," he said, breaking into her thoughts. "That's one more area I need to work on. When Charlotte died so young, I had trouble accepting that as God's will, in my mother's words. My mother believes that everything is in God's hands, and I guess I didn't want to see it that way. In any case," he sighed, "Hanna needs to be in church, and I want to thank you again for taking her."

"You're welcome," she said gently. Maybe she had judged him too harshly, after all. She was about to say as much, but his next words threw her completely off guard.

"Is there some reason you want to avoid being with me?" he asked directly.

She caught her breath, startled by his frankness. Her eyes flew to his face, and she looked him directly in the eyes, wanting to say the right thing. When she realized he was staring at her too, she turned and focused on the clean white lines of the Spanish-style house.

"No, of course not," she answered nervously.

"There's something else I'd like to say." He took a deep breath as though whatever he wanted to say was difficult.

Mary Kate waited, holding her breath. Tension crackled between them like electricity, and her stomach was knotting.

"I would like for you to know," he said turning back to her, his blue eyes suddenly vulnerable, "that I am not a thief. I was innocent of the charges against me."

Mary Kate felt a blush creeping up her cheeks, and she realized with a sinking heart that he knew this was one of the reasons she had been avoiding him.

"I'd also like for you to know that I have not asked another woman out since. . .my wife died."

Mary Kate looked into his face and felt her heart melt. All her defenses tumbled and she knew she was lost. There was no way she could keep on saying no to him.

"I'm honored that you chose to invite me," she said quietly. "And I never thought you guilty of those charges."

There, it was out in the open now. He heaved a deep sigh, as a wide smile flashed over his face. "Thank God."

Mary Kate's eyes drifted toward the house as she thought about the empty afternoon stretching before her. Why not accept his invitation? There was nothing she'd rather do than spend a Sunday afternoon with Hanna and Blake.

"Tell you what," she said with a smile. "I need to go home and see about Bo, and I'd like to change into something more comfortable. Then I really would like to ride over to the beach with you and Hanna."

There was no mistaking the look of pleasure on his face. "That's marvelous. What time should we pick you up?"

"In an hour?" she asked, glancing at her watch.

"That's perfect. Thanks for changing your mind."

Her brown eyes locked with his, and for a moment, neither spoke. Then, awkwardly, she turned in her seat and focused on the key in the ignition. "I'd better get going then," she said, turning the key. "By the way, what if I pack us a little picnic snack?"

"Sounds great. I'll tell Hanna you're coming," he called cheerfully as he got out of the car.

Waving, she backed out of the driveway and drove off, thinking about her afternoon with Blake and Hanna.

An hour later she was surprised to see a white sport-utility vehicle pulling into her driveway when she was expecting the black luxury sports sedan she had seen in Blake's drive. But there was no doubt it was Blake and Hanna. Hanna's face was pressed to the car window, and her eyes were wide with anticipation as Mary Kate hurried out and locked the front door.

She started toward the backseat when the front door was thrust open. "Where's Bo?" Hanna demanded. "He likes the beach, doesn't he?"

Mary Kate wasn't sure Blake would appreciate black cocker spaniel fur on his upholstery. "Yes, he does, but—"

"Dad, Bo can come too, can't he?"

"Absolutely—I'm outnumbered here." Blake hopped out and came around the car, taking the picnic basket from Mary Kate's hands.

"Are you sure, Blake? Your upholstery—"

"Positive. I'll put this in the back."

Hanna jumped out of the car, grabbed Mary Kate by the hand, and dragged her to the house to get Bo.

"What's in the picnic basket?" Hanna asked, her eyes dancing with excitement as Mary Kate unlocked the door.

"Just a snack for later." Mary Kate opened the door and called Bo. He bounded out the door to greet Hanna with a wet kiss. Mary Kate turned to see if Blake had changed his mind about taking her wiggling dog along, but the wide grin on his face told her not to worry. He seemed to be enjoying Hanna's giggles of joy as she dodged Bo's wet nose.

Hanna ran for the backseat with Bo on her heels. Bo stopped, waiting for permission from his mistress before he jumped in behind Hanna.

Hopping into the front seat, Mary Kate smiled first at Hanna then at Blake, after he had settled in under the wheel. They were both wearing shorts and T-shirts and looked relaxed and happy. She sighed with relief. It was nice to see both of them looking this way for a change.

"You've never been to our summer place," Hanna said, her eyes twinkling.

Blake laughed. "We call it that even though we go there year-round. But when Hanna is out of school, we're able to spend a lot more time there, so we refer to it as the summer place."

"Well, it sounds great to me," Mary Kate said, buckling the seat belt over her yellow shorts and matching T-shirt.

"You aren't very tan," Hanna said, staring at Mary Kate's legs.

"Hanna," her father scolded softly, although Mary Kate only laughed as they drove away from her apartment.

"No, I don't have a summer place, nor do I have much free time to spend at one. I'm afraid Bo and I may get spoiled today, Hanna, once we see what we've been missing."

Hanna giggled and squirmed around in the seat whenever Bo sniffed her ear. Blake was concentrating on the traffic and said nothing as he drove along, but his expression was calm and pleasant, as though he were enjoying himself.

He took the bypass around Seabreeze, and soon they were on the road to Seaside with the other Sunday afternoon traffic.

"Don't you go to the beach on the weekends?" Blake asked casually. "Surely you aren't working then."

"You work a lot of weekends, Dad." Hanna frowned at him in the mirror.

He chuckled. "You're right, I do. But I'm going to be doing less of that now." He looked back at his daughter and winked.

"Since I'm the newest reporter, I get called lots of times to cover assignments because the other reporters have seniority and can get their time off. I really haven't minded, because I don't know that many people here. Sometimes my weekends are lonely—no offense, Bo," she said and smiled over her shoulder. After she had made that confession, she bit her tongue. She was getting too personal with them; she hated to admit she got lonely, but of course she did.

Blake darted a curious glance at her. "I should think you'd have plenty of invitations," he replied casually.

She shrugged. "I do, I suppose. Maybe I'm just picky." She laughed, looking at Hanna. "I like being with little girls with big blue eyes and blond hair."

Hanna squealed with laughter. Mary Kate smiled at her, then glanced over at her father, who looked in the mirror at Hanna and grinned.

"Excited, aren't you?" he teased.

She nodded, glancing back at Mary Kate.

They had reached the first strip of tourist shops that always seemed to entice people from other areas. Hanna showed little interest in the shops that advertised T-shirts, caps, souvenirs, even ice cream and hot dogs. She had pressed her hands on the console between the bucket seats and was staring straight ahead, as though watching for something.

"Are you going to tell me where to turn?" Blake glanced at her.

"It's after that second red light," Hanna answered proudly.

"That's right."

As Mary Kate listened to the exchange between the two, she realized it was probably a familiar game they played each time they came to their summer place, with Hanna giving directions, proud that she knew the way.

At the second light, they turned onto a quieter street with small beach houses and an occasional market or restaurant.

"The next light." She pointed and Blake chuckled.

"Right again."

"No, you turn left," Hanna giggled.

"Can't even trick you!"

As Mary Kate leaned back against the seat and let her eyes drift from father to daughter and back again, she wondered why she had ever worried that Blake Taylor was not a good father. He and his daughter were obviously close, despite the terrible hardship they had been through of losing wife and mother, and then the awful charges of theft and the trial that followed.

She blinked and turned back to the road, feeling really sorry for both of them. Hanna was jabbering about a little girl she had met at the beach the last time they were here, as she scratched Bo behind the ears. Mary Kate wasn't really listening, however; her attention was drawn to the exclusive area they had entered. Nice beach houses sat on spacious lots, overlooking the serene blue water. Mary Kate couldn't help being impressed. At the end of the street, Blake turned into a driveway, and she stared at this house. It was different from the others in that it was an A-shaped house, or chalet, like one would expect to see out west or up in the mountains.

"It's different, isn't it?" He glanced across at Mary Kate.

"I like it," she said while Hanna and Bo squirmed on the seat, eager to get out of the car.

Mary Kate opened the door and stepped aside as Hanna and Bo raced up the little walkway that led to the cozy chalet.

When Hanna was far enough away that she couldn't hear, he lowered his voice and explained. "My wife and I enjoyed skiing in Colorado. When we saw this place, we had to buy it, although we would have liked something larger."

At the mention of his deceased wife, Mary Kate felt odd, as though she were trespassing into territory that belonged only to his family. She hesitated, staring at the chalet. Blake seemed to have sensed her sudden reserve because his tone changed to a more casual one.

"Hanna and I come here every chance we get. There's no longer any sadness attached to it."

She turned and met his gaze directly and saw that he did not look sad, merely a bit wistful. She wanted to ask questions about his wife, but she knew that was the last thing she needed to do. She had been invited to come for fun, and she owed it to both of them to keep the conversation pleasant and light.

"Well, I can see why you'd come here often. It's wonderful."

They went up the walkway as Blake reached into his pocket and withdrew a key ring. Hanna was already at the door, jumping up and down, impatient to be inside, with Bo waiting at her side.

After Blake unlocked the door and they entered, Mary Kate took in the simple floor plan. It was a typical chalet, with living room, dining room, kitchen, and a guest bath all on the main floor. The color scheme was a warm yellow, with white wicker furnishings and lots of colorful paintings. A spiral stairway of black wrought iron wound upward to the loft.

"Let me show you my room." Hanna grabbed her hand and Mary Kate followed.

Up the stairs they went to the loft, where two large bedrooms were separated by a huge bath. Hanna's room was decorated in bright blue, and Mary Kate found herself thinking of a summer sky and white clouds, since the furniture was white and the bedspread and curtains were a delicate white eyelet. A small twin-sized bed was filled with stuffed animals.

"This is really pretty, Hanna." Mary Kate turned back to the little girl. "I can see why you love coming here. You're very lucky."

Hanna tilted her head and studied her from an angle, and for a moment, Mary Kate wondered if her choice of words had been wrong. Was she so lucky, after all, losing her mother to a terminal illness and her father to his work? But now he seemed to be making a sincere effort to spend time with her.

"Want to walk down to the beach?" Hanna asked.

"Sure, why not?" Mary Kate smiled as they held hands again and walked down the stairs.

Blake was in the kitchen, checking out the contents of the deep freeze. "We're in luck," he said. "I thought I had left some ground chuck here. Why don't I thaw it out in the microwave and grill hamburgers for us later on?"

"But what about the picnic?" Hanna frowned.

"It's just a snack, really," Mary Kate laughed. "I doubt that it could hold us for long. A hamburger sounds great," she said, looking back at Blake.

"Dad, we're gonna walk down to the beach, okay?"

"Fine. Here, let me unlock the sliding doors."

Blake hurried out of the kitchen into the living room. At the end wall, he unlatched the doors, admitting the fresh sea breeze. As they stepped out onto the deck, Mary Kate's eyes made a sweep of the broad beach and the gentle waves lapping into the shoreline. She sighed.

"Hanna, thanks for inviting me," she said, squeezing the little girl's hand.

"We have to leave our shoes here on the porch and go barefoot. Then we can wash our feet over there when we come back." She pointed to a water faucet, placed conveniently near the steps. It was a comfortable, beautiful place, and Blake seemed to have thought of everything.

Mary Kate and Hanna spent the next hour walking and running up and down the beach with Bo, playing at the shoreline, waiting for the waves as though daring them to catch them, then squealing as the water gushed over their toes. They inched their way backward when the water came too close. Mary Kate realized she had not had so much fun in a long time.

"Having fun?" someone called.

Mary Kate turned to see Blake standing barefoot at the water's edge, watching them with a pleased expression on his face. "I put the picnic basket up there." He pointed to a picnic table. "I'm hungry—what about you two?"

"Great idea." Mary Kate looked at Hanna as they walked across to join him.

"Let's see what surprises you have tucked away in here," he said, leading the way back to the picnic bench.

Mary Kate saw that he had been considerate enough to bring down a plastic picnic cloth, napkins, paper plates and cups, a fresh pitcher of fruit punch, and bowl of water for Bo.

Mary Kate began to laugh. "You two may be in for a disappointment. After offering a picnic snack, I got home and discovered my best fare for sandwiches was peanut butter and jelly!"

"That's my favorite," Hanna said, peering into the basket.

Mary Kate pulled out the plastic-wrapped sandwiches, potato chips, and three large apples.

Hanna had sat down on the picnic bench, eagerly awaiting her food while Bo happily sunned himself in the warm sand. Blake swung his long legs over the bench and sat down, his interested gaze flicking over their snack. "Well, Hanna, I bet you think this is the perfect picnic."

"Mmm," she said, already digging into a sandwich. "I like it better than Sue's fancy old casseroles."

"Come on, now. Sue's a good cook," Blake defended.

Hanna took control of the conversation, relating things from school and projects that had been assigned. Mary Kate was relieved to see that she was opening up to her more, talking freely about her life.

Then when the three of them had finished, Blake stood up, stretching his long legs. "Want to take a walk?"

Hanna darted over and grabbed his hand. "Dad, can we walk down to the pier?"

He glanced eastward to a long pier that looked to be half a mile in the distance.

"Think you're both up to it?" He looked from Hanna to Mary Kate.

"I'm game," Mary Kate answered.

"So am I! Come on, Bo!" Hanna's blue eyes twinkled merrily, and it warmed Mary Kate's heart to see the change that had come over the little girl since the first time she had seen her.

With Hanna in the center, holding each of their hands, they began to walk toward the pier, Bo running ahead and back again. As they walked, Blake talked about the development in this area of the beach, the building codes, and other general topics that interested Mary Kate. Hanna, meanwhile, was more interested in stopping for an occasional seashell. Catching on, Bo sniffed out the best shells for her.

Later, after they had returned to the chalet, Hanna grabbed her sand bucket from the porch and sat down in the sand. The day's frolic had tired her out, and now she was content to sit and play while the exhausted black cocker spaniel napped beside her.

Blake brought out beach chairs onto the deck, and he and Mary Kate sat talking while Hanna built a sand castle.

"She's an adorable child," Mary Kate said, watching her.

"Thanks. And I must tell you, she thinks you're about the greatest person she's ever met. I hope you won't take offense if I suggest that she may be trying to play Cupid."

Surprise widened her brown eyes before realization dawned. She looked at Hanna then at the ocean, slightly embarrassed.

"I'm not offended," she said quietly, "but. . ." Her voice trailed. She had no idea how to express what she was thinking.

"But what?" he asked, studying her thoughtfully.

"I have the impression there is no room in your life for another woman." She turned to face him squarely.

"There hasn't been—before," he replied slowly. "I've been too preoccupied with my own personal problems."

Mary Kate nodded, understanding what he was saying.

"Still, I've missed not having a life, and I haven't had a normal one in what seems like a very long time."

"It's been rough for you, hasn't it?" Mary Kate asked sympathetically.

He nodded. "Still, I've pushed myself too hard for too long. You see," he said, glancing at her briefly, "I've been driven for years to succeed in my work. I suppose I've allowed it to dominate my life for too many years. It became a matter of pride to see how successful I could become, how much money I could make." He sighed, looking far out into the ocean. "Then when Charlotte became so ill, all the money and success couldn't solve the problem. The money helped of course—for awhile." He said nothing more, as though he were deep in thought.

"I've been caught up in my work too. I know the feeling."

He had turned to look at her curiously. "You're a very pretty girl, and you're intelligent and fun. Surely you could have married if you had wanted to do that."

She shrugged. "Guess I just never met the right guy."

"Not that you haven't had offers," he said, testing her.

She smiled. "My parents are very happy together, and I've looked for the same kind of commitment."

The next words came from her heart, an admission of her own philosophy, and she spoke without even thinking how he might react. "They always taught me to pray for the right man, and I have. So I can't take all the credit for not making a blunder. I've relied on God for guidance in making the right choices."

"I see," he said quietly, looking out across the ocean. "You're very religious, aren't you?"

"Religious? Funny, I don't think of myself that way, just a Christian who tries to do the right thing—most of the time," she added with a grin. "But I do see God's hand in things. For example. . ." She hesitated, glancing at the late afternoon sun painting scarlet ribbons across the horizon. "Whenever I see such beauty, I cannot understand how anyone could doubt the existence of God."

"Belief is one thing. Living up to His expectations is more difficult, I think."

"His or yours? I have a feeling you set awfully high standards for yourself, Blake Taylor. No one is perfect."

He stared into her eyes for a moment, saying nothing. Then he took a deep breath and smiled down at her. "I like being with you. I think you're very good for me."

"Blake. . .," she began uncertainly. She wanted to talk with him about Hanna's desire to become a Christian, but she didn't want to seem like she was intruding in their lives. She was wondering how to word it.

"What is it? What did you want to say?" he prompted.

"Well," she said taking a deep breath, "this morning after we left church Hanna was asking me about becoming a Christian. Your mother had already talked with her about it," she added quickly. "I think she was touched by the sermon. I wanted her to talk with you. And I don't want you to think that I'm interfering," she added, watching his face carefully for a reaction.

"I don't think you're interfering at all," he said quietly. "I think you're helping—" He broke off just as Hanna came up the steps.

"That was a great sand castle you made," Mary Kate said.

"Thanks. Want to look at my seashells with me?"

"Sure." Mary Kate stood up, letting Hanna lead the way back inside.

⚓

Later, Blake grilled hamburgers for them, and they ate heartily, their appetites boosted by the sea breeze and the activities of the day. When finally they drove home that evening, Mary Kate felt as though she had been with them for longer than an afternoon. They had discussed many things about their lives and their plans for the future. Blake had even told her of a shopping center he planned to build five miles from their beach house. It had been a wonderful day for Mary Kate, and she felt a stab of disappointment as he pulled into her driveway and she knew the day had come to an end.

Hanna was stretched out in the backseat, sound asleep with Bo curled up beside her as Blake stopped the car and started to open his door.

"You don't need to see me to my door," she said, smiling across at him. She picked her purse up from the floorboard, glanced back at Hanna and Bo one last time, then looked quickly in his direction. "I—that is, we—had a wonderful time. Thank you."

"Thank you for going," he said. He smiled at her, but there was something more in his eyes. Mary Kate didn't want to think about what that was, or what he was thinking, or what she was feeling.

Hopping out of the car, she let Bo out of the backseat without disturbing Hanna, and they hurried up to her front door. Blake waited, his car lights illuminating her path until she had unlocked the door and turned on the inside light. Then she waved again to him and closed the door.

She leaned against the door and sighed. Her heart was soaring with joy, and she knew her plan not to get involved had backfired. She was already involved, and she didn't even care. She had never been so happy.

Chapter 8

Throughout the next two days, despite her efforts to concentrate, Mary Kate's thoughts kept drifting toward Blake, her desire to be with him increasing. She was aware of her coworkers regarding her with puzzled expressions, yet everyone remained tactfully silent.

Everyone, that is, except Coty.

"Guess who I just happened to see over on the pier on Sunday afternoon?"

Mary Kate stared at him for a moment, then remembered that he spent his weekends fishing, and that he had a trailer over at the beach.

"Us?" she whispered, grinning.

"Yes, us," he whispered back, teasing her. "You're grinning like a Cheshire cat every time I see you, and there's a look in those big brown eyes that definitely has not been there before!"

Mary Kate looked up from her work, smiling dreamily.

Coty was shaking his head, looking worried. "I hate to see you get stepped on your first time out, Kid. It *is* the first time, isn't it?"

"He is a very nice man," she snapped, then glanced around to see if anyone was listening. No one was. She lowered her voice. "Your problem, Coty, is that you have no faith in human nature. In fact, you have no *faith*, period. And that's a problem," she added gently.

Coty sighed. "You have a way of setting me straight like no one else. Except maybe Sharon." His big jaw dropped, pain settling over his face like a tragic mask.

"Coty, why don't you two get back together?" Mary Kate looked into his eyes, sensing his pain. "I know you still love her—and she loves you. I was talking to her last week when she came by to leave some mail for you. She still loves you, Coty."

"I'm so lonely without her and the children," he said, leaning against her desk and looking absolutely desolate. "But I just can't believe she'd ever forgive me for the mess I made of our marriage. Once you start lying and deceiving the way I have, Mary Kate. . ." He shook his head. "I don't guess we can work it out now."

Mary Kate stared at him for a moment. Then she reached into her shoulder bag. Plunging into its depths, she pulled out the worn New Testament that Coty had made fun of recently. "Read this, Coty," she insisted. "The answers to all your problems are in that book."

He hesitated, glancing nervously around the newsroom.

"Take it." She pushed it into his hand, breathing a sigh of relief when he accepted it awkwardly then turned and bounded out of the newsroom.

Later that afternoon, she was just clearing off her desk when Carey announced there was a phone call for her. A special twinkle in Carey's eye told her it might be an interesting call, and she noticed that Carey lingered for another second as she answered.

"This is Mary Kate," she said, giving Carey the eye. Laughing, Carey took her hint and strolled off.

"Hi, this is Blake. I know I'm calling you on the spur of the moment, and I apologize, but for the first time Hanna has accepted an invitation to go home with a friend for pizza, and I was wondering. . ."

"Yes?"

"I told Sue to go on and take the night off. That there was no point in her cooking. Could I interest you in joining me someplace for dinner?"

Mary Kate had no plans for the evening, and this time she didn't want to say no.

"As a matter of fact, you could. I'm just leaving work in about ten minutes."

"So am I. Want to meet somewhere?"

"Sure."

"How about a steak?"

Mary Kate rarely splurged that much and the choice appealed to her. "Sounds great. Where?"

He suggested a nice restaurant conveniently located. "So why don't I meet you there in say, twenty minutes? Will that give you enough time?"

"That'll be fine," she said, opening the bottom drawer for her shoulder bag.

After she hung up, she made a dash to the ladies' room to freshen up. She had chosen a polka dot dress today, pale blue with white dots, a scoop neck, and cap sleeves. Her on-the-street interview had been with a young couple who were heading up a charity drive for the summer. She thought a fun type of dress would be appropriate, and now she was glad she had chosen it.

Diving into her bag, she retrieved her pink-and-white-striped makeup kit and unzipped it. She touched up her mascara, added a bit of blusher and lip gloss, then replaced the makeup kit and pulled her hairbrush from the bottom of the bag. Once she had brushed the shine back into her hair, she was satisfied that she passed inspection for a dinner date. Smoothing the wrinkles from her dress, she rushed out of the ladies' room and almost collided with Carey.

"Hmm. Does he look as good as he sounds?" Carey teased.

"Absolutely." Mary Kate gave her an impish grin then rushed on.

Blake was waiting for her just inside the door of the restaurant, still wearing a dark business suit and crisp white shirt. Mary Kate wondered how he managed to stay so neat after a long day. His blond hair was combed neatly in place, and the blue eyes were shining as though he enjoyed seeing her again.

"Hi." She smiled at him.

"Hi. I already have us a table."

A hostess led the way back through the crowded restaurant to a quiet table in the corner where Blake pulled out a chair for her. Once she was seated, she leaned back in the chair and inhaled the wonderful aromas that floated around her.

"Something to drink first?" an attentive server asked, laying menus before them.

"Iced tea, please," she answered.

"Coffee for me," Blake said, then looked back at Mary Kate. "It's been a long day, and I need the caffeine."

"Sounds as though you were really busy."

He nodded. "It was one of those days. What about you?"

She smiled. "It was one of those days for me as well, so maybe we need to think of better things. Like Hanna. I'm glad she's having dinner with a friend."

Blake suddenly looked more serious. "So am I. She's been something of a loner for awhile now."

Mary Kate folded her hands in her lap, remembering her conversation with Hanna about friends. "She said as much to me. Why is that, may I ask?"

He was silent for a minute, staring at the white linen tablecloth. "I guess," he said looking up at her, "it began with her mother's illness. We were unable to have company because Charlotte was so sick. And then after she lost her mother, she seemed to withdraw from the other children. It was as though she didn't want to be reminded that other little girls had normal lives and she didn't. And too," he continued with a sigh, "I'm afraid I gave in to her too much during those last months. It was hard for me to discipline her, even though I realized she was cranky and difficult at times. To be perfectly honest, she probably wasn't very pleasant to be around, and I imagine the kids avoided her as well."

The drinks were placed before them, giving Mary Kate an opportunity to frame a reply. "Well, she seemed to enjoy Sunday school, and there was no problem with her getting along with the other children."

He nodded. "I sensed that. Again, I'm grateful for your help."

She shook her head. "I only took her there. She was the one who interacted, but I will admit that her class is wonderful. I often substitute for Lisa, the teacher. She's a very sensitive, caring person, and she encourages those in her class to treat each other in the same manner. I'm sure they made Hanna feel welcome."

"Ready to order?" A handsome young server stood at their table, ready to explain the specialties of the house. He looked young and eager and kept glancing at Mary Kate as though he recognized her. That was happening more often now, people referring to her as that "TV girl who does the on-the-street thing." She always had to laugh at that expression, but it really didn't bother her.

They both decided on steak, salad, and potatoes.

"I'll have the large T-bone, medium rare, with steak fries," Blake said.

Mary Kate winced. "I'll have the filet, but cook mine longer, please, and I'll have the baked potato."

They both chose the same kind of salad dressing. "At least we agree on that," Mary Kate laughed.

Smiling at them, the server swept up their menus and dashed off.

"Have you done anything that was interesting this week?" she asked conversationally.

"As a matter of fact, I had a great day today. My architect and I left at six this morning and flew up to Highlands, North Carolina, to study an interesting new building there. We got back shortly before I phoned you."

"Highlands! That's a neat place, isn't it? Very small and cozy, but popular with the upper class."

"It's become popular with everyone. It's one of my favorite vacation spots—summer as well as winter. There's skiing nearby, and I like to ski in winter, but in the summer it's really heaven. Nice and cool. The merchants have provided lots of interesting things to attract people year-round. I wanted to study the way they've developed one particular area to get some ideas for my beach development."

Mary Kate nodded. "Very smart of you."

A basket of rolls had been placed on the table, and Mary Kate dived in. Her simple ham-and-cheese sandwich for lunch seemed hours ago. She buttered a bite of roll and popped it in her mouth, then hesitated. Blake was studying her with a little grin, and she couldn't resist asking him what he was thinking.

"I enjoy watching you enjoy yourself," he said, reaching for a roll.

She licked her lips. "Try one of those, and you'll soon be enjoying yourself."

"I already am. I really like being with you. You're very good for me, do you know that?"

She shifted in the chair, suddenly feeling a bit uncomfortable. "Why do you say that?" she asked, concentrating on her roll.

He hesitated for a moment, as though choosing his words. "You help me relax again, to see that life is still fun."

"Of course it is," she said gently, thinking he must have suffered terribly over his wife. "Maybe you need to relax more than you do. Maybe you work too hard."

He sighed. "I do. Work has been an escape for me, I'm afraid. Since the incident with Hanna, my eyes have been opened. I'm trying to do better." His eyes met hers. "You're helping me as much as you're helping Hanna, but you probably don't realize that."

She stared at him for a moment. "No, I didn't realize that," she answered.

Their eyes had locked and now there was a new kind of tension between them, but, strangely, it felt good. She liked being with him, and she was glad she had taken the time to get to know him better.

Their food arrived then, diverting their thoughts, and the rest of the meal passed with general conversation about the city and some of its residents. They decided to split a piece of brownie pie, giggling like teenagers when they were handed two forks and a huge bowl overflowing with brownie, fudge sauce, and ice cream.

"I may not be able to get out of the chair," she laughed, looking across at Blake. Then suddenly something pulled her eyes toward a far corner of the restaurant where Brad and his wife Jane were taking a seat. Brad had already spotted her and his mouth was hanging open.

She quickly looked back at the dessert, but suddenly it didn't taste quite as good. Now all she wanted was to get out of the restaurant, away from Brad's prying eyes.

"I think I've had it," she said, pushing back from the table and folding her napkin over her plate.

"So have I." He motioned for the server. "Are you in a hurry to get home?"

She glanced at her watch. It was eight-thirty. "Do you realize we've been sitting here for two and a half hours?" she asked, amazed.

He chuckled. "No, but I've enjoyed every minute of it. The sitter has to be home at nine, so I guess that answers my question about getting home."

She nodded as they got up from the table and left the restaurant. And she never again glanced in Brad's direction.

⚓

"Brad wants to see you in his office right away," Carey informed Mary Kate as soon as she entered the bustling offices of WJAK the next morning.

Mary Kate suppressed a sigh as she stopped at her desk long enough to collect her telephone messages and place her shoulder bag in the bottom drawer.

"Good morning," she called cheerfully as she entered Brad's office.

His eyes darted up from his cluttered desk, and immediately she read the concern on his face.

"Close the door," he said, staring at her a bit differently.

Please let this be about a news story, she silently prayed, although she had a feeling she knew what was coming. He had not looked pleased about seeing her out with Blake. She closed the door and settled into the chair opposite his desk. "What's up?" She tried to sound casual as she laced her fingers in the lap of her pants suit.

"What were you doing out with Blake Taylor?" he asked in a low voice.

Her mouth fell open. "Brad, I have a right to a life after I leave here. We met for dinner, that was all." She frowned at him. "I wouldn't think my private life should interest you, anyway."

"If you were with Blake Taylor, it interests me." His eyes shot over her head to the glass wall that enclosed his office.

Automatically, she looked over her shoulder to see if someone was there, but nobody was. Then she realized this must be a highly confidential conversation they were supposed to be having.

"Why are we having this conversation, Brad?" She glared at him.

"You can't do that, Mary Kate," he said, his eyes boring through her.

"Do what?" She was thoroughly confused.

"You can't see Blake Taylor socially. Don't you realize there's still a lot of public sentiment where he's concerned? A lot of people were not convinced by the defense that he was entirely innocent."

"And you?" she asked coolly.

"I think his money got him off."

She gasped and stared at him. "That's a cruel thing to say. And very unfair. Brad, he is one of the nicest men I've ever met. He's genuinely nice, and he's devoted to his little girl, Hanna. They've had a rotten time the past

295

year. First, the mother's death and then—"

"I'm well aware of the conditions surrounding his family. If I'm not mistaken, I'm the one who filled you in on those circumstances."

She heaved a sigh and leaned her head against the chair. He was right, he had. She was suddenly at a loss for words. How could she respond to her boss, when in the beginning she had felt the same way he did?

"I think he was misjudged, Brad. I believe he was innocent."

Brad dropped his eyes to his desk and fumbled with a piece of paper for a moment, as though gathering his thoughts. Then he leaned back in the chair and studied her thoughtfully.

"Look, I know he's an attractive man. He has money and he's charming and—"

"Hold it." She put up her hand. "His daughter called me when she ran away, remember? Then I was invited to their house so that he could thank me for helping to locate her. I ended up taking her to Sea World, and then to Sunday school on Sunday."

She paused, wondering how best to explain how she had become drawn into the family so quickly. She looked Brad squarely in the eye and spoke to him as she would her own brother.

"Brad, I don't see the harm of going out with him. After all, he is still a prominent man in this town with lots of friends who believe he was innocent of that theft charge."

He propped his hands on the toppled stacks of work and leaned toward her. "The harm of it is that I don't want you to get hurt. I care about you. Last night the expression on your face was the perfect picture of a young woman falling in love." He paused, clearing his throat as she stared at him, wide-eyed. "Blake Taylor is a very attractive man. I can see why it would be hard for you to resist his advances."

"He has made no advances," she snapped. "And Brad, I am not going to let WJAK dictate how I spend the few leisure hours I have left after giving most of my life to this job. You have no right to do that!"

He sighed. "I understand where you're coming from, Mary Kate." He was speaking in a different tone of voice, a controlled tone that she had heard him use when he was trying to hold onto his logic before he lost his temper. "But I have to warn you. While this man is still such a controversial figure, you could be putting your job in jeopardy if you were to allow this friendship to continue."

Mary Kate stood up and stared down at him, unable to believe her ears. How could he say that? How could one's boss make such an unfair call?

"I'm not sure you have the right to make that kind of threat, Brad." She was fighting her temper now, and she knew she had to get out of his office before she said something she would regret. She turned to go.

"Wait." Brad stood up, staring across at her. "I'm not making any threats, Mary Kate. And I will try to respect your privacy. I'm just asking you to wait awhile. Is that fair enough?"

She hesitated, her hand on the knob. She wanted to turn and yell *no*, but her common sense was slowly returning, and in her mind's eye she recalled her attempts to balance her checkbook each month. She had foolishly overspent after moving here, and now she was trying to get her bills paid off. Furthermore, she liked her job; it had been very important to her, and it still was. *More than Blake Taylor*, she told herself.

She bobbed her dark head slowly and glanced back over her shoulder. "Okay," she said and walked out of the office.

As usual, she became caught up in her work, trying to meet all the demands of her hectic job. She tried not to think of Blake and Hanna when she went home feeling lonely, but by Thursday evening, Blake broke the silence.

The phone rang after she had curled up on the sofa with a book and when she answered, she heard his smooth rich voice.

"Are you having a good week?" he asked, his tone friendly and polite.

She rolled her eyes, thinking he had no way of knowing the veiled threat Brad had tossed at her first thing Wednesday morning. "A typically busy one," she answered. "And you?"

"Typically busy too," he said. "Hanna is already talking about Sunday school again, and I was wondering if I could entice you for Sunday lunch and another trip to our beach house."

Mary Kate took a slow deep breath. What was she going to do? As a Christian, she had to lead Hanna gently along the road to becoming a Christian; but she had to do this without seeing Blake. But then she had another thought. "Could you join us for church?"

He sighed. "Mary Kate, I'm not quite ready for that. But I will be soon, if you'll just give me a little more time. For the first time in a long while, I got my Bible out and read a few passages."

Tears filled Mary Kate's eyes. How could she walk away from this man; on the other hand, how could she defy her boss?

"So could you join Hanna for Sunday school one more time?" he asked.

She nodded her head, hating the conflict that had developed. "I'll be happy to pick her up as usual. But I can't join you afterwards. I'm sorry."

"Oh." She heard the disappointment in his voice, but he quickly recovered. "I should have called sooner, but the week just got away from me and—"

"That's quite all right," she said, more brusquely than she intended. "I understand, and it wouldn't have mattered. I. . .already had plans."

Like watering the plants and reading the Sunday paper.

"Why don't I drop Hanna off at Sunday school then? The least I can do is drive her there, if you're willing to bring her home."

Bring her home. How could she say no? "I'll be glad to do that," she answered, and gave him the time to drop Hanna off. "Also," she added, "please have her come in the side door on Beckam Street. I'll be waiting there for her."

There was a momentary pause, and she sensed he was about to say more, so she rushed to fill the silence.

"So I'll see her then. And thanks for calling," she said hurriedly.

He took the hint and said good-bye. After she hung up the phone, she grabbed a throw pillow and tossed it across the floor. This was so unfair. At last she had found someone she could truly care for, a kind and decent man, and a little girl who needed her. Here was her chance to witness where it was sorely needed, and now Brad had put an end to it. She jumped up from the sofa and began to pace circles around the living room, trying to vent her frustration.

Maybe not an end, just a delay, she thought, consoling herself. If she could keep making excuses to Blake, maybe in time, she could have another talk with Brad, and things would change. Or maybe her desire to see Blake would change. But she doubted that. She sank back onto the sofa, her knees drawn to her chin.

"God, please help me with this situation. I don't know what to do." She sighed, feeling sick at heart.

She thought of the afternoon's conversation with Brad. He had called her into his office and asked her if she would like to audition for anchor of the evening news. Justin, their anchor for the past three years, was accepting a job in Chicago and would be leaving soon. The station's general manager had set aside a couple of hours tomorrow to audition prospects for the job.

"This is a good opportunity for you, Mary Kate," Brad had said with a beaming smile.

Looking at him, she couldn't resist the sneaking suspicion that he was merely trying to make amends for telling her she shouldn't see Blake Taylor. Still, she knew she was fortunate to be offered this opportunity. At one time, it had been her driving ambition, and now she was anxious to see if the job still appealed to her. On the other hand, if that job became available, she would miss her daily contact with people on a personal basis. She had tried to bring some compassion to the world of hard news, inject some kindness and sympathy for those who needed it.

She stretched out on the sofa and reminded herself she had to get a good night's sleep so she would look her best for tomorrow. She couldn't let personal problems get in the way now—not when she had an opportunity for a real career advancement.

Closing her eyes, she tried to rationalize the situation. She would take Hanna to Sunday school, thus keeping her promise to Hanna, and maybe even to God, and she would try out for the anchor job just to please Brad—and maybe herself.

🌴

"With bone structure like yours, today's job is a snap!" remarked Annie, the makeup artist, as she whisked rose blusher onto Mary Kate's smooth, beige skin.

"You're just talented," Mary Kate countered, studying her face in the mirror. Outlined in smoky eye shadow, her brown eyes appeared deeper, more mysterious, while her dark hair, swept back from her face in a sophisticated twist, revealed more prominently her classic features. The look didn't feel quite right, but she kept silent, choosing to trust the opinion of the experts.

Her eyes inched downward to the sophisticated navy linen suit. The straight, tailored look was offset by the bright red bow of a red silk blouse. Somehow the outfit managed to achieve just the right touch of sophistication without being too formal. The wardrobe consultant had suggested the suit, on loan from one of the top stores, as opposed to Mary Kate's preference for loose, flowing dresses.

"You need to look older," the wardrobe lady had stated tactfully.

"Why do I want to look *older?*" Mary Kate had stared at her wide-eyed.

"Because it's difficult to believe you're a day over twenty-one now. This type of job requires a bit of sophistication."

"Then maybe it isn't right for me." Mary Kate sighed, then grinned at the woman. "I'm really a simple gal at heart."

She said as much to the makeup artist now, emphasizing that she didn't want to stray too far from the person she really was. "And I don't think the people of Seabreeze want me to come across drastically changed. It'll ruin my image," she teased, and they both laughed.

"Well, we don't want to ruin your image. What if we just dress it up a bit?"

Mary Kate bobbed her sleek dark hair in an emphatic nod. "I guess that's okay."

The possibility of getting made-up to go before a television camera each evening, looking far too glamorous and sophisticated for her own taste, made

299

her question her interest in being an anchor.

"I don't know why I let myself get talked into this," she mumbled, leaning back in the chair with a regretful sigh. "There are other people more qualified."

"I hear you're the favorite," Annie whispered. "Besides, you mustn't resist opportunity when it knocks!" She winked at Mary Kate as she reached for a can of hair spray and enveloped her in a cloud of mist.

"Mary Kate? You're on next." A technician popped his head around the door. "Come on into the control room."

"Thanks, Annie," Mary Kate said, taking a deep breath as she cast one last glance in the mirror. "You've worked your magic."

"You make my work easy," Annie laughed, tapping her on the shoulder. "Good luck, Mary Kate."

"Thanks again." She hurried out the door and down the long corridor leading to the stairway.

As she climbed the narrow flight of stairs, her heart began to hammer, not in fear, but in response to the step she was taking. *Is this really what I want? To be a television anchor?* The question brought a tiny frown to settle between her brown brows as she opened the door and slipped quietly into the control room.

Squinting against the dimness as the technicians adjusted controls, she peered through the glass window to the stage below where a highly respected anchor from a Jacksonville station sat reading a script to Mr. Lucas, the general manager, seated in the front row.

"You're next," someone whispered, and she nodded in reply, hurrying out the door and down the back steps to the stage.

Mary Kate stood in the background, analyzing the smooth delivery of the man as he finished his last line and glanced expectantly toward the front row. He was answered with a brisk nod before Mary Kate was waved onto the stage.

She squared her shoulders and walked quickly to the small rectangular platform that served as the news desk. Seating herself, she scanned the two typewritten sheets as she cleared her throat.

"You know what to do," one technician whispered as he clipped the tiny microphone to her collar. "Just flash that all-American smile."

Given the nod, she began to read, her voice ringing across the quiet stage as she directed her attention to the camera, only vaguely aware of Mr. Lucas, leaning forward in the front row. After she had finished, she blinked into the bright lights, waiting for a response. When there was none, she stood to leave.

"Ms. Moore?"

She paused, turning back.

"Well done." The silver-haired Thomas Lucas strolled up to her, his hand extended.

"Thank you," she replied, gripping his hand.

"And may I say you do a splendid job with your on-the-street interviews? I assume you're aware of the ratings."

"Yes," she answered modestly, taking in the distinguished man who controlled the firing and hiring of employees with a mere nod of his silver head.

"You don't sound as Southern as we had expected. Normally, we're sensitive about accents, but the public seems to be quite taken with yours. In fact, you've brought a bit of a new dimension to television newscasting."

She shifted uncomfortably, wondering how to reply. She quickly decided to center the conversation on Justin, making a complimentary remark about his popularity as news anchor. Soon, a secretary was waving a telephone toward the older man, and she breathed a deep sigh of relief when he nodded and went to accept the phone call.

Mary Kate returned to her desk, filled with an uneasiness she couldn't define. She had been staring blankly at a stack of telephone messages when Carey tapped her on the shoulder and pointed to her ringing telephone. She dived for it, self-consciously aware that she was the object of a few questioning stares.

As soon as she spoke a quick hello, Hanna's eager little voice filled her ears, bringing a smile of pleasure to her face.

"Hanna, I'm glad to hear from you!" she exclaimed, cradling the phone against her shoulder while she flipped idly through the telephone messages.

"Are we still going to Sunday school this Sunday?"

"Of course. Didn't your dad tell you I was expecting you?"

"Yes. I just wanted to know if you could stay for lunch."

She was about to offer a quick refusal when Hanna spoke again, changing the direction of her thoughts.

"Dad's been called someplace for a meeting Sunday. He's leaving town as soon as he drops me off at Sunday school if you can still bring me home. Sue will be here. She'll fix our lunch."

Mary Kate hesitated. If Blake was not going to be at home, why not have lunch with Hanna? She would enjoy being with her, and she hated the thought of the little girl eating alone. Well, Sue would be there, but still. . .

"Okay, tell you what. I'll stay for lunch and visit awhile. Then I'll have to run."

"I'll see you Sunday," Hanna said, obviously excited about the prospect.

"Right. See you then. Thanks for calling," she added before she hung up.

It occurred to her that Blake might find it odd that she could suddenly change her plans and have lunch, knowing he was going out of town. She sighed. It couldn't be helped. She couldn't please everyone.

She returned to the phone messages that awaited her, trying again to concentrate on her job.

🌴

The announcement became official by the end of the day. Mary Kate Moore was the new coanchor of WJAK evening news. The promotion was received with mixed reactions—surprise and pleasure among her friends, envy and doubt among a few of her coworkers. Brad had been sincere in his congratulations, but she sensed a wariness in Coty, with whom she had worked closely for the past year as her number one cameraman. He seemed to be able to read her mind when others could not.

Mary Kate was not quite sure how she felt. There was no question that she was excited and pleased, in one sense. But somewhere deep in her soul, there was a restlessness, an unease she could not quite define.

Late that afternoon, as she was winding up her work at the desk, her telephone rang. Wearily, she answered it then snapped to attention at the sound of Blake's voice.

Chapter 9

just heard the news," he said. "Congratulations."

"Oh." She ran her hand through her hair and automatically glanced at Brad's office. The lights were out. He had already gone home for the evening. "Thanks. I think."

"You think?" He laughed. "I'm sure you'll be great. This calls for a celebration. How about dinner?"

The truth was, she would have adored going out to a restaurant and having a nice meal with Blake. She was starving. But then she remembered Brad's warning, and she heaved a sigh. "I'm afraid the day has drained me completely. All I want to do is go home and put my feet up on the coffee table."

"That's even better."

She hiked an eyebrow. "I beg your pardon?"

"I'm calling from my car phone, and as we speak I'm turning into the grocery. I'll pick up a few things. I'm in a cooking mood, so just indulge me. You see, you can still go home and put your feet up on the coffee table. And your dinner will be waiting for you. Have I tempted you sufficiently?"

Mary Kate's heart was racing. *How can I get out of this? And why do I even want to?* she thought crossly, as she glared at Brad's empty office.

"Well, the problem is," she said, looking wildly around the newsroom, "I can't even leave this place for another thirty minutes. I'm waiting on a phone call and—"

"That'll be perfect. I'll have dinner ready when you walk through the door. Where do you hide the key?"

"The key?" she echoed, feeling as though every defense she put up was being shot down with lightning speed.

"Every woman keeps an extra key hidden somewhere near her door," he continued pleasantly, "unless you are one of those rare sorts who never locks yourself out."

She couldn't resist laughing at that. He was so right. She did have a key hidden in the flowerpot. And what Brad didn't know wouldn't hurt him. Or her. There was no chance of her running into anyone if they were at her apartment. Furthermore, she had earned a little celebration and she hated the thought of celebrating alone.

"Okay. Look in the flowerpot. On the back side, you'll find a spare key tucked under a long leaf."

He groaned. "That's way too easy. I'll find a better hiding place for you. See you when you get there." With that he hung up, giving her no more time to refuse. *He probably planned it that way,* she decided with a wry grin.

Trying not to remember the state of her duplex, she cleared off her desk and returned a couple of phone calls. By the time she freshened up in the ladies lounge and locked up for the night, she had managed to use up the thirty minutes she claimed as an excuse earlier—the excuse that got her nowhere with Blake.

She smiled to herself as she hurried to her car. It was a summer evening and still daylight. The air felt warm and balmy against her cheeks, and she quickened her steps, looking forward to the evening ahead. She realized that she liked a take-charge man like Blake. He wasn't pushy, yet he wasn't the wimp that Frank Haroldson had been, whom she had dated briefly last year then given up on when she was forced to make all the decisions about where they ate or what movie they saw. Sometimes, after work, it seemed her brain had shut down and refused to function. This was one of those times, and it was actually a relief to have someone else calling the shots.

"Surprise!" Blake greeted her at her door, dressed in jeans and a blue button-down shirt, a dish towel knotted thickly about his waist.

"I like your apron." Mary Kate burst into laughter as she hurried inside and closed the door. She had already taken note of the fact that his black car was conspicuously parked in her driveway, but soon it would be dark, and she was blessed with neighbors who minded their own business.

The weariness that seemed to be dragging at her heels all day suddenly disappeared, replaced by a warm glow tingling through her veins.

"Do come in." He stepped aside, waving dramatically with his arm. "I've timed the meal just right. Are you impressed?"

"Definitely. What is that heavenly smell?" She sniffed the spicy aromas as she followed him back to the kitchen.

"Lasagna."

"Mmm." She sighed, glancing around. To her relief, the place was fairly neat, and Bo was behaving himself as well. She couldn't decide if her little dog was intimidated or fascinated by Blake.

"How did Bo react to you coming in alone?" she asked curiously.

"Suspiciously, at first. Then I gave him a tiny sample of dinner and we've been best friends ever since."

She laughed again, suddenly feeling wonderful. It was so unfair for Brad to deny her of an innocent good time. And how could anyone suspect that this dear man could ever be a thief? It was ridiculous!

"I've been slaving away for hours." He sighed, but he was obviously teasing. He peered into the oven then closed the door and turned back to her. "I hope you're impressed."

Her eyes widened as she took in his neatly combed blond hair and deep blue eyes. "I am," she replied, wondering if she was referring to the meal or the man.

"Used to be one of my specialties," he said, taking her handbag from her and placing it in a chair. Then he led her toward the living room sofa. "Now kick off those weapons and put your aching feet on the coffee table as you had planned to do."

She sighed, pleased to be doing as she was told. "Shouldn't I set the table or something?" she asked, feeling guilty.

"You should do nothing other than look pretty, which seems to be easy for you."

Mary Kate sank onto the sofa and kicked off her high heels. He towered over her, as though waiting for her to obey. Once her stocking feet were placed squarely on the coffee table, he leaned down and picked up a slim foot.

"What do you think you're doing?" she asked in surprise.

"I'm rubbing your tired feet," he said matter-of-factly as her stiff muscles began to relax while he gently rubbed her feet.

She took a deep breath and sighed with relief as the aching disappeared beneath his skilled fingers.

"Why do women wear those uncomfortable things?" he asked, frowning at her three-inch navy spikes.

"Normally, I don't. But this morning we had a meeting with the mayor and his staff, and I was trying to look professional."

His eyes ran down her white linen dress with its matching navy belt and buttons, and he nodded approvingly. "You look very professional. Want to change into something comfortable?"

"I think I'd prefer having my feet rubbed and then watching you prepare my dinner," she said sleepily.

"I wouldn't mind that." The serious blue gaze held her captive for several seconds. The electrical awareness that had surrounded their relationship mounted as they looked at one another. Suddenly, Mary Kate took a breath and forced her attention to the clock on the mantel.

"I think I would like to slip into a pair of jeans."

Just then the oven timer buzzed and Blake leapt to his feet. "Perfect timing," he said, hurrying back to the kitchen.

While he rattled around in the kitchen, Mary Kate hurried to her bedroom and closed the door. For one insane moment, she almost felt an impulse to turn the key in the lock. *What am I doing with this man, letting him rub my feet, cook my dinner, come to my home? Brad asked me to avoid him, and now I seem to be rushing headlong into his arms.*

She hurried to the closet door, yanking down the padded hanger for her dress. She unbuttoned the dress and skimmed out of it, then opened the bureau drawer and reached for her baggy jeans. *Definitely unsexy,* she decided with approval. To further her image she opened another drawer and retrieved the most unfeminine T-shirt she owned. A huge black shirt that begged everyone to save the baby whales. And it hung from her small body as though she too, were a baby whale. *Good, maybe he will lose interest,* she thought, although she dared not ask her heart if that was what she really wanted.

She caught sight of her reflection in the dresser mirror and chose not to put on more lip gloss or dab a powdered brush over her face to alter the shine. Her only concession to good grooming was to grab the hairbrush and swing it through her dark hair, so that it waved neatly about her face. *And I did that for myself,* she argued silently.

She returned to the kitchen, her expression serious, as she assessed the table and realized that there was something she could do after all.

She padded barefoot across to the china cabinet. Opening the louvered doors, she pulled out her best dinner plates, along with her crystal water goblets and gleaming silverware. First she laid out the place mats, then she set the table. She glanced over her shoulder. "Are we drinking water?" she asked matter-of-factly.

He hiked an eyebrow, as though sensing her change in mood. "Yes, Madam, we are. Unless you'd like me to sprint out for champagne."

"I don't drink."

"Good girl. How about a glass of milk?"

She burst into laughter, unable to control herself. She was beginning to remind herself of Frank Haroldson, who usually went to sleep in the movies she recommended. "I did make some fresh tea last night," she admitted. "Does that sound okay to you?"

"Sounds perfect."

She sniffed appreciatively as she passed the stove on her way to the refrigerator. "When did you learn to cook?" she asked, pulling out the pitcher of tea and reaching into the refrigerator for a tiny bowl of sliced lemon.

"During my summers between college. My uncle owned a nice restaurant in Chattanooga and kept me in work and dollars. I quit cooking for awhile," he called from the kitchen as she returned to the dining room table to pour tea. "Then I married a woman who couldn't cook, and I found myself rattling the pots and pans again. I did the cooking during the first years of marriage. Then, as I became more prosperous, I hired a cook who, incidentally, was not nearly as good as Sue. When we moved here, we found a real treasure in her."

"She's a very nice lady," Mary Kate agreed, as she went back to the kitchen for the dish of lemons and her special crystal salt and pepper shakers. She stood assessing the dining room table a moment, wondering if she had missed anything.

Blake came forward, proudly bearing his lasagna in her best casserole dish. Returning to the kitchen, he opened the oven door and pulled out a pan of rolls.

"Compliments of the nearest bakery," he said as she handed him a bread basket.

"I like your honesty," she teased. "I might have been tempted to claim them as some I had spent half the afternoon kneading and coddling."

He shook his head as he swept past her with the rolls. "Nope, you're too honest."

As he removed the towel from his waist, he began to frown. "I forgot to pick up a salad."

"No problem." She walked to the refrigerator and pulled out a jar of applesauce. "Will this substitute?"

"Perfect," he said, as she spooned a generous amount into a small serving bowl and took it to the table.

He turned and pulled her chair back for her. She sat down and motioned him to follow. "Let's get started."

As he took his seat, she bowed her head, offering grace for the meal. When she finished, she unfolded her napkin and lifted her fork, eager to sample his food. After two bites, she sighed and looked at him. "This is delicious. You're an excellent cook."

He shrugged. "I was afraid I might have lost my touch. It's been awhile since I've tied on an apron. But I do hope you enjoy the meal."

She smiled at him, feeling her defenses fly away again. "This was very thoughtful of you, Blake."

"Actually, my motive was more selfish than you think. I figured if I could bribe you with food, I could see you again. I'm beginning to realize something, though." He lowered his fork to his plate, his eyes meeting hers. "Sitting here with you tonight, enjoying a quiet meal together, makes me realize what I've been missing." He turned back to his food.

Mary Kate looked at him with a sinking heart. Of course he had no idea that she had been warned by her boss to stay away from him, at least until the controversy about the trial died down. What was she going to do? She sincerely enjoyed being with this man.

"So are you excited about your new job?" he asked, looking back at her.

Mentally she shifted gears, considering his question. "To be perfectly honest, I'm not sure how I feel about this job." She realized she was aching for someone to talk with. She had already spoken to her parents, but she needed to talk to someone more objective.

She touched the napkin to her mouth and looked into his eyes. "Maybe I should have taken more time before accepting the offer," she admitted, "but it seemed like the sensible thing to do."

"Do I hear a note of uncertainty in your voice?" he asked.

"Maybe. But I would be crazy not to take it." She paused for a fraction of a second. "Wouldn't I?"

He stopped chewing and studied her for a moment. "Not if it doesn't suit you." He smiled, creating a glow in his deep blue eyes. "I think you're just having a slight case of nerves. You'll be great, and I must admit you're a lot prettier than Justin!"

She laughed too, relieved to have someone pointing out the funny side of the situation. "Well, I'll see how it goes. If I despise the job, I can always quit and go back to doing my on-the-street interviews. You know, Blake, I think that's really what's bothering me. I liked the human contact I had with those people."

"You did it so well."

"Thanks. But anyway, I've taken the plunge so I might as well see it through."

She had been so grateful to talk about her new job, then again she remembered Brad's stern warning. This time it depressed her immensely. Maybe she wasn't going to let Brad Wilson be such a dictator, after all.

"Well, in any case, I think you'll do a great job. Hanna tells me she called you earlier about Sunday. Now that you're aware I have to leave town, I really appreciate your taking the time to have lunch with Hanna. You already told me you had a busy afternoon."

She leaned back in the chair, her appetite gone. He was being so nice about this that she actually felt guilty. "Well, how can anyone say no to Hanna?" she asked lightly.

He laughed. "I can't, that's for sure. But I must admit, knowing that you're having lunch at my house tempts me to delay my trip to Montgomery for a couple more hours. But I really can't."

"Duty calls," she quipped, relieved that he wasn't changing his mind.

"Right. Anyway, thanks again for seeing her home and having lunch with her."

"My pleasure," she said, realizing she truly meant it. "Have a safe trip to Montgomery." Then she thought of something else. "You really enjoy your work, don't you?"

He nodded. "Even when I was a little guy, I was always drawing buildings and funny cubicles for shopping centers. Mom and Dad encouraged me to pursue it as a career. In that respect, I've been lucky. What about you? How did you get into television broadcasting?"

"It's kind of funny, actually." Her brown eyes drifted into space, remembering. "Dad owns a small appliance store in Dothan. He sold TVs. He also had a repairman who worked on used ones. One day he brought home a set with just the screen—the insides were missing. He thought his kids could have fun "being on television." The others soon bored with the game, but not me. I would grab a cooking spoon for a mike and report the day's events. Mom was a dear; she always allowed me to interview her."

They both laughed then and began to talk about their childhoods. Mary Kate was pleased to learn that he too, had come from a middle-class background, and they actually had quite a bit in common.

They sat at the table for an hour talking, then Blake glanced at his watch. "Let's get these dishes done, then I have to shove off. I promised Sue she could leave by nine."

"Please. I'll do the dishes. I'd rather you go home and spend some time with Hanna."

He hesitated, glancing over the table.

"I'm serious," she said, coming to her feet. "Thanks for dinner."

"You're welcome."

As they stood up, looking across at one another, Mary Kate realized something was about to happen between them. He leaned forward, tilted her chin back and pressed his lips to hers, lightly at first. Then the kiss deepened, and her heart began to hammer wildly. She had to stop this. *Now!*

She pulled back and looked into his eyes and knew, with a sinking heart, that she was falling in love with this man. *I can't.* Not yet. She had to put on the brakes somehow. Dropping her eyes, she quickly turned her attention to gathering up the dishes and rushing to the sink with them.

For a moment, she caught the flicker of surprise on his face, but he was a good sport about it. "Well, see you. . .soon, I guess."

"Yes, and tell Hanna hello for me," she called from the kitchen. She didn't even offer to see him to the door, for she knew it could lead to another kiss, and she was already more than a little rattled. She had never felt this way about a man, and now that she did, she had fallen for one she couldn't have.

"Good night," he called again as she heard the door open.

"Good night, Blake," she called back, and then the door closed.

She stood at the kitchen sink, staring at the dishes. Even if Brad hadn't warned her, it only made sense to move slowly with a guy like Blake Taylor. Older. Experienced. A widower. And too, she reminded herself, he had told her that she was the first person he had gone out with since his wife's death. She didn't want this to be one of those rebound relationships she was always hearing about.

She sank against the sink, her lips pressed tightly together, her eyes closed for a moment. She could hear his car start up in the driveway, and she only hoped she had not been rude.

She could not have cared less about the dishes at that moment as she looked down at Bo, standing beside her, wagging his tail affectionately.

"You hungry?" she asked. She retrieved his round white bowl from its place beside the refrigerator and filled it with leftovers.

While Bo smacked away, she refilled her tea glass and wandered into the living room. She plopped on the sofa, took a sip of tea, and tried to remember the facts that had led Blake to be charged for jewelry theft.

The jewelry had been found at his house. He had been in the store the same day the jewelry disappeared—what else? He had an alibi for the time the pieces were actually spotted missing from their boxes, but he had looked at those same pieces. She sighed, not feeling so good. That was pretty strong evidence.

What else? There was a designer handbag Mrs. Taylor had admired, along with an expensive silk scarf that disappeared after the couple had been in an exclusive store in town. Mrs. Taylor had been very sick and had leaned heavily on her husband's arm. All due respect had been paid to Charlotte Taylor, but that did not absolve the fact that several thousand dollars' worth of merchandise had been taken.

But Blake could have bought those pieces for her. *Why didn't he?*

That one fact nagged at Mary Kate more than any other. He was obviously doing well in his business; he had the money. So, if his wife liked the jewelry, the handbag, the scarf, why didn't he buy them? And how could he just steal them right from under the noses of the salespeople?

She shook her head, staring into space. It didn't make sense to her. What *had* made sense and constituted the case against him was the search warrant that had turned up the missing valuables hidden in the back of a bureau drawer. With the exception of one exquisite ruby ring. That piece of jewelry was never found, and like the others, Blake claimed to know nothing about it.

The defense hammered hard against the fact that nobody saw him take the jewelry, and that someone could have set him up, then upon fear of being caught, planted the jewelry. To back up this theory, there had been a break-in at the Taylor home which had set off the security system. The police had arrived to find no burglar and, conveniently, the family was away at the time, and Sue, the housekeeper, was not on duty. So nobody could prove that Taylor himself had not broken the glass pane of his French doors to set off the alarm. Countering that theory, however, was the fact that the family had gone to a Christmas play at school, even though Charlotte had gone in a wheelchair. The only item that appeared to be missing was a VCR, which indicated the burglar had not made it past the living room when he heard the sirens coming. On the other hand, the prosecution argued that Blake Taylor could have set this up as well.

His most convincing defense was the fact that he did have a solid alibi for the times the jewelry was actually stolen, and one clerk claimed to have seen the pieces after the Taylors left the store. Since there was no explanation for that, the prosecution paraded out the salesclerk's indebtedness and subtly suggested she might have taken a bribe. It was a low blow on their part, and it had failed to work. Since nobody had seen Blake Taylor take the jewelry, and there was no solid evidence against him, other than finding the pieces at his house, the jury had deliberated for an appalling amount of time, and the opposition had caved in. A verdict of "not guilty" had finally been reached.

As Mary Kate went over the facts, she realized there was enough suspicion still hanging over his head to sully his reputation, even though he was recognized as one of the most talented developers in the state. Still, that was his business life. Apparently, his personal life still suffered. And now she was suffering too.

Life seemed so unfair at times. Her eyes lifted toward the ceiling. "God, I just don't understand the way things go on down here." For years, she had been looking for a man with the qualities of Blake Taylor. She had met some nice guys, but there was always something lacking. Now with Blake, all the chemistry was there. *Too much chemistry,* she thought, kicking at the ottoman. If she didn't keep her distance, he was going to steal her heart. And she just couldn't let that happen. Particularly not now when she was in the limelight more than ever.

Chapter 10

The next day had gone smoothly, and everyone had been wonderful to her.

When she saw Brad she tried to forget that Blake had prepared dinner for her the evening before; instead, she concentrated on the news she would deliver during the six o'clock newscast. And yet, at three in the afternoon she felt a keen disappointment sitting at her desk, watching her replacement leave with the camera crew to cover a story on the animal shelter. It occurred to her that she might have chosen a job that was going to bore her, even though it meant a promotion in status and pay.

At the appointed time, she got up from her desk and went to Annie's office, ready to be "fixed up" for her newscast.

The illuminated numbers on her bedside clock glared a ridiculous 12:10, and still sleep evaded her. It was useless to lie here and flop from one side of the bed to the other. Tossing the covers back, she dragged herself back into the kitchen and made a cup of hot chocolate. The congratulatory flowers from her parents, a flood of phone calls from fans, and today's wide smile on both Mr. Lucas's and Brad Wilson's faces should have combined to make her ecstatic. Or at least give her sweet dreams. So what had happened? Why did she feel such a void in her heart? Was it true, as she had heard, that a long-awaited goal, once achieved, often left one empty and unfulfilled?

Depends on the goal, she thought dully, as she sank into the kitchen chair and sipped her hot chocolate. Bo had come trudging forward from his kitchen bed, sleepy and confused, to see what was going on. Halfheartedly licking her hand, he seemed to sense that she needed consolation for some reason.

"Thanks, Pal," she said with a smile, stroking his soft black fur. "You're a true friend. And a good listener," she added as he tilted his head sideways, enjoying the feeling of being rubbed behind his ears. "It's not as though I've rocketed to the status of a major network anchor, is it? This is merely the top rung of the local ladder—not New York, for heaven's sake." But it was a beginning, if she were serious about pursuing her career.

Oddly, the scene that flashed through her mind surprised her. She saw herself back at Sunday school, laughing with the children, playing games, feeling a warmth in her heart that had come no other way. She doubted that even being a talk show hostess would bring the heady glow she had always thought accompanied such a position.

At least not for her.

"Maybe at heart I'm just a homebody who likes having a cocker spaniel and a little girl like Hanna in my life. Not to mention her irresistible father! But what am I going to do?"

Tears filled her eyes as she finished her hot chocolate and rinsed her cup. This time when she returned to bed, she left the lamp on and reached for her Bible. She needed a kind of wisdom that she would find only there.

On Sunday, she waited for Hanna at the side door, and at exactly the appointed hour, the black sports sedan pulled to the curb and Blake got out. He came around to the passenger's side and opened the door for Hanna, who hopped out, looking beautiful in a ruffled sky blue dress with a small blue satin ribbon in her blond hair. Blake walked her to the sidewalk then glanced up at the door where Mary Kate waved to him. He waved back then got into his car as Hanna ran up the sidewalk to meet her.

"Hi, Mary Kate!" Hanna's blue eyes were glowing.

"Hi, Hanna. You look wonderful. Here, let me do one little thing." She smoothed down a lock of hair near the crown of her head that she had obviously mussed as she sat against the seat in the car. "Ready for Sunday school?"

She nodded happily, linking her arm through Mary Kate's. They turned down the corridor and headed for the eight year old's classroom. A thought suddenly occurred to Mary Kate. "Want to stay for church? I could give Sue a call and tell her when we'll be home."

Hanna tilted her head and looked up at Mary Kate. "I guess so. If the preacher isn't boring."

As it turned out, the preacher's sermon was about the kind of faith that had prompted Noah to build the ark, and Hanna had learned enough about the ark in Sunday school to perk her interest, so she wasn't bored. The music was good, and today's special was given by a group of college students who seemed to interest Hanna. When the altar call was given, Hanna turned and glanced seriously at Mary Kate. For a moment, Mary Kate wondered if she should ask Hanna if she wanted to walk down the aisle and give her heart to God. Then Hanna looked down at her hands, folded demurely in her lap, and the moment passed.

Don't push her, Mary Kate warned herself. *When the time is right, she will know it. And I will too.*

After the church service, they drove home with Hanna talking incessantly. She seemed to be in great spirits and told her all about her week at school. Then she turned in the seat and studied Mary Kate quietly for a moment. "Dad's been in better spirits too. But he was disappointed that you couldn't go to the beach with us this afternoon."

Mary Kate concentrated on turning into the driveway. "Well, as it turned out, he had to go to Montgomery anyway."

"How come you said you couldn't eat with us and then you changed your mind?"

Mary Kate slowed the car and cut the engine. She turned to Hanna. "To be honest, I couldn't stand the thought of you having lunch without your father. But I won't even be able to stay and help Sue with the dishes," she teased. "I'm still busy this afternoon."

It seemed a more logical answer than admitting she had tried to avoid Blake.

The answer seemed to satisfy Hanna as she reached for the door and hopped out of the car. Mary Kate joined her. Arm in arm, they went up the front steps, singing a song Hanna had learned in Sunday school.

Sue met them at the door with a welcoming smile for Mary Kate. "Thanks for joining us. I understand you had a busy schedule."

"Well, not too busy to enjoy being with Hanna."

Sue looked at her curiously for a moment, as though reading what had been left unspoken. *Being with Hanna but not her father.* Then Sue turned to Hanna. "Now, if you'll just run up and change clothes, I'll have everything on the table by the time you get back."

"May I do something to help?" Mary Kate offered, laying her purse on a table and following Sue back to the kitchen.

"Mary Kate?" Hanna paused on the first stair and looked at Mary Kate. "Do you want to see a picture of my mother?"

Mary Kate was taken aback by the unexpected question. Automatically, she glanced at Sue, who had lowered her eyes, offering her no excuse to avoid Hanna's question.

Mary Kate cleared her throat. "Well. . .er. . .if you want me to."

"Come on upstairs," Hanna beckoned.

Feeling more than a little awkward, Mary Kate followed Hanna up the stairs and into a spacious room which Mary Kate instantly recognized as Blake's room. She froze in the doorway, feeling like an intruder.

"Come on in." Hanna looked puzzled by Mary Kate's hesitation.

Mary Kate inched her way into the room, following Hanna to a large, gilt-framed portrait. Mary Kate found herself looking into the face of the striking beauty who had married Blake and given birth to Hanna. A cloud of golden brown hair framed a heart-shaped face, the complexion flawless. The features were small and perfect, the mouth reserved, lifted in only a half smile. Yet the enormous blue eyes were captivating, tilting upward beneath thick lashes.

There was no denying that Charlotte Taylor was one of the prettiest women Mary Kate had ever seen.

"She's very beautiful, Hanna." She glanced down at the little girl who was still staring at her mother.

She nodded. "But she didn't laugh a lot the way you do."

Puzzled by that remark, Mary Kate turned from the picture. Her eyes scanned the room, inspecting the massive furniture of a man's room, inhaling the scent of Blake's aftershave still lingering in the air.

Despite Sue's attempts at housekeeping, the room reflected a lived-in atmosphere. Books spilled over tables, a discarded jacket was flung over a chair, and dusty golf shoes sprawled in a corner. In her innocent sweep of the room, Mary Kate's eyes fell on the intimate photograph resting on the bedside table. It was a picture of Blake and Charlotte with an infant Hanna nestled between them. The couple gazed into each other's eyes as though there were no one else in all the world.

Mary Kate turned away, sick at heart, unable to distinguish whether her pain was born out of sadness for the deep love Blake had lost, or if the picture merely reaffirmed what she had already feared—that no woman could ever replace the beautiful Charlotte in Blake's heart and mind.

"I'll change clothes now," Hanna said, her voice surprisingly lighthearted. They left the room, and Hanna darted down the corridor to the next bedroom. For a moment, Mary Kate stood awkwardly in the hall. "I'll help Sue," she called, feeling a bit silly, for Hanna didn't seem to care.

She turned and retraced her steps back down the stairs to the kitchen. When she entered, Sue was removing something from the oven. The heat had curled the ends of her hair around her rosy cheeks, but her eyes held an odd expression. She turned back to the casserole she was placing on the stove.

"What can I do to help?" Mary Kate asked, her fingers twitching uselessly at her side.

"Well. . .how about putting ice in the glasses?"

"I'm good at that," Mary Kate called cheerfully as she headed for the sink to wash her hands.

"Did you feel funny about that?" Sue asked casually.

Mary Kate frowned, unable to follow the woman's question. "Funny about. . . ?" Her eyebrows rose questioningly.

"About being led up to see a picture of Mrs. Taylor."

Mary Kate looked across at Sue, sensing a friend in this woman, although she had wondered at times. "Awkward might be a better word. But. . .she's a very beautiful woman."

Sue opened the drawer of silverware and reached for a serving spoon. "She was that, but she was a bit difficult, if I say so, which I probably shouldn't."

"Difficult?" Mary Kate paused at the refrigerator.

"Well, what I mean is. . ." She hesitated as though unsure what she did mean. She thrust the serving spoon into the casserole and glanced cautiously toward the open door. "She had lived a very privileged life in Memphis," she explained in a lowered voice. "Her family always had servants, and sometimes she made me feel as though I never quite measured up." She shook her head, lowering her eyes. "Shame on me for saying such a thing about the poor woman. She suffered terribly in the end."

Mary Kate nodded, opening the freezer door and reaching for the ice. "I'm sure she did."

"The thing was," Sue continued in her confidential tone, "she was even more difficult during her illness. There were times when I didn't see how poor Mr. Taylor could endure her tantrums."

The words shocked Mary Kate as she attempted to drop ice cubes into tall crystal glasses.

"I'm sure he loved her very much," Mary Kate said quietly.

Sue hesitated. "He loved her in the beginning, but before she got sick, when she complained so much about living here, I think something happened between them. The week before she was diagnosed with cancer, I heard her ask for a divorce."

Mary Kate caught her breath at that bit of news.

Sue sighed and plunged on. "After she got sick, Mr. Taylor did everything he could to please her. Whatever she wanted, he got for her. But the illness progressed so fast. She was gone within three months after she was diagnosed. I felt sorry for her, but she became more difficult than ever."

Mary Kate realized they were gossiping about a woman who could no longer defend herself, and she felt ashamed to be participating. She glanced at Sue. "I'd rather not discuss this," she said gently.

Sue nodded. "And I should bite my tongue off. I guess the reason I'm saying these things to you is because I saw how Mr. Taylor acted when you were here, like he was happy for the first time in a very long while. And he was really disappointed that you couldn't join them today."

Mary Kate hesitated, tempted to tell Sue the truth, while knowing that was the last thing she should do. Then Sue surprised her even more with her next remark.

"I wanted to testify in the trial but Mr. Taylor wouldn't let me. Said he didn't want to subject me to the publicity."

Mary Kate turned quickly to face her, dropping an ice cube in the process. "What would you have said? In the trial, I mean."

Sue hesitated, reaching into the refrigerator for a tossed salad. "I'm not to discuss it. I promised Mr. Taylor. But believe me," she said, looking Mary Kate squarely in the eye, "he was innocent of those charges against him."

Mary Kate nodded, realizing that she believed this woman completely. She wondered why Blake had not allowed her to testify. Maybe he was confident of his defense, and as she had pointed out, he wanted to protect his housekeeper against more publicity.

At that moment, Hanna bounded into the room dressed in her playclothes.

"Can't you stay awhile?" she asked, tugging at Mary Kate's hand.

As Mary Kate looked down into the little girl's pleading eyes, she almost gave in. "Hey, we're having lunch together, aren't we? And I eat slowly," she teased as the three women headed into the dining room.

"I had hoped my husband would join us," Sue was saying as they took their seats. "He got busy fixing our lawn mower and wouldn't come over, even though I've begged him not to mow our lawn on Sunday. . . ."

While Sue droned on, Mary Kate's mind lingered on the startling news she had just been told, trying to digest everything at once.

It was Hanna who interrupted Sue's rambling with a very sensible plea. "Aren't we going to say a prayer? My Sunday school teacher said we should always thank God for our food."

"That's right." Mary Kate smiled at Hanna. "Want me to volunteer to say grace?"

Hanna nodded and Mary Kate offered a simple prayer. When she finished and glanced at Sue, the older woman looked embarrassed.

"I'm afraid I've failed miserably in that area," she said, picking up a linen napkin.

"We'll have to teach Dad to say a prayer before we eat," Hanna suggested brightly.

Sue nodded, passing the food. "I'm sure Mr. Taylor's mother always said grace at her table. Your dad has just gotten out of the habit."

Sue looked across at Mary Kate. "Mrs. Taylor is a lovely woman and a very religious one."

"She always makes me go to church with her when I visit," Hanna said, taking a large slurp of tea. Her blue eyes twinkled above her glass, and Mary Kate could see that she didn't mind going to church with her grandmother.

"My other grandmother is different." Hanna frowned suddenly. "They never say prayers. Neither did Mother."

Mary Kate cleared her throat. "Sue, this meal looks wonderful. How did you know I adore macaroni and cheese?"

"Because I do!" Hanna giggled.

The rest of the meal passed pleasantly, with no more references to Charlotte Taylor or her family, and Mary Kate began to relax.

"Can't you just play one game of Monopoly before you go?"

Mary Kate hesitated, glancing at her watch. It was only one-fifteen. "If I remember correctly, a Monopoly game can last for hours."

Hanna shrugged. "We'll just play 'til you have to go. Please, Mary Kate. Please, please."

It was useless to refuse and Mary Kate knew it. After all, she had nothing else to do other than get ready for the coming week. And she really enjoyed being with Hanna.

"Okay. I'll play for awhile, but I need to leave in an hour or so."

"Great. Will you help me get the game?"

"Sure."

Sue was chuckling softly as she cleared the dishes. When she met Mary Kate's eyes, she gave her a warm smile. The woman was genuinely nice, and Mary Kate regretted feeling agitated with her the first time they met, after Hanna's disappearance. Now she understood that Sue was merely being protective of Hanna, and she had every right to be.

Mary Kate and Hanna went back upstairs to her room where her games were neatly stacked on a shelf. The room was done in deep hues of pink with only a few pale pink touches. The furniture was cherry with a spindle-post bed and matching dresser and bureau. *The room's more formal than I would have chosen for a girl Hanna's age,* Mary Kate thought; *still, it's impressive.*

"My goodness, look at all these games," Mary Kate said, placing her hands on her hips and shaking her head at Hanna. She was only teasing, of course, and Hanna knew it.

"Sue keeps them organized for me," Hanna boasted, happily taking no credit for the neat room. There was even a card table and four chairs placed beside the end window which overlooked a neat expanse of green lawn. It was a beautiful home, but again she felt that lonely quality that had touched her the first time she entered the house.

As Hanna laid out the board, Mary Kate began to stack the play money and line up the tiny hotels and cards. "You know I used to love to play this game," Mary Kate reminisced.

"You did?" Hanna glanced at her.

"Yep. My brother always beat me, but I just knew that one day I'd out-smart him." She laughed. "I never did."

"Dad's good at Monopoly," Hanna offered, concentrating on the board.

Mary Kate looked sharply at Hanna. Somehow it was difficult to imagine Blake Taylor hunkered down here at the table playing Monopoly with his daughter. She realized she had misjudged him when she once imagined that he spent no time with his daughter, that his life was his work.

She tried not to think about Blake or how she felt about him as they began the game. An hour slipped away, and Mary Kate immediately realized what she had always suspected: Hanna had a very bright mind. Studying the little girl's blond head, tilted over the card she was drawing, Mary Kate found herself thinking of Charlotte. Hanna resembled her father more than her mother, and yet the delicacy that offset Blake's bolder features were gifts from mother to daughter. When finally she glanced at her watch and saw that it was two-thirty, she leaned back in the chair.

"Hanna, I hate to say so, but I really do have to leave now."

"Thank you for playing with me." Hanna beamed. Mary Kate had expected her to complain. To her surprise, Hanna seemed to realize it as she added, "Dad said I must behave better if I wanted to have you come visit us again."

Those words touched Mary Kate, bringing a tightness to her throat. "Well, you have behaved very well," she said tightly, coming to her feet. "Now, I'll help you put the game away."

They began putting everything away, then suddenly Hanna frowned. "I need that little cup I always used to hold my hotels."

"Okay, where is it?"

She frowned. "I don't know. I haven't seen it since the last time Dad and I played."

"When was that?" Mary Kate asked helpfully.

Hanna was staring into space, thinking. "It was when Mom was really sick. Oh, I know. He borrowed it to put something in for Mom." She leapt to her feet. "Come on, you may have to reach it for me."

Mary Kate trailed reluctantly along, uncomfortable at the prospect of trespassing in Blake's bedroom again. They entered his bedroom, and Hanna ran to the closet and flung open the doors where Blake's clothes were lined up neatly on hangers.

Hanna pointed to the shoe boxes overhead. "They kept things put away up here."

Feeling like an intruder, Mary Kate followed orders and pulled down one shoe box after another, but there were only shoes inside the boxes.

Hanna frowned, looking around. "Mom was always looking for containers for her pills." She opened a bedside drawer, plunging around. At the back of the drawer, she found the cup. "Here it is!" She beamed at Mary Kate.

"Yep." Mary Kate removed the pill bottle from the cup for Hanna who had already turned on her heel to go. Mary Kate saw Charlotte's name on the label. As awkward as it would be taking it downstairs to Sue, she just couldn't leave it here within Hanna's reach, even though at eight Hanna was old enough to know better than to take them. Only a few small pills remained in the bottle—no, it was something else. Normally, she would not think to look in someone else's pill bottle, but she had glimpsed something through the amber plastic that aroused her curiosity.

Glancing at Hanna who was walking out of the room, Mary Kate quickly untwisted the bottle cap and peered inside. There at the very bottom of the bottle lay an exquisite ruby ring. Confused, she shook the ring into her palm without thinking. Charlotte had probably taken her ring off during her illness and placed it in the pill bottle when she was half asleep. And then she saw the tiny slip of paper encircling the silver band. *It's a price tag.* The number 1,900 jumped at her. In her haste to replace the ring in the bottle, she almost dropped it. *Think, Mary Kate. Wasn't there one piece of jewelry still missing?* With trembling fingers, she replaced the cap, shoved the bottle to the back of the drawer, and closed it.

Mary Kate stood trembling, staring at the drawer. Should she talk with Sue? Should she ask Blake? Should she call the police?

"Are you coming?" Hanna had returned to the doorway and was peering in at Mary Kate.

"On my way," Mary Kate said shakily. Her mind was spinning in all directions, but she knew she must keep her cool until she got home. Only then would she be able to sit down and digest what she had just discovered.

Somehow she managed to gracefully thank Sue for lunch and quickly left the house. She drove home staring blankly at the traffic, numb with shock. But beneath the shock she knew there were questions simmering in the back of her mind, questions that must be answered.

O God, she prayed, *what am I going to do? Please, please show me the way.*

Chapter 11

Somehow, she managed to drive home without having an accident, park her car, and stumble into the safety of her apartment. Once inside, she felt her knees start to shake, and she fell onto the sofa, her mind still half-frozen in shock. But the seclusion of her apartment gave her security, and now she curled up, hugging a pillow, trying to reason out what she had discovered.

The main question hammering at her now was, *What am I going to do?* She knew she would ask herself this a million times, but only God could give her the right answer.

She had found a ring, a valuable ring, one that had obviously been stolen. Or maybe Blake had purchased it for Charlotte, and she had never taken the tag off. But why not keep it in a jewelry box? Why hide it in a pill bottle?

She blinked, trying to clear her muddled thoughts as her eyes moved slowly across the room and settled on her desk. *Clippings. Newspaper clippings.* Shakily, she got up, crossed the room to her desk, and opened the bottom drawer. She clipped and saved all the articles that were newsworthy in order to keep herself well-informed, and there was always the chance for a follow-up story in the future.

She sorted through several manila envelopes and finally retrieved the one labeled "The Taylor Story." Gathering up the envelope of clippings, she recalled at one point being tempted to throw them out. The aftermath of her interview with Blake had been so bad that she didn't think she would have any desire to conduct a follow-up interview. But she had saved the clippings, prompted by some reason she hadn't quite understood. Had God been acting in her life even then, seeing her future, knowing this moment would someday come? Had He, in His infinite wisdom, known she would be forced to face a truth that would hurt her deeply? And yet she must face the truth.

Scolding Bo for getting underfoot, she made her way to the kitchen table where she could spread out the clippings. She was still wearing heels and her church dress, but she couldn't bother to change. The clippings were more important to her than anything else at the moment.

Carefully, she sorted through each one until she found what she was looking for: the article that detailed the stolen items. The one thing that was never recovered was. . .*a ruby ring,* and Blake Taylor claimed to have no knowledge of that, just as he reiterated that he had not taken any of the other valuable pieces.

She sat back in the kitchen chair, staring blindly into space. She felt as though she held the key to a secret door, but she had no idea what to do with the key. What, in good conscience, could she do? Tell the truth and destroy Blake and Hanna? Hide the truth and live with her scolding conscience? Her eyes strayed toward the phone. She knew the number of the district attorney's office, for she had often called it in getting news.

The clock on the kitchen wall ticked into the silence that imprisoned her, the awful minutes of being held in the grip of indecision.

She turned and looked again at the clippings, trying to analyze her next move. She reminded herself that the trial was over now, old news. What good would it do to rehash the nightmare? After all, Blake had been acquitted. All she had to do was just forget about the ring she had found.

She closed her eyes, feeling miserable. Could she do that? Could she go against everything she had believed in all of her life? Could she live with herself if she did?

Her thoughts turned to Blake and the love she thought she had felt for him. Tears filled her eyes. Had she been that blind to the man's true nature? Was their relationship a part of his game of deception? She couldn't believe that was true. She just wouldn't believe it.

But how could he do such a thing? she wondered, her mind bumping the stone wall of logic. Why would he steal items he could afford to purchase? *Or could he afford those items?* she wondered suddenly. Again, she plunged into the articles, sifting through them, rereading certain ones to refresh her memory. One of the motives for the robberies, according to the prosecution, was that Blake Taylor was deeply in debt. He had been in the process of changing insurance companies when his wife was diagnosed with cancer. None of her medical bills were covered. And the bills were staggering. Numerous hospitalizations, two surgeries, radiation treatments, a host of doctors' bills. What had Blake done under such staggering circumstances?

Sick at heart, Mary Kate carefully folded each article and replaced everything in the envelope. She had a sudden sickening impulse to toss them all in the trash, but she wanted to keep them. She must. This would serve as another reminder to her that she could never be involved with Blake Taylor. She knew that now. Brad had been right to warn her away.

Sue had said he would do anything to please Charlotte toward the end. No doubt, Charlotte was accustomed to the finer things in life, and Mary

Kate could well imagine she would have collected valuable jewelry. *But why resort to theft?* she wondered miserably. Why didn't he sell something valuable to pay his bills? The house. No, of course he would not sell the house with his wife dying inside. The furniture? No. His most logical choice would be to work harder than ever to pay off his bills, and that was precisely what he had done. Everyone called him a workaholic. Even Hanna had hinted that her father had placed work above all else after her mother died. It had seemed a cruel thing for a grieving father to do, but now Mary Kate understood why. The man was desperate. Then, after Hanna had attempted to run away, the scare had forced him back into his fatherly role again.

Tears filled her eyes and rolled down her cheeks while Bo nestled at her feet, seeming to understand her depression. The entire situation was heartbreaking. Still, what he had done was wrong.

Thou shalt not steal. It was a commandment by which she had been reared. If Blake's mother was religious, no doubt he had been taught that commandment as well. *But he was desperate,* her heart argued. His wife was dying. The medical bills were staggering. Could he really be condemned for resorting to almost anything to bring a smile to Charlotte's face, knowing she would soon be gone?

Thou shalt not steal. . . .

Reaching for a paper towel, she mopped the tears from her face and tried to force herself to think clearly. She could still see Hanna, and she would. Her most important mission was to see that Hanna became a Christian, but she would do that and somehow manage to avoid Blake. Hadn't she done so today?

She came to her feet shakily, forcing herself back to her bedroom to undress. Rather than go to the mall to select a few outfits for her new job, she pulled on a nightshirt and crawled into bed, turning off the telephone. She had no desire to shop, to talk, to see anyone. Something inside her had wilted and died. And she knew what it was. She had fallen in love with Blake against her better judgment—against Brad's advice. But that was exactly what she had done. And now she was forced to nurse a broken heart as she would have a physical ailment. Only this one hurt much worse.

🌴

The pressure of a hectic Monday morning did nothing to improve Mary Kate's dark mood as she attempted to bury herself in work.

Carey popped through the door with a fresh cup of coffee. "I must say, you don't look like the happy news anchor everyone expected. Are you feeling ill?"

Mary Kate drew a deep breath and looked at her. "Just a bit. I guess I'm fighting off a virus, but I'll be okay. Thanks for the coffee. I needed it."

She hadn't slept more than three hours, and now she was dreadfully unprepared to face the busy week ahead. She managed to drag through the endless hours, poring over every news report. Then she sank into Annie's chair for her touch of magic before going on for the evening news.

"What are those dark circles doing under your eyes?" Annie frowned down at her.

"I'm fighting off a virus," she said, using the same excuse that had worked with Carey.

"Listen, Girl, you better double up on the vitamins. This is no time to even think about getting sick."

"I know," Mary Kate sighed.

She could hardly believe her bad luck. Just when she needed to look her best, she looked her worst. Just when she should be feeling on top of the world, she felt as though she had lead in her shoes. All because of Blake. She bit her lip, hoping desperately she wouldn't start blubbering. That was all she needed, a crying jag just before she coanchored the news for countless viewers.

"Here." Annie sat a cup of tea before her. "You need a dose of herbal tea and a vitamin." She uncapped a bottle and placed a tablet beside the tea.

Mary Kate's eyes lingered on the innocent bottle of vitamins, but she was seeing again the pill bottle she had discovered only twenty-four hours ago, the bottle that had nailed Blake to the wall, as far as she was concerned.

"Now what's wrong?" Annie asked, the hairbrush poised in midair.

She shook her head. "Nothing." She took the vitamin and drank the tea and did, indeed, start to feel a bit better.

By Wednesday, Mary Kate's spirits were still low, but they plummeted when she studied a news report.

"Look at this!" She waved the report at Mr. Lucas who was sauntering past her desk. "There's a terrific story here, but we're only touching the surface."

He reached for the report, scanning its contents. "A high school student saves a woman from her burning home. How noble."

"But it's far more than noble, Mr. Lucas. Look at that last line. When the reporter asked him how it felt to be a hero, he said he just did what anyone else would have done. Don't you think that's absolutely remarkable coming from a sixteen year old who was running late for school?"

Mr. Lucas lifted an eyebrow and stared at her for a moment. "Why. . .yes. It is quite remarkable." He turned to go.

"But, Mr. Lucas," she persisted, "why doesn't someone interview this boy for a special?" She glanced over the report he had handed back to her. "He risked his life. I think he deserves more recognition than his name and age, don't you?"

Mr. Lucas glanced back over his shoulder. "I'll tell Brad. In the meantime, Ms. Moore, I think you should remember that you're now an anchor, not an on-the-street reporter."

She glared after him, her cheeks flaming with anger. Then she slumped in her chair, staring again at the report, incensed that nobody was giving this boy the recognition he deserved.

"Cool it," Carey whispered as she darted by.

"I don't feel like cooling it!" Mary Kate called after her, not bothering to lower her voice. "When there's some senseless murder, we give the bad guy prime time. When a young boy risks his life, we dismiss it with some flippant good-for-you remark and crowd the story into forty-five seconds. I don't like that, Carey." Her voice rose indignantly.

"Will you settle down?" Brad's sharp words spun her around, and she was looking straight into his icy stare. "You'd better control your tongue, little lady," he warned, spinning on his heel and taking off.

Mary Kate glared after him for a second, then pressed her lips tightly together, determined not to blow up. She took a deep breath and quietly accepted the cool drink Carey placed before her. Sipping it in silence, it occurred to her that she was walking a tightrope these days, torn with conflict over Blake on one side, and struggling with a new job she didn't like on the other.

Her eyes moved toward the closed doors of Mr. Lucas's office. How could she possibly have presumed to tell Mr. Lucas how to run the station? Even Brad would never do that.

She took another sip of the cool beverage then placed it on her desk. Trying to dredge up some enthusiasm for her evening report, she picked up the typewritten pages. And then she knew exactly what was wrong. She missed her interviews—that was it. She missed the opportunity to pursue a Christian approach to news reporting. As she analyzed her feelings, she realized she missed her rapport with the man on the street. Interviewing people had been her main source of enjoyment, particularly people who were an inspiration to others—like the handicapped artist who had been the object of one interview. That interview had ended up gaining national recognition for the artist. When she went home that night, she felt she had accomplished something.

But this—she stared miserably at the news she would deliver this evening.

This was not for her. She only thought she wanted to be an anchor, but now she hated everything about it: worrying about a wardrobe of fashionable clothes, the right cosmetics, the best hairstyle. Just this morning, Brad had pointed out that a female anchor must be pretty enough to win public approval, but not too pretty to detract from the news she was delivering.

Her eyes lifted to the drink in front of her, and she realized she hadn't eaten since breakfast. In fact, she had scarcely touched her meals since. . . Sunday.

Again, the memory of the ruby ring dragged at her. It was becoming apparent to her that she could not just sweep this under her mental rug. She had to deal with it. Even if it meant a long talk with Sue—or even confronting Blake. She just couldn't live with this. It was making her ill.

Just then Brad swept by her desk again and she knew what she had to do.

"Brad, could I speak with you for a minute?"

Chapter 12

You *what?*"

"I want to give up the anchor job and go back to my on-the-street interviews."

He stared at her as though she had slapped him. "I can't believe you're saying this, Mary Kate. Do you honestly know what you're doing?"

She nodded her head. "I honestly do. I'm miserable."

He leaned back in his chair, his arms crossed over his chest. "I don't know what Mr. Lucas is going to say."

She sighed. "If it's a major problem, I'll just resign."

"Resign?" he echoed, more shocked than ever.

"Brad, first you tell me how to run my personal life. Then—"

"So that's it!" He glared at her suspiciously.

"That's only part of it. I could still handle that request if I were happy at work. But I'm not. If I can't go back to the job I had before, I'm leaving."

It occurred to her that maybe she should be leaving anyway. She wasn't sure she could stay in the same town with Blake and Hanna.

"Tell you what," Brad said, his tone more logical, "do the evening newscast, then take tomorrow off and think about what you're doing. I'm sure we can still call the guy in Jacksonville and offer him the job. He really wanted it. Mr. Lucas just favored you." He grinned. "And so did I."

"Well, Mr. Lucas may not look so favorably upon me now," she said with a deep sigh.

Brad pursed his lips. "Let me talk to him. And as I suggested—take tomorrow off and clear your head."

She nodded. "I have something I need to take care of anyway."

He tilted his head and looked at her strangely but wisely asked her nothing more.

After the newscast, she felt as though a load had been lifted from her shoulders, and as she drove home, she felt far more equipped to deal with her personal problems. And she *had* to deal with them; she knew that much.

She drove into the driveway, cut the engine, and hopped out of the car. Once she had unlocked her door and stopped in the living room to pet Bo, she went to the kitchen, determined to eat a sensible meal for the first time all week. She had been existing on sandwiches and microwave dinners, only half touched. Her stomach had rolled over at the thought of food. In all honesty, her stomach had not felt right since she found the ruby ring.

She took a deep breath. She would deal with that later. She decided on bacon and eggs, canned biscuits and honey, a supper her mother often fixed on cold winter nights. She hesitated, thinking of her mother. For a moment, she almost called her to discuss the situation with her. Maybe she would even ride up to Dothan in the morning to talk things out with her. Her mother had that marvelous ability of seeing both sides of a problem and solving it sensibly.

Just then the phone rang. She finished washing her hands under the kitchen faucet and dried them with a towel.

Her merry "Hello" caught in her throat at the sound of Blake's voice on the other end.

"Have I called at a bad time?" he asked.

"No." She took a deep breath and sent a silent prayer winging toward the heavens. "In fact, I'm glad you called."

"Oh? What's up?"

"For starters, I've resigned as anchor. I'm going back to my on-the-street interviews."

"You are?" He didn't really sound surprised at her announcement.

"You're much more calm than my boss was about my decision."

"Because I understand why. You have a special talent with your interviews. A creativity. There's not that much creativity in being an anchor, is there?"

She smiled, relieved that someone had voiced what she hadn't been quite able to pinpoint. "That's exactly right."

"Then I'm happy for you."

She took a deep breath and plunged in. "Blake, there's more. As a matter of fact, I really must talk with you as soon as possible."

"You sound awfully serious."

"Yes, I am."

"Want me to come over?"

She shook her head. She wasn't ready to deal with this tonight. "I'm sure your schedule is filled tomorrow, but I've taken the day off to straighten some things out. Is there any way you could meet me for lunch?"

"I can do better than that. It so happens my eleven o'clock appointment canceled, and I'll have a couple of hours free, so we're in luck. Where do you want to meet?"

She thought it over. "Could I come to your house? It's quieter there, and what I have to say is private."

"You're beginning to worry me, Mary Kate. But sure, we can meet here at the house. I'll have Sue prepare a lunch for us."

"Fine."

"Mary Kate?"

"Yes?"

"Are you thinking of leaving Seabreeze?"

"I'm not sure. There's a possibility I might."

"Then we definitely need to talk. I don't want you to go." His tone was warm and caring, and Mary Kate felt a rush of tears to her eyes.

She had to get off the phone before she started blubbering. "Okay, we'll talk. Now I really need to run. I have several things to do." She knew her voice sounded more formal, but she wanted to keep it that way. She had to be formal with him until she knew the truth. And then there was the possibility that she might be saying good-bye to him. Forever.

When she drove into the Taylor driveway the next morning, her memory returned to her first visit here, when she had come out of concern for Hanna. The relationship between father and daughter had certainly changed since then, but she would not let herself think about how it was going to hurt once she left the house for good. Maybe there was a reasonable answer, or maybe she would never know the real truth. But she had to try and find out, or things could never be the same between her and Blake.

His car was already in the driveway, and again she voiced a silent prayer for strength. This was one of the toughest things she had ever had to do in her entire life, and she wondered if she could even go through with it. But she knew she had to. It was unfair to Blake not to give him a chance to explain.

She glanced one last time in the mirror. She had dressed conservatively in a navy pants suit, with little makeup. She tried to tell herself this was a business meeting and to approach it in that manner. In her heart of hearts, she knew her entire world was turning on what happened here this morning. Again, she told herself, *I have to know the truth*.

She reached for her shoulder bag and got out. As she approached the front steps, the door swung back, and Blake was standing there, still dressed in a business suit minus a tie. His pale blue shirt was unbuttoned, giving him a more casual appearance, and with the blue accenting his blond hair and blue eyes, her heart gave a lurch.

She dropped her eyes to the top step, determined to keep her guard up.

"Good morning," he called. "Although I must admit the look on your face doesn't quite say good morning."

"Good morning," she said, forcing a half smile.

As she entered, she could smell Sue's delicious meal, but Blake took her arm and ushered her into the den. "Sue said it's going to be another fifteen minutes before the roast is done, so we can talk first, if that's okay."

She nodded. "That's fine."

Once they were settled quietly in the den with the door closed, Blake studied her face carefully. He was obviously eager to hear what she had to say.

She looked across at him, saying nothing for a moment. More than anything she had ever done in her life, she hated to say what she had come to say. Or to ask.

"Can I help you get started?" he prompted, suddenly looking serious. "It's obviously hard for you to begin. Does it have to do with me?"

She nodded her head and took a deep breath.

"Shall we play sixty-four questions? Want me to start guessing?"

She shook her head and lowered her eyes, fidgeting with the strap of her shoulder bag. "Blake, I have to know the truth about something." She looked up at him. "And I pray you will be honest with me."

His eyes darkened. "Of course I'll be honest with you, Mary Kate. I always have been. What in the world is it?"

She took a deep breath and lifted her eyes to the ceiling. "I was playing Monopoly with Hanna Sunday and she was missing her little cup. The one that holds the hotels."

He nodded, clearly confused about where this was leading.

"She said it might be in your room, that sometimes your wife kept the cup for her pill bottles."

She watched him carefully, trying to read a difference in his expression, but it did not change.

"Hanna found the cup in the back of the top drawer of your nightstand. It held a pill bottle. I was going to bring the bottle down to Sue—for Hanna's safety—when I noticed. . .a ring in it." She lowered her eyes for a moment then looked at him again. She could see that he was beginning to understand where this was leading. "It was a ruby ring with the price tag still attached. The one ring that was never recovered from the theft."

He heaved a sigh and leaned back in the chair. "And so you think I did steal the jewelry and just forgot about the ruby ring."

"I don't know what to think," she replied honestly.

He pursed his lips and looked across the room at her. "Then you deserve to know the truth."

She waited, her breath bated.

"Charlotte took the jewelry."

"Charlotte?" she echoed, astounded by that bit of information. "But she was sick, she—"

"She felt that being hit with cancer at such a young age was unfair. She became unreasonable, demanding. I spent thousands of dollars on clothes she never wore. Then something changed. It was as if she needed to extend the cruel game she was playing to someone beyond this household. She suddenly began wanting to go jewelry shopping two weeks before she died."

He paused and took a deep breath. "I had exhausted most of my funds on her care by that time, but I still had a little space on my charge card. We went to the jewelry store she liked so much. She was in a wheelchair by then, and we moved from counter to counter. At the expensive counter, she lingered, wanting to look at everything. The salesgirl saw her condition and was very helpful, taking out various expensive items. Charlotte suggested I go over to the front counter and pick up a charm bracelet for Hanna, and I did. I put the item on my charge card and returned to where Charlotte was talking with the salesgirl.

"I noticed the girl seemed upset because Charlotte had been cross with her, demanding to see more and more items. The poor girl took pity on Charlotte, seeing her condition. While I was away, Charlotte had apparently pocketed several items, then closed the case and returned it to the salesgirl, so the girl did not argue; she was trying desperately to please her.

"Amazingly, she got away with it. Then Charlotte sent me to another counter to look for something for her mother, and while I was gone the salesgirl noticed what Charlotte was doing. She discreetly suggested Charlotte take the jewelry out of her pocket or give her a hundred dollars." He shook his head. "Naturally, Charlotte gave her some money, for she was getting quite a bargain with the jewelry she had stashed in her pocket. As for the scarf and the designer bag, she must have picked those up the same day when we went to a department store just down the street. She was always having me get her water or do something for her. She seemed to enjoy having me wait on her."

He sighed, dropping his head to his hands. "Then, there was a break-in which was for real, but the only thing taken was the VCR near the door, because the police arrived just before the burglar made his getaway. The next week, when the jewelry store inventoried their items, they discovered the missing pieces. After checking the sales slips and credit cards, they interviewed everyone who had been in the shop that day. Of course, I knew nothing about the missing jewelry, but Charlotte did. She enjoyed taking the expensive pieces out when she was alone, looking at them, perhaps imagining how life could have been or how it was when she was younger and her parents bought her everything she wanted."

He took a deep breath as though hating to continue, but as his eyes slipped over Mary Kate's face, he forced himself to finish the story. "I was out of town on the day the detective came to the house. When he questioned Charlotte, he detected that she was lying by the way she answered the questions. She was bedfast by then, and thinking she could not have stolen the jewelry herself, they suspected me. He got a search warrant of the house. They were thorough—they found everything but the ring. And now I'll see that it's returned."

When he had finished, Mary Kate sat staring at him, weighing out what he had said. "But why didn't you—"

"Why didn't I tell the truth about it all? The trauma of what had happened made Charlotte worse. She died two days later. On the day before she died, she told me what she had done and why, and she begged me never to tell Hanna. Somehow I couldn't bring myself to go to the district attorney."

"I can understand you were upset, and yet if you had told them the truth. . ."

"Well, of course, there was the funeral which occupied all of us. We had out-of-town guests, and Hanna was distraught. The next week, when the detective called again, I made a decision to avoid telling him for two reasons: One, because I couldn't bear to sully Charlotte's reputation, and two, it may have looked like I was blaming my late wife to save my own skin. I preferred to fight the charges with a good lawyer rather than having Hanna know her mother became a thief. Her parents would never have believed she did it. They always defended her. That was one of the problems—she was very spoiled and pampered. I imagine they would have gone to court to get custody of Hanna if I had said Charlotte took the jewelry. Everyone would have been convinced that I did it, anyway."

A knock sounded on the door.

"Come in."

Sue entered, nodding a hello to Mary Kate. "Lunch is ready."

"Sue, I want you to tell Mary Kate what you would have testified in court."

She looked stunned for a moment, then glancing from Blake to Mary Kate, she walked across the room and settled into a chair.

"I overheard part of a conversation between Mrs. Taylor and the salesgirl from the jewelry store. The girl came here, looking upset, wanting to see Mrs. Taylor. I couldn't help overhearing bits and pieces of the conversation after I left the room and started down the hall. Mrs. Taylor was saying something about paying her more money. The girl said she wanted to go back to Texas. When I told Mr. Taylor about this, it was already too late. The police had been here asking questions, the jewelry had been returned, and Mrs. Taylor was so ill by then. He didn't want to retract what he had already told them, but he had nothing to do with the theft. That's the truth."

Mary Kate looked from Sue to Blake, her eyes filling with tears. How could she have doubted him? Why didn't she trust her heart enough to know she could not love a deceptive man? That this man was a wonderful father, had tried to be a good husband. Her eyes locked with his as she tried to verbalize all that filled her heart.

"I can't tell you how relieved I am—and how sorry I am for doubting you, Blake." Mary Kate swallowed back tears of regret and sympathy. Blake had been through so much; it didn't seem fair for one person to have to endure what he had. Yet, he had not taken the easy way out. He had put his daughter first, even his wife, despite her cruel treatment of him. *How could I ever make up to him for doubting him?* Mary Kate wondered.

Now, looking into his tormented eyes, she wanted more than anything in the world to help him find happiness again. The room was very quiet as both Sue and Blake watched her, and she knew she must lighten the mood before they all started crying.

"Well, Sue," she brightened, "for the first time in days, my appetite has returned, and something in that kitchen smells absolutely divine."

"I'll go finish up then," Sue said, forcing a smile while casting a concerned glance toward Blake as she left the room.

Blake walked across and extended his hand, lifting Mary Kate up from the chair. "You've been carrying a terrible load, haven't you?"

"Not like the one you carried. Oh, Blake, this whole thing must have been horrible for you."

He sighed. "It was. And it would have been worse if I had been convicted. I just kept praying that my innocence would win out. I really knew nothing of any of it until Charlotte told me when she was dying. She admitted what she had done and begged me never to tell Hanna."

He hesitated, running a broad hand across his head as though the memory had set up a terrible headache. When he spoke again, his voice was low and quiet. "It was the day after the salesgirl came. When I questioned Sue, she obviously didn't know what to do. She hadn't been certain she had heard the conversation right, but she was sure of one thing: Charlotte had given the girl money. After I explained to her what Charlotte had told me, then she was certain her ears weren't playing tricks on her. Charlotte had taken the jewelry."

He closed his eyes for a moment, as though a wave of pain had crashed over him. "What would *you* do under those circumstances, Mary Kate? The store had the jewelry back, so all that was left was to fight the charges and the press and try to live down the accusation against me."

She considered his words, wondering what she would have done. Given the circumstances, she wasn't sure she could have been as protective as he had been. But she knew one thing for sure: Blake Taylor had done what he believed was best.

"You did what you thought was the right thing for your little girl, Blake."

He nodded slowly as his eyes drifted over her head to gaze out the window. "I really think Charlotte's mind was affected toward the end. She had a tumor at the brain stem that was inoperable. Most people who are diagnosed with that condition live at least six months, sometimes longer. She only made it for three months."

"Oh, Blake," she said, putting her arms around him, "how could I ever have doubted you?"

"Because you have a head full of common sense. Why wouldn't you doubt me?"

As they looked into each other's eyes, Blake lowered his lips to hers in a sweet warm kiss. Her hands moved up his shoulders and fastened around his neck as he pulled her against his chest and kissed her again.

"Iced tea?" Sue called from down the hall.

Mary Kate broke away laughing. "We'd better go."

"Before we do, there's something else I need to say. I'm in love with you, Mary Kate."

She gasped as tears rose to her eyes. "And I love you, Blake. I have almost from the beginning."

He kissed her again; then hand in hand, they walked out of the den and down the hall to the kitchen.

"Mary Kate, I think maybe I should go back and have another talk with Hal Traina, the district attorney," Blake said, studying the carpet as they walked into the dining room.

Mary Kate stopped walking and looked at him. "Why?"

He sighed. "Because Hanna wants to become a Christian, and I want to rededicate my life. I think it's important to clear all dishonesty out of my past. Maybe I should have told the truth all along."

"You did tell the truth. You were innocent."

"But I knew what had really happened."

Mary Kate stared into his eyes, worried. "But Blake, this could mean they'll drag you back through the press again and—"

"They may," he agreed. "But I feel it's important that I clear my conscience. Then it will be up to the district attorney to decide what to do."

She nodded slowly. In her heart, she was relieved that he was making this decision. It was the right thing to do, even though he had promised Charlotte he wouldn't tell. Still, it was unfair for him to live his life under a cloud of suspicion.

"Then I'm going down there with you, Blake. This time I won't let you face that agony alone."

Chapter 13

The next morning, Mary Kate and Blake sat together in District Attorney Hal Traina's office behind closed doors. Sue had accompanied them, prepared to give a deposition or do whatever was required of her. Blake wanted everything out in the open now. The district attorney had called in the assistant district attorney and the lead investigator. All had been alerted something important was about to be discussed.

Blake began to tell the story, slowly, methodically, each event unfolding in a logical manner. Mary Kate watched the men in the room, wondering why they wouldn't believe him. After all, the truth made more sense than anything else. Shock, then disbelief seized their features, and occasionally they exchanged glances, but no one spoke or asked a single question until he had finished.

For several seconds, there was complete silence in the room. Then Hal Traina looked at Sue. "And you are prepared to give a deposition to what you overheard?"

"I am. And it's more than just overhearing the conversation, Sir. The girl came to our house; I opened the door and led the way up to Mrs. Taylor's bedroom."

"We can make a charge against the girl and you, Mrs. Sampson, for withholding information," the assistant district attorney spoke up.

"May I say one more thing?" Sue asked, clearly not intimidated by any of the men. "Mrs. Taylor threatened her. She told her she would deny everything and see that she lost her job. She threw some bills toward the girl, but I cannot testify for sure that she took the money. I do know that she was threatened. It was not clear to me what Mrs. Taylor would deny until later when she admitted taking the jewelry."

The men exchanged long, meaningful glances, and the district attorney sighed and shook his head.

"Taylor, you've really complicated our lives, you know that? I'm curious as to why you came to tell us this now. You know we can't try you again for the same crime. And all the jewelry has been returned."

"Except for a ruby ring we found yesterday." He removed it from his pocket, still in Charlotte's pill bottle. "Shall I return it to the store or let you take it?"

The three men exchanged shocked glances as they realized what they had put this man through. "We'll take it to the jeweler and explain this to them. But you still haven't answered my question. This case is finally dying down in the public eye. Why would you want to risk stirring things up again?"

"Believe me, Sir, for the sake of my daughter, the last thing I want to do is dredge up that story again. But my daughter wants to give her heart to God, and so do I. And I happen to have fallen in love with a wonderful woman." He looked at Mary Kate, who squeezed his hand. "It doesn't help her reputation for people to think she is seeing a man accused of stealing."

The district attorney shifted uncomfortably in his chair and cast a swift glance around the room. The other men had dropped their heads.

"You've done a remarkable thing for your daughter. And yourself. And these women." The district attorney looked from Blake to Sue to Mary Kate. "I must say I have enormous respect for you all for coming in here today."

Blake smiled weakly. "Thank you."

"As for what you've just told us, give us some time to discuss this." He stood up, signaling that the discussion had ended. "Thank you for coming."

They shook hands, and Mary Kate noticed that all the men were looking at Blake with eyes that reflected their respect as well.

Blake opened the door for Sue and Mary Kate, and they walked quietly out of the complex of offices and down the corridor. No one spoke until they were outside in the fresh balmy air of a pleasant day in Seabreeze.

Sue turned and looked at Blake. "Now what do you think will happen?"

Blake shook his head. "I don't know. But I feel like I've just swallowed the glow of the sun." His eyes rested on Mary Kate, and she looked up at him with love shining clearly in her brown eyes.

"Blake, I've never been so proud of anyone in my entire life," she said with tears shining in her eyes. "Too bad I have to get back to work."

He shrugged. "So do I. But it doesn't matter. I feel like the weight of the world just came off my shoulders! I feel great, Darling. . ."

He leaned down and planted a quick kiss on her lips. "Now remember, we're going to my favorite restaurant tonight, and we're going to have a wonderful dinner over candlelight. And I'm going to whisper sweet nothings in your ears!"

She laughed. "I can't wait." They stared at each other for another long moment, then Mary Kate took a step back from him, forcing herself to say good-bye. "Tonight. . . ," she said. She turned and walked back to her car, feeling as if she had wings on her feet and that she were floating rather than walking.

When she arrived back at the WJAK office, the phones were ringing, as usual. Mary Kate took a deep breath, trying to orient herself as she studied the newsroom. Everyone looked busy. It didn't seem to matter to anyone that she was two hours late for work. As her eyes took in the stacks of papers on desks and the people attached to phones, it amused her to think that her life had changed drastically in the past weeks, and yet nobody really seemed to notice.

She took a seat at her desk and began sorting through her telephone messages. On her desk was one report in particular that interested her. She had been assigned to do a special on-the-street interview of the young high school student who had saved a woman from her burning home. The boy had agreed to the interview, and Mary Kate was ecstatic.

At that moment, Coty entered the newsroom and she waved to him. "We have a great on-the-street interview." She handed him a copy of the report.

He read it over and grinned. "This is great." He laid the report back on her desk, still looking into her face, grinning. "I'm so glad to have you back working with me. And I have something to tell you, Mary Kate."

"What is it?" she asked, studying his face. "And don't make me guess, just tell me."

He leaned down, planting his large palms on her desk. "Sharon and I are back together again, Mary Kate. And I have you to thank for it."

"Back together?" she repeated, staring at him, wide-eyed. "Coty, that's wonderful." But then she was puzzled. "Why are you thanking me? I had nothing to do with it."

"The New Testament you gave me has made all the difference in the world," he said huskily. "I've been reading it, and I'm here to tell you those words have melted this hard heart of mine. I've been turned around from the old beer-guzzling, woman-chasing Coty!"

"I'm so happy for you, Coty!" She smiled brightly, studying the big man, so obviously changed.

"I'll bring your New Testament back in a few days. Sharon is reading it now."

"Coty," she said as she reached forward, gripping his hand, "keep it as a wedding present. You will remarry, won't you?"

He nodded. "Right away. Well, I'd better scoot."

"Thanks for telling me this, Coty," she said, staring after him as he left the room. She sighed, feeling a surge of happiness for the divorced couple who belonged together. Then her eyes fell to the report, and she tried to concentrate on her work again.

The interview—

She jumped up from her desk and barged into Brad's office before realizing he was having a private conversation on the telephone. She stepped outside his office and waited until he hung up, then she rushed back in.

"Brad, I'm sorry I burst in on you like that, but I'm so excited about this." She waved the report. "Thank you so much for allowing me to cover this story."

He grinned. "You were right. It is a good story. And now even Mr. Lucas thinks so."

She sank into the chair opposite him and took a deep breath. "Is he very upset with me about turning down the anchor job?"

Brad tilted his head and looked at her strangely. "You know what he said to me? 'If we had more employees as dedicated to a job as Mary Kate Moore, WJAK could set a wonderful example for other stations.'" He shook his head, clearly dismayed. "I had expected him to be angry, but he wasn't. Which brings up another point."

He got up and crossed the room, closing the door.

Oh, no, she thought, *another lecture about Blake.* She had made up her mind on that point also; if he made the same threat about her not seeing him, she was going to resign. As important as her job had seemed to her, she now realized that nothing was more important to her than Blake and Hanna, and everyone's relationship to God.

"I've just had a long talk with Mr. Lucas about you," he said, taking a seat behind the desk again.

"Oh?" She lifted her brow, waiting for the other shoe to drop.

"It seems that he and Hal Traina, the district attorney, are close friends. He has just enlightened me about some new information on the Blake Taylor case. It seems I owe you an apology, and I imagine all of Seabreeze owes Blake Taylor one, as well."

She gasped. "You know about Blake's meeting with the district attorney?" she asked, amazed that he had heard the news so quickly.

"Just as word of mouth did more to damage his reputation than anything else, I think Hal and his staff decided it would be appropriate if a bit of gossip was now passed along, revealing the truth of the matter. I gather there will be no more trials."

She took a deep breath and tried to hold onto her optimism. "I don't know what will happen. We just left his office this morning. I'm praying that everyone will come to realize what a good man Blake Taylor is."

"I trust your judgment, Mary Kate. After all, you are a people person;

you know how to read people, and you were right about him. I owe you an apology."

"Thanks, Brad," she said, smiling at him.

"Incidentally, I know you were with Taylor today. The district attorney is a very nice guy, actually, and apparently he sensed your delicate situation in the matter. He didn't want your job affected by idiots like me. I'm sorry, Mary Kate."

She leaned back in her chair, at a total loss for words. "I. . .it's okay, Brad. Just as long as people understand, everything is okay. In fact, it's wonderful."

Brad leaned across the desk, his voice lowered.

"Are you in love with him?"

She hesitated only a moment, not because she was unsure of her feelings, but this was the first time she had admitted her love to anyone but Blake. "Yes, Brad," she said quietly. "I'm head over heels in love with him. And I think he feels the same way for me."

"Then let me be the first to wish you all the happiness in the world."

Tears filled her eyes. "Thanks, Brad. And I promise to do my job better than ever."

He nodded. "I'll be expecting that." He had lapsed back to his old teasing manner, breaking the emotional tension between them.

She stood, glancing again at the report. "Now I want to go make some notes on this story so I can do the interview justice."

She dashed out the door, her mind spinning with all that was happening. Last week she had been dragging the ground, and now, this week, she was soaring in the clouds.

Chapter 14

As she prepared for her date with Blake, she took the time for a leisurely soak in her favorite bath oil. So much had happened that it was hard for her to fathom it all. And yet she had always believed in miracles. Her problem was that she never gave God enough time to bring about those miracles.

She captured a clear bubble floating on the soothing suds. Why couldn't she ever get it through her head that God had His own way of working things out? And He always seemed to do things perfectly when given time. She sighed, sinking deeper into the bathwater as she rested her head against the back of the tub.

"My problem," she said aloud, "is that I want to jump in and fix things myself. Maybe this time I've learned," she added softly, feeling a burst of joy in her heart as she thought of Blake and Hanna and the love they now shared.

She closed her eyes for a moment, inhaling the wonderful scent of cinnamon cake candle she enjoyed burning while she took her bath. Her mind drifted toward the evening's date with Blake. She knew exactly what she would wear. Over her lunch hour, she had gone into the boutique that had been beckoning to her for weeks. In the past, she kept walking past the boutique, forcing herself to be frugal. Today, however, she felt that a celebration was in order.

It had been wonderful to go inside the exclusive boutique and wander around the racks of dresses looking for something that suited her mood. She found it quickly—a long flowing skirt of pale blue cotton with a sleeveless blue silk blouse. When she took the outfit to the dressing room and tried it on, it looked as though it had been made for her. The sky blue color accented her dark hair and eyes, and the soft sheer flow of fabric gave her the sensation of floating through the air. And in her heart, that was exactly what she felt she was doing.

She deliberately avoided looking at the price tag, knowing the years of frugal training her parents had instilled might now tempt her not to buy the outfit. She changed back to her other clothes and took the outfit to the counter. Then she spotted a pair of backless silver sandals.

"Those would be terrific with the dress," the young saleswoman assured her.

This was all the prompting she needed. Fortunately, the sandals came in her size, which she considered a good sign. She added the shoes to the outfit then whipped out her charge card, ignoring the total figure.

"This is a lovely outfit," the woman said to her. "Are you going somewhere special?"

Mary Kate nodded. "Very special."

"Then I hope you enjoy your outfit."

Mary Kate smiled at her. "I'm sure I will."

Now, recalling the outfit, she forced herself out of the tub, rubbing down with a thick terry towel. She applied lotion and powder and pulled on a robe. Then she sat down before the mirror to concentrate on her face. Tonight, she would add a bit more makeup than usual—only a small bit. She had already shampooed her hair, but she still had time to touch it up.

Humming a love song to herself, she thought about calling her mother. It was definitely time to tell her about Blake. She and her mother had always been very close, and she wanted to deliver her good news. But as she stared into her sparkling brown eyes, she decided to wait and see what the coming days brought. And she wanted to see how she felt about Blake Taylor after tonight.

As it turned out, there was no point in worrying about the evening. It couldn't have gone better.

Blake arrived wearing a soft tan sports coat and trousers in a chocolate brown. Beneath the coat, his shirt was a soft cream. She thought he had never looked more appealing.

He gave a low whistle when he saw her. "Well, hello."

She smiled up at him. "Hello to you. Want a glass of iced tea or something?"

He shook his head. "Let's allow ourselves enough time to enjoy the drive."

"Fine." Gathering her purse and locking the door, her hand slipped easily into his as they walked out to his car.

Soon they were out of the downtown traffic and onto the beach highway.

"I have a favorite restaurant near the house that I think you'll enjoy," he said above the soothing flow of a nice instrumental in his CD player. "Funny, it's called Summer Place, and maybe that's how we started calling our beach house by that name. Anyway, I thought it was the perfect place for us to go for a celebration dinner."

She nodded, looking across at him. "Sounds great."

He was dressed casually, and he had never looked more handsome to her. He seemed to have dropped several years from his face, his golden blond hair was shining from a recent shampoo, and the blue eyes glowed with happiness as he turned into the restaurant parking lot and cut the engine.

He came around to open her door for her, and they got out and walked up the steps to the quaint little restaurant, nestled on a quiet little strip of land hugging the ocean.

"We'd like a table by the window," he said to the hostess. "I called to request one earlier."

She recognized him and nodded. "We put down your request as soon as you called, Mr. Taylor."

Mary Kate glanced up at him, smiling. "So you called ahead."

"As soon as you said you could go."

The hostess led them back to a table for two by a window that over-looked the sparkling blue water. It was a lovely evening, with the sun beginning to sink on the horizon, dropping a raspberry hue over the ocean.

Mary Kate took a deep breath and sighed. "How lovely."

She felt his hand gripping hers and she turned to face him.

"I'm so grateful for you, Mary Kate. I truly believe God put us together. I've thought a lot about what you said about how you had prayed for the right person." He took a deep breath. "I never did. I'm not saying anything against Charlotte. She was a good person."

Mary Kate nodded. "I know. When I look at Hanna, I realize that."

"What I'm saying is. . .well, I guess what I'm asking is if you think that. . ." His voice trailed as he dropped his eyes to her fingers, entwined in his.

"If I think what?" she asked, squeezing his hand. Then she understood what he didn't seem to have the courage to ask. "If I think you're that man?" she asked tenderly. "Yes, Blake, I do. Without a doubt."

His eyes reached into hers and for a moment there was a sheen of tears glazing the deep blue eyes. He sighed. "Mary Kate, I'm in love with you, very much in love with you. I don't know what I ever did to deserve you, but I promise I'll spend the rest of my life trying to be the person you want me to be."

"Just be who God wants you to be, Blake. And you did that today."

He nodded. "And Sunday I will be joining you and Hanna. After all, we want to start our life together in the right way."

She nodded, feeling her throat tighten. Then suddenly she gave up, as tears began to trickle down her cheeks. "Oh, Blake, I'm so happy."

The waitress stood at the table staring at them, hating to interrupt.

"It's okay." Blake turned to her, grinning. "We just got engaged." He reached into his pocket and pulled out a small navy case.

Mary Kate's breath caught.

"I'll come back," the waitress said with a smile, discreetly slipping away.

He opened the tiny box, and Mary Kate was looking at an exquisite solitaire that took her breath away. "Oh, Blake, it's gorgeous. I don't know what to say."

"Just say yes," he said, slipping the ring onto her finger. It fit perfectly. "If there's another kind you'd rather have, we can go to the jewelry store after work tomorrow night. After all," he laughed, "I've become good friends with the manager."

"Is it the same one that. . . ?" And then she was laughing too.

"Funny thing. He seemed really glad to see me."

Mary Kate nodded, thinking of what Brad had said about word getting around.

"This one suits me perfectly," she said. "Just like you."

They kissed then, not caring who saw them. All they cared about was that at last they had found true love during their darkest hour.

PEGGY DARTY

Peggy is the popular, award-winning author of novels and magazine articles. Peggy, who makes her home in Alabama, has been spinning wonderful tales of romance for several years—and winning awards along the way. She is also the mother of three and grandmother to two little boys.

Treasure
of the
Keys

Stephen A. Papuchis

Chapter 1

Azure seas, intermingled with layers of turquoise and deep blue hues and dotted by many small white-rimmed islands, greeted Ann Langley from the window of the small twin-engine plane. The plane veered to the left, and a display of crimson and gold danced upon the water as the sun made its majestic retreat over the western horizon. *A striking contrast*, thought Ann, *to the dull gray of New York City*, which she had left only hours before.

Ann stirred in her seat with anticipation as the pilot announced that the plane was on its final approach for a landing in Key West, Florida. She ran a brush through her shoulder-length brown hair and put on a dab of powder from her compact, glancing quickly in the mirror at her deep green eyes which had been the subject of innumerable comments by so many potential suitors—suitors who at this time were as far from her mind as Key West was from New York City. For this was no pleasure trip Ann was on. No, for her it was strictly business.

Ann's company, Development Corporation of America, had recently secured the title and appropriate permits to a piece of highly lucrative real estate in Key West. The property was going to be developed into one of the finest resorts on the East Coast, a resort the developers claimed would rival the posh playgrounds for the rich which dot the shores of the Caribbean Islands and the Mediterranean Sea. She was responsible for the marketing and sales of the condominiums to be offered there.

Ann put her compact and brush back into her purse and placed it securely under her seat. She tightened the seat belt around her trim waist, as she could see from her window that the plane was fast approaching the ground. What was once a blanket of blue suddenly gave way to a myriad of browns and greens. Tropical foliage of mangroves, yucca plants, and palms now lay before her. Ann realized instantly that Key West was even more beautiful than Bill, her supervisor, had described it. Yet for all its beauty, it seemed to convey an aura of mystery, as if unknown dangers and hidden secrets lurked in what was essentially the tropical jungle below.

The plane, now landed, taxied into position in front of the small terminal, which was the Key West airport. As it came to a complete stop, Ann rose from her seat, took her purse in one arm and her flight bag in the other, and set forth on the island which for the next four years she was to call home.

The first thing which struck her as she left the plane was that the tropical scenery and topography did not come free of penalty. It was almost twilight, but the heat and humidity lingered on, an immediate discomfort to Ann, who just this morning had put on her favorite yellow cashmere sweater to protect her from New York's early morning briskness. Nonetheless, if she were to make this project a success, she would have to take the good with the bad. If living on a gem of an island in a crystal ocean meant living with hot temperatures and high humidity, so be it.

Having made her way around downtown Manhattan for the past four years, Ann had no trouble getting her bags and hailing a taxi.

"Where to?" asked the cab driver, as he opened the back door for Ann.

"To the Key West Hotel," she replied. "Do you know where it is?"

"Of course I do," the cabbie answered. "That's the island's most popular hotel. If I didn't make at least one trip there a day, I'd think something was wrong."

The driver started the engine and inched the cab along, unperturbed by the steady flow of the late-afternoon traffic which seemed to converge on all sides. As the cab sat idling, Ann caught sight of a light blue van pulling up at the curb nearby. Emblazoned on its side was the sign, NICK'S DIVING SERVICE. As she sat wondering what a diving service would entail, the driver of the van stepped out and hurried around to open the door for his passengers. He was close, so close that she could almost have touched him.

Not moving her eyes from him, she studied him intently as he went about the business of unloading his passengers, the baggage, and scuba gear. He was tall, appearing to be over six feet, and was trim and well tanned. His brown hair was highlighted with streaks of blond—the type of blond one gets from constant exposure to the sun. His muscles rippled rhythmically with his easy handling of the heavy gear. But it was his eyes that so completely held Ann's attention. Large and dark brown, they registered, alternately, friendly exuberance and a distant longing, a combination that struck Ann as contradictory, yet intriguing.

As the cab moved out into the mainstream of the city traffic, she continued to look back until distance obscured him from view.

To Ann's surprise, the cabbie struck up a conversation almost immediately.

"Where are you from, Miss?" he asked, glancing once in the rearview mirror.

"New York."

Ann sat forward in her seat, crossing her arms and resting them on the front backrest.

"Hmmm. I went there once. Didn't like it."

"Why?" Her eyes widened.

"Too big and too cold."

"Well, it's been good to me," replied Ann, somewhat defensively.

"Yeah? How's that?"

"For one thing, my job with DCA, which is headquartered in New York, has allowed me almost endless opportunities—including this tenure here in Key West," was Ann's proud answer.

"DCA," the cab driver replied in a shocked tone of voice, taking his eyes off the road to give Ann a searching look. "You don't mean Development Corporation of America. . .do you?"

"Why, yes, you've heard of us?" questioned Ann, leaning back.

"I should say so!" he retorted in a crisp, bitter tone. "And so has everyone else in Key West who cares two cents' worth about where they live!"

The cold chill which fell across the air with the cabbie's words squelched the happy enthusiasm Ann had felt upon landing and almost sent shivers down her spine. What was it about DCA that its very mention would evoke such a response from a total stranger?

Initially intimidated, she quickly recovered, bit her lower lip, and said to herself, *Forget it, Ann, this guy's probably just some sort of weirdo!*

Silence filled the air for the remainder of the drive, and Ann felt an almost indescribable sense of relief upon arriving at the hotel.

She stepped out of the cab and, without leaving a tip, paid the driver, then followed the bellboy and her luggage into the spacious lobby. At the front desk, Ann received only a silent imposing stare when she told the clerk that all expenses would be paid by Development Corporation of America.

What is it with these people? she asked herself as she left the lobby for her room.

Deciding to forget about both the cabbie and the desk clerk, she checked into her room and proceeded with the tedious task of unpacking and organizing for the days ahead. With so much to do, she hardly knew where to begin. In addition to her personal needs—finding a place to live, having her belongings moved down from New York, and the like—she was to represent the corporation in coordinating final plans for developing the condominiums and for setting up and operating a sales office. Getting the office successfully set up and operational was only the beginning. After that came the real work: sales!

What have I gotten myself into? she worried, as she carefully folded each blouse, placing it in the top drawer of the elegant bamboo dresser.

Although she had worked hard on many large development projects before, during her short tenure with DCA, never had so much responsibility been laid upon her at one time. And never had she felt so alone with her responsibilities. Before, in the bustling Manhattan corporate office, there had always been someone to turn to, someone to collaborate with, or someone's advice to seek. But now there was only Ann.

Perhaps, she fretted, *this time I've bitten off more than I can chew.*

Having put her last blouse away, Ann sighed and stretched out on the large king-size bed. She reached over beside the dresser and switched on the overhead fan. Lying there, she watched the blades spin, feeling the cool breeze across her face. Relaxed, she closed her eyes for what she thought would be a one-minute breather. The fatigue, however, which had been there all day long, overtook her, and she fell into a deep sleep.

The squawking of seagulls awoke her the next morning. She rolled up into a sitting position in the middle of the large bed. She rubbed her eyes, still half asleep, faintly remembering a dream of laughter, which she decided, was the fault of the seagulls, whose noisy calls, when carefully listened to, resembled high-pitched human laughter.

Ann rose from the bed and slowly walked—almost stumbled—to the sliding glass doors, which opened out onto the terrace. She pulled the doors open and was pleasantly greeted with the cool morning air, scented by the refreshing aroma of salt and the sea. The view from the room, which Ann had neglected to check out the night before, now stood before her in sheer majesty. The blue sea lapped against the white-pebble coral coast, which stretched out to the left and ended in a point, piercing the sea as an arrow pierces its target. To the right, the coastline curved back around the main building of the hotel and ended in a basin, which served as a marina at which the hotel's fleet of fishing and diving boats were moored. Beyond the marina, the coast twisted off into the distance and all along was lined with elegant coconut palms. It was a scene of almost indescribable beauty, yet once again Ann had the feeling that for her this unfamiliar landscape held unknown, possibly even unpleasant, experiences.

The gulls which had so rudely awakened her were now squawking and laughing above the water, diving occasionally for morsels of food floating among the waves. Ann watched their amusing antics and thought that if DCA's resort were only half as nice as this hotel, she should have no problem selling every condo offered. She knew, of course, that the plans for the resort far exceeded the size and scope of this hotel, and she felt a sudden surge of pride at being a part of a prestigious organization such as Development Corporation of America, momentarily forgetting the chilly responses her company's name had evoked the previous day.

Deciding not to waste any more time, Ann quickly showered, made up her face and hair, and dressed in a pair of sleek oxford slacks, a light cotton blouse complemented by a blue-and-white-print scarf, and a pair of Top-Sider loafers. Although her clothes were somewhat conservative, she felt that for a woman in her position, they were more appropriate than frilly or daring attire.

Having fallen asleep the night before without eating, Ann's immediate thoughts were on breakfast. Not wanting to spend too much time on dining, however, she decided just to have a quick bite at the hotel's restaurant. She chose a fruit plate filled with all types of tropical fruits native to Key West— mango, papaya, fresh pineapple, oranges, grapefruit, and shredded coconut. *Delicious,* she thought, finishing her meal, *and so exotic.*

Ann charged the meal to her room and leisurely strolled to the lobby for a few minutes of repose before starting her day.

The Key West Hotel, not neglectful of any conveniences which might better serve the guests, had placed to the left of the main entrance a service counter with tourist information. Ann stopped briefly in front of the display and eyed the numerous brochures advertising the various restaurants, museums, and attractions Key West had to offer. She randomly picked up some of the brochures and deliberately took a map of the island to use on her first day's explorations.

She walked to a corner of the lobby where a grouping of rattan furniture was tastefully arranged around a large oval glass-topped table holding a bowl of fresh hibiscus blossoms. Beneath the table lay a handsome blue-and-white Persian rug, and above, an overhead fan whirred, creating a light breeze for the guests seated below. At the sides of the couches stood tall tropical plants set in deep wicker pots, their delicate fronds gracefully bending over the ends of the sofas, adding to the cozy atmosphere. Mounds of cushions were banked in the corners, inviting guests to sit and relax in an area that somehow managed to look both elegant and comfortable. On the east wall hung numerous oil paintings of various Florida settings.

Ann settled herself comfortably in the corner of one of the couches with the stack of brochures in her lap and slowly started flipping through them. Most were advertising typical tourist attractions, only one of which, the pirates' museum, held her attention for any length of time. For some reason, the thought of treasure buried deep beneath the ocean blue was tremendously intriguing. Then suddenly one of the brochures stood out from among all the others. NICK'S DIVING SERVICE, the advertisement read in large bold type. Below the heading was a picture of a brown-haired, brown-eyed man with striking features. For a minute, Ann was taken aback by the photo. "Why, this is the man I saw at the airport," she exclaimed. She stared at the picture, examining the wide cheekbones and striking jaw which outlined the face. The strong, straight nose was flanked on either side by deep brown eyes. As at the airport, the eyes held Ann's attention the longest. Although they were deep and dark, they seemed to sparkle with a friendly radiance which somehow flowed off the page and into the very room where she was seated.

Holding the brochure in her hand, she leaned back on the cushion, closed her eyes, and thought back to the near encounter of the day before, when she had seen the rest of the body that went with this near-perfect face. Suddenly her thoughts were drawn to attention by the call, "Ann."

Startled, she opened her eyes widely to the sight of a blond-haired, blue-eyed woman standing before her.

"Are you Ann Langley?" the stranger asked.

"Why, why. . .yes," she stammered, sitting up on the couch uneasily and focusing her attention on the person who had just broken her reverie. "May I help you?"

"Yes, my name is Virginia Roberts, but please call me Bobbie. Everyone else on the island does. The desk clerk told me I could find you here," she said, barely giving Ann time to catch her breath and collect her thoughts. "I'm from Island Realty," she continued, "and I received a letter last week from a Mr. William Watson, who told me that you would be coming down here this week and would probably be staying for an extended period. He asked me if I would come by the hotel to meet you and show you around the island and maybe help you find a place to live."

Well, this is just great, thought Ann. *Either Bill thinks I'm incapable of finding my own way around, or else he can't wait for me to get out of this nice hotel and into a place of my own just to get off the expense account. Either way, I could get along fine without this Miss Bobbie!*

Concealing her irritation and putting forth her friendliest saleswoman's front, Ann stood up and extended her hand to the woman.

"That's kind of you. I'm sure there is much you can show me in Key West." Ann's green eyes narrowed as she took in this stranger, although she maintained a smiling expression.

"It'll be my pleasure," replied Bobbie. "Would you like to get started today, or shall we set up an appointment sometime this week?"

Bill probably told her to get me out of this hotel today, thought Ann, finding her irritation increasingly difficult to hide. Nevertheless, having no real excuse to put matters off for another day or so, she said to Bobbie, "Today will be fine. In fact, I'm ready to go right now, if it is convenient for you." Her tone of voice was courteous but aloof.

"That's just what I was hoping you would say. Shall we go?"

Bobbie's blond curls bounced as she turned and walked across the lobby of the hotel, with Ann following close behind at a brisk clip. When she reached the front door, Ann stopped briefly at the trash receptacle to discard the stack of brochures she had collected earlier. The last brochure was about to enter the trash when she glanced at the picture beneath the caption NICK'S DIVING SERVICE. She quickly stuffed the brochure into her purse and followed Bobbie out the door.

Though it was not yet ten o'clock, the Southern sun was well into the sky and had warmed the air considerably since Ann had last been out just two hours earlier. The heat, however, was made more tolerable by an insistent breeze, which blew eastward from the sea across the island's interior. This was Ann's first full day on the island, and she immediately took note of how clear and blue the sky was. Across the horizon, were it not for the different tones of blue, one would hardly have been able to distinguish where the sky left off and the blue ocean began.

"I'm parked across the street by the tennis courts," said Bobbie as she walked a few steps ahead. Looking over her shoulder, she continued, "Hope you don't mind riding in a Volkswagen, but the LTD which I usually use when I'm showing clients around broke down on me last week, and would you believe they are having to wait for parts from Miami? Had I known I would have been waiting on parts when I bought a Ford, I would have gone on and bought a BMW."

Ann knew that Bobbie's small talk was just an attempt to be friendly, but she wasn't really in the mood. The fact that Bill Watson didn't leave finding an agent up to her had set her off on the wrong foot with this Bobbie Roberts in the first place, and now the fact that they were going to have to drive around Key West in a cramped little Beetle only added to her bad mood.

"Of course I don't mind," replied Ann, again putting on the front which was so necessary for her profession.

"Well, here we are," said Bobbie as they arrived at the little Volkswagen convertible with the top down.

The two women entered the small car, which purred like a kitten when Bobbie started the ignition. Bobbie shifted the car into reverse and backed out of the parking lot and onto the main road which ran in front of the hotel. The road headed east along the northern coast of the island and was lined with tall coconut palms and island pines, creating a natural portico through which to pass. To the left of the road lay the Atlantic Ocean, with the coastline surprisingly undeveloped.

"Anyplace you would like to see first?" asked Bobbie, glancing in Ann's direction.

"You're the guide. Wherever you decide will be fine with me." Ann shrugged.

Bobbie drove along for a minute more without speaking. Ann was beginning to enjoy the drive along the coast. The wind was blowing through her hair, and the sun, unobstructed by any car top, cast its penetrating rays on her shoulders. She was also beginning to lose her original animosity toward Bobbie and was, in fact, starting to like her. *She seems to be naturally friendly and at ease with herself,* thought Ann, who after having such a curt experience with the first two Key Westerners she met, found it pleasantly refreshing to be with someone so cordial.

To break the now-prolonged silence, Ann offered up some small talk. "You know, Bobbie, I'm surprised you haven't shunned me like everyone else I've met in Key West so far. It seems that as soon as anyone finds out I represent DCA, they treat me as if I had the plague."

Bobbie managed a half smile as she glanced at Ann from the corner of her eyes. "Oh, you know how they are," she replied sarcastically. "The environmentalists in this town will be the death of it yet. You just stick with the right crowd, and you won't have anything to worry about."

The right crowd. . .anything to worry about. What could she possibly mean by that? Thinking perhaps now was not the proper time to pursue the issue, Ann decided just to let it slide and enjoy the tour, which Bobbie was intent on giving.

"This is the main drag through Key West. There are several things along this road which might interest you." Bobbie turned right onto the busy two-lane highway and into the flow of traffic. Along the drive, she pointed out the things which would be of importance for Ann to know, such as the better grocery stores, shopping area, and restaurants. She also showed Ann around some of the tourist attractions, such as the municipal aquarium, the lighthouse museum, the island's oldest house, the southernmost beach, and the conch tour train. They stopped to see Ernest Hemmingway's house on US Route 1, only a few blocks from where the highway ends at the sea. Ann remembered how much she had enjoyed reading *A Farewell to Arms* as she looked at the famous author's home, surrounded by a red brick wall to insure privacy.

Following the tour of Key West, Bobbie took Ann on an extensive house-hunting expedition. She showed her about half a dozen available apartments and condominiums that she thought might be to her liking, but Ann found a drawback to each one. Finally, rolling her eyes in frustration, Bobbie said, "I just don't know what to do with you, Ann. I've shown you some of the better listings available, and you've found something wrong with each one."

"I don't know," sighed Ann, leaning her head back on the car seat. "Perhaps we'd better just call it a day."

"Okay," answered Bobbie. "There's always tomorrow. Now what do you say we go get a bite to eat? I'm starving."

"That's one offer I can agree on," laughed Ann.

Bobbie took Ann to a small delicatessen in downtown Key West that had a group of picnic tables located outdoors on one side where the two women sat while they ate. As she ate, Ann looked around at the part of town they were in. She could tell by the antebellum style of the houses that this was a definitely older section of Key West.

"What do they call this part of town?" she asked.

"Olde Town."

"I never would have guessed," said Ann jokingly.

By the time they finished their meal, the clock was pushing three.

"I guess I'd better be getting you back to the hotel," said Bobbie, after she drank down the last swallow of cola and crunched noisily on the remaining bits of ice.

"By the way," asked Ann, looking around, "which direction is the hotel from here?"

"Why, you are almost there. Half a mile through this neighborhood until you hit the waterfront, turn right along the coast, past the docks, another half a mile or so, and you are there."

"Tell you what," said Ann, rising from the table and taking her purse in hand, "it sounds as if the hotel is close enough for me just to walk back."

"Are you sure?" Bobbie's eyebrows rose. "I'd be glad to give you a ride."

"I'm sure. It's a beautiful day and I could use the exercise. Besides, it will give me a chance to get to know Key West better."

"Okay, then, have it your way. Just be careful."

Ann looked at her questioningly. "Okay, Bobbie, you too."

She then turned and walked away, heading northeast along the sidewalk, which wound through the old neighborhood. The street was well shaded by the large banyan trees, which overhung on both sides. Spanish moss dangled majestically from the lower branches, creating a surrealistic effect, which would have seemed more appropriate to a tropical jungle than an urban neighborhood. The walk through the neighborhood was cool and peaceful, for the road was seldom traveled, used only by residents in their comings and goings.

The neighborhood with its large trees did, however, produce a myriad of noises, most of which were unfamiliar to Ann. These were the sounds made by the large bird population, which occupied the branches of the trees. The squawk of the parrots, the call of the macaws, and the singing of the sparrows all filled the air with a natural orchestration. Ann thought that this would be a pleasant neighborhood in which to live. The houses, though old, were clean and well maintained. They were also some of the largest and most interesting structures on the island, with their many windows, nooks, and crannies. Ann could not help but feel that this neighborhood with the large old homes housed a wealth of unspoken history. From its inception as a haven for pirates through the days of rumrunners and smugglers, Key West was definitely a city with hidden secrets.

The deep blue ocean with its many intermingled hues now lay before Ann. She was surprised at how quickly it was upon her as she left the neighborhood. It seemed just moments ago that she was walking through a densely vegetated area, which, for all its beauty, seemed close, confining, and imposing. Now, however, the open freedom of the sea beckoned its welcome to her. Remembering Bobbie's directions, Ann turned right at the coast and followed it in the direction of the docks. Beads of perspiration were just beginning to break over her brow, and she was about to stop for a rest, even in the sun, when the marina finally came into view. *Good,* thought Ann, wiping the sweat from her brow. *I'll stop there for a soda and cool off for a minute.*

She walked down the path leading to the marina and quickly located the snack bar where she ordered a glass of limeade, advertised to be squeezed fresh daily. *Delicious,* she thought, taking a sip of the frothy liquid. *I guess they really do squeeze it themselves!* She walked slowly down the boardwalk, casually examining the many small boats docked in the inlet. The water lapped at the wooden pilings encrusted with barnacles, and provided a soothing rhythmic melody, which Ann found inherently pleasing. The smells of the marina were not entirely unpleasant either, for they were the smells of diesel fuel, fish, and salt, all combined to form the aroma one would expect and would miss if it were not there.

Resting her arms on the railing, she casually watched a brown pelican floating gracefully among the waves. The sun was slowly sinking in the west, seeming to melt into the ocean where it dipped low on the horizon, spreading pools of deep crimson across the water. An army of cumulus clouds was building to the south, but Ann paid no heed. For although her mind had not ceased its mundane task of executing the physical activities of the body, her thoughts were not centered on any one objective but were mixed and dispersed like the contents of a child's toy box strewn across a large living room floor.

Why had her initial reception in Key West been so hostile? And what had Bobbie meant by staying with the right crowd and being careful?

Raising herself from the railing, she sipped down the last swallow of limeade, now diluted by the melted ice, turned, and walked out along the pier, gently trailing her hand on the weathered railing as she moved slowly forward.

Suddenly, almost instantaneously, the purposeless wanderings of her mind were pulled together like iron filings to a magnet and centered on a common focal point. In front of her was the man who commanded this reaction and who was responsible for such an overpowering assimilation of her thoughts. Unaware of her existence, he was busy with the task at hand—securing his large, sleek cabin cruiser with a frantic urgency.

She watched him with undivided attention. His nimble hands worked the ropes quickly and professionally; with each pull and tug his muscles flexed and contracted almost instinctively. Having the bow of the boat secured, he turned and walked along the narrow deck past the outside of the cabin to the rear.

Although she had seen him only briefly, it seemed to Ann that she knew this man. Vividly she could picture his long muscular legs and trim waist, which slowly gave way to the width of his slightly hairy chest and broad shoulders. Even his blue-and-white-striped swimming trunks and leather sandals stood out in sharp images, but she had not yet seen his face. That is, until he returned on the opposite side of the boat and stood before her.

"Nick!"

Ann grimaced and swallowed hard at having unintentionally spoken his name. Chagrined, she pondered what to say next. How would she explain knowledge of him prior to any introduction? But then, remembering the brochure buried deep in her purse, she immediately came up with an idea.

"Why, hello!" Nick smiled, the shallow of his cheeks folding into deep-set dimples.

A brief moment of silence followed, a moment which seemed like an eternity as Ann dug in her purse for the crumpled brochure. Reaching it, she questioned, "This is Nick's Diving Service, isn't it?"

"That it is," he answered, lifting himself over the stern onto the deck below.

Nick now stood before her. He was so close that she feared he could almost hear her heart beating as she nervously looked out over the water, not knowing what to say next. To her relief, however, Nick continued the conversation. He leaned back on the railing, crossed his arms, and asked, "And you're down here to sign up for a diving trip. Right?"

She looked up at him to answer, but the words were momentarily muted when her eyes met his. It was the eyes which so captivated and held her attention. The effect they had on her from the printed brochure was strong, but now in person they were more than strong—they were mesmerizing! Finally breaking free of their grip, she smiled and answered, "Yes. . .I mean, well, sorta!"

"Sorta!" Nick chuckled. "How do you sorta want to go on a diving trip?"

"Well, it wasn't exactly a diving trip I had in mind, but I'm new in town and was wondering if you might not be available for a sight-seeing cruise."

Ann knew her statement was a lie, for she had stumbled upon Nick quite by accident and had no intention of taking a sight-seeing cruise when there was so much work to be done over the next few days. If she was to save herself the embarrassment of having blurted his name on their first encounter, however, she would need an excuse. And this was it.

Nick gave Ann a searching look, causing her to feel intimidated, as if she were a piece of merchandise on display.

"Tell you what," he answered, raising his chin in a smug manner, "I don't have any trips planned for next Wednesday, and I'll be glad to take you on a sight-seeing cruise then. On one condition."

Ann looked at him suspiciously. "And what might that be?"

"Dinner Saturday night!"

Ann scowled. Normally, she would have been flattered by a dinner invitation and would have accepted without hesitation, especially coming from someone who so captured her interest.

The manner in which Nick asked, however, was smug and arrogant, and she was not going to inflate his ego further by accepting.

"No, thanks," she retorted. "I'm not in the habit of trading dinner dates for sight-seeing cruises. Besides, you don't even know my name!" With that she turned, her brown hair snapping across her shoulders, and started walking down the pier. Realizing that she was leaving, Nick didn't hesitate, but chased after her.

Catching up with her, he took her by the elbow and said, "Listen, I. . . you're right! I don't even know your name, but that doesn't mean I don't want to. What do you say we start over?"

Ann turned and looked up at him. The longing stare in his dark brown eyes was sincere, compelling Ann to give the situation another chance.

"Okay," she answered, the corners of her lips rising in a smile.

"Good!" Nick stood back and extended his hand. "My name's Nick. . . Nick Carmichael, and you're. . . ?"

"Ann. . .Ann Langley," she answered, placing her hand in his.

"Pleased to meet you, Ann."

Nick shook her hand softly, and they shared a long mutual gaze before the rumbling of thunder in the distance suddenly took charge of Nick's attention and caused him to look questioningly at the sky. Ann noticed the seriousness with which he listened to the thunder. "The storm is getting closer," he said. "We'd better get off the dock."

"But there's still plenty of blue sky," protested Ann, looking upward. "Surely the storm is hours away."

"No, these tropical storms can be upon you in a heartbeat. One minute the sky will be crystal clear, and the next minute the lightning and thunder will be all around you. In fact, I'm afraid this storm will be here any minute."

"I'd better get going then, if I'm to get back to the Key West Hotel before it starts raining."

"How are you getting there?"

"Walking."

"All the way to the Key West Hotel?" Nick frowned. "You'll never get there before the storm hits. I'll drive you back."

The large dark clouds which now occupied the majority of the once-blue sky, along with the low rumbling thunder, reinforced Nick's assertions, and Ann agreed to let him drive her to the hotel. Nick locked the door to the cabin, and the two hurried down the pier toward the parking lot.

They reached his van just as the first raindrops fell. He opened the passenger door for her, and Ann stepped up into the van and settled down on the comfortable velour of the bucket seat. She looked over her shoulders at the rest of the van. The interior had been modified to make room for the tools and scuba gear, which occupied all available space. She didn't recognize most of the equipment, but one item she could distinguish—a large, expensive metal detector. *Odd,* she mused.

Nick got in on the driver's side and started the engine. He pulled out of the parking area and onto the coastal highway, turning on the windshield wipers, for the rain was now coming down with a greater intensity.

They drove for a minute in silence, and finally Ann spoke. "I certainly appreciate the ride. I see now that I could never have made it back before the storm."

Nick grinned and said, "Well, this is just the prelude. Experience tells me that the real storm will be upon us in about seven minutes."

Ann wondered about the astuteness of the man who made such precise predictions. Unconsciously, she glanced at her watch. It read 6:03.

They rounded a bend in the road and the Key West Hotel came into view. Nick turned into the parking lot, past the swimming pool and boat docks, and around to the front entrance. Ann jumped out of the van and ran around the front of it, hoping to get out of the rain before getting too wet. Nick opened his door and stepped out also, stopping her just short of the canopy above the front entrance. His stare held her there, and his lips moved slightly as if he were trying to say something but couldn't get the words out. The rain was falling even harder now, and it pelted down on both their heads, running down their necks, and dripping off both their bodies.

"Thanks again for the ride, Nick," said Ann. As she turned to get under the protective shelter of the canopy, he put his hand forward, catching her on the left shoulder and again stopping her short of her desired goal.

"Will I see you Saturday?"

"Maybe," she said, breaking free of his grip and moving under the canopy out of the now-pounding rain. "I'll call you." She then ducked through the front door and into the dry comfort of the hotel lobby.

Pushing back her wet bangs and wiping the water drops from her eyes, Ann walked briskly across the tile floor of the entranceway, straight to the elevator. Entering her room, she hurriedly went to the bathroom for a towel, dried her face, hair, and arms as best she could, and then walked to the terrace doors to open the curtains.

When she pulled the curtains open wide to allow more light into the room, she was blinded by a sudden flash of lightning which filled the heavens and ended with an explosive crack on the ocean's surface. Accompanying the lightning was a thunderous roar, and the rain started falling in violent torrents. Again, the lightning cracked, again the thunder roared while the rain fell harder and harder with such velocity that Ann feared even the ocean itself might overflow its tremendous basin. "This must surely be the storm Nick predicted," she said. She looked at her watch and it read 6:10. It had been seven minutes exactly.

Ann continued to stand at the terrace window watching the storm with hypnotic wonder. A storm like this, a usual occurrence in the Florida Keys, was to Ann a new experience. She had never before perceived anything so violently beautiful.

After several minutes, she turned from the window, leaving the curtains open. She sat down in front of the dresser mirror and began to brush back her still-damp hair, looking at herself in the mirror as she did so.

Ann was a very pretty girl with big eyes and high cheekbones that, at certain angles, made her look like an eighteen-year-old college student instead of the twenty-seven-year-old businesswoman she was. She had a small nose, full lips, and a chin which was neither too flat nor too protruding, but seemed to curve perfectly round to the folds of her neck.

I guess I'll do, she thought as she brushed her bangs down over her forehead.

Turning from the dresser, she removed her damp clothes and started walking toward the bathroom with the intention of taking a shower, but halfway there she decided against it and instead just rubbed her still-damp skin dry with a fresh towel and slipped on a brief sleep shirt. She propped some pillows up on the bed, leaned up against them, and picked up her briefcase. Balancing it on her lap, she opened it and started going through the documents and papers associated with the development project, with the expectation of getting some work done.

The storm had now slacked off to a steady rain, and the roaring thunder could be heard only as a faint rumbling far out to sea. The steady patter of the rain on the terrace created a soothing lullaby, having its own impact on Ann. For the storm had been like the tide of her emotions which had been tossed and turned by the events of the day, much as the waves of the ocean had been tossed and turned by the earth's natural forces. The steady beat of the rain induced a peaceful tranquility. Pushing the briefcase and the papers aside, she curled up in the center of the bed with her head on the pile of soft pillows. She lay quietly listening to the soft patter of the rain as it hit the terrace outside. She heard the faint rumble of the storm far away—the storm which had moved on to inflict its raging fury on some distant land. Then Ann herself moved on to distant lands, to the lands she would visit this night in her dreams, as she fell asleep.

Chapter 2

Clear, fresh air greeted Ann as she threw open the sliding glass door and stepped out onto the terrace, tossing her hair back in the breeze. Everything seemed to have been cleansed by the storm of the night before, and even the distant palm trees stood out in sharp images. The early morning hour provided a crisp coolness to the air, for the eastern sun had not yet started its warming obligation. The sea was calm and blue, and the few small white clouds floating overhead mirrored off its still surface, as did the palm trees, which lined its coast.

Having already showered, dressed, and ordered a room-service breakfast of stone crab crepes, a slice of cantaloupe, and toast with guava jelly, she decided dining on the terrace would be quite enjoyable.

Taking the tray of food from inside, she positioned it on the glass top of the terrace's wrought-iron table, seating herself in one of the two iron chairs. She then removed the covers from her still-warm breakfast, breathed deeply of the enticing aroma, and began to indulge herself in some of the most delicious crepes she had ever eaten. The crabmeat, surrounded by the thin, light crepes, was white and succulently sweet. The cantaloupe was fresh and cool, and the guava jelly with its unique taste, which fell somewhere between a peach and a plum, was delectable on the crisp whole wheat toast.

After wiping her hands with the linen napkin, she tossed it on the table and settled back in her chair. Leaning sideways with both legs over one armrest, she gently stroked her hair while staring out over the horizon. Slowly her thoughts turned to work and the numerous things she must do to get the project off the ground.

The task was tremendous, but it was one Ann had pursued with zeal, at which she was determined to succeed. Having been chosen for the position from a large group of highly qualified candidates (the majority of whom were men) only increased the pressures of success. Ann knew that if she failed to get an office set up on time and on budget, she would be rapidly replaced, bringing a virtual end to her career with Development Corporation of America. A career which at the present was the single most important thing in her life!

Suddenly, the realization of the enormous amount of work yet to be done threw Ann to her feet.

"Got to get to work," she mumbled, collecting the used dishes onto the serving tray. With determination she went inside, settled down at a corner table, and spread her briefcase of documents out before her. For the next three hours, she worked tediously on the task of organizing her priorities, compiling a list of the necessary office equipment, and calling various dealers and suppliers on Key West to obtain price lists.

The corporation had allocated a budget of one hundred thousand dollars to outfit and start up a local office, and Ann was tremendously relieved to find that the majority of the items she needed could be purchased on Key West and at a reasonable price. This was an important matter, for if she could set up the office under budget, it would look very good on her record. Ann had just hung up the phone from the final dealer she needed to contact—an electronics retailer who could supply a business computer, word processor, and telex machine all at a bargain package price—when the phone rang. Hesitant to answer, Ann put her hand on the receiver, wondering who could be calling. She suspected that it was her supervisor, Bill Watson, calling to check up on her, but deep in her heart she hoped it was Nick.

"Hello," said Ann, as nonchalantly as her anxiousness would let her.

"Hi, Ann," the female voice replied. "This is Bobbie."

"Well, hi, Bobbie. How are you?" replied Ann with a sigh, relieved that it wasn't Bill, but slightly disappointed that it wasn't Nick.

"Listen," continued Bobbie in her normal business manner, "I've done some looking and think I've found some places you might like. Would you like to see them today?"

"Sure," answered Ann, looking at her watch. "How about in an hour or so?"

"That will be fine with me, Ann, and by the way, I've found an office that I think you might be interested in."

"Great," said Ann, who was now relieved that Bill had asked Bobbie to help her, for she hadn't realized how much work it required to get the office equipment, much less find an office.

"Tell you what, Ann, suppose I pick you up at the hotel at twelve-thirty, and that will give us time to go office and home hunting both."

"Sounds good to me. See you then."

Relieved at what Bobbie had told her, Ann mentally went over what still needed to be done. *Things are starting to fall into place,* she thought. *If I can get the office rented and equipped, get the power on, a phone with a toll-free number, and a secretary to man the office while I'm out, I'll be in business.*

Before going down to meet Bobbie, Ann moved over to the dresser and put on some eye shadow, lipstick, and a dab of blush. Just before leaving the room, she remembered to pick up the tray of empty dishes out on the terrace and place them outside in the hallway.

Ann took the elevator down to the lobby, went straight to the gift shop to pick up the morning edition of the *Key West Times,* and carried it to the same couch where she had sat the day before, to read and to wait for Bobbie's arrival. Being an avid and rapid reader, she soon finished the bulk of the paper and was about to toss it aside when a full-page ad suddenly caught her eye: STOP THE DESTRUCTION OF KEY WEST! SUPPORT THE CONCH SHELL ALLIANCE. The words stood out in large bold type.

What's this all about? she pondered, lifting the paper for closer examination. She read the entire ad but did not have any better idea what the Conch Shell Alliance was upon finishing it than when she began. For some reason, however, the ad made her uneasy, as if it were directed against her. Frustrated, she crumpled the paper into a tight ball, tossing it into the trash just as Bobbie walked through the front door.

"Hi, Bobbie." She smiled, pleased to see a friendly face.

"Morning, Ann. Ready to go?"

"After you," answered Ann, rising from the couch.

Walking to the car, Ann turned to Bobbie and asked, "Bobbie, what's the Conch Shell Alliance?"

Bobbie stopped and looked at her, a smirk coming across her face. "I take it you saw the ad in this morning's paper!"

"Yeah, I did, but I couldn't figure out what they were talking about."

"They do that deliberately," Bobbie answered, taking her eyes off Ann and continuing to walk to the car. "They'll say something like 'Stop the destruction,' but not tell you what they're referring to. That way they can solicit contributions and gain support from people who don't really know what they're supporting!"

"But who are they? I mean. . .what are their goals, what are they trying to accomplish?"

"Ann," Bobbie's voice sighed, "they're just a bunch of fanatics. Environmental fanatics! They're opposed to any new development in Key West and even campaign for the disbandment of some established developments. They've even done things like lobbying to have the air force base shut down and proposing immigration quotas to stop people from moving here. That kind of craziness!"

A worried look came across Ann's face as she thought about her own development. Would the Conch Shell Alliance be a factor? *Not if I can help it,* she told herself. *After all, we have our permits, and we've done everything by the book—the condominiums will be built!*

On that thought, she put the Conch Shell Alliance out of her mind just as they arrived at the car.

"Sorry about the car," said Bobbie, looking up at Ann as she opened the front door, "but the LTD is still in the shop."

"Oh, no, don't apologize. I really like this car."

"Well, I'm glad somebody does, because as soon as the LTD is fixed, I'm selling it."

What a coincidence, thought Ann, for ironically, she had already had thoughts of buying a car. She did not own one at the present, for in New York City, she could always take a taxi or the subway, and with the heavy traffic and expensive parking fees, a car was not practical. But down here a car was more than just practical; it was a necessity. Everything was so spread out that the small public transportation service available was not adequate to fulfill her needs. *I'm going to buy this car,* thought Ann, having mentally convinced herself of the necessity.

"Tell you what," she said aloud to Bobbie, "before you sell, how about letting me make you an offer? I think I could really use it."

"Sure! If you're interested, I'll let you have first choice."

"Thanks," replied Ann happily.

Bobbie started the engine and drove out of the parking lot and into the light flow of traffic. In less than ten minutes, they arrived at a newly developed commercial area. Bobbie turned into the parking lot of a small new plaza, which was tastefully landscaped. The wood siding of the shops and offices was artistically arranged at sharp angles, which Ann found aesthetically pleasing. Bobbie parked the Beetle in front of a vacant shop and said, "Well, this is the office I was telling you about. It just became available last week."

"It looks good from here. Can we see the inside?"

"Certainly."

After a thorough tour of the office and about thirty minutes of discussion—going over the terms of the lease, rental price, restrictions, and the like—Ann decided to take a lease on the office. She was especially pleased that it was available for occupancy immediately and that she could arrange for prompt delivery of the equipment she had ordered only that morning.

"One down and one to go," she said, as Bobbie locked the door to the office behind them.

"After we do some house hunting for you, we can go back to the realty office and sign a lease. Maybe we can take care of both places with one trip to the office, and I can give you the key to your office then."

"Fine," replied Ann. "But there's just one thing—I'm not sure if I want to go on another house-hunting trip."

"What do you mean?" Bobbie frowned. You haven't found a place on your own already. . .have you?"

"No, no, nothing like that. It's just that. . ."

"What?"

"Well, do you remember that older neighborhood I had to walk through on the way back to the hotel yesterday?"

"Yes."

"I was wondering if you might have something available in that neighborhood."

"So that's it!" laughed Bobbie. "You had me scared there for a moment, but you're in luck. I just listed a house in that section recently. I would have shown it to you first, but I had no idea you'd be interested in renting one of those large old houses."

Leaving the office, the two drove to the old neighborhood and down the familiar street with its large, overhanging banyan trees. Ann felt a sensation of comfort and belonging in the densely vegetated neighborhood. Maybe it was because she had left an area which was largely composed of asphalt and concrete and highly lacking in natural vegetation. Or maybe it was because her childhood in Long Island had been spent in an older, established neighborhood, and her subconscious felt its stability. Whatever the reason Ann was not sure, but she was sure that she liked this neighborhood and wanted to live here.

Bobbie turned the car down one of the side streets, pulled in front of one of the larger houses on the block, and stopped. "This is it," she said, motioning to the large white house on the right.

Ann looked up, and she couldn't have been more pleased. The house had a large front yard filled with all types of mature tropical plants: burning orange poincianas, deep purple bougainvillaea, and the very fragrant frangipanis. Yuccas and palms bordered the front yard, displaying the stately beauty that comes with age and maturity. Almost in the center of the yard, slightly to the left, was a huge banyan tree, its low, spreading branches providing an umbrella of shade over a small brick patio. The house itself was two stories high, with a row of arched windows on either side of the front door. Four black iron posts supported an upstairs patio, which was rimmed by a black wrought-iron fence of intricate design. The roof of the house had a low pitch, necessary to support the handsome red tile shingles which overlaid it.

"Want to see the inside?" asked Bobbie.

"Sure," said Ann, "but it's only academic. I can tell you now I want it."

The two walked across the yard to the front door and into the noble house. The entrance foyer opened to spacious rooms on three sides. High ceilings and thick walls helped provide natural cooling in the tropical heat. Ann was very pleased to see that each room also had its own overhead fan.

The kitchen was large and well arranged, and although the house was old, all new, modern appliances had been installed. A screened porch opened from the kitchen to the fenced backyard, and a spiral staircase led to the three upstairs bedrooms, which were positioned around a central bath. It had another full bathroom downstairs, and both baths were tastefully furnished with antique basins and large, deep tubs, which sat on legs shaped like bear paws.

"I'll take it," said Ann, while standing in the entrance foyer still examining the many intricate features.

"Good," answered Bobbie, smiling. "Shall we go sign a lease?"

"Let's go!"

The two then left and drove to Bobbie's office at Island Realty.

Entering the Island Realty building, they walked past several people busy at their desks, to Bobbie's private office in the back, where she prepared the necessary lease papers, explaining the terms, obligations, and fees. Ann signed the two leases, and Bobbie turned over the keys to her.

The two then sat there for several more minutes making small talk and enjoying each other's company. Ann told Bobbie about the events of her career which led up to her moving to Key West, and the things that had happened to her since she had been there. "And yesterday I met the most interesting man," she said. "His name is Nick and he runs a diving service at the docks."

"You don't mean Nick Carmichael, do you?" exclaimed Bobbie, genuinely surprised.

"Yes, that him! And you know him?"

"Well, let's just say I know of him. . .as does everyone else on the island."

Bobbie's words had an almost sarcastic, gossiping tone to them, which caused Ann to retreat in a defensive posture. What was it about Nick, a man she found so enticing, that caused her (supposedly) new friend to snicker? Ann was torn between wanting to leave the room in order not to hear any more and pressing Bobbie for further details. Finally, her curiosity got the better of her, and she asked, "What is it, Bobbie? What's there about Nick that gives him such a reputation?"

"He's a nut."

"What?" Ann exclaimed.

"I don't mean he's a real nut—like being insane or anything—it's just that he does a lot of crazy things."

"Like what?" Ann pressed.

"Well, for one thing, everyone knows he's obsessed with hunting a treasure that doesn't exist!"

"A treasure!"

"Yeah, sunken treasure. I tell you, Ann, if he devoted half the energy he spends searching for buried treasure to his diving business, he'd be a rich man by now."

"But maybe he'll find a treasure someday," Ann injected, somewhat in defense of Nick.

"Yeah," laughed Bobbie, "and maybe someday we'll have a ski slope here in Key West!"

A long moment of silence followed before Ann spoke again. "This is all very interesting, Bobbie, but if it's all right with you, I'd like to get back to the hotel. It has been a long day."

"Sure, Ann," said Bobbie, getting up from her desk.

On the drive back to the hotel they hardly spoke, for Ann's thoughts were in too much turmoil for small talk. Mostly she thought about Nick. Surprisingly, her new knowledge about this unique individual did not lessen her interest; in fact, it seemed to further increase her eagerness to know him better.

Arriving at the hotel, Bobbie broke the silence by saying, "Ann, if you would like, I could stop by sometime tomorrow, and we can talk about a deal on the car. I'm sure my LTD will be ready by then, so I'd be willing to go ahead and sell this Beetle."

"That will be fine, Bobbie. What if I just call you sometime tomorrow?"

"Okay, Ann. Take care."

After stopping at the hotel desk to check her mail, Ann went up to her room, took off her shoes, and tossed them into a corner. She lay down on the bed, staring up at the ceiling. Over and over, she told herself to put Nick out of her mind, but her mind wouldn't listen, for something greater, stronger, and more dominant than any sensible rationale was controlling her thoughts.

Finally, after many mental arguments and self-evaluations, she picked up Nick's brochure and slowly dialed the number printed on the front. Nervously she listened as the phone rang: once, twice, three times. Just as she was about to hang up the receiver the phone clicked, and a voice at the other end answered, "Hello, Nick's Diving Service; Nick speaking."

Chapter 3

The sound of Nick's voice on the other end of the line snapped Ann to attention and sent her courage plummeting. She almost eased the telephone back onto the hook—but, taking a deep breath, she found herself saying in her calmest and most self-assured manner, "Hi, Nick. This is Ann Langley. I was just calling to see whether the offer for Saturday night is still open."

The enthusiasm in Nick's voice as he replied instantly, "You bet it is," eased Ann's tension and brought a smile to her face. "I was just this moment planning to give you a call."

"Oh. . .well, that's wonderful."

A moment of awkward silence followed. Ann did not know whether she should continue with some trivial pleasantry or wait for Nick. She waited.

Then, slowly, as if he were giving serious consideration to the evening, he said, "I have a suggestion. What if I pick you up at the hotel around six o'clock and give you a guided tour around the area before dinner? Sound okay?"

Not wanting to confess that she had already had an extensive tour of the island with Bobbie, she replied eagerly, "I think that sounds wonderful! I would love it."

"Okay, then. See you Saturday at six."

Well, Ann, she mused, hanging up the phone, *looks like you've got yourself a date.*

🌴

The following morning Ann spent conducting business from her room. It was almost eleven before she left for the lobby, stopping briefly at the desk for her mail and a copy of the *Key West Times*. Surprisingly she had only one letter. A single white envelope with her name typed on the outside and no return address!

Positioning herself at the corner of the now-familiar couch, she looked at the letter curiously. *I wonder who this is from?* Slowly she opened the envelope and removed the single white page from inside. As she unfolded the page and read the message it held, her heart skipped a beat, and the palms of her hands broke out in a cold clammy sweat. For there, boldly typed in the center of the page, were only five words: GET OFF THE ISLAND NOW.

Quickly she stuffed the letter back in its envelope and shoved it deep to the bottom of her purse. There she felt for the familiar can of mace, which she had always carried in New York City. She had hoped that, once in the Keys, she could do away with the strictly defensive weapon. But now she feared that it might prove even more necessary than ever.

With adrenaline still pumping through her veins, Ann looked nervously about the lobby. Finally, with a deep sigh, she rested her head back on the soft pillows of the couch. *Relax,* she told herself. *You're getting too upset over nothing. This letter could even have been a joke.* Her heartbeat was slowing at last and the nervous fear almost gone when suddenly she was frightened to her feet by the call, "Ann!" which came from behind. Blood raced through her veins with a renewed intensity, and her heart pounded violently as she turned around.

"Bobbie!"

Bobbie's face was smiling, but the smile quickly disappeared when she noticed the panic in Ann's eyes.

"Ann, I'm sorry. I didn't mean to startle you."

"That's okay," said Ann with a deep sigh of relief as she sat back down on the couch. "I've just been a little on edge lately, that's all." How she wished she could show Bobbie the threatening note! Desperately she needed someone to confide in, to talk to, but now was not the time. Although she considered Bobbie a friend, she did not know her well enough to confess her growing fears. Nor would she tell anyone, at least not until she had found out herself the reason she had met with such hostile resistance.

"Anyway," said Bobbie, sitting down on the couch beside her, "the reason I stopped by is because I've gotten the LTD out of the shop and I'm ready to sell the Beetle, if you still want it. Do you?"

"Yes, sure, I'll be needing a car. How much did you say you wanted?"

"Fifteen hundred."

"Fifteen hundred! Bobbie, you drive a hard bargain, but I'll take it." Although she felt that Bobbie might be gouging her, Ann had no enthusiasm for car shopping in a strange city where she had no friends and no close contacts except Bobbie. She then wrote Bobbie a check, and Bobbie handed over the title and the car keys.

"Congratulations!" chortled Bobbie. "You now are the owner of a not-so-new Volkswagen Beetle." The two women talked for a few minutes more before Ann finally asked, "Say, Bobbie, do you know of a place that sells casual outfits, but sort of on the dressy side?"

"Sure. There is an excellent little shop not far from here."

"Good. I want to get something new to wear for Saturday night."

"For Saturday night?" Bobbie's voice rose in curiosity. "Something serious?"

"Oh, nothing serious," said Ann nonchalantly, "just a date."

"A date! Tell me, with whom?"

"Nick Carmichael," answered Ann calmly.

"Nick Carmichael? Ann! I thought I warned you about that kook."

Ann frowned. "Well, actually, it's nothing serious, just dinner. Anyway, I'd like to find out for myself what this guy is like."

"Suit yourself, Ann. But after dinner if he takes you to the library to read about sunken Spanish galleons, don't say I didn't warn you. Now, about that boutique. What if I just go with you? I've been wanting to do some shopping anyway."

"Sounds good to me," answered Ann, somewhat relieved that Bobbie had asked to go, for she had not yet fully recovered from the threatening note.

The two left the hotel. Ann drove and Bobbie gave directions as they made their way to the boutique. Here Ann picked out a light blue all-cotton sundress that hung low on the shoulders and was tied at the waist. The dress had small ruffles around the neck and sleeves, as well as the hem. It was not the type of dress she would have chosen a week ago in New York, but for here in the Keys, it seemed to be most appropriate—not too fancy, not too casual, just cool and comfortable and lovely.

"You look super!" commented Bobbie, as Ann looked at herself in the full-length mirror of the boutique.

In addition to the dress, Ann bought several pairs of shorts and matching tops, a pair of sandals and tennis shoes, a striking one-piece bathing suit and a revealing two-piece, which she tried to talk herself out of, but finally decided to buy after rationalizing that she would use it only for private sunbathing.

By the time the two were on their way home, the back seat of the Volkswagen was piled high with packages. Ann dropped Bobbie off at her office and headed out alone. Carefully maneuvering her way through the late-afternoon traffic, she successfully found her way back to the hotel in her car filled with new clothes.

The next few days were busy ones in which the time passed quickly, and Ann's mind stayed occupied with thoughts other than those of Nick or of the troubling encounters she had experienced. Demonstrating the efficiency that had won her this position, she managed to get the office furnished and operating and hired a secretary to staff it permanently. The girl's name was Stephanie, and, although she lacked some of the experience and education which Ann sought, she had a dynamic personality and a willingness to work that Ann found a redeeming virtue.

During these days, Ann also managed to get her personal belongings, furniture, and clothes moved into her new home. She was, however, still living in the hotel, as there were a few improvements yet to be made before the house would be ready for occupancy. She had ordered a light ivory carpet for the living room, which still had to be laid, and the draperies for both that room and her bedroom had not been hung.

Before Ann knew it, Saturday was upon her. In her mind, she had designated four o'clock as the hour to begin her preparation, allowing herself a leisurely two hours to get ready. She could, in fact, be ready to go in less than half that time, but for her this evening had a special appeal, and she wanted to be able to spend the hours of preparation in a relaxed, unhurried manner, reveling in the mounting sensations of excitement and anticipation.

Latin music was playing on the radio as Ann stepped out of the shower. Moving rhythmically to the beat, she patted herself dry, wrapped a towel around her wet hair, and headed for the dresser. Breaking routine, she applied moisturizer over her entire body and then dusted herself with a lightly scented powder. She carefully filed her nails and applied a coat of soft pink polish. Next came the face. She highlighted her green eyes with black pencil, put on a coat of light blue shadow, and finished the job by putting a dab of mascara on her long lashes. Some blush, which she applied lightly, served to enhance her high cheekbones, and her light pink lipstick complemented the nail polish already applied.

She gave careful attention to her hair, drying it all to a full, rich fluff and then curling the ends under in her usual casual style.

Makeup and hair complete, Ann finished getting ready by putting on her new dress, a pair of white semi-high-heeled shoes which matched her small white purse, and jewelry. Putting on her jewelry was her favorite part of getting fully dressed, and she spent several minutes pondering over the many selections in her jewelry box. She finally decided on a gold ball necklace with matching earrings and bracelet.

When all was finished, she stood in front of the full-length mirror giving herself a thorough evaluation. She decided that her appearance and choice of attire were fine. Her makeup and dress, with the ruffled neckline and low sleeve-line, seemed brighter than her usual preference for conservative attire would demand. But things here were different and she felt different. *This,* she thought, *is Key West, a land of fiery red sunsets and turquoise blue water, a land where the colors and traits of nature are intensified and where life itself seems more daring and exciting!*

The clock on the dresser showed the time to be 5:45. *Still a few minutes to relax,* thought Ann. Opening the sliding doors to the terrace, she walked out and stood looking out over the still, blue ocean. She thought about the evening yet to come and what it might offer. She then let her thoughts wander far away—back to her home on Long Island, to a warm summer day long ago when she was just a little girl. She was swinging on the green-and-yellow swing set in her own backyard, her father pushing her. "Higher, Daddy, higher," she said. She then remembered the fall and how upset her father had been as he scooped her up in his arms and ran into the house, pressing her tear-filled eyes close against his large welcome shoulders. And then the soft, tender rocking that followed to soothe and comfort her after the not-so-tragic disaster. "It's okay, Honey, it's okay," she heard her father whisper.

Just as the memory was beginning to fade, the phone rang. Ann jumped, half startled by the loud ring, and went inside. She let the phone ring an extra time, so as not to appear too anxious, for the time was exactly 6:00, a telltale sign that the caller was Nick.

"Hello," said Ann in a friendly, yet almost sultry, tone.

"Hello, Ann," the deep voice on the other end replied. "This is Nick."

"Hi, Nick. Are you in the lobby?"

"That I am. Are you ready to go?"

"Be down in a minute."

Not wishing to appear too eager, she deliberately took her time as she picked up her purse and took one last long look in the mirror before leaving the room.

Almost immediately after getting off the elevator, she saw Nick. He was standing in the lobby with his arms crossed over his chest, apparently engrossed in the numerous oil paintings which hung on the lobby's east wall. Ann stood there for a minute watching him. She was slightly surprised at what she saw, although not sure why. It was the same Nick she had met on the docks, the same Nick whose picture appeared on the brochure, but something seemed different. For some reason, he didn't evoke the perception of an outdoorsman or a divemaster who spent the majority of his daylight hours out on the high seas. Instead, he seemed almost the perfect image of a sharp young businessman or Madison Avenue sales executive. He was wearing a neatly pressed pair of khaki slacks with a brown leather belt, a light blue button-down sports shirt, and a white lightweight sports coat. She noticed that his brown hair was neatly styled in a contemporary feathered fashion. Such a contrast, she thought, to the wet, stringy locks she remembered from their last encounter in the storm.

Ann started walking in his direction, and at the same time Nick turned from the wall which had held his attention. He looked up and their eyes met. A wide smile appeared on his face, as it did on Ann's.

There was a moment of silence as the two stood there, each capturing the other's attention with equal intensity. Nick finally broke the silence.

"Good evening. You do look lovely."

"Why, thank you," replied Ann. "You look nice yourself."

"I'm sorry that I didn't see you come in. I was too involved in studying these paintings."

Ann's eyebrows went up slightly in surprise above her green eyes.

"Then you like art?"

"Yes, very much. I must say that visiting the art museums is one of the few things I miss about living in New York City."

"Oh, you're from New York?" asked Ann with genuine surprise.

"No, but I did live there for several years."

This discovery pleased Ann, for she felt that now they might have several similar interests to talk about during the evening.

"Shall we go?" asked Nick, as he motioned to the door with one arm. The two walked out of the hotel side by side. Ann's eyes scanned the parking lot looking for the familiar van, but Nick did not seem to be walking toward one. After a short distance, they stopped in front of an elegant brown Volvo, and he opened the passenger door.

"I thought you drove a van," she said.

He laughed. "No, that's the business truck. Tonight we're going to ride in air-conditioned comfort."

Sinking down in the luxurious cushioning, Ann noticed the rich white leather interior, done in attractive European styling, and thought to herself that Nick must be doing pretty well with his diving business.

She felt relaxed and quite at ease as Nick pulled onto the coastal highway. He drove along the coast until the road intersected the overseas highway, the major link which spanned the Keys and connected with the mainland just south of Miami. He turned left on the highway, heading northeast away from Key West.

"I know a nice little Greek restaurant on Big Pine Key, thirty miles up the highway. I thought we might go there, and you could see some of the lower Keys on the way."

"Fine, I'd like to see some more of the Keys, but this restaurant must be really good to rate a sixty-mile drive."

"It is," answered Nick. "You can decided for yourself, but I'll guarantee you won't be disappointed."

The drive from Key West to Big Pine was delightfully scenic. From Key West to Big Pine, they crossed twenty bridges connecting twenty-one islands. Some of the islands were so narrow that the Gulf of Mexico could be seen on one side of the road and the Atlantic Ocean on the other. Others, however, were so large that it was easy to forget you were on an island. Some of the islands were largely undeveloped, mainly because the lack of water and power made the development too expensive. Others, such as Sugarloaf Key, were extensively developed, even to having their own airstrip. Ann was especially intrigued by the many tiny islands which could be seen from the highway. One especially beautiful little green island stood alone like an emerald set upon a turquoise band.

"Does anyone own the small islands?" asked Ann.

"Oh, yes. In fact, the majority are privately owned, and some even have self-contained houses on them, totally self-sufficient with their own power generators."

"Really?" answered Ann with great surprise. "They look so small, I would have never believed there were houses on them." Nick crossed the South Pine Bridge, and the two were now on the island of Big Pine. "This is the largest island of the lower Keys chain," boasted Nick, "and in my opinion one of the prettiest."

The island was indeed beautiful, the home of some of the most exotic plant and animal life found in the entire Keys chain. The thrinax palm, the small and dainty tree that was one of the few native flora of the string of islands, could be found there. The island also hosted the largest commercial pineapple plantation in the continental United States.

Most of the development on Big Pine Key was of a residential nature, and only a few hotels or commercial establishments existed. This, coupled with the fact that large tracts of the island were permanently set aside as game preserves, made it quite unique among the Florida Keys chain.

Nick turned the car off the main highway and headed north along a two-lane road, which ran almost down the center of the island. They had driven about a mile when Ann asked, "Is this the way to the restaurant?"

She had noticed that there was no traffic on the side road, and even a pickup truck that had turned off the main road behind them was no longer in sight. And while she had felt Nick's unmistakable charm and attraction and had been excited by this date, she now was having second thoughts about being alone with this man she barely knew.

"No," said Nick in reply to her question, "the restaurant is in the other direction, but there's something this way that I want you to see."

Ann remained silent, her fears steadily increasing.

They drove on for another three or four miles, passing a few small housing developments, but for the most part, the landscape consisted of undisturbed tropical forest.

Finally, Nick turned off to the left into an area with a large open field on one side and a dense forest on the other. After he had driven for about a half mile and the open ocean could be seen ahead, he pulled the car off to one side and turned off the engine. To the right of the car was a field with a small thicket of yuccas and pine trees near the center. To the left was a densely vegetated forest. Not quite understanding Nick's intentions, Ann exclaimed almost sarcastically, "Is this what you brought me way out here to see—an empty field?"

"Wait just a minute," said Nick, "and they'll be here."

What will be here? wondered Ann, but before she could give voice to her thoughts, three deer appeared. They came from the woods toward the open field and crossed the road almost directly in front of the car.

"Do you see them?" asked Nick softly. But the question was not necessary, for the three tiny deer that were crossing the road had already captured Ann's undivided attention, replacing her fears with amazement.

They were the tiniest deer she had ever seen, barely larger than a small dog. Their soft brown coats and snow-white tails made them instantly adorable.

"Those are Florida Key deer," Nick explained, "and they are full grown."

"But they are so tiny!" said Ann in an almost disbelieving tone.

"Yes, and no one really knows why, but these elfin creatures are found nowhere else in the world except right here on Big Pine Key. There are only about three hundred of these deer left, and all live right here where we are now on the Key Deer Refuge."

"I would never have believed it if someone had told me such tiny, beautiful creatures existed," replied Ann.

"Just another one of the many mysteries harbored by the Keys!"

Nick and Ann watched the deer for several more minutes as they walked leisurely across the field and disappeared into the thicket. "Well, that's what I brought you here to see. Now, how about dinner?"

"Sounds great!" Ann smiled at Nick with immense relief and pleasure in this shared moment.

He started the car and drove back in the same direction from which they had come. The two hardly spoke as Nick drove to the restaurant. Ann was still thinking about the beautiful little deer and of her unfounded worry, and Nick was busy driving.

The sun had now set, and a velvet blanket of darkness was rapidly descending upon the island. Nick turned on the headlights, and they cast a warm glow across the road. They reached the main highway from which they had originally turned, but Nick crossed the highway and continued on in a southerly direction. With the main business district behind them, Ann was beginning to wonder where this restaurant could be.

They drove for another half mile until they reached what seemed to be the southernmost tip of the island, and there, situated on a peninsula which extended into the sea, was the restaurant.

It was a medium-size building, artistically positioned on the tip of the peninsula. In front was a large parking lot and canopied entrance. The other three sides were constructed with a glass framework, which provided a waterfront view for the majority of the patrons. To the left of the building was a small pier to which were moored several small fishing boats.

Nick parked the car and, making a small comment about having arrived, opened his door and got out. Ann reached for the handle on her door, but before she opened it decided otherwise, for Nick was already halfway around the front of the car. *Well,* she thought, *if he wants to open the door for me, I'll let him. After all, we are on a date.*

Nick opened her door and extended his hand. Thanking him with a pleasant smile, she took it and stepped out of the car.

Once out, she expected Nick to let go of her hand, but instead he simply pushed the car door shut and started toward the entrance. Hand in hand, they walked across the parking lot, looking as if they might be longtime lovers instead of the virtual strangers that they were.

As they approached the entrance, a deeply suntanned man wearing jeans and a cap pulled low over his forehead stepped out of an old blue pickup truck directly in front of them. He stared at them both, especially at Nick, as if trying to be certain of his identity.

"Pardon me," said Nick, drawing Ann around the man and walking toward the entrance.

"Well," said Ann softly, so that she could not be overheard, "he certainly doesn't look like a dinner guest to me."

"Probably came to sell Tony some fish," said Nick. "Anyhow, clothes don't mean anything down here."

Ann said nothing more, but as Nick opened the door for her to enter the restaurant, she looked back just in time to see the blue pickup leaving the parking lot.

Once inside the restaurant, Ann realized that the simple exterior gave no indication of the elegant dining establishment it housed. The large dining room was shaped like a half-moon with two levels separated by a single step. The upper level was large and open with many tables symmetrically arranged. The lower level had a single row of tables, each butted up against the glass walls and circling the entire establishment. Every table was covered with a white linen tablecloth and decorated with a crystal vase holding a single rose in the center.

Large plants hung from the ceiling, creating a warm, cozy atmosphere, which was punctuated by Greek music flowing out of unseen speakers.

As Nick and Ann waited in line to be seated, Ann took the opportunity to further examine her surroundings. She spied two island pictures, hung on opposite walls, which she thought were especially appropriate in this setting. One was an aerial view of the Florida Keys chain: the many islands connected by the overseas highway, which stretched across the ocean and disappeared into the horizon. The other was a view of a different island chain—islands that were larger and more mountainous than the Florida Keys, but nonetheless beautiful—islands which she recognized as the Greek Isles in the Aegean Sea.

Finally reaching the front of the line, they were greeted by an elderly gentleman with dark hair and a bushy mustache.

"Hello, Nick," said the man with a slight accent. "It is always good to see you."

"It is always good to see you too, Tony. This is Ann Langley, a new arrival to Key West. Ann, this is Tony Agnostapolis, the owner of this fine establishment."

Ann smiled and extended her hand, which Tony took in his and gently shook. "It is a pleasure to meet you, Ann. Beautiful girls such as you are always welcome here in the Keys."

Ann laughed and said, "Thank you. I wish everyone in the Keys shared your hospitality."

Tony raised his hands in the air in a typical southern European gesture. "Well, enough talk! I'm sure you two are ready for dinner, and I have just the table, so if you would, please follow me."

They followed Tony to the lower level where he seated them, in cozy privacy, at a small table located at the far end of the dining room. The glass wall against which the table was situated provided an unobstructed view of the water. The moon had now risen considerably in the Southern sky, and its reflection off the calm sea provided a spectacular view, creating an unparalleled romantic atmosphere.

"Will this be okay?" asked Tony, pulling out a chair for Ann.

"This will be fine," said Nick.

"Good. Here are your menus, and enjoy your dinner."

"Thank you," said both Nick and Ann as they opened their menus.

The menus were beautiful, with an impressive listing of Greek dishes, seafood, and steaks. Ann opened the conversation by saying, "Tony is certainly a nice gentleman. You must come here often to know him so well."

"I come here occasionally, but I know Tony more from his lobster business than from the restaurant. When I first moved down here, before I got the diving business started, I worked for him setting lobster traps. It was good experience for me because I learned how to navigate these waters extensively, which has more than once proved to be a valuable asset."

"I see. The boats docked outside—are they his?"

"Yes. He used to sell lobster on the open market, but his restaurant has grown so much that now he fishes just to supply his own needs. By the way, if you like lobster I highly recommend it. Tony prepares it with a special flair, and I can guarantee it's fresh daily."

"That sounds good; I think I'll try it."

The waitress had now arrived. She was a young woman with dark brown hair and looked as if she could be Greek herself. "Are you ready to order?" she asked. "Or would you just like something to drink for now?"

"No, I believe we're ready," said Nick.

Ann ordered a lobster and an artichoke with lemon sauce. Nick ordered a steak with rice pilaf. They both ordered small Greek salads and tall glasses of lemonade.

The waitress brought the drinks first, and Ann sat quietly, contentedly sipping her beverage and looking out over the water. Greek music played softly in the background, and the combination of the effects of the water and the music brought to Ann memories of Greece—memories of a vacation she had taken there the summer she graduated from college. She remembered sitting in a small café on Patmos and looking out over the water, thinking how wonderful it would be to live on an island. And now here she was, sitting in a restaurant on an island once again. Only this time she was not just a vacationer—she was a resident, at least for the present.

Soon the waitress arrived with the salads and the main course at the same time, in the tradition of most southern European countries. The salad was delightful, consisting of a generous combination of cucumber, tomatoes, onion, Feta cheese, and olives all drenched in olive oil and vinegar and sprinkled with dill.

Ann's lobster was large and succulently sweet. The artichoke had been steamed to perfection, and the lemon sauce served as a delicious complement.

Nick's steak had been charred on the outside and was pink and tender on the inside. The rice was a delicious combination of wild and long-grain white, seasoned with parsley, dill, and lemon and served over a bed of grape leaves.

For dessert, they both ordered Key lime pie and coffee. Nick explained to Ann that the pie was made from miniature Florida Key limes, a variety of limes found nowhere else in the world. The pie was delicious—a delightful combination of sweet and sour that teased the taste buds, for it was almost impossible to determine which was the dominant flavor.

After dinner, they both sat for a minute sipping their coffee and looking at each other.

Conversation over dinner had been light, and now feeling very relaxed, Ann finally asked the question that had been burning on her mind.

"Tell me about yourself, Nick. Are you really the obsessed treasure hunter I've heard you are?"

"Obsessed treasure hunter! Where did you ever get an opinion like that?"

"Do you know Bobbie Roberts?"

"Yes, I know Bobbie," responded Nick in an exasperated tone while rolling his eyes. "Bobbie sold me my condominium when I first moved down here. But since then, I wouldn't say we've been the best of friends."

"What happened?" asked Ann with genuine concern.

"Let's just say we have differing opinions—on a variety of subjects. Anyway, if she's the one who described me as 'obsessed,' let's just say she's wrong. I do hunt treasure, but it's actually nothing more than a hobby—something to fill the time between dive trips."

Ann nodded her head in agreement, wondering to herself if there might not be more to Nick's treasure hunting than just a hobby.

"Well, then," answered Ann, "earlier you said that you lived in New York. Did you move down here strictly to start your diving business?"

"No, not exactly. I moved down here originally to get away from New York. The diving business and treasure hunting came after I'd been here awhile."

"Oh, come on now. New York isn't that bad!"

"No, it's not, and it wasn't just New York I was getting away from. Actually, it was the entire lifestyle I was living there."

"Really?" said Ann, not pressing the issue further, but Nick continued on without hesitation.

"Have you ever heard of Cagney and Sons?" he asked.

"Of course," said Ann, instantly recognizing it as one of the largest stock brokerage houses in the country.

"Well, at twenty-six, I was one of the most successful brokers on the books. I started with the company in my hometown of St. Louis shortly after graduating from college. I advanced quickly and soon found myself trading for them directly on the floor of the New York Stock Exchange in Manhattan. It was great for the first few years. I was swinging all sorts of million-dollar deals and making money hand over fist, but all along there was something missing. My entire life was devoted to the stock market. When the market closed, I studied annual reports; when the market was open, I was on the floor trading. I soon found myself drinking too much and sleeping too little. My temper rose as well as my blood pressure. Then one day I almost got into a fight with another broker on the floor of the New York Stock Exchange. My boss decided I should take a vacation."

"And then what happened?" asked Ann, who was beginning to find Nick's story intriguing.

"At first I argued," he answered. "I didn't want to leave New York, but more than that, I didn't want to leave Wall Street. My boss finally made it clear, however, that if I didn't take a vacation, my career with Cagney and Sons would be over. So I took five thousand dollars in cash and a suitcase full of clothes and flew down here to Key West. At first, I spent my time sitting around the pool at the hotel, but then I got bored, so I took a scuba diving course. After that, I started going out with a guide almost every day. It didn't take long before I was hooked."

"So that's why you moved down here and started the diving business?"

"That's part of it, but something else, even more important happened to me, something that completely changed my goals and priorities in life. My daily dive trips and time spent on the ocean provided me with an exposure to the wonders of nature that I had never before experienced, and through them I discovered my taproots to God."

"My taproots to God." Whatever did he mean by that? Bobbie had said Nick was a kook, an obsessed treasure hunter, but could he be one of those religious fanatics too? Although she considered herself a Christian, for the past several years, with the exception of holidays or weddings, Ann had not been in a church. She kept telling herself that when she had accomplished certain goals she would have time to return to church on a regular basis. With each accomplishment, however, came a new goal, and time for church and for God was once again put aside.

But here was a handsome, muscular divemaster discussing his "taproots to God"! Ann did not know quite how to respond to such openness. But her response wasn't necessary. With hardly a pause, enjoying her rapt attention and obvious interest, Nick continued.

"After that, it was only a matter of time. I knew I must make the Keys my home, so I sold all my private securities, moved down here, bought a condo at Western Shores and the cabin cruiser, and eventually found myself running a successful diving business."

"That is certainly an interesting story," said Ann, who was truly captivated. She thought to herself that he must have been quite successful in New York, for a single-bedroom suite at Western Shores cost over a hundred thousand dollars, not to mention a cabin cruiser and the capital required to start a business.

Unable to suppress her curiosity, she asked, "But wasn't it difficult to turn your back on New York and all that money?"

"No, not at all. I did, however, catch a lot of flak from my family and friends, who told me I was running away from life. But when they said that, I just told them I wasn't running away from life, but to it."

It was almost eleven o'clock. The evening had flown. However much they regretted ending such a delightful evening of good food and interesting conversation, Nick and Ann both realized that it was time to go. Nick paid the bill and the two walked to the car, again hand in hand.

At the car Nick stopped and took Ann by her arms. His eyes looked deeply into hers, his head moved slightly forward, and his lips opened as if he had something essential to say. Instead, he just asked, "Did you enjoy your meal?"

Ann, sensing that the question was not Nick's original intention, eased the situation by putting her arms around his neck and giving him a slight hug. "Yes, Nick. It was marvelous."

On the long drive back to Key West, the night air was cool, and the full moon followed them along, reflecting brightly off the dark water. Conversation was held to a minimum, as Nick and Ann were both quiet and reflective, not wishing to break the spell of the enchanting evening.

Ann was truly intrigued by what she had learned about Nick. It appeared that this man with the golden tan and trim physique, the man who by the very nature of his profession she assumed to be a carefree, independent fun seeker, was serious about his relationship to God. Surprisingly, her new knowledge about this handsome Christian did not lessen her interest; in fact, it seemed to further increase her eagerness to know him better.

At the hotel Nick got out first and again opened Ann's door for her. "I really enjoyed myself," she said as the two stood there before the hotel entrance.

"I did too, and Ann. . .there's something I wanted to do earlier."

Just then, Nick bent over, and their lips met in a soft and gentle but lingering kiss. Ann's lips fitted perfectly with Nick's, and excitement darted through her body.

Nick pulled away slightly and Ann stood there, her head tilted back and her eyes looking into his.

"Will I see you again Wednesday?" he asked.

She turned toward the hotel entrance as if she hadn't heard his question. But their hands were still locked, and before they became totally separated, Ann turned once again toward Nick and gave him a quick brush with her lips.

"See you Wednesday," she said, turning to enter the hotel.

Chapter 4

Wednesday was finally here. The three days of anticipation had seemed like three years. Not only had Ann been longing to see Nick again, but she was also excited at the prospect of seeing Key West from the water, possibly even getting a look at the property her company planned to develop.

Following Nick's advice, she ate a large breakfast (once again outside on the terrace), deliberately leaving a piece of toast on the railing for her seagull friend before heading back in.

Inside, she quickly showered, prepared a small day bag, and put on her makeup. *Now, what shall I wear?* she wondered. She hesitated between shorts or a bathing suit and beach coat, finally deciding on the latter. Putting on her bikini, which she had originally bought for private sunbathing only, she went over to the full-length mirror and looked critically at herself in the skimpy suit. It fit perfectly and looked great, clinging to the smooth curves of her trim figure, but the longer she looked, the less appropriate it seemed. Finally, she said to herself, *What in the world are you doing?* This isn't you!

And she was right. Although Ann looked fine on the outside, she knew that if she wore the suit she would be uncomfortable on the inside, for it just didn't fit her modest, conservative demeanor.

She took off the bikini and put it back in the dresser drawer, replacing it with the stylish but modest one-piece suit. She then threw her white knit beach coat over her shoulders, put on a pair of white sandals, picked up the day bag, and made her way to the lobby. She was just getting off the elevator when her eyes caught sight of Nick coming in the front entrance.

"Good morning," said Nick happily. "What a lovely suit."

"Thank you," replied Ann, smiling to herself at having made a choice that evoked an immediate compliment from Nick.

"If you're ready to go, I have the van parked out front."

"Fine. Just let me leave word with the front desk that I will be gone for most of the day, and I'll ask them to save any messages." She quickly did so, hoping that there would be no repeat of the plain white envelope with its brief cryptic note.

The two walked out of the lobby and to the blue van. It was just a short drive to the docks, and in no time, Ann was helping Nick unload scuba gear from the van and into the boat. "What do we need all this stuff for?" she asked, raising her eyebrows in a questioning manner. "I thought we were going on a sight-seeing tour."

"I thought you might like to give diving a try."

"Oh, I'd love to, but is it safe? I've never been before."

"If you just remain calm and keep a positive attitude, it should be perfectly safe. And may I add that I am a certified diving instructor."

"Well, if you think it will be all right, I'd love to try it."

"You'll do just fine," said Nick reassuringly. "I'll be right there with you the whole time, and then if you like it, you might consider taking a course and becoming a certified scuba diver."

"I believe you're trying to drum up a little business," said Ann, laughing.

Nick instructed Ann on how to secure the gear in the boat. Care needed to be taken because it was not uncommon to suddenly encounter rough seas, and the last thing a person wanted in rough weather was to have heavy gear falling about the deck.

Gear all secured and stowed away, Nick completed the final preparations necessary for a successful cruise. He worked swiftly, checking the instruments and various fluid levels. It was a task that almost came as second nature to him, for it was one he performed on a daily basis.

"Well, everything looks in order. Ready to cast off?"

"You're the captain," said Ann. "Ready when you are. Just one thing," she added, as she pulled a map of Key West from her day bag and pointed to an area of the island. "Do you think we'll be going by this section of the island? I'd really like to see it from the water."

"Sure. It's on the far side of the island, though. How about if we go there on the return trip?"

"Fine with me."

At that, Nick started the engine of the sleek cabin cruiser. He allowed it to warm up for a minute as he untied the lines that had secured the boat to the pier.

Walking around from the bow along the outside deck, Nick took a seat at the helm of the boat and motioned to Ann to join him. She stepped up and took a seat on his left, next to him at the helm. Looking at her with smiling approval, Nick put the boat in reverse and backed away from the pier and into the harbor.

Ann looked over the side of the boat and realized for the first time how sparkling clear the water actually was. She was amazed at how easily she could see the sandy ocean bottom from her high perch.

The hum of the engine created a tranquilizing effect as the boat moved out of the harbor toward the open sea. A trail of white foam created by the rotating propellers followed the boat, and several seagulls flew ahead as if leading the way.

Nick and Ann did not speak as the boat made headway. To do so would have interrupted the peaceful harmony of the morning. The blue water, clear skies, warm sun, and cool breeze all converged to form a seemingly unattainable accord that was as fragile as it was transient.

Ann experienced a sense of belonging that transcended the simple recognition of physical presence.

Nick too was experiencing sensations and feelings similar to Ann's. Her presence next to him seemed as natural as it was actual. Her absence, in fact, would have left a void, and the harmonious combination of sun, wind, water, man, and woman would not have been possible.

Nick piloted the small craft expertly out into the open ocean. The island of Key West lay behind them as only a narrow brown streak on the horizon. Finally it disappeared entirely, and the two were surrounded by nothing but miles of deep blue water as far as they could see. Even the friendly seagulls that had accompanied them at the outset had now disappeared, having returned to their familiar habitats near the coast.

Suddenly Ann felt an overwhelming sensation of loneliness and isolation. It was not that the day had lost any of its former beauty or charm, but the sudden realization that there was not another human being around for miles had a definite impact on her. Then she felt Nick's leg brush against hers and remembered that she was not alone. She inched over in her seat closer to him, so that their sides were almost touching. Sensing her apprehension, Nick put his left arm around her to bring her even closer.

Instead of being nervous at Nick's sudden show of affection, Ann felt a sense of security and safety in his closeness. In her soul too, she felt another sensation—an assuredness growing out of the knowledge that all around her was the overwhelming presence of an invisible power—power that controlled and brought order to the great infinite expanses of water which surrounded and dwarfed them and the tiny boat.

Gradually, the smooth surface of the ocean was replaced by gently rolling swells which, little by little, increased in intensity until they reached the height of several feet. With each swell, the bow of the boat rose and crashed back to the ocean surface, sending a large spray of water out either side. Ann found the ride becoming excitingly invigorating and felt like a true sailor as each spray of saltwater splashed across her face. Undaunted by the rough water, Nick plowed on. The engine changed tones with each rise and fall of the boat but continued relentlessly to push the craft on toward its final destination.

After about fifteen minutes of rough sailing, the ocean calmed to an almost glass-smooth surface. It was as if someone had shut an open window, blocking out the disruptive wind.

Somewhat amazed, Ann asked, "What happened to the waves?"

"Well," said Nick, "we have just entered an offshore atoll, an area of coral reefs situated in a circle. The reef heads break up the wave action and allow a still lagoon to form in the center."

"How interesting! A calm spot in the middle of a turbulent sea!"

"Right. This area also serves as a haven for marine life of all types. The reef provides food and shelter for the smaller creatures, which in turn attract the larger ones. The end result is a fierce predatory battlefield, each species of marine life competing for its own special niche in the ecosystem of the coral reef."

"It almost sounds dangerous," said Ann.

Nick laughed. "Only if you are one of the smaller creatures, or if a shark happens to pay a visit."

"A shark!" Suddenly Ann felt a deep sense of apprehension. Not only were they miles out in the ocean with land nowhere in sight, but now there was the possibility of an encounter with a shark. Even Ann, a novice to the world of the ocean and its undersea inhabitants, knew that certain species of sharks could kill a man with a single blow. Sensing her apprehension, Nick patted her leg just above the knee.

"Relax, normally the reef is perfectly safe and can provide one of the most beautiful encounters with nature a person could possibly hope to experience."

"Okay," said Ann, "but if we see a shark I'm hiding behind you."

"Don't worry!" Nick laughed, giving her a reassuring hug with his left arm.

Nick then maneuvered the boat into an area of the atoll which he knew to be one of the most scenic. He dropped anchor, secured the boat, and proceeded to teach Ann how to handle the scuba gear. He gave detailed instructions on the use of each piece of equipment, showing her breathing techniques, methods of equalizing pressure, and ways to clear her mask should it somehow fill with water.

After an hour or so of instruction and of having her practice with the equipment, Nick decided that, with his assistance, Ann was ready to make her first dive. He helped her put on the gear and then suited up himself.

The two sat on the edge of the boat together with their feet in the water. Nick looked into Ann's dark green eyes.

"Ready?"

"Yes," Ann said with a nod.

"Okay, then, start breathing through the regulator, and at the count of three we'll jump. Now remember to hold your mask as we go in, and don't forget to breathe."

Nick gave Ann a last-minute squeeze of assurance and putting his regulator in his mouth began his count, holding up his fingers. One. . .two. . .three!

Spheew, sounded the splash as the two jumped into the water. Quickly the waves covered their heads. Ann breathed rapidly, nervously, as the bubbles from the splash rose around her head, obscuring her vision. "Relax, be calm," she remembered hearing Nick say. This advice she put into practice and her nervousness began to ease. The bubbles soon cleared and Nick, holding Ann's hand, started swimming toward the bottom, away from the boat. Ann let him pull her along, allowing herself to move into a horizontal swimming position.

The scenic beauty of the undersea garden now stood before Ann in great majesty. She stared with awe at the tremendous coral heads, which rose from the ocean bottom like mountains from a dusty plain. Intricate coral formations of brilliant colors that rivaled the most dazzling terrigenous flowers speckled the undersea landscape. Hundreds of species of fish and marine life swam in and about the coral, each with its own individual beauty and each adding its own contribution to the living undersea forest of the coral reef.

Nick and Ann swam together just a few feet above the tops of the coral. Hundreds of sea fans of sparkling pink or orange clung to the top of the reef and swayed in the ocean currents like leaves being blown by a gentle breeze. Suddenly, the flat surface of the top of the reef ended in a sharp cliff that dropped twenty feet or more to the sandy ocean bottom.

Ann felt her heart drop and experienced a sudden sensation of fear—fear of falling over this steep cliff. Instead, however, the two just glided smoothly over the edge and started a slow descent toward the bottom. Ann again relaxed and let herself enjoy the sensation of being able to fly. *I'm flying over the cliff,* she thought, *like a bird soaring over the peaks of the Grand Canyon.*

The unique sensation of weightlessness one experiences when scuba diving was one Ann was becoming accustomed to and enjoying immensely. Daringly, she let go of Nick's hand and swam ahead of him down the face of the cliff. She turned her head just once to check that he was still there and continued her descent, studying the features of the cliff all the while. The many nooks and crannies of the cliff were all immensely interesting to her, for each harbored its own special inhabitant. Sea urchins sat deep in some of the holes, their long slender spines extending out, catching food and sensing for predators. Small brightly hued fish, the type Ann had seen before only in saltwater aquariums, darted freely in and out of the many passages of the coral ledge, and vivid sponges, animals that appear to be a type of marine fauna, grew in patches of bright orange, deep red, and fluorescent yellow.

Soon Ann reached the base of the cliff and found herself standing on the bottom in a large semicircle of white sand. The area reminded her of a clearing in a dense forest. Three sides were bordered with steep coral ledges. The fourth side was open, but the fine white sand bottom gradually gave way to a thicket of deep rust-colored staghorn coral, the type which grows with many segregated branches like those of a barren oak tree.

Ann positioned her fins on the sandy bottom and managed to stand for a minute by waving her arms for balance. She turned just in time to catch sight of Nick making his final descent. She expected Nick to take up a position next to her or to swim on past. Instead, he swam directly to her, hovering above her, his mask facing hers. He put one arm forward and around her neck, and pulling himself toward her, pressed his mask directly against hers so that their eyes could meet through the glass partition.

She felt herself floating upward, being drawn toward Nick by the magic of his deep brown eyes. As together they floated weightless through the clear warm water, Nick moved his arms down around Ann's back, and she put hers around his shoulders. Together they swam through the open clearing, with only the many colorful fish which inhabited the reef to witness the moment.

Their closeness thrilled Ann. Perhaps it was the fact that their romantic interlude was taking place thirty feet below the ocean's surface, or perhaps it was just the fact that is was taking place with Nick. Ann did not know. All that mattered was that it was happening.

Nick released Ann from his embrace but still holding her hand swam out and away from her. She resumed a swimming position, and hand in hand the two continued to explore the intriguing reef.

Nick pointed out some of the more subtle aspects of the reef, such as the Christmas tree worm, which protrudes from the face of the coral beds like a plume of feathers and then disappears with lightning speed into its protective tube when threatened by a diver's fingers. He showed her the spiny tentacles of a Florida lobster extending from a crevice in the coral bed, and he disrupted the repose of a sleeping skate that was buried in the sand, visible only to the experienced eye.

Together they collected as souvenirs several starfish, sand dollars, and sea biscuits, which resembled a sand dollar that had been inflated with air. Just when Ann was beginning to think that she had seen and done all the marvelous things the reef had to offer, Nick surprised her with the most interesting display of the day.

He pulled from his diving bag a pouch of small fish and held one up in the water. In less then a minute a large silver angelfish was circling it cautiously. The fish moved closer and then, without further hesitation, took a quick bite. It darted off, but quickly returned for another nibble. Before long the fish was eating leisurely from Nick's hand and was soon joined by three others. Nick fed the four fish directly from his hand until his supply of the small fish was totally exhausted. Ann had seen many new and exciting things, but this last display of interaction between man and nature left her filled with awe.

Nick swam over to Ann and indicated to her on the gauge of his regulator that their air supply was almost gone. Together they swam back toward the boat, slowly making the steep ascent.

They were halfway to the surface when suddenly Nick stopped. *What is it?* thought Ann, experiencing an immediate sense of fear. *Is it a shark?* In panic she looked all around, fearing the worst, but to her relief, no shark could be seen, only the colorful tropical fish of the living reef.

Nick pointed to a spot near the bottom and then motioned Ann to join him as he swam downward. By now, Ann was totally confused. They were dangerously low on air and were supposed to be heading toward the surface. Instead, Nick was insistently making another descent toward the bottom. What was the reason?

As they neared the bottom, Nick excitedly started pointing toward a spot in the coral ledge. At first, Ann struggled to find what had so captivated his attention, and then, like a flash of lightning, she saw it!

Embedded in the coral was a chain—a solid gold chain! Brilliantly it sparkled in the clear water, and Ann was so excited now that she totally forgot about her low air supply.

Nick pulled his diving knife from its case and frantically started chopping at the coral surrounding the chain. It was only minutes, but to Ann it seemed that Nick worked for hours. She could see that he was making progress, but the chain still seemed firmly entrenched in its coral housing.

Watching intently, Ann realized that each breath of air was becoming increasingly difficult to obtain. She looked at her air supply gauge. The needle was dangerously in the red, indicating just a fraction above zero. Ann grabbed Nick by the shoulders and pointed to her gauge. He nodded his concern, then held up a single finger, indicating one more minute, before returning to his work.

Becoming increasingly nervous with each breath of air, Ann wished that Nick would hurry. And then it happened. A large block of coral broke loose from the ledge and tumbled to the sandy bottom below, dragging the golden chain with it. Nick reached out for the chain, and pointing upward, indicated to Ann that she should start swimming toward the surface. *We're going to make it*, she thought, experiencing a tremendous sense of relief. This relief, however, was destined to be short-lived. For as she neared the surface, almost in reach of the noonday sun sparkling across the waves, she took her last breath of air. Desperately she drew on the regulator, but to no avail. The tank was empty! Panic-stricken, she thrashed through the water, desperate to reach the surface and the life-giving oxygen, which would relieve the burning sensation mounting in her chest. All she could see through her mask was a blur of blue, and in her fear she even forgot that it actually was the blue ocean. It seemed that a blue film was enveloping her, suffocating her, closing her off from the rest of the world which she would never see again. When she thought that she could go on no longer, that her life actually was coming to an end, she broke the surface.

Jerking the regulator from her mouth, she breathed deeply, inhaling volumes of air into her hot, burning lungs. Still gasping, she trod water, turning in search of Nick. The heavy gear weighted her down, and it was all she could do to keep herself afloat and struggle to breathe.

Nick! Where is he? What must I do?

She vaguely recalled some remark he had made about how she should inflate her buoyancy compensator in an emergency. In her panic, she could not remember what he had said. She only remembered that he had told her something—then had said, "But never mind. I'll be there with you all the time."

But he wasn't. Fear almost overwhelmed her, but her years of exercise at the health spa to maintain her trim physique paid off with the extra strength she needed. Just when she thought she could last no longer, she saw him. He broke the surface only a few feet away, gasping for breath, but still holding the coral-encrusted chain tightly in his grasp.

"I got it, Ann!" he exclaimed between gasps, holding the chain high in the air. "I got it."

"Help, Nick, help!" she cried frantically. "I can't last much longer."

"Pull the cord on your CO_2 cartridge, Ann, and inflate your B.C.," he shouted across the water.

Ann fumbled for the cord on the pocket of her buoyancy vest, gave it a jerk, and found herself floating easily on the surface.

By now, Nick was at her side.

"Look, Ann," he said excitedly, holding out the chain for her to see.

"Nick, I nearly drowned!" shouted Ann angrily. "I'm not interested in that chain or in anything else except getting back in the boat—if you don't mind." This last remark was made with a touch of sarcasm, but with a tremor in her voice that revealed how real her fright had been.

Hastily Nick hoisted himself into the boat and then assisted Ann in boarding. As he lifted the tank from her back and helped her remove the rest of the gear, he repeatedly apologized. "Ann, I'm sorry. . .I'm truly sorry. I acted very unprofessionally. . . I really was careless. Please forgive me—I wouldn't have frightened you so for the world. . . I promise you it won't happen again. Can you forgive me?"

By now Ann was seated and had calmed down. Although her legs still ached from the exertion and trembled from her fright, the pleading in Nick's brown eyes together with his continued apologies convinced her of his sincerity.

Nick brought her a glass of ice water, and the cool liquid tasted wonderful to her after breathing the compressed air and swallowing some of the salty seawater.

"Okay, Nick," she finally responded, "let's see this so-called treasure that nearly made me drown."

Nick held it out for her to see, excitement over his find returning to his voice. "I'm getting close, Ann. This chain is sixteenth-century Spanish. It's the third artifact I've found in this general area, and if I'm not mistaken, they all came from the same wreck."

Having chipped the last bit of coral away, he held the chain high in the air, allowing the sun to sparkle brilliantly from its dazzling surface.

"Yep," he exulted, "I'm awfully close; soon I'm going to find the wreck! It has to be near here."

Ann stared in awe at the gold chain. Now that her fear was gone, some of his excitement began to rub off on her, and she could understand the lure of the sunken treasure.

Neither of them saw a tiny boat on the horizon. Its occupant also observed the chain through high-powered binoculars.

Nick put the chain away, turned to Ann, and said, "Now, how about a picnic on a beach somewhere, to make up for my bad manners?"

"Sounds great," responded Ann, her eyes twinkling a smile. "Let's go."

Nick started the engine and carefully navigated the cruiser out of the coral atoll and into open water. He opened throttle, and the breeze created by the cruiser's speed combined with the salt spray and warm sunshine filled Ann with renewed exhilaration.

Nick had set as his destination an uncharted island he had discovered when blown off course by a sudden tropical storm. The island, small but exquisitely beautiful, Nick had named Galilee, because it was there that he not only found refuge after being lost in the storm, but where he also found God.

Soon the small island came into sight. From the boat, one could easily see it from end to end. The total land area was slightly more than ten acres and was highly vegetated with tall palms, short palmettos, and other tropical foliage.

"How about this place for a picnic?" asked Nick.

"It's beautiful, but can we stop here? I mean, doesn't anyone own it?"

"Sure, we can stop here. And as for the ownership, it belongs to the state of Florida, as do all of the uncharted islands in these waters."

"You mean nobody has even seen this island before?" asked Ann.

"Oh, no, I'm sure other people have seen it in passing, but it's just that it's never been reported and put on a map. Others just cruise on by, I guess, without paying this little island much attention."

"How odd, and it's so beautiful."

"I know. I've been coming out here for years when I want to get away to think and to meditate, and to this day I've never seen signs of another human being."

Nick maneuvered the boat alongside the island, into a small cove that was bordered on two sides by eroding coral ledges and on the third by a long stretch of white sand beach. Palm trees swayed in the gentle breeze, and the sounds of tropical birds could be heard emanating from the island's interior.

He dropped anchor in the center of the cove, explaining to Ann that the shallow depth of the water made a closer approach to the shore impossible. He then put on a pair of sandals and jumped over the side into the clear blue water. Ann was surprised to notice that, although they were a good hundred feet from the beach, the water barely came above Nick's knees. Nick extended his hand to Ann to assist her in getting out of the boat. She was expecting to step into the water and walk with him to the shore when, with one swift motion, he lifted her out of the boat and into his strong arms. Startled and surprised, Ann threw her arms around his neck. "Thought you might like a ride," he said with a large grin.

"Very chivalrous," laughed Ann.

Nick carefully carried Ann to the shore, shuffling his feet to insure that he didn't step directly on a stingray that might be sleeping on the sandy bottom. Having safely arrived, he gently set her down on the white sand beach. She was amazed at how soft and fine the sand was. *It's almost the texture of flour,* she thought, *or a newly fallen snow.*

"Be back in a minute," said Nick as he returned to the boat for the picnic supplies. In a few minutes, he had spread out before them a large blanket to sit on and a generous assortment of sliced meats, cheeses, and fresh fruit. For their drink Nick had brought a cooler of lemonade, to which he had added several fresh-sliced limes.

"You certainly know how to put on a picnic," said Ann as she placed a slice of cheese on a cracker.

"Thank you. Actually I didn't know what you'd like, so I just brought a little of everything."

"And everything you brought I like," said Ann in a pleased tone.

Having finished eating, the two stretched out on the blanket to relax and watch the water lap at the pristine shoreline. "This is a lovely island," said Ann.

"I'm glad you like it, since this island is special to me."

"Nick, remember the other night at dinner when you told me that down here you had found God in nature?"

"Yes."

"I hope I'm not prying, but what did you mean by that?"

"Well, it's just that here I can see the works of God and the wonders of God in everything."

"You mean such as the beauty of the reef where we dived?"

"Yes, but also in each simple thing, the things we so often take for granted. Take this sand dollar here," Nick continued, lifting a sunbleached sand dollar from the beach. "The legend of the sand dollar tells us that this small simple creature is a symbolic example of God's love. The star in the center is a reminder of the Star of Bethlehem, which appeared at Christ's birth, and the five holes represent the wounds Christ suffered when He died for us on the cross."

Nick then broke the sand dollar open. A surprised look came across Ann's face as he did so, for she did not know the reason why he would destroy such a beautiful seashell. He then emptied the contents of the shell into the palm of his hand, and, as he did, Ann instantly recognized the five pieces.

"Doves," she said softly.

"Right. Doves of peace, representing the love and peace God wants for us all."

"That's so beautiful," sighed Ann, almost with tears in her eyes. "I wish I could see God like that."

"But you can," said Nick reassuringly. "All you have to do is look."

With that he put his arms around her and brought her close to his chest in a warm embrace. Ann looked up into Nick's eyes, longing to understand this strong, independent man who had turned his back without regrets on the business values she held in such high esteem.

Nick looked at Ann—compassion and desire mingled in his deep brown eyes. "Ann, I must confess that ever since I first saw you out on the pier I've wanted to hold you. . .to kiss you."

With that their lips met. The warmth of Nick's lips against hers sent Ann's pulse racing and caused her body to tingle down to her fingertips and to her toes. Nick lightly stroked her neck and shoulders, and his fingertips felt cool to her skin, still warm from the sun's touch. Little shivers of delight ran down her spine. The kiss ended and she dropped her head on his shoulder, breathing a deep sigh of contentment.

"I've never known anyone like you before, Nick," she said in a tremulous voice, hoping with all her heart that he felt the same way.

To her delight, he replied, "And I've never known anyone like you," and clasped her tightly to him. It could have been an eternity or it could have been only seconds that the two stayed locked in that close mutual embrace.

Ann wished they could stay there on the beautiful little island forever, but the duties of the everyday world demanded their return, and soon she found herself sitting next to Nick at the helm of the boat with her arms around his neck and her head resting on his shoulder. They were heading back to Key West, for the sun was slowly descending in the western horizon. The events of the day had been so completely different from anything Ann had ever experienced that the whole day seemed but a dream, a beautiful dream filled with wonder, nature, love, and excitement.

As the coastline of Key West came into view, Ann realized that the events of the day were soon to come to a close, and the mundane task of running a business would once again be hers.

"The area you wanted to see should be around here somewhere," said Nick, his remark paralleling Ann's train of thought and reminding her of her primary duty and reason for being on Key West in the first place. Nick slowed the boat almost to a stop, and Ann concentrated on the flat coastline, looking for some indication that would guarantee the area she was looking at was that which was to be developed. Then she saw it.

"There it is!" she exclaimed excitedly. "Do you see the sign? That's the property!"

The large sign stood above the flat property. It was nailed to three large posts and read: COMING SOON ON THIS SITE. 84 LUXURY CONDOMINIUMS. PRECONSTRUCTION PRICES START AT $99,999.00.

"Yes, I see it," answered Nick coldly after a moment of hesitation.

Ann sensed the change in his tone of voice and realized that something was bothering him. "What's the matter?" she asked. "Is there something wrong?"

"Yes, there's something wrong," Nick answered tensely. "That's the property that's going to be developed by DCA."

"I know," said Ann. "That's why I wanted to see it. I work for DCA."

"What!" Nick turned abruptly, his dark eyes piercing Ann with a fierce intensity. "You never told me that."

"Well, you never asked," Ann retorted somewhat defensively. "Anyway, what does it matter?"

"It matters to me," answered Nick through quick breaths.

A long moment of silence followed. Finally, without looking at him, Ann spoke. "I don't understand you, Nick. Just like I don't understand half the people on this island. It seems that the only one I've met who understands what a benefit DCA can be is Bobbie, at least she—"

"Bobbie!" Nick interrupted angrily. "That money-hungry real estate agent would sell her own brother for the price of a bus fare."

"That's not true, Nick, and you know it! Bobbie is a fine and decent person, and she happens to be the only friend I have down here." Ann's face was cross and flushed, for Nick's condemnation of Bobbie angered her even more than his disdain for DCA.

"Yeah? Well, I've known her a lot longer than you, Ann, and I think I know her better."

"I don't want to hear anymore, Nick!"

The entire trip back to the dock was spent in uneasy silence. Once there, Nick secured the boat and put the gear away, speaking only the necessary instructions that Ann was to follow.

He drove her back to the hotel, looking solemn and depressed the entire way, saying nothing. At the hotel entrance, they bid each other farewell with crisp good-byes, and Ann went on into the hotel and up to her room.

At first she felt like crying. *Everything was going so well,* she thought. *What went wrong?* Then the sadness was replaced with anger.

Just who does he think he is? she said to herself. *He had no right to treat me so coldly. I didn't do anything.* The more she thought about it, the angrier she got. Finally, she slammed her fist on the dresser. *Just who does that Nick Carmichael think he is, anyway?*

Chapter 5

Stephanie slammed the phone down on the receiver, causing Ann to turn suddenly from the file cabinet where she was standing.

The young secretary's face was tense and drawn, alternately displaying the signs of worry and anger. She looked up at Ann, shaking her head as if to say, "I've had enough!"

"Another one of those calls?" asked Ann. Stephanie nodded. "Only this one was worse. They called me a murderer."

Shaking her head in disgust, Ann walked over and knelt down beside her.

"Were they on long enough for you to get a tape?"

"No," sighed Stephanie. "They hung up too soon."

"Well, we'll get them next time," assured Ann. "And when we do, this harassment is going to stop!"

Ann banged her fist on the desk as she stood up, causing Stephanie to jump in surprise. She then turned and walked to her office in the back, slamming the door behind her.

It was this type of harassment—insulting phone calls, threatening notes and letters—that kept Ann on edge the majority of the time. Since the opening of the new sales office, the harassment increased daily. There was not much Ann could do except live with the harassment until the police could catch the perpetrators, who, she suspected, were members of the Conch Shell Alliance.

Regardless of the harassment, the new sales office got busier by the day, with prospective clients continuously calling for information, and the home office frequently checking with Ann regarding the progress being made to ready the site for construction. Stephanie, her secretary, was an indispensable help in handling the day-to-day functions of the office and weathered the harassment well, but she was not prepared to deal with the more important details involving coordination of the building contracts, obligations with the corporate office, and prospective buyers' inquisitions. All of these major functions were left to Ann. Consequently, by the end of the day she was totally exhausted.

After several visits to the building site with the architect whom DCA had employed to coordinate locally the final plans for the condominiums, Ann realized that the entire ten-acre site was nothing more than a low-lying swamp with no high and dry land. She acknowledged that DCA had purchased the land at a reasonable price, but she questioned the feasibility of developing the marshy site into a superior resort.

Her concerns, however, were quickly put aside by the architect, who explained to her the process of dredging and filling, by which the entire site could be built up to a usable level. Visiting the site with her, he explained how the process would work. First, a deepwater basin would be dredged up through the center of the property, a process which would require the blasting and removal of the underlying coral formations. This material would then be dumped on the surrounding marshland to provide a fill, to which topsoil would be added. The condominiums themselves would be built on deep-driven pilings, which would act as a very stable foundation. The end result would be a marvelous new resort with a deepwater marina where the original dredging was done. Beautifully landscaped grounds would exist where once just a mosquito-infested swamp had stood, with the grounds graced by the finest condominium development in the Florida Keys.

The architect spread his arms out wide as he spoke and beamed with excitement at the thought of constructing such a marvelous new development. His enthusiasm managed to excite Ann with a renewed pride and joy at being a part of such a major undertaking.

A nagging thought, however, kept making its irritating way into her mind. She couldn't quite rationalize to herself the cost-effectiveness of such a massive undertaking. Although her expertise was in marketing and not construction, she could not help but feel that helping to dredge one-third of the land to act as fill for the other two-thirds was a tremendously expensive process. *Wouldn't it be cheaper to build on existing dry land?* she wondered. *Oh, well,* she told herself, *Bill Watson is very experienced at land development; I'm sure he knew what he was doing when he bought this land.*

With that conclusion, Ann decided to forget about the development for awhile and relax on the sofa in her living room with a good book. Fortunately, she had finally moved out of the hotel and into her new home. The gracious walls provided a solitary retreat to which she could escape from the stressful pressures of day-to-day business. She curled up amid the colorful cushions that decorated the sofa, but found herself finishing entire pages without even knowing what she had read. She had successfully pushed the problems of the office from her mind, but now troubling thoughts of a different nature intruded—thoughts which were irritating, confusing, and puzzling—thoughts of Nick.

Repeatedly she told herself to get him out of her mind. The image of his handsome face and muscular physique, however, would not depart from her memory. She remembered in detail their first encounter on the boat dock. She recalled in depth the lovely dinner they shared and the evening they spent together, which ended with a tender passionate kiss. The memories that haunted her most, however, were those of the dive trip they had taken together. *So beautiful*, she mused pensively as she remembered the sparkling coral reef over which they dove hand in hand. The tiny island with its secluded cove and powdery white sand stood out in her memory as if she were there. And then there were the moments of tender embrace.

If only we hadn't gone by the land, said Ann bitterly to herself. Everything was fine until then. Such a beautiful relationship had been developing, only to be ended for some unknown, pointless reason.

But perhaps it was not some unknown, pointless reason, she worried. *Perhaps he got so angry because he doesn't want to see the condominiums built. Perhaps he's even a part of the Conch Shell Alliance!* The thought alone filled her with a deep sense of despondency. *No, no, no,* she told herself. *He couldn't be! He's too. . .too gentle and religious! But why then? Why the behavior?*

Over and over in her mind Ann debated the situation, but to no resolve. Finally, she berated herself for even worrying about it, telling herself to forget about it completely—and Nick!

She told herself these things hoping to believe them, but somehow she knew this was not what she really wanted. Without her being consciously aware of it, the Keys had had an impact on her. She was starting to appreciate the small things in life, to enjoy living in tune with nature, and to feel that perhaps there was more to life than making money and moving up a corporate ladder. These feelings, however, were buried deep within her soul. On the surface, she again told herself to forget about Nick and to concentrate on the awesome task she faced—the task of sales, sales of condos, which were going to be built with or without the concerns of Nick Carmichael!

The next day Ann busied herself with the routine of running the office. She checked proposed layouts for advertising, called on prospective customers, visited the site and prepared progress reports for the home office, and generally strove to perpetuate the success of the corporation.

It was shortly after lunch. Ann had sent Stephanie on an errand and was alone in the office when the phone rang.

She looked at the phone apprehensively. Was it another of those calls? Once, twice, three times it rang. Knowing full well that she must answer it, she put her hand on the receiver and hesitantly lifted it to her ear. "Development

Corporation of America," she answered, expecting the worst. "Ann Langley speaking."

"Hello, Ann," came the masculine voice from the other end, a voice she instantly recognized as Nick's.

Ann sighed. "Yes, Nick?"

"Ann. . .I need to see you. Could I stop by this afternoon?" There was urgency in Nick's voice that could not be denied.

Ann sat down at her desk and resting her head on her left arm, shook it slightly and answered, "I don't know, Nick. After the other day, I just don't know if we should see each other."

"But it's the other day I want to talk to you about!" he interrupted. "I owe you an explanation. . .and an apology."

Nick's voice took on a soft, gentle tone that soothed Ann's vexed emotions, causing her to think, *I guess I do owe him a chance to explain.* Maybe there was some good reason.

"Okay," she answered. "But not today. I'll be tied up all afternoon."

Ann cringed at the lie. She was busy, but not too busy to squeeze Nick into her schedule. Regardless, she needed to buy herself some time—time to collect her thoughts and compose herself before seeing Nick again.

"Tomorrow then," he insisted. "Perhaps we could get together over lunch."

"Let's see," answered Ann, looking at the calendar needlessly. "I think I might be able to make it tomorrow."

"Good. What if I come by the office around twelve?"

"Hmm! Better make it twelve-thirty," answered Ann, delaying the time for no real reason.

"Okay, twelve-thirty it is! And Ann, I do apologize for the other day."

"That's all right," she said as she smiled, rising from her seat and walking around to the side of her desk. "We'll talk about it tomorrow. Bye now."

She hung up the phone and leaned back on her desk, crossing her arms. A half smile came across her lips as she thought about the conversation. Maybe it was nothing after all. No, it was something—but what?

Ann shrugged and sat back down at her desk, returning her attention to the mounds of paperwork before her.

Time passed quickly for the rest of the day, and Ann soon found herself back at home reading the same book she had tried to read the night before. This time, however, she read quickly and thoroughly, for the conversation she had with Nick somehow seemed to have eased the nagging and intruding doubts which had interrupted her thoughts for the past several days. She also slept soundly that night, undisturbed by the irritating worries that had made the previous night's sleep restless and unsatisfying.

The next morning Ann awoke and enjoyed a simple breakfast of fresh fruit—fruit she had picked herself from the many trees which grew stoutly in her own backyard. She derived immense pleasure from harvesting and preparing her own food. Her life in New York City had provided very little exposure to, and therefore comprehension of, the particulars underlying everyday ordinary existence. Life in the Keys, however, took on a different perspective. Ann knew that the fruit on her table came from the trees in her backyard and that the fish she had for dinner came from just off the coast. This awareness provided a sharper, more acute understanding of the interrelationships of life, which in turn gave her a deep and serene satisfaction.

Filled with anticipation over the upcoming luncheon date with Nick, Ann took a little extra time in choosing her dress for the day. She wanted to look like the executive that she was, but she certainly did not want it to appear that she had chosen her outfit strictly for Nick's benefit. With this in mind, she decided on a modified version of the familiar shirtdress—a very simple green dress with large white buttons placed asymmetrically to one side from the round collarless neck to below the waist. The covered belt sported a large white buckle to match the buttons. Ann felt completely herself in the plain, modest dress, but the color turned her green eyes into deep crystal pools, and its very simplicity accentuated her own natural beauty.

Slipping her feet into comfortable white sandals, she left for work in her little Volkswagen. The sun was shining brightly, and there was not a cloud in the sky on this particular morning. Following her usual custom, Ann drove with the top down, and the cool breeze blowing through her hair further lifted her already high spirits.

As she entered the office, she greeted Stephanie with a cheerful "Good morning!"

Stephanie looked up from her typewriter and smiled. "My, you seem to be feeling chipper this morning," she commented, noticing at once a change in Ann's attitude when compared to that of the past several days.

"Just had a good night's sleep, that's all," replied Ann while unlocking the door to her private office.

"I see," Stephanie remarked without further comment. However, her female intuition told her that Ann's high spirits were due to more than just a good night's sleep.

Stephanie and Ann worked diligently all morning. Sounds of paperwork and typing were frequently punctuated by the ringing of the telephone, interruptions which could have led to impatience and created a tense atmosphere. Instead, however, the two women remained cheerful and industrious, often exchanging pleasant comments. Around ten-thirty, Ann sat down next to

Stephanie and said, "I'm going out for lunch today, and I don't really know what time I'll be back. Would you mind staying on through lunch?"

"Not at all, Ann. I'll just order something from the deli down the street and eat it here."

"Fine, then. Thank you!"

Ann rose from her seat and was halfway to her office when Stephanie's curiosity finally got the better of her, and although she knew she shouldn't, she asked, "Important business date?"

"No," answered Ann, looking over shoulders. "Just a luncheon date."

"Oh, I see," said Stephanie, returning her attention to the computer with a satisfied smile.

The rest of the morning went by quickly, and as twelve-thirty approached, Ann's eyes were frequently focused on the front door. Shortly after twelve-thirty the door flew open and in walked Nick. He was wearing a pair of white tennis shorts and a sleeveless but stylish blue sweatshirt. His golden tan and friendly smile made him look as handsome as ever.

Stephanie immediately stopped typing and stared before greeting Nick with a well-practiced, "May I help you?"

"Yes. Is Ann Langley in?"

"She's in the back office. If you would like to have a seat, she'll be out in a moment."

Ann, hearing Nick's voice, quickly put on a dab of blush from her compact, picked up her purse, and started for the front office.

"Hello, Nick," she said upon entering.

"Hello, Ann. You look lovely."

"Thank you." After giving some last-minute instructions to Stephanie, Ann left with Nick. Stephanie sat at her typewriter, watching them leave and smiling to herself.

Nick was driving the familiar blue van, the only difference being that it now carried a large fiberglass canoe strapped to the top. Although Ann thought this was unusual, she didn't bother questioning him about it. Their conversation to this point had been light and cheerful, and she didn't want to press him with any prying questions, at least until she had heard what he wanted to tell her.

Nick drove to a small downtown restaurant called the Seafood Shack. Ann had seen it several times but had never eaten there. To her it looked old and rundown, for it appeared to be nothing more than an open-faced outdoor bar with wooden stools and a roof made of dried palm fronds that reminded her of a South Pacific tiki hut.

Her initial impression changed quickly, however, after sitting down at the bar. The restaurant was old but was exceptionally clean and was imbued with a rustic, tropical atmosphere reminiscent of a scene from an old Humphrey Bogart movie.

"What are you having, Nick?" she asked, looking up at him.

"I'm afraid we're both going to have the same thing. This restaurant has a one-item menu."

"You're kidding! What is it?"

"Fried shrimp. Fresh and hot and as much as you can eat."

"Sounds good to me—I love shrimp."

Nick ordered two iced teas, and the waiter began to serve the shrimp. They were tender and delicious, lightly breaded and fried to a golden brown.

"These are the largest shrimp I've ever seen," commented Ann, holding one in the air for closer inspection.

"Key West pinks. That's what they call them. Each shrimp is born and raised in the warm waters off the Florida Keys."

They continued eating until they had filled themselves with the golden shrimp. Although Nick was attentive and courteous, he had kept the conversation on impersonal matters, and Ann was beginning to think that he really had nothing special to say to her. Finally, his hand reached for hers and his voice took on a serious tone. "Ann, I feel I owe you an explanation for my behavior," he stated, his dark eyes focusing on hers.

"That's all right," she answered, breaking free of his grip and staring at the floor. "If you wish, we'll just forget about it."

"No," he protested, taking her lightly by the elbow. "I really need to tell you this!" Ann looked up at him. The cheerful sparkle of a few moments earlier had left his face, replaced by a somber expression that bordered on desperation.

"Okay," she answered firmly. "What is it?"

Nick turned in his stool, clasped his hands, and rested them on the bar. Staring straight ahead, he began to speak. "The other day, when we went by the property. . ." Nick hesitated. "Ann, I just want you to know that the way I acted is not my normal behavior. It's just that the development of that property has been an important issue I've been opposed to since it was first announced. You see—"

"Nick!" Ann interrupted. "Before you go any further, there's something I must know."

Nick stared at her questioningly.

Breaking contact with his eyes, Ann bit her lower lip and asked, "You're not part of the Conch Shell Alliance, are you?" She cringed at what the answer might be. Desperately she wanted to hear him say, "No! Of course not!" but her mind could only imagine the worst.

A brief moment of silence followed before Nick laughed.

"No, of course not!"

"Thank goodness." Ann sighed with relief.

"Ann, I am opposed to the Conch Shell Alliance, their goals, tactics, and methods! However. . .I can't help but side with them on this one particular issue. . .as do most people in Key West."

"But why, Nick? Why? What is it about the development that everyone is opposed to?

Nick took Ann by the hand and tenderly answered, "I'm afraid you've got it all wrong. It's not the development itself that people are opposed to. It's the area it's going to be built in."

"The swamp?"

"Yes, the swamp. You see, that was a restricted area, an area to be protected from development. That is, until DCA obtained a permit."

Ann looked at him with disbelief. "I still don't see the importance, Nick. After all, that's just a useless old swamp, not good for anything!"

"Oh no, Ann. That swamp is very useful and is important to everybody."

"What do you mean?"

"Tell you what, if you have an hour to spare, instead of explaining, I'll show you."

"Okay," answered Ann, rising and taking her purse in hand. "Show me the importance of that wasteland!"

Nick then paid the bill, and the two left in his van in the direction of the property in question. Before reaching the site, Nick pulled the van off on the side of the road into a clearing, which had easy access to the water.

"What are we doing here?" asked Ann. "This isn't the property line."

"The only true way to see this property is by water. How about a canoe ride?"

Ann looked at him with suspicion, but reluctantly agreed.

Nick then put the trim little boat in the water and assisted Ann in boarding. She sat in the front, facing the back so that she could see Nick as he paddled.

Nick cast off and paddled the canoe with strong, swift strokes. His muscles flexed with each stroke of the paddle, displaying the trim physique which Ann found so appealing.

The canoe glided smoothly through the still water. Ann leaned her head back and let her hand dangle over the side, creating a small ripple in the water's surface.

Had the ride been taken under different circumstances, she could have imagined she was some pre-Civil War Southern belle being courted by her beau on a lazy Southern river. The importance of the trip, however, left little time for daydreams.

"Almost there," said Nick, causing Ann to open her eyes. She turned to see the bright green mangroves that marked the edge of the property fast approaching.

In no time, the canoe was in the midst of the mangrove trees. Ann thought Nick would stop paddling, but instead he pushed on several feet into the dense thicket.

"Here we go," he said, dragging his paddle and allowing the canoe to come to a stop. "Now let me show you the importance of the marsh."

He took a fine mesh net from the bottom of the canoe and swept it through the water in several wide arcs. He dumped the contents of the net into an inch or two of water in a bucket that lay in the bottom of the canoe.

"Look!" said Nick, gesturing toward the bucket.

Ann peered in, not knowing what she'd find or even what to look for. She noticed that the water was alive with wiggling, frantically jerking organisms. Nick reached into the bucket, cupped a palm full of water and held it up for Ann's inspection. She immediately recognized the tiny creatures: shrimp. More than a dozen of the crustaceans, each only a fraction of an inch long, stirred in the water in his hand.

"There are so many of them," she exclaimed, "and they are so tiny!"

"At this youthful stage," explained Nick, "they congregate by the millions in the warm, shallow, protected waters of the mangrove swamp. Later, as they mature, they will migrate out into the open gulf, where they will form an important link in the food chain for the ocean creatures, as well as provide food for human enjoyment, such as we had today."

"So that's why the swamps are so important—as a haven for baby shrimp?"

"Actually, that is only part of the reason. . .swamps also serve as nurseries for lobster, crabs, snails, and all types of fish. The shoots of the mangroves trap nutrients from the sea, as well as from the land. The unending supply of decaying matter provides a perfect medium for bacteria and other micro-organisms that are at the very heart of the food web. These swamps are in fact one of the richest and most productive ecological systems in the world. An acre of the best Iowa farmland doesn't produce nearly as much vegetation as an acre of mangrove swamp."

Nick finished speaking, and as he did the silence of the marsh was broken by the rustling of leaves and the flapping of wings.

An ungainly clapper rail, a gray-brown bird with long legs and a sharp beak, rose from its nesting place in the swamp into swift, silent flight.

"That's another benefit of the swamp," said Nick. "Areas like this serve as ideal nesting places and feeding grounds for all types of migratory birds."

"I had no idea," she said softly, still watching the clapper rail in the distance.

They sat there in silence for a few minutes. Finally Ann spoke. "Nick, could you take me home now?"

Her mind was filled with turbulent thoughts. On one hand, she was very interested in what Nick had told her and was pleased that he had. On the other hand, she now realized what impact the condominiums would have on the environment. These mixed emotions were difficult, if not impossible, for her to reconcile. The last thing she wanted to do was to hurt the Keys, which she realized she had grown to love. But her career, to which she had given her whole life since college days, demanded that she execute the successful completion of a condominium development on this very site, destroying the swamp.

Nick paddled the canoe slowly back to the bank. He realized the dilemma this new knowledge created for Ann, and he felt a bit guilty at having given her the cause of her anxiety. He was beginning to care deeply for Ann and did not want to see her hurt in any way.

They arrived at the shore, and after loading the canoe, Nick headed back toward the office so that Ann could pick up her car. Ann barely spoke as they drove; she simply looked out the car window at the now-familiar town of Key West.

She sat deep in thought. The events leading up to her arrival in the Keys, her past and future career with DCA, her growing relationship with Nick, with whom she now allowed herself to admit she was falling in love—all these varied facets of her life milled about in her mind in conflicting confusion.

Nick turned into the parking lot and slowed the van to a halt directly in front of the new DCA sales office.

Ann opened her door and was about to step out when suddenly she turned to Nick and asked, "How do you think it happened, Nick? How did DCA obtain a permit to build in a protected area in the first place?"

Slowly Nick shook his head. "I don't know, Ann. That's one question I was hoping you would be able to answer."

Chapter 6

Ann awoke early the next morning to the sound of birds singing in her backyard. What would normally be a pleasant and welcome beginning to her day was at this moment nothing more than an annoying nuisance.

She rubbed her eyes, which were heavy with sleep, and dragged herself out of bed and into the bathroom. She turned the tap water on hard and cold, splashing it briskly against her skin. She cupped her hands, allowing them to fill with water, and then doused her face with the cold and stimulating liquid.

Turning off the faucet, she looked up at herself in the vanity mirror. Her eyes were bloodshot and rimmed with dark circles. The night had been one of the most restless she had ever spent. Over and over she had tossed and turned, debating the events of the day but never coming to any concrete conclusions. Finally, her extreme fatigue, both mental and physical, was given some relief by a few early morning hours of sleep. The sleep came too late and morning came too early, however, for the brief rest to do her much good. Now the dark circles which rimmed her eyes were a telltale sign of the sleepless night. She left the bathroom and walked slowly to the kitchen.

There she prepared her morning coffee and then sat quietly at her kitchen table, gazing out toward her spacious backyard at the large mature trees, which were home to so many tropical birds. The early morning dew dripped slowly from the leaves of the lower branches, biding its time until it would be dried up by the warm morning sunshine.

Ann got up from the kitchen table and, wrapping her robe tightly around her waist, walked out of her back door into the crisp morning air. The air had a sweet smell to it, the smell of yellow honeysuckle, which grew along the backyard fence and was in full bloom in the morning sun. She walked to the fence, enjoying the pleasant aroma given off by the funnel-shaped yellow blossoms, and rested her hand gently on the top of the fence as she looked down the long row of flowering vines. Turning, she scanned the confines of her backyard, a yard she loved and found perpetually interesting. *Such a lovely day,* she thought, briefly forgetting her own fatigue and original animosity toward the morning. *I think I might just take the day off. There is so much in Key West I haven't seen yet, and so much I have seen that I would like to see again.*

With that thought, Ann went inside and immediately phoned the office, explaining to Stephanie that she was taking the day off and that she would have to handle the office alone. Stephanie cheerfully agreed, somehow sensing that Ann needed the time to herself.

Following a light breakfast of fruit and cereal, Ann went upstairs, made her bed, and unhurriedly showered and dressed. She had no particular plans for the day and, in fact, did not know exactly why she had the sudden urge to take the day off. She knew only that she was not ready to return to the office and to the project with the insoluble dilemma it now presented. She felt the need for a relaxing day, a day that she might spend getting to know the Keys better.

She looked through the new casual clothes she had bought and decided to wear a pair of khaki culottes and a light cotton blouse. She tied a scarf loosely around her neck and put on a pair of brown plastic shoes, the type typically worn by white-water rafters or beachcombers. Going slowly down the stairs, she took one last long look around her lovely home—at the soft, thick, ivory carpeting in the living and dining rooms, at the deep, plush, off-white sofa, at the long draperies with their colorful design of flamingos in a tropical garden, at the many cushions on the sofa that picked up the colors in the draperies, at the heavy oak pedestal dining table and the hanging stained-glass Tiffany chandelier above it—all these representing many happy hours of choosing just the right thing for the right place. She let out a deep sigh, a sigh of satisfaction with her surroundings, but a satisfaction clouded by the uncertainty of the future and a realization that nothing in life ever seemed to be permanent. Even this beautiful old house, so stable and secure, was not for her a permanent home.

With a final glance over her shoulder, Ann went out the front door and into the warm morning air of another Key West day.

The Volkswagen was parked in the driveway with the top up. She carefully lowered the top, allowing the fresh air and morning sunshine to enter freely, started the car, and backed out into the two-lane road in front of the house. In one direction, the road led southward toward the sea until it intersected with the coastal highway. The other direction led into the commercial district of downtown Key West. Ann debated for a minute as to which direction to take. She really didn't have any idea where she was going or, for that matter, what she wanted to do. She only knew that she needed a day to regroup her feelings, her priorities, and her resolves. Finally deciding on a drive by the sea, she put the car in gear and headed off.

The road she was traveling was the one on which the Key West Hotel was located, as well as the marina where Nick's boat was docked. As she drove slowly by the marina, Ann noticed that Nick's boat was not there. *He must be out on a dive,* she thought.

Ann was about to drive on, when suddenly her attention was drawn to a large, burly man standing in the vicinity of Nick's mooring. She slowed the car almost to a halt and watched intently as the man poked about the mooring, apparently in search of something. He was obviously in a hurry and was constantly looking over his shoulder, as if to insure he was not being observed.

She had been watching only a few seconds when, as if by instinct, he turned and locked his eyes upon her. They were dark, piercing eyes, made even more intimidating by thick eyebrows which turned inward in a scowl. Immediately she recognized the man. He was the same one she had seen in the restaurant parking lot on the night of her dinner date with Nick. Without hesitation, Ann stepped on the accelerator, but as she drove away, in her rearview mirror she could see he was still staring—a stare that continued until she rounded the bend, out of view.

I'll have to tell Nick about this, she told herself, with a deep sense of foreboding that somehow this man meant trouble for Nick.

When she reached the overseas highway, again Ann didn't know which direction she wanted to take. After a few seconds of hesitation, she turned the car to the left, heading northeast along the overseas highway toward the upper Keys and the mainland Florida coastline.

Across the Key West Bridge she drove to Boca Chica Key. She intended to turn around after a few miles, but for some reason she found herself driving on. Over Big Coppitt, Saddlebunch, and Sugarloaf Keys she went. Past Cudjoe, Summerland, Big Torch, and Ramrod she drove until after thirty-three miles she found herself on the familiar island of Big Pine.

On Big Pine Key, Ann stopped the car at a roadside park and got out, stretching her arms and breathing deeply of the clean, fresh air. The park bordered the Atlantic Ocean and was quite small, with less than an acre of usable space. Several picnic tables were spaced along the shoreline, shaded by simple wood-frame canopies, and at one end of the park stood a small concession stand staffed by a single individual. Ann walked to the stand and ordered a cherry snow cone, which tasted cool and refreshing in the hot Florida sun. She sat down at an empty picnic table and ate the snow cone while looking out over the clear blue water. A cool breeze blew from the sea, providing an exceptionally comfortable atmosphere in which to rest and think.

While sitting there staring out at the horizon, she let her mind wander back to her visit to Big Pine Key with Nick. It had been a perfect evening. She thought about the tiny Key deer, which Nick had introduced her to and about how vulnerable they seemed in their limited environment. She remembered the elegant dinner she and Nick had shared and the interesting conversation. In her mind, she could see Nick's face as plainly as if he were presently there in front of her. *He's such a contradiction,* she thought. *If only I could understand him better. The new resort will surely bring in more scuba divers, which would help his business; yet, he doesn't seem to care about that, at least not at the expense of the mangrove swamp! His appearance and profession are those which should belong to a carefree Casanova, yet he is so full of compassion and understanding and talks freely about his relationship to God and Christ.*

Regardless of how hard she tried, Ann could not assimilate her thoughts into a definite conclusion. While her problem seemed complex, it really was simple: She had fallen in love—fallen in love with both Nick and the Keys. Old values and emotions were rapidly deteriorating, stepping aside and making room for the growing emotion of love which demanded its full share of her heart and soul. While these realizations about life were ones Ann enjoyed and wanted to grasp and hold tightly, she experienced unsettling confusion and distress in the abandonment of the old values. Everything she had held important prior to her move to Key West now seemed shallow and superficial accretions to the true meaning of life. These old values, however, were so deeply ingrained into her psyche that total abandonment of them at this time was impossible.

Having finished her snow cone, Ann returned to the car and drove once again out onto the highway, still heading northeast toward Miami. She reached the turnoff Nick had taken which led to the Key Deer Refuge, home of the tiny Key deer. She almost turned left, thinking she might pay the deer another visit. Instead, however, she stayed on the northward course, deciding to explore the Keys even further, and visit areas she had not yet discovered. The road remained relatively straight for a mile or so. It then turned sharply to right and the end of the island could be seen ahead. As far as she could see, there was nothing but a blanket of blue, disrupted only by the white face of the overseas highway which extended across the surface of the ocean like a monstrous snake, disappearing finally in the distance. As she approached the end of the island, she could plainly read the large billboard posted to the side of the road. SEVEN MILE BRIDGE: LONGEST SINGLE SPAN IN THE WORLD. Ann felt a surge of excitement at reaching the Seven Mile Bridge, for even though she had limited knowledge of the Keys prior to her assignment there, she had heard of the famous span.

It was indeed impressive. Completed in 1982, it replaced the narrow, older bridge, which had originally been the old Flagler Railroad Bridge. Ann could see the old span off to the left. The two new wide lanes allowed traffic in either direction to cross safely and easily the great expanses of water, which separated Big Pine and the rest of the lower Keys from Marathon and the remaining upper islands. Gradually the highway rose in a steady incline as the flat surface of the island gave way to the raised surface of the Seven Mile Bridge. For several miles, Ann enjoyed the massive blue expanse of water surrounding the bridge.

Looking off in the distance, she caught sight of a school of porpoises swimming out to sea. Every few seconds, the backs of two or three porpoises would break through the surface of the water, exposing the large dorsal fin which, to the inexperienced eye, were often mistaken for those of the dreaded shark.

To the left of the bridge, she happened to see a single shrimp boat slowly returning to shore, riding low in the water, its hull filled with the highly prized pink shrimp found in abundance in these warm shallow seas. She considered the fate of the fishermen and how their very livelihood depended on the availability of mature shrimp in and around the Florida Keys. She remembered her visit to the swamp with Nick and the vast numbers of baby shrimp he caught with a single sweep of the net.

The importance of the swamp to the ecosystems of the entire Keys chain was now clear. Also clear was the hostility so many of the residents expressed toward her and her company. The damage to the area would be tremendous and permanent. How was it that DCA obtained a permit, especially in a protected area? Something was not right!

She wished fervently that the project could somehow be carried out without the destruction of the swamp; but Ann was a pragmatist, and she realized that plans had been made and permits issued, and that regardless of her own personal feelings, doubts, and suspicions, the resort would be built. But if only there were some other way!

Halfway across the Seven Mile Bridge, Ann began to appreciate the immenseness of its span. She had driven for miles, but the shore of Marathon Key was still far off in the distance. Finally, the shoreline came into view. To the left stood a marina, with boats of all kinds moored securely to stout wooden piers. The road made a gradual decline down to the flat surface of Marathon Key. She noticed immediately how well developed it was in comparison to the lower Keys chain. Every usable inch lined the road on either side, behind which sat residential dwellings, hotels, and condominiums.

Seeing a small convenience store beside the road, Ann pulled off and went inside the market for a soft drink to quench her thirst resulting from the long hot drive. Sipping the soda, she debated where to go next. She had already driven halfway to Miami and, considering the time, decided it would probably be best not to go farther. This left only one more place to go—the place when there is no place else: home.

With that decision, she started her car and turned back out into the highway. She headed southwest, back over the bridge, past Big Pine, Ramrod, and Big Torch Keys. On she drove home—home to Key West.

Turning into her driveway, Ann gave a big sigh of relief and satisfaction at being home. She had seen and done much this day, but the fundamental questions which she had set out hoping to find answers to were still hanging in limbo, unanswered.

Thinking she might feel better after the long drive in the Florida sun if she freshened up a bit, she took a shower and got dressed in some cool casual clothes. She then went downstairs and fixed herself a bowl of vegetable soup, a slice of toast, and a cup of tea, deciding to let this light meal serve as her dinner, for it was now five o'clock. She sat for some time pensively sipping her tea. She got up, cleared the table, and put the dishes in the dishwasher. She then walked into the living room and curled up in one corner of the couch and started reconstructing the events which had led to her problem. At once, she felt a sudden sensation of isolation and loneliness. She wanted—needed—human companionship. Putting aside her usual regard for proper etiquette, she picked up the phone, called Nick, and invited him over. He said he would be there in about an hour.

Normally under such circumstances, with a guest on the way, Ann would have been rushing around the house doing last-minute cleaning and straightening. Instead, she just sat there mulling over the many questions concerning her life that needed clarifying—questions that she hoped Nick could somehow help her answer.

After about forty-five minutes, a knock came at the door, and as she expected, it was Nick. She opened the door with a happy smile.

"Come in!"

"Hi," said Nick, giving her a small hug as he entered.

"Please have a seat. May I get you something to drink?"

"No, thanks," replied Nick, sitting on the couch she had indicated.

"Did you have a good day?" questioned Ann, sitting down beside him. Nick nodded.

"I drove by the marina, but your boat wasn't there. Another dive?"

"No, not today," answered Nick. "But I was out on the ocean."

"Oh?"

"Yes, it's funny, Ann. I awoke this morning with the strangest feeling— a feeling that today I would find the treasure."

An excited look came over Ann's face. "Any luck?"

"Well, yes and no. I didn't find the treasure, but I did locate an area of several large timbers. You know, the type from which the main body of the galleon would have been constructed."

Ann looked puzzled.

"The central area of the ship," Nick explained, "where the treasure would've been stored."

"I see." Ann nodded.

"I did find one more thing, though," Nick continued. "Something that makes me certain I'm on the right track. Something I'd like you to have."

Nick reached into his pocket, and Ann stared in awe as he slowly removed a golden cross.

It was the most beautiful thing she had ever seen, intricately made with what must surely have been hours of painstakingly meticulous work. Set in the center of the cross was a bright green emerald, and on each of the four points, deep red rubies! Snow-white ivory was inlaid around the edges, and from the top dangled a chain—a solid gold chain, each link hand-formed.

Nick placed the chain around Ann's neck.

"Nick!" she gasped. "I couldn't possibly accept this. I mean it's beautiful, but it's so. . .priceless!"

Nick placed his hands lightly on her shoulders.

"To me, it is priceless. That why I want you to have it. I could never sell it, so please, take it. You see, Ann, I'm not searching for this treasure for any monetary gain. All I want is to recover it and see to it that it is never sold. I could not imagine beautiful items like this being melted down, destroying a part of human history that will never be repeated. I guess what I really want is to see the treasure secure in a public museum, displayed for generations to come."

Ann stared up at Nick through her deep green eyes. *How I misjudged him*, she grieved to herself, finally understanding the driving force behind his obsessive passion.

Ann lifted the cross in her hand, turning it ever so slightly, causing the jewels to sparkle in explosive brilliance.

"Thank you, Nick." The words came in a soft whisper. "I will treasure it always."

Nick smiled at Ann's acceptance of his gift. She too smiled and looking at him said, "You know, Nick, I realized something today, something that I guess I've known for a long time but had not yet admitted to myself."

"And what is that?"

"How much I love these islands."

A soft smile came across Nick's lips. It was a smile of joy and approval that someone he cared about so much was in love with the same thing he was.

"That's wonderful!" he said. "I hoped, even prayed, that you could see the beauty and wonder in these islands that I do."

He then gave her a long hug—a hug of tender compassion, almost one of congratulations and thanks for sharing the same feelings about the Keys that he did.

"But now the very company I'm working for is doing something destructive to these islands, and I don't know what to do about it," confided Ann with a tone of anguish. "You have shown me how important the swamp is and why the resort should not be built there. Nick, I just can't help but feel that there's been some mistake with the permit. I couldn't imagine anyone at DCA deliberately damaging the environment. At least, I hope this is not the case. I just have these nagging doubts. . . I don't know." She sighed. "What can I do?"

Nick listened intently as Ann talked about her problem. She said she did not feel that she could be an active participant any longer in the destruction of the swamp, but even if she resigned from her job, that would not solve the problem. No, someone else would step in and take over—one of the many competitors she had successfully surpassed in winning the management of the Key West office. And to think of resigning now was almost unimaginable.

Ann told Nick how hard she had worked for this job and, in fact, how hard she had worked for most of her remembered youth. As an only child, she had tried hard not to disappoint her parents, who had always expected the best from her. And she had succeeded. From high school, where she had been a member of the Beta Club and president of the student body, on through Dartmouth, where she had made Phi Beta Kappa. She had lived up to the high expectations her family held for her and that she held for herself. The only big dilemma she had faced previously had been the choice of positions open to her upon graduation. And that had not been a real problem, for all the offers had been good. But she had gone against her father's advice in accepting a position with DCA, and now more than ever she wanted to prove she could succeed in this highly competitive, growing corporation.

Like Ann, Nick felt that even if she left the company, the swamp would still be doomed, so he could only listen sympathetically as she talked. He had no doubt about what his own actions would be, but he did not feel that he could impose his values upon her. Nick had long ago set his own priorities straight and did not willingly or knowingly participate in any activity destructive to God's world. But even though he knew this decision had to be Ann's alone, her turmoil became his and he reached out to her.

Gradually Ann became aware of a change in atmosphere. As he listened, Nick had taken hold of Ann's hand and held it gently. Now his fingers began to stroke her arms ever so lightly, creating a tingly sensation. His hands crept up to her shoulders and his dark eyes held her entranced. She nervously licked her lips, and the small movement only intensified the charged atmosphere.

She knew he was going to kiss her, and she wanted him to. Without intent, even without her willing it, her hands lifted of their own accord and her fingers ran through his fine brown hair, coming together around his neck as he leaned forward and captured her lips with his own. She felt a marvelous warmth seep through her veins as he feathered kisses lightly across her face. She rested her head on his shoulder, trembling with the pleasurable sensations he had made her feel.

"Ann. . .Ann," she heard him whisper.

He spoke softly, close to her, and she felt more than she heard his voice as its deep masculinity vibrated in her ear.

"Ann?" He spoke again, his voice rising with a questioning urgency this time.

"Yes, Nick?"

"Ann, you know I must leave."

She was torn, not wanting this moment to end, yet knowing he was right.

"You are an extraordinary person, Ann, a resourceful person, and I know you will find an answer to your problem. And you know how I feel. You know you have my support."

"Yes, yes, Nick. I know. Thank you for coming."

"Whenever you want me, Ann. Anytime you need me, I'll be here."

With a big hug and a warm good-night kiss, he was gone. Suddenly Ann realized that she had forgotten her resolve to tell Nick about the swarthy stranger poking around his moorings at the dock. She removed the cross from her neck and draped it over the lampshade. As she watched it sparkle in the lamp's warm glow, she was once again alone with her thoughts.

Chapter 7

Not being one to give up easily, Ann continued to sit on the couch and search for answers to her problems. Suddenly, a thought flashed through her mind. Maybe, just maybe, it might work! She got up and walked quickly to her desk and picked up her briefcase, which contained all the papers associated with the construction project. She sat down, opened the briefcase, and began mulling over the various documents. She found copies of all the estimates that were submitted by different contractors, each soliciting Development Corporation of America for the initial "fill job." Every estimate was different, but all were similar in one respect—they were all high. The more Ann studied, the more she realized how terribly expensive it was to "create" land from marsh.

Why is it that they took this route? she questioned. *Is the location of the site that superior, or is dry land just too expensive?* She took out her calculator and started comparing figures.

Time passed quickly, and toward the wee hours of the morning, she had come to a definite conclusion. Considering all the cost factors involved, she had determined that if DCA could purchase some waterfront property for under two thousand dollars per front foot, they could save money by building on an existing dry site. Could they not find a dry site for this price?

I'm going to call Bobbie as soon as the office opens, she decided, *and find out for myself.*

With that thought in mind, she finally allowed herself to get some sleep. Although she knew her alarm would be going off again in a few hours, it didn't matter. All that did matter was that she got to the bottom of things and found out the truth!

At the sound of the alarm, Ann sprang up in bed. Unlike the previous morning, she awoke with a sudden burst of energy, for she knew that she had much to do. She had reached a decision that might affect the rest of her life.

She showered, dressed quickly, and hurried down to the kitchen. There she enjoyed a few minutes of solitude while having a light breakfast of fruit and toast. During these few minutes, her decision of the night became solidified in her mind.

If I find an existing dry site that meets our requirements, I'm going to propose moving the resort. Surely Bill will give it some consideration, especially after he realizes how damaging it would be to build on our present site.

But what if he doesn't? He can be exceptionally narrow-minded sometimes, and the original site location was his choice. He'll probably hear nothing of moving the location, probably even resent me for suggesting it.

But so what! If nothing else, at least my proposal could be a good excuse for returning to New York and finding out for myself what went on with the issuance of the building permits! With that came the end of Ann's moment of solitary thought. She got up from the table, paused briefly to rinse out the few dishes, and went upstairs to brush her hair and put on a dab of makeup. Then with her purse in one hand and her briefcase with its new calculations in the other, she headed out the front door.

When she arrived at the office, she was pleased to see Stephanie already at work.

"Good morning, Stephanie," she said as she walked through the front door.

"Good morning, Ann. Your 'in' box is full of documents, and there are a million messages on your desk. I've arranged them in what I thought you'd consider an order of importance."

"Thank you. I take it you had a busy day yesterday."

"The busiest we've had so far."

"Well, I guess I picked a good day to take off then," laughed Ann as she walked to her desk in the back office.

"That you did!"

Once at her desk, Ann went over the stack of papers that had accumulated the day before. *Nothing here that can't wait,* she said to herself as she laid the last sheet to the side. Then with her new plan in mind, she reached for the telephone and dialed the number of Bobbie's office.

"Good morning, Island Realty," came the voice from the other end.

"Could I speak to Bobbie Roberts, please?"

"May I ask who's calling?"

"Yes, this is Ann Langley with Development Corporation of America."

"One moment, please."

Ann tapped her fingers lightly on the desk as she waited for Bobbie to answer. After what seemed like ages, the phone clicked.

"Hello, Ann!" Bobbie's voice was warm and friendly. "How's everything been going?"

"Oh, about as well as can be expected, considering all the hassles we have to deal with."

"You're not having any problems with sales, are you?" questioned Bobbie with genuine concern.

"No, sales are fine. Our main problem now is dealing with the harassment from the environmentalists. Seems it gets worse every day."

"I know what you mean," Bobbie sympathized. "Anyway, how have things been going with you and Nick?"

Nick! Ann's eyebrows narrowed. *Why would she ask about him?*

"Fine. . . ," she answered, somewhat hesitantly. "Why?"

"Oh, I don't know. It's just that you two have become somewhat of an item down here."

Ann's face crossed. "Yeah, how's that?"

"You know! Local gossip, the land developer and the environmentalist. Makes for the kind of item people like to talk about."

"I didn't know we were such a popular subject!" Ann retorted, somewhat sarcastically.

Bobbie's voice hesitated as she continued in a serious tone, "Ann, this is a small town, and word gets around—especially in our business! I know it's none of my affair, but as a friend, I feel I should tell you this. I'd be careful of that Nick Carmichael!"

Ann frowned. "What do you mean, Bobbie?"

"Ann, please don't be offended, but it's just that you can never be sure whose side he's on."

A tense moment of silence followed.

"Thanks for the advice, Bobbie, but I believe I can take care of myself!" Ann's words were hard, punctuated by crispness which could not be denied.

Bobbie's voice took on a soothing, apologetic tone. "I'm sorry, Ann, I should've kept my mouth shut! It's just that—"

"That's okay, Bobbie," Ann interrupted, not letting her finish her sentence. "We'll just forget about it. But please, let's leave Nick out of things from now on, okay?"

"Sure, Ann, not another word. Now, what can I do for you? I'm sure this wasn't just a social call."

"Well, to be honest with you, it wasn't." Ann rose from her desk and stood at the east wall, eyeing the poster-sized map of Key West that occupied the majority of its available space. "The reason I was calling is that I want you to find me a piece of property."

There was a moment's hesitation.

"But Ann, whatever for?"

"I'm considering moving the location of the resort. What I'm interested in is about five to ten acres of dry land located on the water. Think you can help me?"

"I guess so. I mean, sure I can. But do you mind if I ask why? You've got a good site now, plus all the dredge and fill permits, which I might add aren't too easy to come by. Why would you want to move the resort?"

No need to give her all the details, thought Ann. *She'd never understand my reasons, anyway.* With that decision in mind, Ann replied, "It's purely a matter of economics, Bobbie. It looks like it's going to cost more to fill the site than the original estimates indicated. That's why I'm calling you. If you could find me a dry site for around two thousand dollars a front foot, we could probably save money by building there."

"I see," answered Bobbie.

"Well. . .can you help me?"

"I suppose so. . .just one more thing, though. Does the property have to be on Key West, or would one of the other Keys be acceptable?"

"I hadn't really thought about it," answered Ann. "I suppose I just assumed it would be on Key West, but there is no reason not to look at other islands, provided one could meet all the requirements. Let's just keep all our options open."

"Okay, then, I'll get on the computer and see what is available, and I'll be back with you early this afternoon."

"Fine, I'll be looking forward to hearing from you as soon as possible."

Bobbie went straight to work, researching the available listings on Key West first and then those on the lower Keys. Ann went back to work on the stack of papers that had accumulated from the day before.

With her eagerness to hear from Bobbie, time passed slowly for Ann. At noon she took a break and joined Stephanie for lunch. They turned on the automatic answering machine and hung a BACK IN THIRTY MINUTES sign on the front door, deciding to go out for subs. At lunch, Ann very much wanted to tell Stephanie about her plans for a new site. She decided against it, however, thinking that if everything worked out, she would find out soon enough, and it would be better if no hint of a change leaked out to prospective buyers.

Back at the office, Ann settled down at her desk, anxiously awaiting Bobbie's call. Sure that each ring of the phone would be Bobbie, she answered the phone herself, but each brought a renewed anticipation only to be followed by another disappointment.

At 1:30, the phone rang again. This time Ann didn't even bother answering it, for she had become accustomed to the disappointment. Finally, Stephanie, noticing Ann's reluctance, picked it up on the third ring.

"Development Corporation of America," she answered in a pleasant voice. "Why, hello, Bobbie, we've been expecting your call." Ann looked up from her desk at Stephanie's words, with sudden excitement showing in her face. Stephanie noticed Ann's response and immediately transferred the call.

"Hello, Bobbie," said Ann. "How did it go?"

"Pretty good. In fact, I've found something that I think you might be interested in."

"Great! Tell me all about it."

"What if I come on over and we go out and look at the property? I can fill you in on the details on the way."

"Fine. See you in a few minutes."

Ann quickly repacked her briefcase and prepared to leave. She explained to Stephanie that she was going off with Bobbie for awhile and did not know when or if she would be returning that day and that she should lock the office if they did not return before closing time. Ann had no sooner finished giving instructions than Bobbie pulled up out front.

Ann rushed out before Bobbie could get out of the car. In no time at all, they were cruising down the overseas highway away from Key West toward what might be a new location for Development Corporation of America's premier Florida Keys resort.

"I take it this site is not on Key West?" asked Ann as they drove over the Key West Bridge.

"No, it's not. It's not far, though—just seven miles up the road here on the lowermost of the Saddlebunch Keys." Bobbie talked on, excitedly telling Ann everything she knew about the site.

"I thought about this place when you first asked about a new site, but I had to do some checking first to insure that it was still available. It is essentially a small eight-acre private island. Several years ago, some local developers had dreams of building a big hotel on the island. They spent all the capital they had building a bridge and installing water, power, and sewer lines to the place. Everything was going well for awhile, but then their major financier pulled out, and the money just dried up. The island has been sitting empty now for several years. There have been some interested parties looking at it, but no one with enough capital to cash the current owners out."

"It certainly sounds interesting. But do you think it would make a good site for a resort?"

"The best."

With that, Bobbie turned the car to the right, off the main highway and onto a small dirt road. The road wound around a thick growth of yuccas, saw palmettos, bodocks, and pines.

"The land we're on now is actually part of the site," explained Bobbie. "It was intended by the original developers that this land could be used eventually as a parking lot, and they would then provide a shuttle service out to the island where the main resort would be located."

"That certainly sounds like the bridge was good, although that is probably what broke them financially."

The dirt road abruptly came to an end at the water's edge. It was continued by an impressive concrete and steel bridge several hundred feet long, at the other end of which lay the eight-acre island.

Bobbie drove up on the bridge with casual ease. The ocean was a mere five feet below the road's surface and Ann could tell that at a particular point the ocean itself was very shallow.

"I wondered why they built this bridge so low," she said. "Now I see that no large boats could pass through here anyway." After a minute or so, Ann and Bobbie were once again on solid land. Bobbie turned the car to the right and stopped the engine. "Road ends here. We'll have to walk the rest of the island."

For the next two hours, Ann and Bobbie walked the coastline of the entire island. Ann was thoroughly impressed. On the Atlantic side of the island was a private white sand beach which ended in a natural inlet that could easily be turned into a marina. In her mind, she visualized the resort being built on this island. She could mentally picture the main building, swimming pools, and tennis courts tastefully positioned amid the tropical foliage of the island paradise.

Finally, Ann asked Bobbie the most important question. "How much do they want for the island?"

"Well, everything I've shown you today, including the land on the main island, could be bought for four hundred thousand dollars."

"Hmm," murmured Ann, biting her lower lip while surveying the surroundings. "Let's see what that comes out to per foot."

Pulling a small calculator from her purse, she quickly started making the calculations, occasionally jotting down figures on her notepad. Finally, a wide smile came across her face.

"Well?" asked Bobbie.

"We could do it!"

"Buy this island?" Bobbie's voice rose in excitement, matching Ann's.

"Let's just say it would be economically feasible. But as far as buying the island, I don't know. That decision would have to come from New York."

Ann quickly put her things away and turning to Bobbie said, "Let's get out of here! I'm going to catch the next flight to New York!"

"Sure, Ann," replied Bobbie. "But couldn't you wait until tomorrow and catch a flight at a decent hour?"

"No, in my business, time is money. The sooner I present the home office with my new proposal, the better the chance they'll buy it. In fact, we have already lost precious time as well as money working with the first site."

"Okay, then, let's go."

The first thing Ann did upon arrival at her house was to call the airport. "We have a nonstop flight leaving for New York City at 5:10 P.M.," the clerk at the other end of the phone said.

Less than an hour away, thought Ann. *I can make it, though!*

"Reserve one seat for Ann Langley, please," she said to the clerk. "I'll see you in thirty minutes."

Ann hung up the phone, and while Bobbie waited, she hurriedly began collecting her things. She packed a suitcase with enough clothes to last for a week, guessing from experience what the New York climate would be like this time of year. She also packed an overnight bag with personal items and makeup. She then gathered all the important papers and documents associated with the Key West development. These she arranged securely in her briefcase along with the new data she had received from Bobbie concerning the alternative site.

Ann then phoned the office. Stephanie had already left for the day, so she left a message on the answering machine explaining to her what was going on and instructing her to maintain the office as usual until she returned.

Next, Ann wrote a short message to Nick on some of her personal stationery. She sealed the message in an envelope and was about to hand it to Bobbie and ask her to deliver it, when suddenly she changed her mind. *I'll just mail it from the airport,* she thought, stuffing the letter into her purse.

Ready to leave, Ann turned to Bobbie and said, "Looks like that's about it. Ready to go?"

"Sure," Bobbie replied. "Would you like me to give you a ride to the airport?"

"No, thanks. I want to drive myself so I'll have my car there when I return. If you'll just run me by the office to get the car, I'll be on my way."

Immediately upon arriving at the office, Ann threw the car door open and stepped out. Bobbie leaned out the window as Ann was stepping into her car and called, "Ann, have a safe trip, and good luck in New York. We'll get together when you return."

Ann arrived at the airport in the nick of time. Rapidly the desk clerk checked her in and issued her a ticket, which she charged on her company credit card. She boarded the plane with just seconds to spare, sat down at her seat, and took one long last look out the window at the island which she had grown to love—the island of Key West.

Chapter 8

The lights of New York City sparkled on the ground below like so many diamonds tossed across black velvet in a jeweler's showcase.

"We are now approaching our final descent into LaGuardia International Airport," the voice over the intercom said. "Please fasten your seat belts, and return all seats and food trays to their full and upright positions."

More out of habit than as a response to the stewardess's instructions, Ann did as directed. She looked out the window at the lights of the city below. A warm feeling came over her, for although she had grown to love the Florida Keys dearly, she had lived happily in New York for many years. From her tiny window, she could see the famous landmarks which were so familiar to her. The Statue of Liberty stood majestically in Liberty Harbor, bright and fresh from the improvements just recently completed. Behind this enduring symbol of freedom stood the twin towers of the World Trade Center, highest buildings in the city, and off in the distance she could see the pinnacle of the Empire State Building shining brightly across the dark evening sky.

Several times the plane circled as it waited its turn to land at LaGuardia, one of the busiest airports in the world. Finally, Ann could feel the steep descent as the plane approached the runway. Below she could see the ground fast approaching; she felt the plane level out and then the impact as the large jet landed. Once again, she was back in New York City! Having disembarked, Ann worked her way through the crowded airport to the baggage claim area, so different from the small, quiet airport of Key West. After about thirty minutes, she had successfully retrieved her bags and found herself standing at the airport entrance, debating what to do next. She couldn't go back to her own apartment, because she had sublet it prior to moving to Key West. The only other alternative was to rent a hotel room or call a friend. In her hurry to come with her new plan for DCA, she had not thought out such details. *Wait a minute*, she thought. *The last train to central Long Island doesn't leave until 8:45, and I could always go out to my parents' house. That's it*, she decided. She called her parents to let them know that she was in town and would be coming out soon. They both were excited to hear from her and, although Ann argued otherwise, insisted on waiting up until her arrival.

Ann then hailed a cab to take her out to the train station. The cabbie hardly spoke to her the entire way. The only words she could actually remember him saying were, "Where to?" and "That will be seventeen dollars."

Once on the train, she began to think about the New York she had left and the one to which she had returned. Although she still had some affection for this tremendous city, it had lost a great deal of the charm and excitement it once held for her. Looking out the window at rows of tenements passing by in the darkness, she thought that the city seemed to be bigger, dirtier, and more hostile than when she had left it only a short time before.

The steady clatter of the train wheels against the tracks provided a most relaxing rhythmic melody. It was good that Ann's day could wind down with a long quiet train ride, for the two previous nights had offered little sleep, and the day itself had been exceptionally demanding. But much had been accomplished in the past twenty-four hours. Ann had calculated the cost-efficiency of moving the location of the condominium development and had, with Bobbie's assistance, found a new location that would be ideal. She had packed, taken care of last-minute business, bought a plane ticket, and flown to New York all in a single afternoon. And now here she was on a train out to her parents' home on Long Island.

Since it was past the rush hour, the train was not full of passengers, and Ann looked around at them as they rode along. Most of them seemed to be business people returning to their homes in the suburbs after a day's work in the city. Toward the front of the car, there were a couple of young people who appeared to be college students, and in the very front, sitting alone in one of the corner seats, was a single elderly lady.

Ann looked at the lady sitting there in her faded print dress. She was small and slightly hunched over, with stringy gray hair that hung to her shoulders. A tattered sweater was all that shielded her from the early fall weather. On her feet was a pair of thick cotton socks covered by dirty white tennis shoes. Between the lady's feet, on the floor, was a paper shopping bag. The bag appeared to be full to the top, and those items that could be seen were mostly useless junk. Ann had often seen women like this before, for they were a common sight in New York City. "Bag ladies" they were called—homeless old women who lived on the streets and whose entire worldly possessions were generally carried in a single shopping bag. Yes, Ann had seen women like this before, but never, until now, had she ever really looked at one. She suddenly felt her heart going out to this woman. She wondered where she got the money for the train ride and where she could be going. She saw her not as another faceless piece of humanity, but as an individual, a person, a person deserving of the respect and dignity endemic to being a human.

Suddenly Ann came face-to-face with a love that could die for someone this helpless.

Christ gave His life for me too, she realized, humbled. *I need Him as much as she does.* Freedom seemed to fill her soul.

The train came to a stop, and Ann watched as the old woman got off. She continued watching as the train pulled away from the platform, leaving the woman standing there alone in the darkness.

The sincere compassion Ann felt for this single lady was not a spontaneous incident, but a result of the redirection her life had taken since her tenure in the Florida Keys. She now saw things on a wider and different scale, with a heightened insight into the nature of life and the relationship between people and between man and God. Her increased reverence and appreciation for His works in nature had begun to include an appreciation for another of His creations—mankind.

The tall skyscrapers of New York City had now given way to the residential dwellings of suburban Long Island. The terrain began to take on a familiar look, and occasionally Ann would catch a glimpse of a well-known landmark, for she had made this trip many times in the past. The train went around a sharp bend, and she felt an overwhelming sense of familiarity. With the slowing of the train, she caught sight of the platform sign glowing in the cool evening air. The sign announced the name of Ann's stop: her hometown, Hempstead.

Although Ann had been born in Boston, her family had moved here when she was just a child and it was here that she grew up. As a little girl she played, carefree, among the tall oaks and maples lining the yards of the spacious homes.

Hempstead was a quaint, lovely New York town, one for which Ann had many fond memories. It had not, however, always been that way. As an adolescent, she couldn't wait until graduation from high school so she could go on to college, away from Hempstead, away from the confines of home and parents. During college, her goals and objectives became centered on a successful career, and Hempstead gradually became a thing of the past. Now, returning with her new and broadened insights not so centered on herself, she saw Hempstead in a different light.

The town seemed to her to be a monument to stability and constancy. It neither grew nor declined, but maintained a consistent, stable population that respected the traditions and values of generations past, yet was willing to change and adapt in order to survive in a modern world. As the train slowed, Ann remembered the Gothic cathedral which stood at the center of the town, its tall spire continually reaching for heaven and its bells, which rang every

Sunday, reinforcing old truths and reminding the people of the existence of a power greater than themselves.

With one long shriek of the air brakes, the train jerked to a halt. Ann rose from her seat and took her baggage down from the storage compartment above. Wearily she lugged the baggage down the aisle and off the train onto the station platform. She was just about to phone for a taxi when from around a corner came her parents.

Her father was a large, burly man with thinning gray hair and a thick mustache. He was wearing his usual dark blue business suit and wing-tipped shoes. His gray hair was partially covered by a stylish gray hat, and in his right hand was an ivory-handled walking cane. Her mother was a petite but stout woman who stood at her husband's side with her back straight and her chin up. In reality, she was quite friendly, but an initial impression of her would be that of a snobbish Boston blue blood.

Ann was taken aback with surprise at the sight of her parents, for they had given no indication that they would meet her at the train station. They came up to her, her mother smiling. Ann dropped her bags and threw her arms around first her father's neck and then her mother's.

"We're so glad to see you," her mother said, giving Ann a hug.

"It's good to see you too. I must say you took me by surprise. I wasn't expecting you to be at the train station."

"Well, we thought we might surprise you by meeting you down here," her father answered. "Come on, now, let me take your bags and let's go home. I'm sure you must be exhausted."

Ann's father took the bags and led the way to the car parked out front, opened the car trunk, and placed her bags inside. He then opened the car doors for both Ann and his wife, displaying the courtesy his generation and social stratum always extended to ladies, even family members.

On the way home, Ann's father questioned her about her assignment in the Keys. She told him all about her experiences there and how beautiful the islands were. She also told him about her new plans to relocate the development on existing dry land. Offering his opinion on the subject, he cautioned her, "Just don't rock the boat. After all, you've only been with DCA a few years, and you don't want to do anything that's going to make somebody angry."

"Don't worry, Father. I know what I'm doing," Ann answered. She had said the words with much assuredness, but deep down she knew that her father was right. She actually had no idea how her plan would be received at the New York office or if she would discover what she sought. All she could do was hope and pray for the best.

Once home, Ann and her parents settled down in their spacious living room for some more conversation prior to going to bed. Ann's father sat back in his dark leather easy chair. "Tell me, Ann, do you have any more news for us from Key West?" he asked.

"Well," Ann hesitantly answered, "I have met someone, someone quite special."

Her mother's eyes opened wider at her words, for she could tell from the tone in Ann's voice that she was not just talking about a casual new friend.

"His name is Nick Carmichael," Ann continued. She then went on to tell her parents all about Nick. Excitedly she told them about his past, his experience as a stockbroker, his present occupation as a divemaster, and his unending search for treasure. She told them about diving on the reef and finding the gold chain and what she had learned from Nick about the Florida Keys environment. Finally, she told them about the golden cross embedded with sparkling jewels he had given her just before she left.

Finally, her father rose from his chair. *"Hmmph,"* he snorted. "Anyone who would turn down a position on the floor of the New York Stock Exchange to take people out in a boat and search for sunken treasure isn't playing with a full deck."

With that and a final "Good night," he turned and left the room. Ann felt her heart sink. She was so proud of Nick and assumed her parents would feel the same way. But now her father not only didn't show any interest in him, but even insinuated that he was crazy!

She turned to her mother. "What do you think, Mom? You don't feel that way, do you?"

"Ann, Dear, I don't know," her mother replied, a slight frown on her forehead. "Nick sounds like a nice person, but your father has made a good point. And I am surprised that a man who has walked away from an excellent position is attractive to you, since you have so much ambition yourself."

Again, Ann felt a twinge of disappointment at her mother's words. To her Nick was a wonderful person, and her hopes had been high that her parents would see him as she did.

"Come on, now," her mother said, noting the disappointment in her face. "It's been a long day, and I'm sure you must be tired. Let's go to bed."

They both stood up and walked toward the back bedroom. Ann's mother had long ago converted her daughter's former bedroom into a guest room and replaced the original furniture with sleek contemporary furnishings. At the bedroom door, she stopped and took Ann by the shoulders.

"Now don't let yourself get upset," she said. "I'm sure everything will work out with your job, and as for Nick, someday he'll only be a distant and pleasant memory."

Ann didn't answer. She simply said, "Good night, Mother," gave her a kiss on the cheek, and closed the door behind her.

So they don't like Nick, she said to herself, crossing her arms and leaning back against the bedroom door. *Well, I'm not going to let it bother me. I'm an adult and capable of making my own decisions. If I decide to see Nick, that is my business!*

With that last bit of self-reassurance, Ann undressed and got into bed. The crisp cool sheets and the fluffy down blanket felt comfortable against her smooth skin. Ann laid her head down on the soft pillow and thought only briefly about the events of the day. She then cleared her mind of all thoughts, even those of Nick, and fell into a deep, deep sleep.

The alarm sounded early. Too early for Ann, for it seemed only minutes ago that she had fallen asleep. The bright morning sun shining through the crack of the curtains, however, reinforced the announcement of the alarm clock that morning was here.

Quickly she showered and dressed. There was much that needed to be done this day, and Ann was going to insure that every available minute was meticulously utilized. In no time at all, she was ready to go. She had even applied her makeup and fixed her hair, and not more than thirty minutes had elapsed since the alarm first rang.

Ann's mother was already in the kitchen in her bathrobe, sipping a cup of coffee and reading the morning paper. Her father had left for the office, for it was Friday and he had to start early in order to see that all his employees got their paychecks on time.

"Good morning," her mother said as Ann walked into the kitchen. "How about some coffee?"

"Thanks," Ann replied, pouring herself a cup from the nearly full pot before sitting down at the kitchen table. She and her mother talked briefly while she drank her coffee and ate a quick bowl of cereal. Sipping down the last swallow of coffee, Ann rose from the table and said, "Well, I guess I'd better be going. I want to catch the 8:15 train to the city."

"Wait just a minute while I slip on a dress," her mother replied, "and I'll give you a ride to the station."

"That would be nice," answered Ann with a smile. At the train station, her mother kissed her good-bye without leaving the car, and Ann got out and walked up to the station platform. She bought a ticket to Manhattan and assumed a position in line. Although the train wasn't due for fifteen minutes, people were already lined up, for the 8:15 express to Manhattan was probably the most heavily traveled train of the day.

In due time the train arrived, and fortunately Ann found a seat. Minutes later, she was again watching the New York countryside pass by as the rumbling commuter train made its way into New York City.

Although the scenery was pretty and the train crowded, she paid no attention to either of them. Her thoughts had returned to the monumental task ahead. She was concentrating on what she would say once she arrived at the office, how she would present her plan for relocating the site of the development, and how she would go about researching the building permits. Over and over, she rehearsed her presentation. Time and time again, she pictured herself confronting Bill Watson about the proposed site change.

She flipped through the documents in her briefcase, studying every aspect of the plan carefully. Going over the mounds of paperwork, she wished that she had given herself more time to prepare for the presentation. *If only I had waited a few days, I could have prepared a formal presentation that would have been more compelling and thoroughly convincing,* she told herself. It was too late now to fret over the situation, however, for the New York City skyline was coming into view over the horizon. She would just have to make do with the information she had brought and give the best presentation possible.

The scenery outside the train window had now changed from the gently rolling hills of Long Island's suburban countryside to the bleak gray of Long Island's lower industrial harbor. The skyscrapers of Manhattan dominated the view, reaching seemingly forever toward the infinite sky above.

With a *rickety-rack,* the train hit the bridge spanning the narrow body of water, the East River, which separates Long Island from Manhattan. Below the bridge, freighters chugged their way in and out of New York Harbor, delivering goods to and from ports the world over. Gradually, the bridge declined until the tracks flattened out and the train rolled firmly onto the surface of Manhattan. After a half-mile run, the train entered the first of many subsurface tunnels through which it would pass on its way to its final destination, Penn Station and the Empire State Building.

Slowly the train rolled into the station, coming to a full stop at the end of platform four. The crowd of commuters on the train all seemed to rise from their seats at the same time. Ann too rose with the crowd and jockeyed for position as the mass of people headed toward the sliding doors. She held tightly onto her purse and briefcase, unconsciously reverting to the necessary habits of the New York City dwellers.

Out on the platform, the mass of people who had been traveling together for the past hour now dispersed, each one going his separate way to lead separate lives, never to be together in exactly the same grouping again.

The escalator from the lower level of Penn Station took Ann up to the street, where she stepped out of the station doors onto the bustling sidewalk of Seventh Avenue. The Empire State Building towered high above her. Macy's Tower, the Chrysler Building, the PanAm Building, and the other familiar skyscrapers rose above midtown Manhattan. The sights and sounds of the city were all around her. People were scurrying about in every direction; cars, buses, and taxis crowded the busy streets. From every street corner street vendors were selling their goods: hot dogs, roasted nuts, magazines, and newspapers.

"Good old New York," said Ann with a sigh as she surveyed the noisy commotion taking place around her.

The main office of Development Corporation of America was not far from Penn Station, so instead of spending her time hailing a taxi, Ann decided to walk. Into the crowd she went, walking briskly and keeping her eyes straight ahead, a habit she had long ago developed as a New Yorker. At last, after several blocks and many busy intersections, she stood in front of the twelve-story gray building which housed the corporate headquarters of Development Corporation of America.

She entered the building. On the street level was a large, spacious lobby with a white marble floor. At the far end was a receptionist's desk with a directory to the building hanging above it, and on either side of this desk were the elevators, two on each side.

Ann took one of the elevators to the eighth floor where her division, the Southeast Development Division, was located. The southeast division handled the development and marketing of property from Myrtle Beach, South Carolina, south to the Florida Keys and east to the Mississippi coast. In addition, there was a northeast division, a southwest and California division, and a Pacific Northwest division, each occupying its own space in the twelve-story office complex.

The Southeast Development Division of DCA, with the advantages of operating in an area undergoing a boom but still with property values not too inflated, was the most profitable. Ann considered herself quite fortunate to be a part of it, for it was a division envied by the entire corporation.

The elevator doors opened into a large office complex. Directly in front of the doors was the receptionist's desk. Behind her were many other desks and tables, some made more private by partitions. Sounds of the office were everywhere. Phones rang, keyboards clicked, and the copy machine hummed.

"Good morning," said Ann to Leah, the receptionist, as she stepped off the elevator.

"Good. . .why, good morning, Ann," answered Leah with a startled look. "This is certainly a surprise."

"Important business," answered Ann, walking to the side of the desk.

"Is Mr. Watson in?"

"Why, yes, he's already in his office."

"Good. He's just the one I want to see."

As Ann walked across the large room to the back where Bill Watson's private office was located, she took the time to greet her coworkers, who were each equally as surprised to see her as Leah had been. The most surprised of all, however, was Bill, and it showed on his face as Ann entered his office.

"What in the world are you doing here?" he asked, sitting straight up at his desk.

Ann explained that she had an important proposal to discuss with him and requested an hour of his time to listen and discuss it. Although Bill was hesitant at first, explaining that he had a busy schedule that day, he agreed to hear her out, for he assumed it must be something important for her to drop everything in the Keys and fly back to New York.

Ann set up her presentation and calmly but firmly laid it out before him. She explained about the sensitive nature of the mangrove swamp and the adverse effect filling it would have on the environment. She then presented her alternative proposal, stressing the lack of environmental damage and the other excellent advantages of the new location. She showed Bill graphs and charts she had prepared, outlining the cost-effectiveness of her proposal versus the original site. Ann finally wound up her presentation by saying, "I think it would benefit everyone, especially the company, if my proposal were given serious consideration."

Ann felt she had made an excellent presentation, and indeed, she had. Bill had been polite and courteous, listening intently to Ann's statements. For this reason, Ann thought she had made a positive impression on him and was totally surprised when he made the single comment, "Ann, as much as I'd like to consider your proposal, I'm afraid it is out of the question."

He then stood up, as if to escort her from his office.

"But Bill," Ann protested, "surely there—"

"I told you there is no way we can change the plans," snapped Bill, interrupting Ann in midsentence.

"And furthermore," he continued in a harsh tone, "your job is in sales, not planning! So I suggest that you get back to Key West and get to work."

Ann had not expected immediate acceptance of her proposal, but neither had she expected such an adamant refusal to consider it. Giving no indication of her surprise and disappointment, she replied simply, "Yes, Sir." Experience in corporate politics had taught her the value of patience.

"I'll be leaving this weekend," she added coolly as she collected her papers and left the office.

She hurriedly left the building, not even stopping to say good-bye to her colleagues. She was hurt and seething with anger, and in her disappointment, she walked briskly and purposefully out onto the sidewalk. She had nowhere in particular to go and nothing pressing to do, but she walked nonetheless with a frantic urgency.

For thirty minutes or more, Ann walked blindly through the streets of New York, oblivious to the people around her, until at last she came to rest on a bench at the entrance to Central Park.

There she let her emotions calm and her anger subside as she relaxed on the park bench. For the next hour she sat there, not thinking about anything in particular, but simply watching the people pass by. There was probably nothing she could do about the situation with DCA. This realization imposed an uneasy sense of despair and frustration. For the first time in her life, she felt totally helpless to take action on an issue that was important to her.

With this feeling of despair and helplessness, Ann decided that she might as well spend the rest of the day in the city; she refused to run home like a child to her parents. She then spent the rest of the day frequenting some of her former haunts. She took a stroll through Central Park, did some window-shopping on Fifth Avenue, and finally found herself at one of her favorite lower Manhattan places: Chinatown.

The afternoon had passed, and since it was already close to dinnertime, she decided to have a bite to eat at her favorite Chinatown restaurant, the Jade East. It was a small family run business, but the food was excellent and Ann had come to know the owner, Ho Ng, from the many visits she had made there while living in New York. He recognized her immediately as she entered the restaurant and greeted her enthusiastically in his thick Oriental accent.

"Ann! It's good to see you again. It's been long time since you visit me!"

"I know. I've been out of town for the past few months. But it's good to come back to the Jade East. What do you have on special today?"

"Oh, you in luck! Today's special is shrimp in lobster sauce. The shrimp is fresh from the Florida Keys." He smiled broadly as he spoke, sure that Ann would be pleased with his suggestion.

Instead of showing pleasure, however, Ann's face sank. Ho's innocent statement only served to remind her of the beautiful Keys and the destruction that would take place if the development were built to the present design. Forcing a smile to her lips, she answered, "No, thanks, Ho. I'll just take a bowl of wonton soup."

Ho nodded, sensing that his suggestion was not received with enthusiasm. Ann took a seat toward the front of the restaurant where she could look out the window at the people passing by. In a few minutes, she was sipping at a steaming hot bowl of wonton soup, complemented by a cup of Chinese tea.

As Ann let the hot liquid ease the tightness in her throat, she looked out the window and thought about what Ho had said. *"The shrimp is fresh from the Florida Keys." Even New York City benefits from the mangrove swamp,* she thought. She let her mind wander back to Nick, who had taught her so gently about the benefits of the swamp and its place in God's world. Again she thought about Bill Watson, and how relentlessly he had objected even to considering her alternative plan, which would have allowed the swamp to be saved. The more she thought, the less sense it made. Why wouldn't Bill consider the alternative site? It was economically feasible, environmentally conscientious, and most attractively located on the small island.

In her mind, she went over and over the conversation with Bill earlier that morning. She analyzed in detail every aspect of it, trying to find some reason for his unbending attitude, but she could find none. Finally, in an exasperated, almost bitter tone, she mumbled to herself, "There's more here than meets the eye! Just as I've suspected all along." Ann was not by nature an inquisitive sort of person, but once curiosity overcame her, there was no stopping her until she got her answer.

She paid Ho for the soup then hailed a cab to midtown Manhattan. The cab stopped in front of the familiar building that housed the headquarters for DCA. She stood alone in the near darkness looking up at the massive gray structure. Everyone would have gone home by now—everyone, that is, except for the night guard and a few cleaning ladies.

Fortunately, Ann knew Charlie, the night guard on duty, from the many nights she had worked overtime when she was still in New York. He only smiled and nodded when she entered the lobby, not once questioning her reason for being there at this late hour. Ann smiled back, and even though she wasn't doing anything wrong, she still felt a bit apprehensive about being in the office after hours.

Taking the elevator to the eighth floor, she stepped off into an eerily dark office. The place was deathly silent, such a contrast to that morning when busy sounds filled the room.

Ann knew where she wanted to go, and without hesitation she went there: the computer room. The computer memory banks housed the data on all of DCA's current projects, and there was what she wanted to see—the data on the Key West development. She sat down in front of one of the several terminals and turned on the switch. The screen came aglow with a bluish hue.

Using the computer was nothing new to Ann, and since she knew the log-on code and the password, she had no trouble accessing the file on the Key West development. As she requested information, rows of figures came across the screen. Most of it looked fairly routine—initial cost estimates, scheduling, bid proposals, and the like. Ann studied the figures. She wasn't really sure what she was looking for, but something had to be there. Bill must have some reason for not considering the alternate plan. Suddenly something near the bottom of the screen caught her attention: SUBFILE PERSONAL AND CONFIDENTIAL. "I wonder what that's all about?" she asked herself. "Why would someone create a private subfile in the original?"

To access this subfile, Ann knew that she would have to find the password. She also knew that she should not even try to access the file, but her curiosity was too great, and the stakes too high for her to give up without trying to find a way. She knew that the only person with the authority to create a private subfile was Bill Watson, so the password would have to be one he invented.

For the next hour, Ann tried different passwords that she thought Bill might have used, but her efforts were to no avail. She tried every word she could think of relating to the site and to its Key West location. Then she tried the words relating only to Bill—the names of his children, his wife, his cars, even his pets, but none of them worked. Almost ready to quit, exhausted, Ann stopped and thought for a minute. It has to be some common name, one he would remember; perhaps—maybe—yes! The name of the street he lives on. Quickly Ann typed in the name "Telfair," and almost instantaneously the computer responded, "Command." She had done it. She had accessed the secret file.

When the information housed by the file came across the screen, it did not merely surprise Ann—it shocked her. Not even in her most doubtful moments had she suspected what was now being disclosed. The file read:

KEY WEST DEVELOPMENT

ITEM:	Sale of Property
SELLER:	William Watson
PURCHASER:	Development Corporation of America
PURCHASE PRICE:	$1,000,000.00
ITEM:	Application for Building Permit
DATE APPLIED FOR:	1/8/96
STATUS:	Rejected
DATE APPLIED FOR:	1/22/96
STATUS:	Rejected
DATE APPLIED FOR:	5/17/96
STATUS:	Rejected
ITEM:	Transfer of Funds

AMOUNT TRANSFERED: $25,000.00
FROM ACCOUNT: 1251267, Bill Watson
TO ACCOUNT: 8983721, Earl Snead
ITEM: Application for Building Permit
DATE APPIED FOR: 2/8/97
STATUS: Permit Issued
END OF FILE

So that's it! she gasped. Bill could secure a building permit only after making a twenty-five thousand dollar cash payment to Earl Snead, head of the Florida Department of Ecology. . .bribery! And the purchase price of the property, one million dollars! That's ten times what the official records show. He bought the property for the resort from himself and pocketed nine hundred thousand dollars! That's embezzlement! *No wonder he wouldn't consider my plan.*

Ann's hands went clammy with the discovery of Bill's criminal activity. Quickly and nervously, she typed a few more commands and was about to log off the computer, when suddenly the door flew open.

Startled, she turned. There, silhouetted in the doorway, stood. . .Bill Watson!

Chapter 9

A surge of fear raced through Ann's body, and she momentarily went numb at having been caught at the terminal.

"What are you doing here?" Bill demanded.

"I. . .I. . ."

He started walking toward her.

Instantly she hit the clear button, erasing the screen and its incriminating evidence.

"I'm working!" she answered, her voice breaking.

Bill gave her a long hard stare, as if to say, I don't believe you. "At seven o'clock on a Friday night?" His question had a sarcastic tone to it.

"Yes!" Ann retorted, rising from her chair. "I have some potential clients here in New York whose phone numbers I needed. You do still want me to sell condominiums. . .don't you?" Ann's brown hair snapped across her shoulders as she turned from Bill toward her briefcase. Reaching it, she hurriedly collected her things and started for the door.

"I'm going home now. I'll be returning to Key West Monday," she said.

"Good! And let's see if you can manage to stay there a little longer this time!" Bill sneered as she left the room.

Entering the elevator, she let out a tremendous sigh of relief. Trembling slightly, she balanced herself against the handrail and swallowed hard as the full realization of what could have happened swept over her.

Surprisingly, she felt no guilt at the lie she'd told when confronted by Bill. Although it wasn't a complete lie—there had been potential clients' phone numbers on file—she knew full well that was not her reason for being there. But somehow the words had come as if not from her. They had just rolled off her tongue, as if someone else were speaking through her mouth.

Since it was dark outside, Ann called a cab from the lobby of the building and allowed it to take her to the train station. It was only a short distance to the station, but she knew better than to walk the street of the city alone at night.

The station was not very busy. The majority of the commuters had left the city for the day, and the street people of New York were now out. Ann was glad when she was finally settled on a seat in the train to Hempstead.

Not wanting to inconvenience her parents, she took a taxi home from the station. Her mother had prepared a large dinner of pot roast and mashed potatoes, and even though it was late, her parents had waited for her arrival before eating. Ann felt obligated, therefore, to have a bite with them, although she was not hungry after her soup at Jade East.

The dinner conversation was simple, with Ann's parents asking her about her day. She couldn't tell them about her meeting with Bill and especially not about her discovery of his involvement in the bribery scheme. This fact was something so important that Ann felt she couldn't tell anybody, at least not until after she had decided what she was going to do with this new knowledge.

She went to bed early, but, in spite of her busy day and the physical exercise she had walking about New York City, sleep would not come. What should she do now? The fact that Bill had bribed the head of the Department of Ecology in Florida kept pressing on her mind. She knew that if she exposed him, the development might be halted and the swamp could possibly be saved. But this change in the project might also mean the end of her career with Development Corporation of America, or, if not the end, at best a demotion and return to New York. To Ann this result would be almost as devastating as filling the swamp would be, for her career with DCA and her growing relationship with Nick were currently the two most important areas of her life.

Over and over, her mind wrestled with these possibilities, but she could not reach any conclusions. Finally, she decided to get out of bed and look for something to read. The sleek new furniture in the guest room did not include a bookcase, so she slipped down the hall to the den, walking quietly in order not to disturb her parents.

One entire wall of the den consisted of bookshelves, and Ann hardly knew what to choose. Finally, near the bottom, she noticed some volumes that appeared dingy and rather dog-eared. She pulled one out and discovered that they were her own books—her favorites from childhood. She was touched to think that her mother had kept her old books all these years, and the thought of her parents' love for her and their expectations of her success added to the dismal weight of the decision she now faced.

She thumbed restlessly through a few of the books and came across her high school yearbook. She turned the pages, smiling at the youthful appearance of the seniors. She remembered how adult she had felt at the time, a feeling shared by her classmates. She turned to the pages showing the Senior Superlatives, and there was her picture under the heading "Most Likely to Succeed." Although this honor had made her parents very proud, it was one that she secretly would have given up to be voted "Prettiest Girl of the Senior

Class." Now, despairingly, she thought that she did not deserve the other honor either, as success was surely about to escape her. She closed the book with a sigh and crept back to her room for the few hours left of the night.

🌴

At the first glimpse of daylight, Ann rolled wearily out of bed, took a shower, dressed, and went into the kitchen. Her mother was already there, seated at the breakfast table, reading the morning paper.

"Morning," she said as Ann entered the room.

"Morning, Mom," replied Ann in a tired voice.

Mrs. Langley sensed at once that Ann had a problem, but not wishing to pry, she simply said, "How about some coffee?"

"That sounds good," said Ann.

Her mother poured her a cup of coffee, and the two sat down for a few minutes of conversation.

"Your father has gone into the office for a few hours," said Mrs. Langley. "They have been so busy lately that he can't seem to get caught up."

"I'll have to go in for a few hours myself. There are some loose ends I failed to tie up yesterday."

"Work, work, work," her mother said, throwing her hands into the air. "You and your father. Oh well, like father, like daughter, I guess."

Ann smiled, finished her coffee, and said, "Well, I'd better get going."

"But you haven't even eaten breakfast," her mother protested.

"That's all right, Mom. I'll get a bagel once I get to the city." Ann rose from her seat, lifting her purse over her shoulder.

"Well, all right," her mother answered as she too rose from the table. "But at least let me give you a ride to the station."

In no time at all, Ann was seated once again on the morning train to midtown Manhattan, this time with only a few Saturday commuters. The day was overcast, and a cold bleakness seemed to settle on the city as the train rolled into Penn Station.

As on the previous day, Ann walked to the office from the train station. Although only a few people were there, she was a bit apprehensive about entering the office, especially after her confrontation with Bill the day before. Knowing what she did about him, she was certain she wouldn't be able to look him in the eye. She hoped desperately that he would not be there and that she could get her things and leave unnoticed. But this was not to be, for as soon as the elevator door opened on the eighth floor, there stood Bill.

"Back again?" he asked, looking sharply at her as she stepped off the elevator.

"Just returning to pick up a few things I forgot," she replied crisply. "Just pretend I'm not here, and I'll be gone in a bit." As she spoke, she strode past him, purposely not letting her eyes meet his.

Ann was now more nervous than ever as the item for which she had specifically returned was something she definitely did not want Bill to see. She bided her time, hiding her nervousness by casually talking to the few employees there and finding things to do while Bill was around. Eventually he left the office, taking the elevator down.

Immediately Ann sprang into action. If she were to get out without anyone noticing what she was doing, she would have to act fast. She went directly to the copy room where the printer was located. The printer was running, as it would be all weekend, printing files that had been requested Friday to be ready Monday. Ann started going through the stack of paper already printed. Finally, she found what she was looking for. Disconnecting her printout from the rest of the stack, she quickly slid it in her briefcase. She then left the copy room and went straight to the elevators and pushed the down button. As the elevator bell rang and the door opened, out stepped Bill. Ann passed him getting off as she got on.

"Well, did you finally finish this time?" he asked in a somewhat sarcastic manner as they passed.

"You got it. Three hours on a Saturday is enough."

"Yes, but remember that I'm expecting you to be back in Key West on Monday," Bill called as the elevator door closed.

"Whew, barely made it!" Ann said to herself as the elevator started down.

Clutching her briefcase tightly, she immediately left the building, walked back to Penn Station, and bought a ticket for the first train back to Hempstead. She had gotten what she had come for; there was no need to stay in the city any longer.

During the train ride back to Hempstead, Ann pictured the confrontation that would take place if she went to Bill with her knowledge. Over and over in her mind, she acted out the role she would play and the dialogue that would ensue during such a confrontation, and each time the end result was the same: one with unequivocally devastating consequences for herself and her career. She could picture Bill denying any knowledge of the bribery and ultimately discrediting and disgracing her for her accusations. She could picture her termination—or firing—that would take place afterward, putting an end to her career with DCA and placing a permanent black mark on her record.

The more she thought about these consequences, the more fearful she became. She now felt certain that if she confronted Bill with what she knew, it would mean the end of her job.

The train's arrival in Hempstead did nothing to lift her spirits, and in a state of dejection she left the train and walked slowly down the platform to the street below. She didn't bother calling her parents, nor did she hail a taxi. She simply walked. Oblivious to anything or anyone around her, she walked down the long wide street which led to her parents' neighborhood.

A steady cold wind was blowing, scattering the first few brown leaves which had fallen from the trees. Almost unaware, she pulled her jacket up around her neck to protect it from the chilly autumn breeze.

Suddenly a flock of geese appeared overhead, flying in formation toward the Southern Hemisphere. Their honking roused Ann from her dejection, and she looked up and marveled at the grace and beauty of the magnificent birds on their migratory flight to a warmer climate. She thought she knew where the geese were heading, because she remembered Nick's words about the importance of the marsh as a winter nesting ground. "For all types of migratory birds," he had said, and now his words came back to her.

Just as the migrating geese served to remind her of the beautiful Keys and the abundance of wildlife they nurtured, so the walk through the town of Hempstead with its successful and prosperous neighborhoods served to remind her of her own desires to become successful and prosperous. Such was the dilemma she faced and the difficulty of the decisions ahead.

As Ann walked along, the crisp wind scattered the dry, yellowed leaves across the walk in front of her. In despair she said to herself, *I may as well try to stop these leaves from blowing about as to try to stop the development from going on as planned.* All her plans and exuberant hopes that she had had when she left Key West were now but yesterday's dreams. Sorrowfully she realized that things don't always work out as planned.

Engulfed in the dark cloud of her fears and doubts and confusion, she trudged on as evening approached, barely noticing the familiar sights around her. Suddenly she was almost startled to see close upon her the bright lights of her parents' home.

A quiet stillness, interrupted only by the steady tick of the antique clock which hung above the fireplace, filled the room as Ann entered the door. Taking off her coat, she hung it on the adjacent rack and looked questioningly around.

"Anybody home?" she called.

Within seconds, her mother entered from the lighted hallway that led from the kitchen. "Oh, hi, Ann. We didn't hear you come in." She had a towel in her hands, and still wiping them with it, asked, "We were just about to have a bowl of soup. Care for some?"

"Sure, Mom. Give me a minute to freshen up and I'll be right in." She approached her mother as she spoke, and to her parent's surprise, gave her a slight hug before disappearing in the hallway toward the back of the house.

Within minutes she reappeared in the kitchen. Her mother smiled from the stove where she was standing, while her father remained seated at the kitchen table, engrossed in his magazine. "Evening, Dad," she greeted pleasantly as she sat down next to him. "What're you reading?"

Her father looked up from his magazine and smiled before closing it and laying it aside. "Oh, just the financial news," he answered, crossing his arms and resting them on the table. "Looks like the price of gold will continue to fall. If your friend ever does find a treasure he won't be able to sell it for half what he could have four years ago."

"Guess not," Ann agreed, deliberately neglecting to tell her father what Nick's intentions for the treasure were—should he ever find it.

"Anyway," her father continued, "how was your day?"

"Okay," she answered, attempting to hide the uncertainty in her voice.

"Well, now," her mother exclaimed, arriving at the table, "dinner is served." She set the tray down in the center of the table. Three large bowls of steaming hot clam chowder complemented by crackers and sliced cheeses filled the space.

"Mom! New England clam chowder! My favorite! How'd you remember?"

"You mean how could I forget?" She laughed, sitting down next to Ann. "You used to insist on it every Saturday night, remember?"

Ann was just about to answer when she was interrupted by the ringing of the telephone.

"Never fails!" her mother grumbled. "Someone always calls just when we're sitting down for supper!" Quickly she rose from the table and picked up the receiver.

"Hello," she answered in an exasperated manner. "Yes, she's here. One moment please." Turning toward Ann with a quizzical look on her face she said, "It's for you."

A hot surge of adrenaline raced through Ann's body at the announcement. Why would someone call her at home—especially at her parents' house? No one even knew she was here, except, possibly. . .Bill Watson! Her heart fluttered as she lifted the receiver to her ear and cautiously answered, "Hello? . . . . Nick!" Next came a sigh—a tremendous sigh of relief given through several long breaths.

"Ann," he answered, "you sound exhausted! Is something wrong?"

"No, Nick. I'm just relieved it's you, that's all. I wasn't expecting any calls, so when I was told the phone was for me, I didn't know what to expect."

"Ann," Nick questioned with genuine concern, "you sound worried. Are you sure nothing's the matter?"

"Oh, Nick, I don't know. . ." Ann turned from her parents and cupped her hand around the mouthpiece. "Things really haven't gone the way I expected. But then again, I don't know what I expected. Some miraculous solution, I guess, and now I realize there isn't one." A brief moment of silence ensued before Ann spoke again. "But what about you? Is everything going all right in the Keys?"

"Oh, about as well as can be expected, I guess, considering all that happened today." Nick's voice had a solemn tone to it.

"What, Nick? What happened today?"

"You mean you haven't heard?"

"No, tell me! What are you talking about?"

A long moment of silence followed before Nick spoke again. "We'll talk about it when you return, Ann. I'd rather not go into it over the phone. Anyway, I really just wanted to call to tell you how much I miss you, and that you are in my thoughts and prayers continually."

"I miss you too, Nick," Ann whispered, "and I'll be back soon, I promise. . . thanks for your prayers. . ."

"Ann?"

"Yes, Nick?"

"There's just one more thing. I. . ." Nick hesitated.

"Yes?"

"I'll be looking forward to seeing you soon," he answered, somewhat awkwardly.

Nick's answer was not what Ann hoped it would be, but regardless of her disappointment, she simply said, "And I'll be looking forward to seeing you too, Nick. Bye now."

With the click of the receiver the conversation ended. Ann turned and stood for a minute before hanging up the phone. *What happened today to make Nick sound so depressed?* she wondered. *And his last statement, "I'll be looking forward to seeing you soon. . ." Was that what he really wanted to say, or perhaps could he have been going to say, "I love you"?* The question hung unanswered in her mind.

Supper ended without much ado, and while Ann was helping her mother clear away the dishes, she was suddenly taken off guard by the question: "You really care about Nick. . .don't you, Hon?"

Momentarily she paused, and looking at her mother answered, "Why. . . why, yes, of course I do."

"And apparently he cares about you," was her mother's reply. "After all, he did call you long distance from Key West, when you've only been gone two days." A half smile came across her lips as she spoke.

"I don't know, Mother. . ." Ann hesitated. "It's just that. . ."

"He's never told you such?" her mother questioned.

Ann sighed. "Yes. . .that's it. I mean, I feel that he cares about me. . .even loves me. But he's never said anything!"

Ann rinsed the last bowl and slammed it down into the dishwasher.

"There, there," her mother comforted. "I'm sure Nick feels the same about you as you do him. He's probably just not able to put his feelings into words yet. A lot of men are like that." Mrs. Langley placed one finger under Ann's chin and lifted her bowed head so their eyes could meet. "Your father was."

Ann smiled. "Really?"

"Yes, really. But he came around, and I'm sure Nick will too. Just give him time."

Ann wiped her still-damp hands dry and placed one arm around her mother. As they walked away from the kitchen toward the dining room, she said, "You know, Mom, I was under the impression you were against my seeing Nick. I mean. . .after the other night—"

"Let's forget the other night," Mrs. Langley interrupted. "It was just hard for me to believe you would be attracted to someone like Nick. But after seeing the expression on your face tonight when he called, well. . .I knew I was wrong."

Ann took her arm from around her mother, looked her in the eyes, and smiled. "Thanks, Mom." She then gave her a kiss on the cheek and said, "I think I'll go on to bed now."

"All right, Dear, sleep well."

Before leaving the den, she stopped briefly at the recliner where her father was seated watching TV, gave him a kiss on the forehead, and said, "Good night, Dad."

"Good night, Ann," he called as she left the room.

Once in bed, Ann stared restlessly at the ceiling and wondered what she should do next. Eventually, she began to rationalize. *Perhaps the development as planned wouldn't be so terrible, after all*, she thought. *The plans have been made and the permits secured. If the development proceeds, I can remain in the Keys with Nick, and no one except myself will be the wiser. People have already accepted the fact that the development is going to take place, so even though I failed to get the location moved, they won't hold me responsible; after all, I tried.*

And what if the development doesn't take place? What then? I would have to leave Key West and Nick. I might not ever see him again. So went her reasoning.

Even though Nick had not yet told her he loved her, deep within her heart Ann felt sure he did—he must! And she had to be near for this love to develop, to blossom. It was this last single thought that gave the most impetus and acceptability to her line of reasoning.

That settles it, she told herself. *The development will take place as planned. I'm going to say nothing.*

With this final bit of reassurance to herself, she rolled over, pulled the covers up, and fell into a fitful, restless sleep.

The smell of fresh-brewed coffee and bacon frying greeted Ann as she awoke the following morning. A golden ray of sunshine entered through a crack in the curtains and shone on the bedspread below, giving evidence that the dull overcast of the previous day was past and a bright new morning was here.

Ann rolled over and struggled for a minute with the sheets that had become tangled around her during the fitful night. Free from their confines, she got out of bed and put on her slippers and housecoat. She paused briefly at the mirror, ran a brush through her tangled hair, and rubbed the sleep from her tired eyes before going to the kitchen.

The kitchen in her parents' home was large, with a breakfast nook to one side where the kitchen table was located. Her mother was standing behind the stove in her robe, busily frying the bacon and intermittently cracking eggs into a large plastic bowl. Her father was seated at the kitchen table, sipping a cup of coffee. Although it was still early, he was already dressed in a gray pin-striped suit. For as long as Ann could remember, it had been his habit to shower and dress prior to breakfast.

"Good morning," they both said almost simultaneously as Ann entered the room.

"Good morning," Ann replied from behind a yawn.

"Breakfast is almost ready, Dear," her mother said.

"Here, let me give you a hand," Ann answered as she walked around the bar which separated the kitchen from the breakfast nook.

"No, no, just go sit with your father. I will be with you in a minute."

Ann readily complied with her mother's urging and went to the table and sat down beside her father. The Sunday edition of the *New York Times* was spread out before him.

"How about a section of the paper?" he asked as she sat down.

"Fine. Let me see the business section."

"Oh, no. You'll have to wait on that!"

Ann managed a laugh. "Well, then, just hand me the front page."

Ann skimmed the paper, paying little attention to most of the articles, when suddenly one headline jumped out from the page at her. TREASURE FOUND OFF KEY WEST, it read in large bold type, below which was the subcaption, LARGEST RECORDED FIND IN HISTORY!

Ann clutched the paper intently and read the article as if in a panic. As the article progressed, she realized the treasure was discovered in the general area in which Nick was searching. She recognized immediately the coral atoll being described as the very one over which she and Nick had dived. Voraciously Ann studied the article, looking for Nick's name or for some clue as to who had discovered the treasure, but there was none—that is, until she turned the page and saw a picture. He was standing on the beach proudly displaying a cache of silver and gold bars, but the man in the picture was not Nick. He was not, however, a complete stranger. Ann instantly recognized the man. His thick beard and dark eyes stared at her from the page as intensely as they had when she'd first seen them in the restaurant parking lot and again when she had watched him from her car.

The pieces of the puzzle now fell together perfectly. *He'd been spying on Nick,* Ann told herself, *trying to discover his secrets!*

Ann crumpled the paper on the table and ran to her room, leaving her parents staring in confusion.

As she threw herself on the bed, she cried, "Why didn't I warn him? I'd seen the man around his dock! I knew something was suspicious! Why, oh why, didn't I tell Nick?" As the initial shock wore off, she began to realize the extent of her guilt. *I've been too selfish,* she berated herself. *That very evening when Nick came over, I was too concerned with my own problems to consider his. Even when he gave me the cross and told me how close he was to the treasure, I didn't remember to tell him. And now it's too late.*

As Ann's cries turned to muffled sobs, she repeated the question, "Why didn't I tell him? Why didn't I tell him. . . ?"

Then it seemed a voice spoke softly in her ear, *Call Nick.* The message was so plain and clear that it broke Ann's depression, causing her to bolt upright in the bed. For a moment, she sat there in silence. Then the message came again: *Call Nick.* This time the message was louder and clearer than before, causing Ann to look around the room in search of its origin. It only took a second, however, to confirm she was indeed alone. Befuddled, she rose from the bed, opened the door, and looked cautiously down the long hallway. Not a soul in sight. For a moment, Ann pondered the possibility that her mind was playing tricks on her. But no, the message was too strong, too convincing. She must call Nick.

On the third ring, Nick answered.

"Nick! I had to talk with you!"

"What's the matter? Is there something wrong?"

"I. . .I read about the find in today's paper. Nick, I've seen that man before. The day before I left, I saw him on the dock. . .near your boat. Oh, Nick. . .I meant to tell you, but with so much going on, I—"

"Now, now," Nick interrupted, "it's all right! There have been some new developments since that article was written that I'm sure you're not aware of. I'll tell you all about it when you return, but right now I'm on my way to church. You understand, don't you?"

"Of course I do, Nick, and I can't wait."

"Good. And Ann. . .will I be seeing you soon?"

"Yes, Nick. Very soon."

As she hung up the phone, Ann thought about Nick's words and the calmness of his voice. He didn't sound at all depressed today, but why not? *Someone else has found his treasure, and the swamp is all but doomed.* Yet he sounded happy—and was on his way to church!

Ann sat in silence by the telephone, resting her head in her hand, her elbow on the chair's armrest. It was a peaceful moment, but one cut short when her mother entered the room.

"Ann, care for some breakfast now?"

Her mother had a concerned look on her face.

Ann looked up at her and smiled. "Sure, Mom. Sure."

Following breakfast, while still seated at the table, Ann's mother hesitantly asked, "Would you like to go to church with us this morning, Ann? Several churches, including ours, are having a joint service at the cathedral. Dr. Tomlinson, that dynamic speaker from California, will be addressing the congregations and conducting the service. It should be an excellent sermon."

A few minutes of silence followed the invitation. Ann's initial thought was to decline the offer, for she was still feeling depressed over everything that had transpired. Then she remembered Nick's words and the fact that he would be in church this morning. With him as her inspiration, she momentarily put aside her problems and turned to her mother and said, "Yes, Mom, I think I would like that."

Looking pleased, her mother answered, "Good, then. The service starts at ten, so we'd better clean up this mess and start getting ready."

Ann helped her mother clear the table and load the dishwasher. She then showered, dried and curled her hair, and sat down in front of the dresser to put on a dab of makeup. Hair and makeup complete, she took from its hanger a conservative navy blue dress, which for some reason she had impulsively packed at the last minute. At the time, she didn't know why she would need the dress, but she was now very pleased that she had brought it.

She had gotten ready quickly and was surprised when she left her room to find her parents waiting on her. Her mother was wearing a gray wool dress, which went well with her father's gray pin-striped suit. Ann looked at her parents and thought that even at their age and after so many years of marriage they still made a perfect couple.

The three of them rode together in her father's sedan. They had to park rather far away from the cathedral because of the large crowd that turned out to hear Dr. Tomlinson speak. The air was crisp and cool, but the sun was warm on their backs as they walked to the cathedral from the car. As they approached the majestic building, Ann could hear the organ music coming from the front entrance. The Hempstead Cathedral housed one of the largest and most beautiful pipe organs in New York State, and it was always a privilege to hear it, even for Ann, who had grown up in Hempstead and had heard the organ since she was a little girl. Although it was still early, the cathedral was already filling up with people when she and her parents arrived.

The long central aisle, carpeted in muted violet, stretched out before them. On either side of this aisle were long rows of hand-hewn wooden pews. In true Gothic style, beyond these pews on either side were two more aisles, with still another set of pews on either side of them butting up to the cathedral walls.

The walls were entirely of stone, except for the large stained-glass windows placed at equal intervals down the entire length of the cathedral.

At the front of the cathedral was the altar. A speaker's podium sat to the left, and a massive wooden cross hung on the back wall in the center. At the rear of the cathedral, in a balcony, were located the choir loft and organ. The tremendous pipes of the organ rose almost to the ceiling on either side of the loft, and the instrument itself was positioned at the center.

The organ music was loud and clear, resonating throughout the entire sanctuary. As Ann and her parents took a seat near the center, she recognized the prelude the organist was playing as Bach's "Jesu, Joy of Man's Desiring," one of her favorite classical compositions.

In a short while the sanctuary was filled, and the service about to begin. At the sound of the chords to the opening hymn, the congregation rose and joined the choir in song.

After the opening hymn and some traditional formalities, the guest speaker, Dr. Tomlinson, was introduced. Even though he was a renowned doctor of theology, Dr. Tomlinson was dressed in a simple blue suit and looked almost humble as he attempted to adjust the microphone to his above-average height.

When he began his sermon, Ann realized immediately why he was such a popular speaker, for he spoke with a positive dynamism, which could almost be felt as well as heard.

"My friends," he said, "as we look out at the world around us today, we are blessed with the beauty for which an adequate description is impossible. I feel certain that God has given us such a wonderful creation because He has great plans for it and for us. All creation is good! Over and over in Genesis we are reminded of this, for with each creation we hear the refrain, 'And God saw that it was good'!"

"What is the message in this? I feel very strongly that it is clearly a basic truth that indeed all the world is good and precious; it is God's handiwork, His gift to us to treasure and cherish.

"God entrusted this colossal, yet intricate, delicate world to us—surely not to exploit and brutalize, but to utilize constructively to the benefit of all its inhabitants. If we do this, then surely we will be better prepared to care for the world yet to come, the world in which we will live as one with God."

At the end of his sermon, Dr. Tomlinson thanked the congregation and returned to his seat beside the podium.

The service continued, but Ann was only vaguely aware of it. Her ears were still ringing with Dr. Tomlinson's words. The message of the sermon had made its way to the depths of her heart and soul. The decision she had made the night before—to ignore what she knew about the development and to let it go on as planned without her interference—now seemed to be a callous wrong that she could not let take place. Yet, her career was at stake. The opposing values increased in magnitude, and Ann mentally tried to reconcile them, but the more she thought, the greater the conflict became, until at last with the stress burning on her mind, her soul cried out, *God, what am I to do?*

Immediately a warm feeling, coupled with a blanket of peace, overcame her. Her feelings of peace and relief were bolstered by a strong sense of power and determination. Ann had her answer. She knew what she was going to do.

Tomorrow she would confront Bill Watson.

Chapter 10

I need to talk with you," said Ann as she walked unannounced into Bill's office, his secretary trailing her in protest.

"That's all right, Christina," said Bill to his secretary. "If Ann thinks something is so important that she can barge in here without notice the first thing on Monday morning, I guess I can give her a few minutes." The tone of his voice was stern, and there was a scowl over his eyes as he spoke.

Ann felt an immediate sense of apprehension at Bill's words. Perhaps she should have waited, made an appointment to see him; but no, she had given herself, and Bill, enough time.

She could have called him Sunday afternoon immediately after making a decision to take some sort of action. Instead, she had spent the time debating the options open to her: As a divisional director, Bill reported directly to Mr. Michael Van Pelt, president of Development Corporation of America, and she could go straight to him with her story; she could even go to the legal authorities, since the bribery involved a public official; or she could go to Bill himself. This last option was the one she chose to take. She would explain that she knew all about the bribery and possibly even embezzlement but that she was willing to keep silent if he would right his wrong: to return to the company any overpayment for the land and to relocate the development in an environmentally acceptable location.

It had taken much soul-searching for Ann to come to this decision. She knew that perhaps, ethically, she should turn Bill in regardless of any restitution he might make, but she really wanted to give him a chance to right his wrongdoing.

Ann closed the door behind her. She and Bill were now alone.

"I hope you have a good excuse for this intrusion," Bill said from behind his executive desk. "You are supposed to be on your way back to Key West."

"That is just what I'm here to talk about—Key West development. I'm going to come right out with it," she continued as she crossed her arms and walked to the side of the desk, removing herself from a position of subordinance. "I know a lot about the development, a lot more than you think. In fact, I know everything about it."

"Everything?" Bill asked, raising his eyebrows and half smiling in a smirking, questioning manner.

"Yes, everything."

Ann placed her hands on Bill's desk and bending over slightly, she looked him directly in the eyes and said, "Bill, I know that you sold the Key West property to the company at an inflated price. I also know that you bribed the director of the Florida Department of Ecology in order to get a permit to fill the swampy site you sold."

Rising, Bill walked around to the right side of his desk, opposite Ann. He dropped his head slightly and rubbed his chin with his right hand. There was a strong silence in the room, a silence made even more intense by the heightened tension between the two adversaries. Finally, he broke the silence. "Those are serious charges, Ann. I hope you know—"

Not giving him a chance to finish his remark, Ann started into her rehearsed speech. "I know the seriousness of the offenses, but I'm willing to overlook them—even forget them—if you'll just do two things—"

"What do you want? Money?" he interrupted in an angry bitter voice.

"No, nothing like that. All I want is for you to return to the company the money you overcharged it for the property and to relocate development on a dry, environmentally safe location."

Ann felt a great relief at having said what she had planned. She was certain that Bill would agree without objection to her conditions. After all, she was agreeing to remain silent about his wrongdoing, and all he had to do was to correct the mistakes he had made.

Her positive attitude that things would turn out right as she had anticipated proved to be very short-lived. No sooner had she finished speaking than Bill lifted his head and looked directly at her with a fiery, evil look in his eyes.

"Listen here, Ann," he said, shaking his finger in her face. "I couldn't care less for what you want, and, furthermore, I'm not returning any money to anyone."

His voice became louder, angrier, and his brow wrinkled above eyes, which were filled with fury. "Girl," he shouted, "you are way out of your league. I could ruin you with just one phone call."

Ann was beginning to feel a bit nervous. Never before had she seen Bill act like this. He was behaving in a violent manner, and she wished that they were not alone in the office. He lifted his arm, and for a moment, she feared he was going to strike her, but, instead, he grabbed her by the elbow and pushed her toward the door.

"I'm not going to put up with any more of this," he said through his teeth in a nasty, hissing manner. "If I hadn't given you that promotion, I'd fire you now, on the spot. I'm going to go clear this with Mr. Van Pelt right now!"

Ann jerked her arm loose from his grip, turned, and said angrily, "Get your hands off me! Don't you dare touch me again."

Releasing Ann's arm, Bill opened the door and spoke to Christina, Ann standing directly behind him.

"Christina, will you please call Mr. Van Pelt and see if he is in? I have an urgent matter to discuss with him."

Ann was so agitated she did not know whether she felt relief or fear when Mr. Van Pelt proved to be in his office and agreed to see Bill.

"You can wait right here, Ann," said Bill. "This won't take long."

Ann sat in a chair beside Christina's desk while Bill went upstairs to the executive offices. Fortunately, her new position had required Mr. Van Pelt's approval, and now it would require his decision for her termination. She could only wonder nervously what conversation might be taking place in his office. She knew well the story behind Michael Van Pelt. He had founded Development Corporation of America thirty years earlier as a one-room real estate office, and his skill and managerial expertise had been the driving force behind the transformation of DCA from a small local business to a multinational corporation. She had no idea what his personality was really like, and although at one time she had held him in extremely high esteem, she was now becoming fearful of what the consequences to all this would be. For all she knew, he might be as deceitful and unscrupulous as Bill had turned out to be. Perhaps he might be even worse.

Her train of thought was interrupted by the ringing of the phone on Christina's desk, and in her nervousness she jumped at the loud sound.

"Bill Watson's office," answered Christina. "Yes, Sir. I understand, Sir. Yes, right here, Sir."

Placing the receiver back down on the desk, Christina turned to Ann. "Mr. Van Pelt would like to see you in his office, Ann. Now." Ann could see the question in Christina's eyes and her sympathetic smile, as Ann picked up her briefcase and headed back through the large office full of desks and people to the elevators. Distractedly she nodded to her friends on what seemed a mile-long walk. Her knees felt like water, and as the elevator door closed, she slumped against the wall, her heart pounding. She pushed the button for the top floor, thinking that this was not at all the way she had hoped the confrontation would end. It seemed now that her worst fears had materialized.

She stepped out into the plushly carpeted lobby of the twelfth floor. No receptionist's desk greeted her, nor was there an office index, since anyone venturing to the twelfth floor was either an invited guest or an executive who knew his way around.

Three hallways radiated out from the circular lobby, one to either side and one directly in front of the elevator door. The center hallway led into an expansive square area containing a secretary's desk, several leather chairs, and a bookcase wall. Large paintings of resorts built by DCA adorned the other walls. Behind the secretary's desk was a massive set of oak doors, intricately and elaborately carved, with doorknobs and an inlaid nameplate apparently made of solid brass.

It was the nameplate that caught and held Ann's attention. It read, "Michael Van Pelt." Ann swallowed, her throat dry with nervous tension.

"Mr. Van Pelt is expecting you, Ann," said his secretary, getting up from behind her desk and starting for the heavy door.

Slowly the door swung open, and there on the other side, wearing a dark blue suit, stood Mr. Van Pelt. Ann had seen him only twice, both times only as a formality when she was hired and subsequently promoted, and she had almost forgotten what he looked like. He was a large, elderly, but handsome gentleman; his silver gray hair was conservatively styled, and his thick mustache neatly trimmed.

Large dark eyes sat deep within their sockets, and as they met Ann's they seemed to emit a gentle warmth that calmed her frazzled nerves and somehow reminded her of Nick.

Bill was sitting in front of Mr. Van Pelt's desk, and as Mr. Van Pelt spoke to Ann, he motioned for her to take the seat beside Bill. He then sat down behind his desk.

"Now, Ann," he began, "Bill tells me that you are creating some serious problems in the Key West development; that you are trying to get the site changed, not following company procedures, and, in fact, are deliberately obstructing the progress of the development. Are these accusations true?"

"Only in part. I do want the site moved, but there is a very good reason, and I think the move would prove to be very beneficial to the company in the long run."

"Then tell me your side of the story."

Ann then calmly told her story. She began with the sensitivity of the mangrove swamp and how she didn't want to see it filled. She told about her alternate plans and how it was Bill's refusal to consider them that led her to discover, in a confidential file of the computer, the facts concerning the purchase of the site and the bribery scheme.

Bill jumped up from his chair and heatedly and emotionally accused Ann of lying.

"She's only making these accusations to destroy me in order to guarantee her own advancement in the company. There's not a shred of truth in what she is saying. And, Sir, I suggest that she be terminated immediately!"

"Mr. Van Pelt," said Ann, "unfortunately I am telling the truth. I have already told Bill what I know. I should not have gone to him first, but I wanted to give him a chance to right his wrong, and so I went to him first, in confidence."

"She isn't telling the truth," said Bill. "There's no confidential file in the computer, never was."

"I don't know what is in the computer now, but I'm telling the truth." Ann spoke softly but firmly.

"Then prove it. . .prove it!" shouted Bill.

Ann opened her briefcase and pulled out a thick computer printout. She dropped the printout on Mr. Van Pelt's desk and said, "There's your proof."

"What good is that? Just some ordinary printouts of the day's work."

"No, Bill. You see, Saturday when I returned to the office, it was to pick up this stack of paper. This is a computer printout of the Key West development file. I had accessed the file on the computer Friday evening and requested the printout before you walked in on me. Everything is here, Mr. Van Pelt," Ann said, turning toward him. "Even the confidential file which records all the bribery transactions."

Bill's face turned as white as a sheet, and he put his hand on the desk to stabilize his balance.

Ann had said what she had to say. Things had not turned out as she had anticipated, and she did not have any idea what was going to happen now. All she knew, all she thought as she turned and walked toward the door was that she was certainly not going to be a part of it.

"Where are you going?" asked Mr. Van Pelt as Ann opened the door.

"I'm leaving. And Mr. Van Pelt," she added, "please consider this my resignation."

Chapter 11

The bright sunshine, scattered into sparkling bits by the dancing waves, filled Ann with a sense of serenity as she looked out the window of her small Volkswagen. Across the horizon she could easily recognize the fishing boats as they headed out to sea from their harbor on Key West. The shrimp and other fish soon to be caught and loaded on these boats might have had as a birthplace the very mangrove swamp she so hoped to save.

These thoughts buoyed Ann's spirits with the feeling that she had done the right thing before she left New York. Even though her actions had cost Ann her job, and even though she had no guarantee that the condominiums would not still be built on the original site, she at least had the feeling, deep inside, that she had done everything in her power to prevent the annihilation of the swampland so vital to the ecology of Key West and of Florida. And she felt a deep satisfaction over the severance of her ties with the iniquitous element that had precipitated such a corrupt and callous development in the first place.

It was good that she could now experience these positive emotions, for during the days following her resignation from Development Corporation of America, she had been burdened by a deep, dark depression—a depression which she could not seem to shake—and the cause of which she could not then explain to her parents. Remembering her father's advice not to rock the boat had not helped her feelings either. It had only served to make her retreat further from the reality of the present.

Now, staring out the car window, she relived every detail of those agonizing days.

The day following her resignation Ann did not venture from her room, nor did she eat. She sensed, rather than saw, the worry and concern her parents were feeling. She knew they were waiting and wishing with all their hearts that she could soon break out of her self-inflicted shell and return to her normal, determined self.

Fortunately, their hopes were soon confirmed, for on the following day Ann emerged from her room with a new determination—a determination to start her life over. But they had not anticipated the announcement she was to give them: She had resigned from Development Corporation of America and was intending to return to Key West, look for a job, and live there permanently. After they realized that Ann was adamant, despite their dismay, they gave her their blessings and a loving assurance that as long as they lived there would be a home for her in Hempstead—a home where she would always be welcomed with open arms.

With happiness now and the renewed conviction that she was doing the only thing she could do for her own peace of mind and well-being, she quickly went about the duties involved in carrying out this momentous decision. She managed to free herself from the lease on her apartment in New York, to change her mailing address, and to secure a one-way plane ticket from New York to Key West.

Now and then during her lonely flight, doubts and fears kept entering her mind, nagging her like so many little stinging, sticky gadflies. She tortured herself with the thoughts: *Now that I'm back in Florida, in Key West, what will I do? What about my career? What about Nick?*

Nick! Deep down in her heart, she knew—but was not quite able yet to admit to herself—that Nick was the motivating force behind her move from New York to Key West. But why? She knew she loved him—as she had never loved anyone else—and that she wanted to be near him, with him always, for the rest of her life. But did he love her in the same way? *What if I'm chasing a will-o'-the-wisp?* she thought. *Or looking for the elusive pot of gold at the end of the rainbow?*

She felt that he loved her too, but how could she be sure? He was kind, thoughtful, sweet, attentive, even passionate at times—but did that mean he really loved her? After all, he had never actually put into so many words the depth of his emotions for her.

As she drove, Ann wondered what she might do to sustain herself now that she was no longer involved with Development Corporation of America. The road she was on went directly in front of the small shopping and business complex, which housed Island Realty.

Hmm, she said to herself, as she drove past it. *I'm good with sales and I know the real estate business. Perhaps I could go to work for Bobbie.* She entertained this idea for a minute, but she soon put it aside, realizing that in her present situation a job that paid a consistent salary and not just a commission would be more practical. Suddenly a troubling thought entered her head. She realized that without the generous salary she was earning from DCA, she would not be able to afford the lovely antique house she had rented. This realization proved as distressing to her as any of those she had faced earlier, for she loved the house dearly and wanted very much to continue living there. At least the rent was paid through the end of the month. *Maybe by then,* she consoled herself, *I can find a position; at least I'll enjoy the house until then.*

With this new thought, Ann drove directly home. The wide banyans and mature coconut palms hung in thick profusion over the roads in Olde Town, providing such a large amount of shade that here the air felt several degrees cooler. As she drove through the familiar streets of her neighborhood, a growing anticipation filled her heart, for she was almost back to the house that she loved, on the island she loved, and close to the man that she loved. Perhaps tonight. . .no, certainly tonight, she would give him a call.

Ann made the turn around the final bend in her street, and her house came into view. She was instantly pleased at seeing her home, but the excitement was dampened and replaced by anxiety as she saw a car in the driveway and realized that there were two people sitting on her porch. *Who are they? What are they doing sitting on my porch?* she wondered. As she drove closer, the anxiety was replaced by great excitement as she realized that one of the men was Nick! *But who could that be with him?* she wondered, squinting her eyes to get a better look. That older gentleman wearing the pink Hawaiian shirt and white bermuda shorts—could it be? *Is it? It is! Mr. Michael Van Pelt!*

Ann felt a hot flash of nervousness at the realization that Mr. Van Pelt was sitting on her front porch. *What could he be doing here?* she asked herself as she turned the car into the driveway. Nick had risen from where he was sitting and had walked to the driveway to greet her as she brought the car to a stop. He put one hand around the back of her neck, and, without saying a word, brought his lips to hers. He kissed her tenderly for an extended moment, and then breaking his lips free from hers, he pulled her head tightly against his chest. As he hugged her he said, "It's so good to have you back. I've missed you terribly."

"I've missed you too," Ann responded. "And it's great to be home. But tell me, what in the world is Mr. Van Pelt doing here?"

Nick pulled back and rested his arms on the car door. "He's here to see you. We both descended on poor Stephanie at the office at the same time this morning, and when we found out that she didn't know your plans, I called your parents' home and talked to your mother. She said you flew out of New York this morning, so we've been waiting here on the porch for you for the past two hours."

"But I don't want to see him," Ann protested. "I don't know whether he's told you or not, but I've resigned from Development Corporation of America."

"He's told me everything. He's really a very nice man, and I think you should give him a chance to say what he's come here for." There was a certain seriousness in the tone of Nick's voice.

"All right," Ann replied. "I'll talk to him."

Nick took Ann by the hand and assisted her out of the car. He then put his arm around her shoulders, and together they walked toward the front of the house. Mr. Van Pelt stood up and smiled as Nick and Ann walked up the front steps of the porch.

"Ann, so good to see you again," he said, extending his hand.

Ann relaxed a bit at the friendly tone in Mr. Van Pelt's voice. She had no idea what he wanted and, upon seeing him, she had even entertained the possibility that he was here to accuse her of some involvement with Bill Watson's bribery scheme. She now thought otherwise, however, for if Mr. Van Pelt were here to accuse her of some wrongdoing, he surely wouldn't have such a happy, enthusiastic tone to his voice.

"How do you do, Mr. Van Pelt?" replied Ann courteously.

"Please," he answered, "call me Michael."

Ann was almost aghast at the modest behavior of Mr. Van Pelt, considering the level of his achievements and the status he held in the business world.

"Yes, Sir, Michael it is. Won't you come in?"

"Thank you."

Ann unlocked the front door, and the three entered the house. She escorted Nick and Michael to the living room and asked them to please take a seat.

"I'm going to put on a pot of coffee. Could I get either of you a cup?"

"That would be good," answered Michael.

Nick simply shook his head in a negative response.

Ann went into the kitchen and returned in a few minutes with two steaming cups of coffee and a plate of Danish butter cookies. She set the plate down on the coffee table and handed Michael his cup. She then sat down on the couch next to Nick.

Michael took a sip. "Delicious," he said.

Ann too took a sip of her coffee, but she did not speak.

"Ann," Michael said, "I'm going to get right to the point with this. I'm here to ask you to come back to work for DCA."

Almost immediately, Ann shook her head. "I'm sorry, Michael, but my decision was final."

"Please let me explain. I'm not asking you to come back to your former position; I'm asking you to come back and head up the Southeastern Development Division. I like a person with courage and integrity, and you have proven you have a full measure of both."

Ann could not believe her ears. Here was the founder and president of one of the country's largest real estate development companies asking her to head up its largest and most lucrative division.

There was a moment of silence.

Finally, Ann asked, "But what about Bill?"

"Well, this is a sad story, Ann. After going over the computer printouts which you left on my desk, and after two days of intensive investigation into Bill's business affairs, past and present, we had no choice but to terminate his connection with Development Corporation of America. Our investigation revealed that the director of the Department of Ecology here in Florida was involved, not only with Bill but with companies all over the state, in incidents of bribery and extortion. Now he and Bill both may have to face federal charges."

"I'm sorry to hear that," said Ann solemnly.

"Yes, I was too. It is especially tragic since Bill was such an intelligent and talented individual. He just didn't have the moral fiber to succeed in a company like DCA. But Ann, I believe that you do, and right now, we need somebody. So I'm asking you to please come back."

A long moment of silence followed.

Ann stared out across the room and then at Nick. Nick only smiled. He knew that the decision was entirely hers, but that he would support her regardless of what it was.

Finally Ann spoke. "Mr. Van Pelt, if I accept the position, am I correct in assuming that I will have to return to New York?"

"Yes, that is correct."

"I'm sorry, then, but I'm going to have to say no. You see, Michael," she continued, "before I came here, there was nothing that could have stopped me from taking a position like that. But I've found something here that I didn't have before, and it is here that I'm going to stay."

Another moment of silence followed. Ann looked at Nick and she could see that he was smiling. He was smiling because he knew what she was talking about when she said she had "found" something here in the Keys. It was the same thing that he had found years ago, the same thing that caused him to move here permanently.

Mr. Van Pelt leaned back in his chair, crossed his arms, and said, "I was afraid that would be your answer, so I came prepared with an alternative offer. If you won't come back to New York, perhaps you will stay here and take charge of the Key West development. I would be willing to give you broad leeway over site location and marketing strategy, and after the condominiums are sold you could stay on as the permanent manager—if you would like."

Ann couldn't believe his words. He was offering her a chance to stay with the company and also to stay in the Keys. She turned again to Nick, who was now smiling broadly. This time he nodded his head in decisive approval.

His encouragement, however, wasn't necessary, for Ann already knew her answer. "Yes, Michael, I'll accept your offer," she said, smiling as she stood up and extended her hand. Michael stood up and extended his also. He shook her hand enthusiastically and said, "And while I am here in Key West, I would like very much to see the site you have in mind for our condominiums—that is, if there is enough time." He looked at his watch. "Two and a half hours until flight time. Is that enough?"

"Plenty," answered Ann. "The site is not in Key West, but it is only a short drive, and I would like very much to show it to you."

"Then let's go. You too, Nick."

Ann had been to the new site only once with Bobbie, but she had no trouble in locating it again. She showed Michael as much of the island as time permitted and described in detail her thoughts and ideas relative to converting it into a beautiful, luxurious resort area. Michael listened carefully and from time to time nodded his approval or asked pertinent questions.

It was time for Michael to get back to the airport and New York. The three returned to Ann's house, where they all shook hands. Promising to keep in close touch with Ann on developments to follow, Michael drove off in his rented Continental.

Now Nick and Ann were alone. They walked slowly to the porch swing and sat down, Nick putting his arm around Ann's shoulders. For a few minutes they sat there, rocking gently in the swing but saying nothing. To herself, Ann was reliving Michael's surprise visit and reveling again in his words of praise, support, and encouragement. Finally, Nick broke the silence.

"Ann, I know it's been a long day for you, but I'm so proud of you and so happy to have you back that I feel like celebrating. What do you say we take the boat and escape from everything for awhile?"

Ann looked up into Nick's dark brown eyes, and she could see the joy and excitement within.

"That sounds like fun, but where shall we go?"

"You'll see," answered Nick with a wink.

The two then rose and went inside the house. Ann changed from the suit she had worn on the plane into some shorts, a shirt, and tennis shoes, while Nick prepared provisions for a picnic.

After a short drive to the marina, where they readied the boat with gas and oil, they once again found themselves seated side by side at the helm of Nick's cruiser, heading out to sea.

The late afternoon sea was incredibly still, and the trim craft cut the ocean's surface freely, sending rolls of white foam out on either side. A cool breeze generated by the moving vessel chilled Ann slightly, and she snuggled closer to Nick, resting her head on his shoulder. Nick responded tenderly, putting his arm around her and gently stroking her hair.

In time, the island chain of the Florida Keys disappeared behind them, and once again, they were surrounded by an infinite expanse of blue. This time, however, Ann did not experience the lonely isolation she had felt on her first excursion with Nick. Instead, she experienced a sensation of contentment and oneness with him and God.

For Ann, time as a dimension ceased to exist. She could have stayed as she was forever, alone with Nick on the vast blue ocean. At his prodding, however, she looked up.

"Recognize it?"

Ann peered out across the horizon, and for the first time noticed the small patch of green they were rapidly approaching.

"Galilee," she whispered, "your island."

Nick slowed the craft into the lagoon where he and Ann had first picnicked on the white sand beach. He dropped anchor and stepped overboard into the warm shallow water. Ann handed him the provisions and then stepped off herself, and together they walked hand in hand to the beckoning shore.

As Ann laid out the supplies, Nick busied himself by collecting pieces of driftwood which had been washed ashore by the never-ending tide.

The sun was rapidly setting and now burned as a brilliant orange ball, making a final display of glory before retiring below the horizon. As the sun dipped out of sight, the velvet darkness of night enfolded them. Nick quickly built a fire, bringing the once-dead wood alive with bright efflorescent colors of orange and red. The moon rose above the horizon, reflecting off the cool still water, the palm trees silhouetted against it.

Together Nick and Ann sat close to the fire, mesmerized by the dancing flames and the soft crackle of the burning wood. The food they had brought sat off to the side, forgotten, replaced by the nurturing quality of the fire's warm glow.

"Ann?" His voice broke the long silence.

"Yes?"

"There's something I've been wanting to talk to you about." There was a moment of hesitation before he continued. "I've realized over the past few days, while you were away, how much I need you, how much I. . .love you."

At last! The words she had so longed to hear—at last they had been spoken. How could she have doubted?

A great joy swelled her heart and spilled over her whole being, and so overwhelming was the emotion, so strong its power, that she sat silent, unable to speak.

Nick reached into his pocket and took out a small box. Taking both her hands into his, he put the box in her hands and closed them, clasping them for a moment within his own.

Slowly Ann freed her hands and looked at the box. Trembling slightly, unable to contain her excitement, she opened it. In the firelight, the large diamond sent flashes of red, yellow, blue, green, and violet in every direction.

Nick took the ring and slipped it on Ann's finger.

"My darling, I don't ever want to be without you again. Please, will you marry me?"

As their lips drew close, she softly whispered, "Yes, my love, oh, yes."

For a long moment they sat there locked in an embrace, neither speaking. Finally, Ann broke the silence. She whispered, "Oh, Nick, you've made me so happy. Everything in my life has fallen into place better than I could've dreamed. But you—the treasure you've searched so hard for and dreamed of finding has now been taken by someone else." There was a quiver in Ann's voice as she spoke.

Nick only smiled and pulled her closer. With a slight chuckle, he said, "Ann, it doesn't really matter. You see, that man who found the treasure, the one in the photograph, was from the University of Miami's Department of Archeology. The treasure will be recovered and preserved just as I'd hoped, and I've been asked to manage the recovery."

"But doesn't it matter to you that you weren't the one who actually found the treasure?" Ann questioned.

Nick smiled. "But I *was* the one who found the treasure!"

Ann looked up at Nick through her large green eyes, a puzzled expression on her face.

"You, Ann. . .you are my treasure."

With his words their lips once again met. As the kiss ended, Ann laid her head on Nick's shoulder and stared out at the moon reflecting off the shimmering water. While the waves gently caressed the shoreline and the fire softly crackled, Ann realized that she too had found a glorious, wonderful treasure. Her love of Nick and her newfound love of God and His islands would always be her treasure of the Keys.

STEPHEN A. PAPUCHIS

Stephen lives in Nashville, Tennessee, with his wife Carol and their four children Leah, Stephanie, Christina, and Michael. He and Carol are avid boaters and recreational scuba divers. They vacation frequently in the Florida Keys, whose lush tropical scenery, clear waters, and living coral reef served as the setting for his first **Heartsong Presents** novel, *Treasure of the Keys.*